30 p

GW01418135

# THE
# Wo
# Handbook 1976

Compiled by Brian Glanville

**A Playfair Publication**

**Queen Anne Press London**

© Brian Glanville

Also published by Queen Anne Press
Goalkeepers are Crazy and other stories 45p

Cover photo by courtesy of Colorsport
Super-Cruyff befuddles the Uruguayan defence

Published in association with *The Sunday Times* by
Queen Anne Press Limited
12 Vandy Street
London EC2A 2EN

Made and printed in England by C. Nicholls & Company Ltd
The Philips Park Press, Manchester

# Contents

# CHAPTER ONE

# The European Football Championship 1974–76

Once again the teams were divided into eight qualifying groups whose winners would contest the quarter-finals on a home and away knock-out basis, the semi-finals, final and (alas) the third place match to take place on the territory of one of the four semi-finalists.

---

**GROUP 1** ENGLAND, Czechoslovakia, Portugal, Cyprus.

---

It was a little hard on England's new team manager, Don Revie, that he should not have the slightest chance of a 'warm-up' before his team was plunged into the maelstrom of the Nations Cup, receiving the Czechs and Portuguese at Wembley. Making a number of changes from the team which had toured Europe so successfully in the summer, he pulled the Czech match out of the fire thanks largely to a bold late substitution which brought on Dave Thomas to run at the defence; his first international and a remarkably successful one.

The Portuguese match was not to be redeemed. Foolish optimism had been bred when Portugal lost badly to the Swiss in the previous friendly game, but at Wembley they were a different, highly defensive, proposition, and England could not crack them.

The Czechs held out for 70 minutes, and even threatened to lead when their excellent, blond, attacking full-back Pivarnik, hit the bar from long range. If the Czechs scarcely confirmed the good reputation they came with after some 'friendly' victories, the England approach work was drab. Czechoslovakia fell apart in the end chiefly through weariness, though Thomas' spirited attacking certainly cracked their defence. The first goal came when the Czechs could stop him, on the right, only by fouling him. Brooking pushed him the free kick and Channon headed in his cross.

A pass and a cross from Channon made the next two goals for Colin Bell, who had had a fine all round game. But the fact that the result was illusory was shown when the Portuguese held out with little trouble, and breached the English defence a couple of times with Octavio's lovely through balls. England's midfield failed totally, and a Frank Worthington-figure (if not Worthington himself) was manifestly missed in attack. For all Revie's fine talk of Total Football, the renunciation of harsh and cautious football such as he had first promoted at Leeds, his insistence that the crowd sing *Land of Hope and Glory* (rather than *Give Us A Goal*), there was plainly far to go.

Cyprus should have been met in February, but the pitch and the political situation in Limassol were equally unsatisfactory, so the match was postponed till May. In April, Cyprus came to Wembley.

By scoring all England's five goals against Cyprus at the Empire

Stadium, Malcolm Macdonald equalled the international goal scoring record shared by G. O. Smith, Steve Bloomer, and Willy Hall. Four of the goals were headed, and there should have been another, in the first half, when he was put clean through by Channon's pass and a defender's miss, only to hit Alkiviades, the brave goalkeeper.

Macdonald's opportunism was to be praised, but it is highly doubtful whether he could have scored such goals against even a second rate international team, and England's performance as a whole was depressing. Far too seldom did they find the way round the flanks of a nine, even ten, man defence, though the late arrival of Dave Thomas, in place of an unimpressive Channon did improve things. He made Macdonald's fourth goal, immediately, with a long right wing cross, and the fifth when he exchanged passes with the clever Ball and got to the goal line. Keegan set up two of the others, while the first came from Alan Hudson's free kick in the second minute.

The fielding of Kevin Beattie, in his first international, at left-back was not really a success. His physique and pace, or lack of it, fit him much better for the back four, though he did push further up the left flank in the second half, and forced Alkiviades to leave the field after colliding with him, on a disallowed goal.

The Cypriots, two of whose players had been killed in the recent war, were negligible opposition, Savva had some good runs in the first half, on a promising debut.

Czechoslovakia proceeded to score nine goals in two games; most surprisingly, five of them were against Portugal, who had perplexed England at Wembley. The Portuguese, fresh from a 2–0 win in Paris, were no match for a dazzling Czech team for whom Petras, the 1970 World Cup star, reappeared and scored. It was an ominous result for England, themselves due in Bratislava in October. In the Cyprus game, Panenka, the Czech midfield player, was brought into the side, and scored three of the goals. Bicovsky, another midfield man, scored twice against Portugal.

In Limassol, on a farcically bad pitch which resembled a sand dune, England won a dreadfully tedious match against Cyprus 1–0, with little credit. The goal came as early as the sixth minute. Kevin Keegan forced a corner on the left, Dave Thomas took it, and Keegan rose on the near post to head it into the far corner. Thereafter, though the Cypriots three times cleared off the line, there were no more goals. Cyprus played a cautious game, but did break sufficiently, especially after half-time, to give England much more space than they enjoyed at Wembley.

England played with a 4–2–4 formation which left them rather sparse in midfield. Watson and Todd were admirable central defenders, Clemence in goal had one free-kick to catch, Tueart came on to win his first cap, and Channon had some good second half runs when switched to the left. But the bleakness of the game belied the sunshine.

Wembley, October 30, 1974
    England (0) 3                        Czechoslovakia (0) 0
    *Channon, Bell (2)*

*England:* Clemence (Liverpool); Madeley (Leeds U.), Hughes (Liverpool); Dobson (Everton), (Brooking (West Ham U.)), Watson (Sunderland), Hunter (Leeds U.); Channon (Southampton), Bell (Manchester C.), Worthington (Leicester C.), (Thomas (Q.P.R.)), Francis (Q.P.R.), Keegan (Liverpool).

*Czechoslovakia:* Viktor; Pivarnik, Capkovic (Vojacek), Ondrus, Varadin, Bicovsky (Kuna), Pekarik, Gajdusek, Masny, Svehlik, Stratil.

Wembley, 20 November 1974
    England (0) 0                 Portugal (0) 0

*England:* Clemence (Liverpool); Madeley (Leeds U.), Cooper (Leeds U.); (Todd (Derby Co.)); Francis (Q.P.R.), Watson (Sunderland), Hughes (Liverpool); Thomas (QP.R.), Brooking (West Ham U.), Channon (Southampton), Clarke (Leeds U.), (Worthington (Leicester C.)), Bell (Manchester C.).

*Portugal:* Damas; Artur, Alhinho, Humberto, Osvaldinho; Octavio Martins, Alves, Texeira, Nene (Romeu), Chico (Oliveira).

Wembley, 16 April 1975
    England (2) 5                 Cyprus (0) 0
    *Macdonald 5*

*England:* Shilton (Stoke C); Madeley (Leeds U.), Watson (Sunderland), Todd (Derby Co.), Beattie (Ipswich T.), Bell (Manchester C.), Ball (Arsenal), Hudson (Stoke C.), Keegan (Liverpool), Channon (Southampton) (Thomas (Q.P.R.)), Macdonald (Newcastle U.).

*Cyprus:* Alkiviades (A. Constantinou); Kovis, Kyzas, Pentzaras, Koureas, Theodorou, Michael, Marcou, Charalamdous (Constantnous), Savva, Stylianou.

April 20
    Czechoslovakia (2) 4            Cyprus (0) 0
*Penanka 3 (1 a pen), Masny*

April 30
    Czechoslovakia (3) 5            Portugal (0) 0
*Bicovsky 2, Nehoda 2, Petras*

Limassol, May 11
    Cyprus (0) 0               England (1) 1
                           *Keegan*

*Cyprus:* A. Constantinou; Covis, Kyzas, Stylianou, Pantziaras, Michael, T. Constantinou, Miamiliotis (Papetas), Savva, Charalambous, Panayiotou (Antoniou).

*England:* Clemence (Liverpool; Whitworth (Leicester C.), Todd (Derby Co.), Watson (Sunderland), Beattie (Ipswich T.) (Hughes (Liverpool); Bell (Manchester C.), Ball (Arsenal); Thomas (QPR.) (Tueart (Manchester C.)), Channon (Southampton), Macdonald (Newcastle U.), Keegan (Liverpool).

7

June 8
  Cyprus (0) 0                        Portugal (1) 2
                                       *Nene, Moinos*

**Remaining fixtures:** 29.10.75 Czechoslovakia v England; 12.11.75 Portugal v Czechoslovakia; 19.11.75 Portugal v England; 23.11.75 Cyprus v Czechoslovakia; 3.12.75 Portugal v Cyprus.

---

## GROUP 2  WALES, Austria, Hungary, Luxemburg.

---

In this group, Austria and Hungary resumed their eternal rivalry – they seem fated to be drawn together in qualifying groups, whether they be for the World or Nations Cup – Wales set out under new management, Luxembourg made up the number.

The new Welsh manager was . . . an Englishman, the young national coach Mike Smith, once a Corinthian-Casuals amateur. He immediately impressed the players with his thoroughness, which included the provision of distractions on away trips, and showed his boldness by giving the 33-year-old Wrexham inside-forward, blond Arfon Griffiths, his second cap. Griffiths, once an Arsenal man, responded, in the good old tradition of Ted Robbins, Smith's remote predecessor, by rising splendidly to each occasion.

Like Don Revie, Smith unfortunately had to jump in the deep end with a Nations Cup match in Vienna which he lost. Griffiths actually gave Wales the lead with a header after the Austrian defence had made a mess of Leighton James' centre. Austria, however, were technically much the better, and turned the game after the coloured Koegelberger had come on as substitute on the hour. Though Sprake made some excellent saves, Kreuz, home from Holland, and the prolific Krankl gave them the game.

The Hungarians, given a surprising amount of trouble in Luxemburg and relying somewhat arbitrarily on young players, were well beaten in Cardiff. Meanwhile, they'd lost their new manager, Josef Bozsik, with heart trouble.

The Welsh were much the more incisive team, with Leighton James in glorious form. He it was who set up both goals, in the second half, beating several men before finding Reece, whose centre was eventually put in by Griffiths – again – and later crossing for Toshack to head the second. Luxemburg, lacking two of their best men were predictably no match for the Welsh at Swansea, Griffiths scoring again in their easy 5-0 win; the first Welshman to score in three successive internationals since Trevor Ford, 21 years earlier.

Wales' victory in Budapest was indeed a famous one; the first three against Hungary, in tournament football, for 30 years, the first by a British international team for an incredible 66. Moreover, it was well deserved, and would have been clearer had not John Toshack missed a penalty. Dai Davies, the 27-year-old Everton goalkeeper, crowned a fine season with an admirable display in the Welsh goal.

Indeed, it was only when the team relaxed, in the closing stages, that Branikovits was able to outpace Phillips and slip the ball past Davies.

Wales should have scored after 13 minutes, when Mahoney was brought down by Balint, after Wales had struck the bar. Toshack's penalty, however, was splendidly saved by the diving Meszaros. A cross from the right by the ebullient Leighton James allowed Toshack to make amends, and give Wales the lead.

After 59 minutes, the injured James gave way to little Brian Flynn of Burnley, another talented newcomer who, ten minutes later, took Toshack's pass, beat Balint and centred for Mahoney to chip into goal. It was another considerable success for the young Welsh manager, Mike Smith and his rapidly evolving team.

Vienna, 4 September 1974
| | |
|---|---|
| Austria (0) 2 | Wales (1) 1 |
| *Kreuz, Krankl* | *Griffiths* |

*Austria:* Rettensteiner; Eigenstiller, Winklbauer, Krieger, Kriess, Walzer, Stering, Kreuz, Krankl, Starek, Schlagbauer (Kogelberger).
*Wales:* Sprake (Birmingham C.); P. Roberts (Portsmouth),Phillips (Cardiff C.), D. Roberts (Oxford C.), J. Roberts (Birmingham C.), Yorath (Leeds U.), Mahoney (Stoke C.), Griffiths (Wrexham),Reece (Cardiff C.), Toshack (Liverpool), James (Burnley).


October 13
| | |
|---|---|
| Luxemburg (2) 2 | Hungary (2) 4 |
| *Dussier 2 (1 pen)* | *Horvath, Nagy (2), Balint* |


Cardiff, 30 October
| | |
|---|---|
| Wales (0) 2 | Hungary (0) 0 |
| *Griffiths, Toshack* | |

*Wales:* Sprake (Birmingham C.) (Phillips (Chelsea)); Thomas (Derby C.), P. Roberts (Portsmouth), Mahoney (Stoke C.), England (Tottenham H.), L. Phillips (Aston Villa), Griffiths (Wrexham), Yorath (Leeds U.), Reece (Cardiff C.), Toshack (Liverool), James (Burnley).,
*Hungary:* Meszaros; Torok, Balint, Mucha, Kantor ,Halmosi, Fekete Toth (Poczik), Fazekas, Kiss, Nagy.


Swansea, 20 November
| | |
|---|---|
| Wales (1) 5 | Luxemburg (0) 0 |
| *Toshack, England,* | |
| *P. Roberts, Griffiths,* | |
| *Yorath* | |

*Wales:* Sprake (Birmingham C.); Phillips (Aston Villa), Thomas (Derby Co.); P. Roberts (Portsmouth), England (Tottenham H.), Mahoney (Stoke C.) (Flynn (Burnley)), Reece (Cardiff C.), Yorath (Leeds U.), Toshack (Liverpool), Griffiths (Wrexham), James (Burnley).
*Luxemburg:* Thill; Fandell, Da Grava (Romer), Flenghi, Hansen, Trieweiler, Pilot, Zwang, Dussier, Langers (Martin), Braun, Phillip.

April 2 1975
Austria (0) 0                          Hungary (0) 0

Budapest, April 16
  Hungary (0) 1                        Wales (1) 2
    *Branikovits*                        *Toshack, Mahoney*
*Hungary:* Meszaros; Torock, Balint, Nagy, Horvath, Toth, Csapo,
Kocsis, Branikovits, Kozma, Mate.
*Wales:* Davies (Everton); Page, Roberts (Birmingham C.), Phillips
(Aston Villa), Thomas (Derby Co.); Mahoney (Stoke C.), Yorath
(Leeds U.), Griffiths (Wrexham); Reece (Cardiff C.), (Smallman
(Everton)), Toshack (Liverpool), James (Burnley) (Flynn (Burnley)).

Luxemburg, May 1
  Luxemburg (1) 1                      Wales (2) 3
    *Phillipp*                           *Reece, James* 2
*Luxemburg:* Moes; Fandel, Hansen, Pilot, Marque, Trierweiler,
Zuang, Phillipp, Zender, Marten, Braun.
*Wales:* Davies (Everton); Thomas (Derby), Page (Birmingham),
Yorath (Leeds), Roberts (Oxford), Phillips (Aston Villa), Griffiths
(Wrexham), (Flynn (Burnley)), Mahoney (Stoke C.), Reece (Cardiff),
Toshack (Liverpool), James (Burnley).

**Remaining fixtures:** 24.9.75, Hungary v Austria; 15.10.75, Austria v
Luxemburg; 19.10.75, Hungary v Luxemburg; 19.11.75, Wales v
Austria.

---

**GROUP 3**  NORTHERN IRELAND, Sweden, Yugoslavia, Norway

---

Northern Ireland, who made an emotional return to Belfast after long
absence when they played Yugoslavia in April, made an early and
uneven beginning in Scandinavia. Unexpectedly losing to Norway
in a careless performance, they just as unexpectedly beat the Swedes,
heroes of the World Cup.

In Oslo, the Irish even threw away the advantage of a third-minute
goal, scored by a newcomer, Tom Finney of Sunderland, after a
Norwegian pass to the 'keeper went astray. In the second half they
had no answer to the admirable Tom Lund, who scored twice to sink
them.

It was a very different story in Stockholm, where concentration and
spirit alike reached a far higher level. Even Edstroem and Sandberg,
devastating in the World Cup, could not penetrate a stout Irish defence
in which Chris Nicholl, winning his first cap on his father's Irish birth,
not only played stoutly, but also headed their first goal from an early
corner. O'Neill scored the second with a tremendous shot from outside
the penalty box. Ireland held that lead in the second half.

The Yugoslavs, who had lost their manager, Miljanic, and several
players – through injury and conscription – beat Norway without
10

excelling. Two of the goals were scored by their big, hard stopper, Katalinski, in the second half, after the first had ended 1–1, Vukotic equalising a goal from the irrepressible Tom Lund.

In the event, Northern Ireland's performance was fully worthy of this, their first match in Belfast for four years. Yugoslavia were beaten much more clearly and comfortably than the 1–0 score suggests, and Dave Clements thus made a very heartening debut as player manager. True, the absence of Dragan Dzajic hindered Yugoslavia, but the Irish performance remained impressive, not least that of Sammy McIlroy, the gifted young Manchester United inside-forward, while Spence of Bury made a vigorous debut at centre-forward.

The goal, after 23 minutes, was a combined Ipswich affair. At an earlier corner, Chris Nicholl had had a header cleared off the line by Buljan. Now Hunter, on the far post, headed McIlroy's corner, and Bryan Hamilton, with another header, made sure it was home. The one possible blemish on the goal was that Derek Spence seemed to have pushed Buljan to gain the corner.

With the exception of an early, anxious moment when Branko Oblak – back after long absence – flicked over the bar, Ireland were in clear command. Only a fine save by O. Petrovic prevented Hamilton scoring again, and just after half time the same player almost got a touch to Spence's fast cross, after a spectacular run.


Oslo, September 4
   Norway (0) 2                 Northern Ireland (1) 1
   *Lund* 2                        *Finney*
*Norway:* Karlsen; Goa, Birkelund, Brakstad, Groendalen, Johansen, Austboe, Kvia, Fuglset, Lund, Hestad.
*Northern Ireland:* Jennings (Tottenham H.); Rice (Arsenal), Craig (Newcastle U.) (Dowd (Glentoran)), O'Kane (Nottingham F.), Hunter (Ipswich T.), Clements (Everton), Hamilton (Ipswich T.), Cassidy (Newcastle U.), Finney (Sunderland), McIlroy (Manchester U.), McGrath (Tottenham H.).


Stockholm, October 30
   Sweden (0) 0                Northern Ireland (2) 2
                               *Nicholl, O'Neill*
*Sweden:* Hellstroem; B. Andersson, Karlsson, Nordqvist, R. Andersson, Tapper, Larsson, Torstensson, Kindvall, Edstroem, Sandberg.
*Northern Ireland:* Jennings (Tottenham H.); O'Kane (Nottingham F.), Nelson (Arsenal) (Blair (Oldham Ath.)), Jackson (Nottingham F.), Hunter (Ipswich T.), Nicholl (Aston Villa), Hamilton (Ipswich T.), Dowd (Sheffield W.), McIlroy (Manchester U.), O'Neill (Nottingham F.), Morgan (Aston Villa).


October 30
   Yougoslavia (1) 3            Norway (1) 1
   *Vukotic, Katalinski* (2)      *Lund*

Windsor Park, Belfast, April 16, 1975
   Northern Ireland (1) 1          Yugoslavia (0) 0
   *Hamilton*
*Northern Ireland:* Jennings (Tottenham H.); Rice (Arsenal), Nicholl (Aston Villa), Hunter (Ipswich T.), Nelson (Arsenal), Clements (Everton), O'Neill (Nottingham F.), Jackson (Nottingham F.), Hamilton (Ipswich T.), Spence (Bury), McIlroy (Manchester U.)
*Yugoslavia:* O. Petrovic; Muzinic, Hadziabdic, Perusovic, Katalinski, Buljan, Jankovic, Oblak, Vukotic, Jerkovic, Surjak.

June 4
   Sweden (1) 1                    Yugoslavia (1) 2
   *Edström*                       *Katalinski, Izevic*

**Remaining fixtures:** 9.6.75 Norway v Yugoslavia; 30.6.75 Sweden v Norway; 13.8.75 Norway v Sweden; 3.9.75, N. Ireland v Sweden; 15.10.75, Yugoslavia v Sweden; 29.10.75, N. Ireland v Norway; 19.11.75, Yugoslavia v N. Ireland.

---

**GROUP 4**  SCOTLAND, Spain, Denmark, Rumania.

---

This group was blemished and even farcified by the case of Roberto Martinez. Real Madrid's Argentinian-born forward played and scored in the 2–1 victories away to Denmark and Scotland, although the two Basque clubs, Bilbao and Real Sociedad, had been angrily insisting that his birth certificate was forged, and he was no Spaniard at all. The Scots were very passive about it, the Danes asked for an investigation. UEFA, in their customary perverse way, reminiscent of Joseph Heller's novel *Catch 22*, finally told the Danes that a rule existed (a Cheats' Charter?) whereby if you wanted to protest, you had to do so within 48 hours of the particular match. Matters were further complicated when Spain announced that the decision would be made by their courts.

Not that Scotland, who might well have won the return match in Valencia, had anyone to blame but themselves for their failure at Hampden. A weak midfield and a missed penalty cost them a game which they began impressively. After only 10 minutes, a 92,000 crowd was encouraged when Bremner hooked in a corner; but thereafter lack of match fitness took its toll, while Souness and Hutchison, who missed the penalty 11 minutes later when Migueli handled, were flaccid figures.

So the fine opportunism of Quini, with a shot on the turn after 32 minutes and a fast break and follow up after 61, gave Spain the match. They'd already won in Copenhagen, where Iribar made some admirable saves, and Martinez scored an enterprising goal from the narrowest of angles.

In Valencia, where the 33-year-old Charlie Cooke was recalled with much success, Scotland scored in the very first minute, Joe Jordan heading in after Burns had hit the bar. Alas, they could not consolidate their early superiority. Some rough, unchecked Spanish tackling impeded their rhythm, and Spain equalised after 56 minutes. The blond Rexach went round Cooke to cross, and the substitute Megido scored, though Buchan tried to keep the ball out with his hand and Willie Ormond claimed, erroneously and ill-advisedly, that it should have been a penalty.

Hopes for the Scots flickered again when Spain, despite scoring early and dominating play, could only draw with Rumania in Madrid, showing lack of drive in midfield, while UEFA's Control and Disciplinary Committee reviewed the Martinez Case. Unfortunately, this was now the province of the Spanish courts; with every prospect that delay would be both long and finally decisive.

Rumania then had a shattering 6–1 win in Bucharest over the Danes, their young forwards Georgescu and Crisam scoring a couple of goals each.

Short of a benign resolution of the Martinez Case, Scotland's hopes virtually disappeared when they failed to beat Rumania on June 1 in Bucharest; though a 1–1 draw was a good result, especially without Bremner and Co. of Leeds, and in the shadow of the 5–1 thrashing by England. Brown of Sheffield United made his debut in goal, and seemed to be at fault when Georgescu headed Rumania's goal, after a fine dribble and cross by the elegant Lucescu. His save from Dobrin's drive, just after half-time, atoned for this.

With 23 minutes left, Scotland brought on Hutchison and Robinson, and managed to equalise, despite the heat, in the last moments. Kenny Dalglish took a free kick, the ever adventurous McQueen hooked it in.

25 September, 1974
| Denmark (0) 1 | Spain (2) 2 |
| *Nygaard(pen)* | *Claramunt(pen)*, *Martinez* |

13 October
| Denmark (0) 0 | Rumania (0) 0 |

Hampden Park, 20 November
| Scotland (1) 1 | Spain (1) 2 |
| *Bremner* | *Quini* 2 |

*Scotland:* Harvey (Leeds U.); Jardine (Rangers), Forsyth (Manchester U.), Bremner (Leeds U.), McQueen (Leeds U.), Burns (Birmingham C.), Johnstone (Celtic), Souness (Middlesbrough), Deans (Celtic) (Lorimer (Leeds U.)), Jordan (Leeds U.), Hutchison (Coventry C.) (Dalglish (Celtic)).

*Spain:* Iribar; Castellanos, Benito, Capon, Migueli, (Sol), Costas, Martinez, Villar, Quini, Planas, Rexach.

Valencia, 5 February
| Spain (0) 1 | Scotland (1) 1 |
| *Megido* | *Jordan* |

*Spain:* Iribar; Sol, Benito, Costas (Migueli), Camach, Villar, Claramunt Asensi, Castro, Garate (Megido), Rexach.
*Scotland:* Harvey (Leeds U.); Jardine (Rangers), McQueen (Leeds U.), Buchan (Manchester U.), McGrain (Celtic), Bremner (Leeds U.), Dalglish (Celtic), Cooke (Chelsea), Hutchison (Coventry C.); Jordan (Leeds U.) (Parlane (Rangers)), Burns (Birmingham C.) (Wilson (Celtic)).

17 April
  Spain (1) 1                    Rumania (0) 1
  *Velazquez*                    *Crisan*

11 May
  Rumania (2) 6             Denmark (0) 1
  *Georgescu* 2, *Crisan* 2,
  *Lucescu, Dinu*

Bucharest, 1 June
  Rumania (1) 1             Scotland (0) 1
  *Georgescu*                *McQueen*
*Rumania:* Raducanu; Cheran, Satmareanu, Sandu, Anghelini (Kun), Dumitru, Dinu, Georgescu (Balaci), Crisan, Dobrin, Lucescu.
*Scotland:* Brown (Sheffield U.); McGrain (Celtic), McQueen (Leeds U.), Munro (Wolves), Forsyth (Manchester U.); Rioch (Derby C.) (Hutchison (Coventry C.)), Dalglish (Celtic), Miller (Aberdeen); Parlane (Rangers), Macari (Manchester U.) (Robinson (Dundee)), Duncan (Hibernian).

**Remaining fixtures:**
3.9.75, Denmark v. Scotland    12.10.75, Spain v. Denmark    29.10.75 Scotland v. Denmark 16.11.75, Rumania v. Spain 17.12.75, Scotland v. Rumania.

---

**GROUP 5** Holland, Poland, Italy, Finland.

---

Probably the strongest group of all, a particular irony putting Italy against the Poles, the team who knocked them out of the 1974 World Cup, and whom they were accused of trying unsuccessfully to bribe. Though Gorski, the Polish manager, mysteriously withdrew his published allegations, the story persisted. Offers, it was said in Polish circles, had actually been made to their players while on the field; Gorski had been ordered to withdraw his remarks to a Warsaw journalist by 'the authorities'.

Meanwhile the Poles began the season uneasily, their players manifestly sick of football, the brilliant Deyna threatening to retire at the end of the season, Gadocha demanding to go first to Munich then, when this was refused, to Nantes, Zmuda, the young centre-half and revelation of the World Cup, being suspended for wanting to leave his club. He was amnestied only just in time for the match against Italy, in Rome.

The Italians themselves, after an almost unbelievable attempt to appoint as their overall manager that great cultivator of referees, Italo Allodi, gave the job to the 68-year-old Fulvio Bernardini, once a great attacking centre-half, and later a most successful club manager. He unceremoniously threw out both Rivera *and* Mazzola, which was some sort of solution to that unending dualism, but found the way hard. Two very severe decisions in what was already an uphill struggle against the Dutch, in Rotterdam, stopped Italy from doing better than lose 3–1. Roberto Boninsegna gave them a very quick lead, and should have had a penalty when he was obviously fouled, while one of Cruyff's two goals – Orlandini could not hold him – seemed well offside.

The Poles had unexpected difficulty in winning their opening match against a spirited Finnish team, which scored after only three minutes. Szarmach equalised, and a splendid run by Kasperczak early in the second half gave Lato what turned out the winner. The return, predictably, raised fewer problems; but it was still scarcely the World Cup Poland.

In Rome Italy played a dull 0–0 draw against Poland, who were far from the dazzling team which had beaten Italy at Stuttgart in the World Cup. They complained that they were greatly affected by the heat and seemed happy enough to draw. Very few chances were made by either side, though Tomaszewski once saved from Graziani with his foot, and Pulici came close on another occasion. Italy used the huge striker Giorgio Chinaglia in a strange, deep-lying role.

1 September 1974
  Finland (1) 1         Poland (1) 2
  *Rahja*             *Szarmach, Lato*

25 September
  Finland (1) 1         Holland (2) 3
  *Rahja*             *Cruyff 2, Neeskens (pen)*

9 October
  Poland (2) 3         Finland (0) 0
  *Kasperczak, Gadocha, Lato*

20 November
  Holland (1) 3         Italy (1) 1
  *Rensenbrink, Cruyff 2*     *Boninsegna*

19 April 1975
  Italy (0) 0          Poland (0) 0

**Remaining fixtures:** 5.6.75, Finland v. Italy; 20.8.75, Holland v. Finland 10.9.75, Poland v. Holland; 27.9.75, Italy v. Finland; 25.10.75, Poland v. Italy; 22.11.75, Italy v. Holland.

Getting away to a splendid start, Eire made this group one of the most exciting and interesting of all. They thrashed the prosaic Russians with a hat trick by Don Givens, causing an agonising Soviet reappraisal and a decision to base the team on Dynamao Kiev. Next, they took a commendable point in Turkey, whom the Russians, some months later, emerged from hibernation to beat in Kiev.

Inspired by the splendid generalship of their player-manager, Johnny Giles, the Irish were far better than the Russians, in Dublin. Nor were they upset by an incident at a corner when Kaplichniy, the Russian stopper, broke Terry Mancini's nose, and was promptly felled by an Irish forward. He and Mancini were both expelled.

Givens, whose hat trick was the first by an Eire player since the war, leaped high to head his first goal from Joe Kinnear's cross midway through the first half. His second and third goals were knocked in with the Russian defence in disarray. Liam Brady, the 18-year-old Arsenal inside-forward, brother of two former Irish internationals, made a promising debut.

In Ismir, Givens again was the Irish scorer, coolly running through alone on to Giles' fine pass to evade the goalkeeper. The unfortunate Conroy had headed Mehmet's corner into his own goal to give Turkey the lead after 54 minutes. By and large, Ireland were cautious but compact.

Russia now took desperate and effective action, deciding to base their team on the successful Dynamo Kiev, winners of the Championship, and, later, winners of the Cup-Winners' Cup. No fewer than nine from Kiev played – in Kiev – against Turkey the following April. Russia won 3–0, two of the goals coming from the penalty spot through the clever inside-forward Kolotov, Blokhin getting the other. This made it almost inevitable that the group would be settled in Eire's hectic three games in May.

A desperately mediocre game in Zurich saw the Swiss draw 1–1 with the Turks, who equalised ten minutes after Kudi Muller had given Switzerland the lead.

Eire began their hectic ten days with a well deserved and unflattering 2–1 win in Dublin over Switzerland. As early as the second minute, Mick Martin threw himself at a centre by Ray Treacy to head the first goal. The second came 26 minutes later when Johnny Giles crossed from the right, Conroy and Givens had shots blocked, and Treacy finally thumped the ball in. Giles, Conroy and Brady ran the show, and the Swiss had much to thank Burgener, their goalkeeper, for. It was a little ironic that theirs should be the only goal of the second half; a breakaway, a cross by the experienced Kuhn, a volley by Kudi Muller.

Though Steve Heighway returned for their game in Kiev, Eire did not do so well. Dynamo Kiev, having won the European Cup-Winners' Cup but four days earlier, now put on their other hat, or shirts, to represent the Soviet Union, en bloc. Against UEFA's laxly applied rules, the match had duly been switched from Moscow to Kiev.

Russia, or Kiev, should have won more easily than 2–1. Their own inadequate finishing, fine goalkeeping by the Manchester United reserve Paddy Roche, and a 79th minute goal by stopper Eoin Hand, beating two defenders to a through pass, frustrated them.

Oleg Blokhin, hero of Basel, scored first after 14 minutes, having 'nutmegged' Joe Kinnear, while after 29 minutes, Viktor Kolotov headed the second.

The following Wednesday, in Berne, Eire surprisingly and disappointingly lost to Switzerland, thus severely compromising their chances, and raising Russia's hopes. They looked a weary team, and lost to a goal 14 minutes from time by the substitute Elsener, after Hand had collided with Conroy. Johnny Giles, who had injured a calf, then had to give way to the substitute, Daly; and Eire's hopes evaporated.

Dublin, 30 October
Eire (2) 3                        USSR (0) 0
Givens 3
*Eire:* Roche (Manchester U.); Kinnear (Tottenham H.), Mulligan (Crystal Palace), Mancini (Arsenal), Holmes (Coventry C.), Martin (Manchester U.), Giles (Leeds U.), Brady (Arsenal), Heighway (Liverpool), Givens (Q.P.R.), Treacy (Preston N.E.).
*USSR:* Pilgui; Nikolini, Olshansky, Matvienko, Kaplichny, Lovchev, Eremecvc, Onishenko, Kolotov, Fedotov (Feodorov), Blokhin.

Izmir, 20 November
Turkey (0) 1                      Eire (0) 1
Martin (o.g.)                     Givens
*Turkey:* Yasinl; Alpaslan, Ismail, Ziya, Zekeriya, Egin, Selcuk, F. Mehmet, B. Mehmet, Camil, Metin.
*Eire:* Roche (Manchester U.); Kinnear (Tottenham H.), Mulligan (Crystal Palace), Hand (Portsmouth), Dunne (Bolton W.), Martin (Manchester U.), Brady (Arsenal), Giles (Leeds U.), Heighway (Liverpool), Conroy (Stoke C.), Givens (Q.P.R.).

1 December
Turkey (1) 2                      Switzerland (1) 1
Ismail, B. Mehmet                Schild

2 April
USSR (1) 3                        Turkey (0) 0
Kolotov (2 pens), Blokhin

30 April
Switzerland (1) 1                Turkey (0) 1
Muller                           Alpasian

17

Dublin, 11 May

Eire (2) 2                          Switzerland (0) 1
*Martin, Treacy*                    *Muller*

*Eire:* Roche (Manchester U.); Kinnear (Spurs), Dunne (Bolton W.), Mulligan (Crystal Palace), Hand (Portsmouth), Brady (Arsenal), Martin (Manchester U.), Treacy (Preston N.E.), Conroy (Stoke C.), Giles (Leeds U.), Givens (QPR.).
*Switzerland:* Burgener; Hasler, Hree, Bizzini, Guyot, Kuhn, Rutschmann, Schild, Jeandupeux, Nuller, Botteron.

18 May

Russia (2) 2                        Eire (0) 1
*Blokhin, Kolotov*                  *Hand*

*Russia:* Rudakov; Konkov, Matvienko, Fomenko, Troschkin, Kolotov, Muntijan, Veremeyev; Onishenko, Burjak, Blokhin.
*Eire:* Roche (Manchester U.); Kinnear (Spurs), Hand (Portsmouth), Mulligan (Crystal Palace), Dunne (Bolton W.); Martin (Manchester U.), Brady (Arsenal), Giles (Leeds U.); Conroy Stoke C.), Heighway (Liverpool), Givens (QPR.).

21 May

Switzerland (0) 1                   Eire (0) 0
*Elsener*

*Switzerland:* Burgener; Bizzini, Trinchero, Guyot, Fischbach; Kuhn, Hasler, Botteron; Rutschmann (Pfister), Muller (Elsener), Jeandupeux.
*Eire:* Roche (Manchester U.); Dunne (Bolton W.), Mulligan (Crystal Palace), Hand (Portsmouth), Holmes (Coventry C.); Martin (Manchester U.), Giles (Leeds U.) (Daly (Manchester U.)), Brady (Arsenal); Conroy (Stoke C.), Treacy (Swindon T.), Givens (Manchester U.).

**Remaining fixtures:** 12.10.75, Switzerland v. USSR; 29.10.75, Eire v. Turkey; 12.11.75, USSR v. Switzerland; 23.11.75, Turkey v. USSR.

---

**GROUP 7**   France, Belgium, East Germany, Iceland.

---

The most astonishing result of the group so far has certainly been Iceland's 1–1 draw in Magdeburg against East Germany, who utterly belied their World Cup form in the opening months of the season, failing to win any of their first three Nations Cup games. Well coached by the old Leicester centre-half, Tony Knapp, the Icelanders surpassed themselves, refusing to despair when Streich gave the Germans an early lead. When Mathias Halmgrimsson was left unmarked five yards from goal he duly equalised, and Iceland's 4–4–2 formation repelled all further pressure. In June, Iceland beat them 2–1!

The Germans were unequally unable to win at home to Belgium, but deserved to win in Paris, where two very late goals pinned them back, Gallice heading the equaliser. Iceland then sunk them.

In Brussels, the French had lost to Belgium, a 'derby' game they might have saved were it not for a couple of defensive errors, Baratelli letting Martens' shot fly through his legs in the first half, Lacombe getting caught in possession, giving Van der Elst a goal, in the second. Previously Coste, the new international from Lille, had equalised, and France had had the better of the first half, especially in midfield.

France went to Iceland in May and were held to a goalless draw on a difficult pitch, dominating the second half but failing to score.

8 September 1974
Iceland (0) 0                          Belgium (1) 2
                                       *Van Moer 2 (1 pen)*

12 October
East Germany (1) 1                     Iceland (1) 1
*Hoffman*                              *Hallgrimsson*

Belgium (1) 2                          France (1) 1
*Martens, Van der Elst*                *Coste*

17 November
France (0) 2                           East Germany (1) 2
*Guillou, Gallice*                     *Sparwasser, Kreische*

7 December
East Germany (0) 0                     Belgium (0) 0

25 May
Iceland (0) 0                          France (0) 0

5 June
Iceland 2                              East Germany 1

**Remaining fixtures:** 3.9.75, France v. Iceland; 6.9.75, Belgium v. Iceland; 27.9.75, Belgium v. E. Germany; 11.10.75, E. Germany v. France; 15.11.75, France v. Belgium.

---

**GROUP 8**   West Germany, Greece, Bulgaria, Malta.

---

World and European Cup holders, West Germany found themselves with a team to rebuild. Müller, Overath, and Grabowski retired from international football after the World Cup. Paul Breitner was transferred to Spain. Their remodelled team made a shaky beginning, drawing in Greece with some difficulty, and only squeezing through in Malta, a result which looked better when the Maltese proceeded to beat the Greeks, who had previously drawn with, then very easily beaten, Bulgaria, though the one goal margin in the latter game was flattering to the Bulgars.

In Athens, the Germans were twice behind to a Greek team which recalled the skilled 33-year-old inside-left Domazos with success, and played another 33-year-old in the centre-forward, Papoinnou. The German team clearly missed Gerd Müller's finishing, Rainer

Bonhof was missing, too – suspended – and his club colleague, Herbert Wimmer, headed the equaliser only seven minutes from time.

A goal by Cullmann gave them their narrow win in Malta, and the Maltese excelled themselves by defeating Greece. Well organised in defence by their Italian coach Polverini, they kept the Greeks at bay on the rough pitch and opened the score through 20-year-old Richard Aquilina, playing his first international, after 32 minutes. The Greeks' heads dropped, Malta cleverly played possession football, and ten minutes from time Magro scored the second from a bizarre angle.

West Germany recalled both their Real Madrid players, Paul Breitner and Gunter Netzer, for the match in Sofia against Bulgaria, but could still do no better than a 1–1 draw, each side scoring from a penalty, Breitner giving away the Bulgarian spot kick, but gaining Germany's when he was brought down on one of his overlaps. Bulgaria, under their new manager Ormandjiev, fielded a very young team, which excluded even Bonev.

12 October 1974
   Bulgaria (3) 3                Greece (1) 3
   *Bonev, Denev 2*           *Antoniadis, Papaionnou, Glezos*

20 November
   Greece (1) 2               West Germany (0) 2
   *Delikaris, Eleftherakis*       *Cullmann, Wimmer*

18 December
   Greece (2) 2               Bulgaria (0) 1
   *Serafis, Antoniadis*          *Denev*

29 December
   Malta (0) 0                West Germany (1) 1
                            *Cullmann*

23 February 1975
   Malta (1) 2                Greece (0) 0
   *Aquilina, Magra*

27 April
   Bulgaria (0) 1            West Germany (0) 1
   *Kolev (pen)*              *Breitner (pen)*

June 4
   Greece (2) 4                Malta (0) 0
   *Mavros, Antoniades,*
   *Iosifides, Opapaioannou*

**Remaining fixtures:** 11.6.75, Bulgaria v Malta; 11.10.75, West Germany v Greece; 19.11.75, West Germany v Bulgaria; 21.12.75, Malta v Bulgaria; 28.2.76, West Germany v Malta.

# CHAPTER TWO

# European Cup 1974–75

Leeds United became only the second English team to reach the final of the European Cup; but not the second to win it. Having overcome Barcelona and Cruyff in the semi-final, they fell in a contentious, ill-starred final to the holders, Bayern Munich, in Paris, in a match most dubiously refereed and further blemished by violence from the Leeds fans. UEFA then banned Leeds for three years.

Leeds' achievement in getting so far was remarkable, given their turbulent beginning to the season; Brian Clough's stormy 44 days. Jimmy Armfield, who succeeded him, brought calm and order, though he might have made more adventurous use of the splendid forward Clough left behind – Duncan McKenzie. The indications were that McKenzie, for all his talents – and perhaps even because of them – was not wholly *persona grata* with the close knit, long established team.

Beating Zurich, Ujpest, then Barcelona, Leeds went from strength to strength where Bayern tottered. They, too, sacked one manager and appointed another, little Dettmar Cramer, the ex-FIFA chief coach, succeeding Udo Lattek at the turn of the year and finding what he called 'a dying team'.

Even in the final, Bayern looked no more than a parody of their splendid Cup winning side of 1974, playing dourly in defence, luckily surviving two penalty appeals against Beckenbauer (their outstanding player) and what looked a good goal by Peter Lorimer. Then, in two late breakaways, Roth and Müller struck, Leeds had lost the Cup, and their fans, behind the Bayern goal, rioted shamefully on the terraces.

Jimmy Armfield, the new manager, from Bolton Wanderers, was an altogether less flamboyant figure, a former England right-back, who set about picking up the pieces. His critics accused him of indecision, yet he had the strength of character to pull Bremner off late in the home game with Anderlecht, to rest him, and the shrewdness to turn Frankie Gray, a reserve outside-left, into a splendidly successful left-back. If he was strangely reluctant to use the enterprising, unorthodox McKenzie, he took Leeds farther in the European Cup than Don Revie himself had ever done, for in the 1970 semi-final Leeds lost both legs. Moreover, their 1975 team was as put upon as 1970's, in terms of fixtures. The home leg against Barcelona was the seventh game in a fortnight.

The 'natural' Final seemed from the outset to be Bayern against Barcelona, but by the turn of the year, both teams had shipped abundant water. Bayern, losing Paul Breitner to Real Madrid, and dreadfully weary after their players' efforts in Bundesliga, World Cup, European Cup, and an ill-judged series of friendlies, fared disastrously in the League, eventually sacking Udo Lattek, their manager, at the turn of the year, and bringing back little Dettmar Cramer, from the USA, to take his place. The move incurred the justified wrath of the Americans, who had recently put him under contract as their national coach, and the satisfaction of Franz Beckenbauer. But for many weeks, things went no better in the League.

Fortunately, Bayern were able to raise their game for the European Cup matches, particularly when, in the Second Round, Fate pitted them against East Germany's Magdeburg, winners of the Cup-Winners' Cup in 1974, a team whose star was Jurgen Sparwasser, scorer of the World Cup goal which had beaten West Germany, including numerous Bayern players, in Hamburg.

Sparwasser duly scored in both legs, but Bayern showed finer recuperative powers, and Gerd Müller his old opportunism. They began the first leg, in Munich, appallingly, Hansen, their Danish full-back, putting through his own goal and Sparwasser snapping up a second. In the second half, however, the more gifted and sophisticated Bayern team found its rhythm, Müller scored three, including a penalty, and the game was won, 3–2. In Magdeburg he scored two more, to Sparwasser and Magdeburg's one, and Bayern had come through with credit.

This gave them the long winter hiatus to get themselves better together, and the draw favoured them by giving them the ex-Russian Champions from Armenia, Ararat Erevan, just deposed by Dynamo Kiev.

Ararat played a cautious, defensive game in Munich, and held out until Bayern brought on Uli Hoeness, who had long been absent after a cartilage operation, and then had a nasty stud injury to his ankle. Hoeness scored a superb goal after dribbling past several Russians; Tortensson, the Swede, who had also had much injury trouble, added a second, and these late goals saw Bayern through. In Armenia, the clever Andriassian got the only goal of the game in the first half, but Ararat could contrive no more.

Barcelona also foundered, with Johan Cruyff, in his second season, now receiving much rougher treatment from opponents, and scant sympathy with referees. The arrival of his compatriot Johan Neeskens was of surprisingly little help, particularly as it meant omitting the little Peruvian forward Sotil, who had fed off Cruyff so well the previous season. Barcelona resourcefully – if that is the word – got round the problem of the 'extra' foreigner by discovering Spanish origins not only for Argentina's Juan Carlos Heredia, whom they had had to lend elsewhere, but even for Mario Marinho, who had actually played for Brazil in the World Cup!

Their clash with Feyenoord in the Second Round was a considerable one. In the first leg, at Rotterdam, Barcelona defended to a degree, and were fortunate that the dreadful weather impeded Feyenoord's almost ceaseless attacks. They themselves, in fact, had three foreigners in Kreuz, Ramljak, and Kristensen. Van Hanegem hit the bar in the first half, Jansen in the second. Neeskens devoted himself simply to marking Van Hanegem.

Jansen marked his Dutch international colleague Cruyff with great success, and the Spanish hero was unquestionably Mora, the lesser known of their two goalkeepers, who had to give way to Sadurni 17 minutes from time. Cruyff splendidly created good chances for Clares and Rexach in the first half, but both were missed.

Carlos Rexach was much less forgiving in Barcelona, where it was a different ball game. Though without their Spanish international inside-forwards Asensi and Marcial, one hurt, the other suspended, Barcelona were dominant after the first half hour. Neeskens was dominating, Cruyff spectacular, and the clever Van Hanegem again found his ex-team mate Neeskens a hard opponent. Perhaps the Dutch were too cautious, leaving out their strikers Kreuz and Schoenmaker in the first half. By the interval they were already two down, Cruyff's crosses making both for Rexach, who converted another of them after 71 minutes; an impressive win.

Much less impressive was their double victory over the Swedish Champions Atvidaberg, who most controversially agreed to play both matches in Barcelona, since their own ground was at that time of year unplayable. There was nothing, however, to stop their home leg being played in Stockholm; or even in a neutral country.

The dark horses, meanwhile, were the French champions Saint Etienne, welded into a fine, combative, resilient side by their old captain, Roby Herbin. Even when they astonished some and enraged others by transferring their international captain, left-winger Georges Bereta, between the Second Round and the quarter-finals, they maintained their momentum.

With the Yugoslav veteran Curkovic in goal, the Argentinian cap Piazza at centre-half, the brothers Revelli in attack, Larqué dropping back successfully to midfield, and young Barthenay emerging as a splendid half-back, they recovered sensationally against both Hajduk and the powerful Poles, Ruch Chorzow.

In the Second Round, Hajduk thrashed them 4–1 in Split, but when they brought their Franco-Greek striker, the forceful Triantafilos, on late in the return game, everything changed. His two goals enabled them to lead 4–1 at the end of normal time, then score again in extra time to go through on aggregate. True, Hajduk badly missed Oblak, ruled out by an Achilles tendon injury, but it was a glorious recovery.

So was that against Ruch Chorzow, inspired by such fine players as Masczyk, a World Cup hero, and Bula, in midfield. At one stage in Chorzow Saint Etienne were 3–0 down, but they fought back again to lose only 2–0, and finished the job 2–0 in France. Alas for them, the next draw obliged them to play the first rather than the second leg at home, and wily Bayern pegged them to a goalless draw, finishing the more dangerous side.

Leeds rose on stepping stones of their moribund League selves to trounce Zurich 4–1, hitherto undefeated all season. Though Bremner, so often the driving force, was under suspension, Leeds steadily gained their old confidence to control the game, with Johnny Giles genially orchestrating their play. Not only did they get four goals, two of them Allan Clarke's, but they struck the woodwork four times; Clarke twice, Lorimer twice more. Botteron had bright moments in the Zurich attack, and Katic scored a very late goal, but the die was plainly cast. True,

Leeds lost 2–1 in Zurich, giving the poorest display of their European Cup run; but they would put this behind them.

Zurich, surprisingly, dominated the game, after Clarke's splendid individualist's goal in the 37th minute had put the tie out of their reach. In the second half, David Harvey had to play like a hero to keep the score down to two; but at least Leeds were through, which was more than could be said for Celtic.

The Scottish Champions, destined to lose their Championship, were most unexpectedly put out in the First Round by the Greeks, Olympiakos, who thoroughly deserved their success. Not till the clever Uruguayan, Viera, who had lobbed a fine goal ten minutes from half time, was expelled ten minutes from the end after pulling Hood's jersey, did Celtic manage an equaliser through Paul Wilson. Celtic never mastered the gifted Delikaris in midfield.

Even without Viera, Olympiakos were too good for Celtic in Piraeus. Making light of the bumpy pitch, the Greeks led through the excellent Kritikopoulos after only three minutes, when he dived to the admirable Delikaris' free kick. The second goal came from another free kick, which Stavropoulos simply drove through the porous Celtic wall.

So it was left to Leeds, who girded themselves for a magnificent victory over the fine, experienced Hungarian team, Ujpest, themselves past European Cup conquerors of Celtic. Leeds won the first leg 2–1 in Budapest, despite having Duncan McKenzie sent off for a hot-headed retaliation after the last of several painfully provocative fouls. They then overwhelmed the Hungarians 3–0 at Elland Road.

Leeds, as Jimmy Armfield said, 'caught Ujpest cold' with a goal after only 13 minutes. When the Ujpest keeper, Rothermel, fumbled the ball, McKenzie got it across to Peter Lorimer, who scored from a very slim angle. Nine minutes later Gordon McQueen, who played a dominant game at centre-half, as he would so often do in the competition, forsook defence to head Johnny Giles' free kick inside the right hand post. It gave Leeds back the lead, Fazekas having scored for Ujpest, and had Lorimer not hit the post with a late penalty, it would have been 3–1. Ujpest themselves had Harsanyi sent off a few minutes later.

The return was one way traffic. Leeds, with Bremner and Clarke back in the side, were utterly superior. Ujpest could match them for technique, but not for pace, commitment and incision. The big McQueen headed another goal, the first, from Giles' free kick, after half-an-hour. A minute after the break, Cooper shot, Szigeti turned it for a corner, Giles found Lorimer, who crossed, Yorath headed against the bar, Bremner headed in. It was a goal to crown Bremner's happy return to the team, for he had missed 22 games and played only a League Cup tie. Clarke missed a number of chances, but Terry Yorath himself headed the third goal after a delightful move, Clarke finally heading him Paul Madeley's centre.

Four months later, it was Anderlecht, the Belgian Champions, whom Leeds had to play; and they did another double. Anderlecht had not had a good season, floundering in the League, beaten by Olympiakos in Piareus, after overwhelming them in the first leg in Brussels. But any teams with so many Belgian internationals, with the fine veteran Paul Van Himst in midfield, the flying Dutchman Rensenbrink in attack, had to be respected.

The first leg, at Elland Road, took place in such thick fog that it had to be abandoned for fifteen minutes in the first half. Anderlecht played defensively, and Leeds took the lead in the 11th minute, a splendid pass by Norman Hunter releasing Joe Jordan, whose shot Ruiter should have saved.

It was touch and go whether the match could be continued, but the fog lifted sufficiently for it to be resumed, and Leeds, though often caught by Anderlecht's offside trap, scored twice more. One of Giles' insidious free kicks was headed across goal by Jordan, and headed into goal by McQueen, yet again. Loeck missed a wonderful late chance to score when Rensenbrink pulled the ball back from the left goal line, and Anderlecht lived to regret it when Lorimer scored a third, after Eddie Gray's shot was blocked.

The weather in Brussels was vile, too, though this time it was a case of snow, sleet, and rain, not fog. Leeds left out Eddie Gray and Giles, played an economical but highly effective game, and had David Stewart to thank for a couple of splendid saves in each half, Reaney for heading off the line from Thissen in the first. Their goal, after 75 minutes, was a jewel. Lorimer crossed from the left, Bremner ran in from the right, breasted the ball past Broos and lobbed delicately over Barth, who sportingly shook hands with him. The Leeds defence was admirable.

The semi-finals gave Leeds Barcelona, and Johan Cruyff. Surprisingly, Jimmy Armfield left out both Lorimer and McKenzie – eligible again after suspension – from the home leg at Elland Road. The consequence was territorial domination but few chances. Barcelona inevitably packed their defence, with Marinho as sweeper, Cruyff often dropping back, but it was a case of number rather than quality; banal mistakes were legion, and Eddie Gray ran elegant rings around De La Cruz.

Leeds scored after only ten minutes from yet another free kick by Johnny Giles. Crossing from the left, he saw the ball flicked on by Joe Jordan to a surprisingly unmarked Billy Bremner. Bremner, on the right of the goal, had abundant time to control the ball, steady himself, and shoot past Sadurni's right hand.

Cruyff, in dazzling fits and starts, was always dangerous, and McQueen twice intervened splendidly to rob him after he had left first Madeley, then Yorath. Just before half-time, Eddie Gray left De La Cruz standing, for a cross which Jordan struck mightily, only for Sadurni to turn it one handed over the bar; a glorious save.

So it was that 19 minutes into the second half, Barcelona were able to equalise. Cruyff's fine through pass sent Heredia away, Reaney was penalised for his tackle, Cruyff rolled the free-kick to Asensi, and Asensi shot low through the wall.

It was a sickening reversal for Leeds, who no longer looked the power they'd been in the first half; partly because too much was expected of Bremner in terms of bursts down the vacant right flank. But with thirteen minutes left, Madeley, preferred to Hunter as second stopper, nicely found Paul Reaney, who flew down the right flank, beat his man, and crossed. Once again Jordan headed across goal, and this time Allan Clarke banged the ball home. Would 2–1 be enough?

In Barcelona, Leeds scored a goal in seven minutes, gained a 1–1 draw despite the expulsion of Gordon McQueen, and became only the second English team ever to reach the final of the European Cup, seven years after Manchester United became the first.

Their performance in the first half was remarkable for its poise, authority, and cool excellence. With Frankie Gray playing splendidly against the talented Carlos Rexach, to whom so many Barcelona balls were played, Terry Yorath showing a new skill and maturity ('I've grown up'), Jordan immense courage, Barcelona were reduced to high, hopeful crosses.

Peter Lorimer scored a splendid early goal which took the uncertain Barcelona defence by surprise, moving on to Jordan's back header, after a long clearance by Stewart, to drive a relentless right-footed shot by Sadurni. True, Barcelona might have scored even before that, when Heredia got his head to De La Cruz's fine right wing cross and was only a little wide, but Leeds now took control.

They lost it in the second half when Barcelona brought on Rife for Asensi and pushed up Marinho, who had been wasting time as a sweeper. Jordan, meanwhile, had had four stitches in his cheek after being brutally elbowed by Migueli, Neeskens committed several unpleasant fouls, Gallego was booked for a savage tackle on Bremner, while Heredia, just before Barcelona's free kick and goal, kicked Yorath with impunity.

Though Cruyff never began to dominate the game, and Jimmy Armfield's decision to play Madeley merely on the right flank rather than use him as Cruyff's shadow, was justified, Barcelona won the midfield. Perhaps over caution was at the root of Leeds' decline. Had it not been for the glorious goalkeeping of Stewart, whose one handed save from Cruyff's deflected shot, ten minutes from time, was astonishing, Leeds might have gone down.

As it was, the only goal Barcelona got came after 68 minutes, when Clares neatly headed in Gallego's free kick from the right.

Twenty-five minutes from time, McQueen, in a moment of wild aberration, felled Clares, and was sent off the field. Now it became a matter of sheer survival. Stewart, who had already made a wonderful save from Heredia's header, made his still better one from Cruyff and, after 89 minutes, flung himself successfully at the Dutchman's feet, as Neeskens headed the ball down. A memorable performance.

In Munich, Bayern duly got the better of Saint Etienne, both goals coming from defenders, but their performance was drab and a timid one. When Beckenbauer scored from Hoeness' cross as early as the second minute, all seemed set for a jamboree by Bayern. Instead of which they closed up the game, kept only two men upfield, let Saint Etienne attack, and were fortunate that the French team should do so down the blocked middle, rather than on the wings.

The final, on the disgracefully inadequate, deceptively green, pitch of the Parc des Princes was a sombre affair. In the first minutes, a lamentable tackle by Terry Yorath, after the referee, M. Kitabdjian, had whistled a foul against Frankie Gray, lamed Andersson, and put him off the field. Later Uli Hoeness, hurt when he tackled Frankie Gray, also had to be substituted, by Klaus Wunder. As Cramer said, it took Bayern half-an-hour to digest these changes. For all that, their bleak defensive posture was deplorable.

Twice in the first half Leeds seemed to have good claims to a penalty, first when Beckenbauer handled to stop Peter Lorimer dashing through, then when Beckenbauer palpably tripped Allan Clarke. They played, most successfully, to Joe Jordan's head; but when they did make chances, they found Sepp Maier in superlative form. He dived to catch Jordan's right footed shot, on the turn in the first half, while in the second he stopped a point blank shot from Bremner, after Madeley headed on Lorimer's free-kick, which would have given United the lead.

In the 67th minute, Giles took a free kick, Madeley's head was there again, a defender headed out, and Lorimer, with a glorious volley, beat Maier. After hesitation, and a word with his linesman, M. Kitabdjian, having refused both penalties, disallowed the attempt for offside – 'against three Leeds players'. One, Bremner, was in an offside position, but scarcely interfering with the play, and he claimed, in any case, that the shot had hit an opponent.

It was then that the violent Leeds supporters began breaking up seats and savagely bombarding the field, knocking out a ball boy and a policeman, blinding a photographer in one eye, menacing Sepp Maier. When Bayern rashly attempted a full lap of honour, they bombarded them, too. It was a sorry end to a depressing evening. As for the Bayern goals, both were excellent. Roth, newly restored to the team, scored the first after 72 minutes, Müller and the previously invisible Torstensson setting him up for a low left footer into the right hand corner. Müller swept in the second, right footed, after Kappelmann's fine work on the by-line. So the Cup was dashed from Leeds United's lips. . . .

## ROUND BY ROUND RESULTS

**First Round**

| | |
|---|---|
| Leeds United (3) 4 | FC Zurich (0) 1 |
| *Clarke* 2, *Lorimer* (pen), | *Katic* |
| *Jordan* | |

*Leeds United:* Harvey; Reaney, Cooper, Yorath, McQueen, Hunter, Lorimer, Clarke, Jordan, Giles, Madeley.
*Zurich:* Grob; Heere, Rutschmann (Marti), Ziglerlig, Bionda, Kuhn, Martinelli, Katic, Jeandupeux, Stierli, Botteron.

| | |
|---|---|
| FC Zurich (2) 2 | Leeds United (1) 1 |
| *Katic*, *Rutschmann* (pen) | *Clarke* |

*Zurich:* Grob; Hiera, Bionda, Zigerlig, Stierli, Martinelli, Rutschmann, Kuhn, Katic, Jeandupeux, Botteron.
*Leeds United:* Harvey; Reaney, Cherry, Yorath, Madeley, Hunter, Lorimer, Clarke, Jordan, Bates, Gray, F. (Hampton).

Celtic (0) 1       Olympiakos (1) 1
*Wilson*        *Viera*

*Celtic:* Connachan; McGrain, Brogan (Lennox), Murray, McNeill, McCluskey, Johnstone, Hood, Dalglish, Callaghan, Wilson.
*Olympiakos:* Kelessidis; Kyrastas, Aggolis, Siokos, Glezos, Perssidis, Losanda, Viera, Kritikopoulos, Delikaris, Stavropoulos.

Olympiakos (2) 2     Celtic (0) 0
*Kritikopoulos, Stavropoulos*

*Olympiakos:* Kelessidis; Liolios, Siokos, Glezos, Anglies, Persidis, Kyrastas, Delikaris, Losanda, Kritikopoulos, Stavropoulos (Davroulis).
*Celtic:* Connaghan; McGrain, Brogan, Murray, McNeill, McCluskey, Dalglish (Lennox), Callaghan, Johnstone (Hood), Deans, Wilson.

| | |
|---|---|
| Feyenoord (3) 7 | Coleraine (0) 0 |
| *Schoenmaker, Kreuz* 3, | |
| *Van Hanegem* 3, *Ressel* | |
| Coleraine (0) 1 | Feyenoord (2) 4 |
| *Simpson* | *Schoenmaker* 3 (1 *pen*), |
| | *Kreuz* |
| Universitatea Craiova 2 | Atvidaberg 1 |
| *Oblemenco* 2 | *Augustsson* |
| Atvidaberg 3 | Universitatea Craiova 1 |
| *Andersson, Ahlqvist* 2 (1 *pen*) | *Balin* |
| Levski Spartak (0) 0 | Ujpest (1) 3 |
| | *Horvath, Bene, Dunai* |
| Ujpest 4 | Levski Spartak 1 |
| *Bene* 2, *Dunai* 2 | *Voinov* |
| Valetta (1) 1 | HJK Helsinki (0) 0 |
| *Magno* | |
| HJK Helsinki (3) 4 | Valetta (0) 1 |
| *Rahja, Pettoniemi, Hamalainen,* | *Iglio* |
| *Forsell* | |
| SK Voest Lunz (0) 0 | Barcelona (0) 0 |
| Barcelona (3) 5 | SK Voest Linz (0) 0 |
| *Asensi, Clares* 2, *Carlos, Rexach* | |
| Viking Stavanger (0) 0 | Ararat Erevan (0) 2 |
| | *Makarov* 2 |
| Ararat Erevan (1) 4 | Viking Stavanger (2) 2 |
| *Makarov* 3, *Bonderenko* | |
| Hvidovre (Den.) (0) 0 | Ruch Chorzow (0) 0 |
| Ruch Chorzow (1) 2 | Hvidovre (0) 1 |
| *Bula* 2 | *Pederson* |
| Saint Etienne (1) 2 | Sporting Lisbon (0) 0 |
| *H. Revelli, Bereta* | |
| Sporting Lisbon (1) 1 | Saint Etienne (1) 1 |
| *Yazalde* | *Synaeghel* |
| Jeunesse D'Esch (0) 2 | Fenerbahce (1) 3 |
| *Mond, Melle* | *Osmàn* 2, *Cerril* |

Fenerbahce (1) 2                         Jeunesse D'Esch (0) 0
Slovan Bratislava (3) 4                   Anderlecht (0) 1
*Nvotny, Masny 2, Svehlik*                *Coeck, Van Himst*
Anderlecht (2) 3                          Slovan Bratislava (0) 1
*Van Himst, Coeck, Thissen*               *Masny*

**Second Round**

Ujpest (1) 1                              Leeds United (1) 2
*Fazekas (pen)*                           *Lorimer, McQueen*

*Ujpest:* Rothernel; Kellner, Harsanyi, Nagy, Horvath, Dunai I,
Fazekas, Toth, Zambo (Duani II), Fekete, Bene.
*Leeds United:* Harvey; Reaney, Cooper, Madeley, McQueen, Hunter,
Lorimer, Yorath, Jordan, Giles, McKenzie.

Leeds United (1) 3                        Ujpest (0) 0
*McQueen, Bremner, Yorath*

*Leeds United:* Harvey; Reaney, McQueen, Hunter (Cherry), Cooper
Bremner, Madeley, Giles, Lorimer (Harris), Clarke, Yorath.
*Ujpest:* Szigeti; Kolar, E. Dunai, Sarlos, Kellner, Toth, Fazekas,
Zambo, Fekete (A. Dunai), Bene, Nagy (Torocsik).

Feyenoord (0) 0                           Barcelona (0) 0
Barcelona (2) 3                           Feyenoord (0) 0
*Rexach 3*
Hajduk (1) 4                              Saint Etienne (1) 1
*Jerkovic 2, Gungul, Miac*                *Revelli*
Saint Etienne (1) 5                       Hajduk (0) 1
*Triantafilos 2, Barthenay,*              *Jovanic*
*Synaeghel, Larqué*
*(after extra time)*
HJK Helsinki (0) 0                        Atvidaberg (1) 3
                                          *Almqvist 2, B. Hasselberg*
Atvidaberg (0) 1                          HJK Helsinki (0) 0
*Almqvist*
Bayern Munich (0) 3                       Magdeburg (2) 2
*Müller 3 (1 pen)*                        *Hansen (o.g.), Sparwasser*
Magdeburg (1) 1                           Bayern Munich (0) 2
*Sparwasser*                              *Müller 2*
Ruch Chorzow (1) 2                        Fenerbahce (1) 1
*Kopicera, Beniger*                       *Niazi*
Fenerbahce (0) 0                          Ruch Chorzow (2) 2
                                          *Kopicera, Chojnacki*
Anderlecht (3) 5                          Olympiakos (1) 1
*Rensenbrink 3 (2 pens),*
*Ladinsky, Van der Elst*
Olympiakos (2) 3                          Anderlecht (0) 0
*Galakos 3*
Cork Celtic (0) 1                         Ararat Erevan (1) 2
*Tambling*                                *Zanazanyan, Kazaryan*

Ararat Erevan (1) 5                     Cork Celtic (0) 0
*Pogosyan 2, Zanazanyan,*
*Ishtoyan, Andriassian*

**Quarter Finals**
Leeds United (2) 3                      Anderlecht (0) 0
*Jordan, McQueen, Lorimer*
*Leeds United:* Stewart; Madeley, F. Gray, Bremner (Yorath), Mc-
Queen, Hunter, Lorimer, Clarke, Jordan, Giles, E. Gray.
*Anderlecht:* Ruiter; Van Binst, Broos, Van Den Daele, Thissen, Dockx,
Verheyen, Vanderelst, Coeck, Van Himst, Rensenbrink.

Anderlecht (0) 0                        Leeds United (0) 1
                                        *Bremner*
*Anderlecht:* Barth; Dockx, Broos, Van Den Daele, Thissen, Van der
Elst, Coeck, Nicolaes (Denul), Ladinski, Van Himst, Rensenbrink.
*Leeds United:* Stewart; Reaney, McQueen, Hunter, F. Gray, Bremner,
Yorath, Madeley, Lorimer, Jordan, Clarke.

Bayern Munich (0) 2                     Ararat Erevan (0) 0
*Hoeness, Torstensson*
Ararat Erevan (1) 1                     Bayern Munich (0) 0
*Andriassian*
Barcelona (1) 2                         Atvidaberg (0) 0
*Marinho, Clares*
Barcelona (1) 3                         Atvidaberg (0) 0
*Gallego, Asensi, Neeskens*
(*both games in Barcelona by arrangement*)
Ruch Chorzow (2) 3                      Saint Etienne (0) 2
*Masczyk, Beninger, Bula* (pen)        *Larqué, Triantafilos*
Saint Etienne (1) 2                     Ruch Chorzow (0) 0
*Janvion, Revelli (pen)*

**Semi-Finals**
Leeds United (1) 2                      Barcelona (0) 1
*Bremner, Clarke*                       *Asensi*
*Leeds United:* Stewart: Reaney, McQueen, Madeley, F. Gray, Bremner,
Yorath, Giles, Clarke, Jordan, E. Gray.

*Barcelona:* Sadurni; De La Cruz, Marinho, Migueli, Gallego, Costas
(Rife), Neeskens, Heredia, Asensi, Rexach, Cruyff.
Barcelona (0) 1                         Leeds United (1) 1
*Clares*                                *Lorimer*
*Barcelona:* Sadurni; Marinho, Gallego, De La Cruz, Miguell, Nees-
kens, Rexach, Heredia, Cruyff, Asensi (Rife), Clares.
*Leeds United:* Stewart; Cherry, Gray, Bremner, McQueen, Hunter,
Madeley, Yorath, Lorimer, Jordan, Clarke.

Saint Etienne (0) 0                     Bayern Munich (0) 0

30

Bayern Munich (1) 2                          Saint Etienne (0) 0
*Beckenbauer, Dürnberger*

**Final**   Paris, 28 May, 1975
Bayern Munich (0) 2                          Leeds United (0) 0
*Roth, Müller*

*Bayern:* Maier; Beckenbauer, Dürnburger, Schwarzenbeck, Andersson (Weiss), Zobel, Roth, Kapelmann, Torstensson, Müller, Hoeness (Wunder).
*Leeds United:* Stewart; Reaney, Madeley, Hunter, F. Gray, Bremner, Yorath (E. Gray), Giles, Lorimer, Clarke, Jordan.


CHAPTER THREE

# European Cup-winners' Cup 1974-75

For the first time, a Russian club won a major European trophy. Dynamo Kiev were thoroughly worthy of their success, winning the final with masterly ease, eliminating in the semi-final a team as powerful as PSV Eindhoven. True, goalkeeping errors helped them both in the Kiev leg against PSV and in Basel against a disappointing Ferencvaros, but their display was of a quality, enterprise, and authority which quite belied the monotony of Russian football over recent years; and, indeed, this very season, Dynamo Kiev, in the meantime, had won the Russian League, and been chosen, *en bloc*, to represent the Soviet Union in the Nations Cup.

The British contribution was somewhat inglorious, and faded away in the Second Round. Ferencvaros, now managed by their old centre-forward Florian Albert, and drawing successfully on past glories rather than present difficulties, put out first Cardiff then Liverpool, in the course of an impressive run. Dundee United surprisingly fell to the obscure Turks of Bursaspor, against whom they could not even manage a goal. Ards, the Ulster representatives, were unlucky enough to meet the prolific PSV team from Eindhoven in the First Round, conceding ten in Holland and another four at home to Ralf Edstroem, Van der Kuylen, and company. They may have been consoled to see that in the next round, PSV actually thrashed Legia 5–0 in Warsaw. How Legia must have missed their fine young stopper, Zmuda, suspended because he wanted to leave them for Wroclaw.

Mate, the talented winger, was the star of the Ferencvaros attack in the opening rounds. He scored one of their four goals in Cardiff, where the home team belied its fine reputation in the tournament, and got a wonderful solo equaliser at Liverpool, gliding past man after man on the right.

Liverpool previously had made most of the running, but had been consistently thwarted by Geczi, the Hungarian goalkeeper, now remarkable, now lucky. Liverpool had contrived but one first half goal, when Ray Kennedy knocked down a ball from Brian Hall to Kevin

Keegan, who scored. A sharp contrast to their opening game, when their eleven goals against the unfortunate, admiring Norwegians, Stroemsgodset, beat their previous record of ten in European football. Everyone but Hall and the goalkeeper Ray Clemence scored; but Kennedy alone scored in Norway.

Ferencvaros, who had won at Anfield in 1968 – one of the only two European teams to do so – held Liverpool 0–0 in Budapest. Liverpool lacked imagination in attack, and the ploy of using Keegan in midfield did not bring success. Kennedy was given a rough passage, Mate had another clever game for Ferencvaros, and when a brandy bottle was thrown on the field towards the end, Tommy Smith collapsed. Protests were vain, UEFA punished Smith, who they said had feigned injury. A sorry affair.

While the Russian national team laboured, Dynamo Kiev strode on apace, their attack strengthened by the acquisition of Onishenko. A goal in each game by their other international left winger, the blond Blokhin, gave them a useful double over their fellow Communists CSKA Sofia. Busaspor were no problem to them. Onishenko got the only goal of the game in Turkey, and the defence stood firm again in Russia, with the celebrated inside-forwards Kolotov and Muntijan scoring. Kolotov, Onishenko and Blokhin were all on the mark in Kiev in the first leg of the semi-final, when PSV, for all their foreign stars, were overcome with surprising ease.

A particularly piquant feature of the competition was the meeting of Real Madrid and Red Star Belgrade in the semi-final; Miljan Miljanic, Yugoslavia's World Cup manager, had just left Red Star for Real, after spending his whole career with the Yugoslav club.

Since Red Star had lost a host of players, too, in one way and another (Karasi, Acimovic, Bogicevic), Real were strong favourites. They themselves had materially reinforced with Paul Breitner, playing splendidly in midfield rather than at full-back, and Roberto Martinez, the Argentinian from Espanol, who scored both goals in their opening match in Iceland. FK Austria were the next to go, then Real beat Red Star 2–0 in Madrid with a goal in each half – the second by West Germany's Gunter Netzer, following up a penalty – and that seemed that.

It wasn't. In Belgrade, Dragan Dzajic headed a splendid goal, then when Breitner gave away a penalty, it was converted by O. Petrovic, the current Yugoslav 'keeper. When extra time produced no further goals, Petrovic it was who now *saved* a penalty in the conclusive series, to take Red Star through.

Perhaps it was PSV's misfortune that they should meet Dynamo Kiev in the first leg of the semi-finals on the very ground where nine of their players, a week earlier, had helped Russia trounce Turkey. These players participated in another 3–0 win, Kolotov's goal being followed by one each from the international wingers, Blokhin and Onishenko. In Budapest, however, Savic's goal for Red Star ensured that they retained a good chance, despite their 2–1 defeat by Ferencvaros.

As expected, PSV's deficit was too great to make up in Eindhoven.

32

Their Swedish star, Ralf Edstroem, scored twice, enabling them to beat Dynamo Kiev 2–1, but Kiev thus entered the final; first Russian team ever to get as far in any European competition.

In Belgrade, 100,000 saw Ferencvaros reach the final with a spirited performance against Red Star, though in the end it took a penalty by Mate, seven minutes from the end, to make sure. Rather surprisingly, and commendably, Ferencvaros attacked from the first, adding to their lead through Pustai after only seven minutes. Though without the brilliant Dzajic, Red Star improved after the interval, equalised, then took the lead with 12 minutes left. Ferencvaros recovered, and when Magyar was brought down in the box, equalised, and reached the final.

Russia's extraordinary, mesmeric spell over Hungarian football was confirmed in Basel, when Ferencvaros were outplayed in the final. Dynamo Kiev, now strolling, now accelerating, beat them with ease, dominating the midfield through Kolotov, Muntijan, and Troschkin, punching holes in their defence through Onishenko, Blokhin, and Burjak. Ferencvaros, it is true, were somewhat under strength, but the fact is that they mustered only one truly dangerous shot, when Rudakov saved splendidly from Mate's powerful drive, in the first half.

Geczi, the Hungarian goalkeeper and captain, was certainly responsible for the second of Onishenko's two first-half goals, and might have done better with the first. This came from a dazzling individual run on the left, and a cross shot for which Geczi might have been better positioned. The second, five minutes from half-time, was an unexpected shot from outside the penalty area; unexpected certainly by Geczi, who allowed it to fly over his head and in off the crossbar.

He had no hope with the third, which came after 67 minutes, Blokhin, on the right, leaving his defender standing on the outside, rounding Geczi, then scoring, in off another defender.

## ROUND BY ROUND RESULTS
**First Round**

| Liverpool (5) 11 | Strömsgodset (0) 0 |
|---|---|

*Lindsay (pen), Thompson 2,*
*Boersma 2, Heighway, Cormack,*
*Hughes, Smith, Kennedy,*
*Callaghan*

*Liverpool:* Clemence; Smith, Lindsay, Cormack, Thompson, Hughes Boersma, Hall, Kennedy, Callaghan, Heighway.
*Strömsgodset:* Thun; Wroelner, Karlsen, Nostdahl, Pedersen, Amundsen (Wibe), E. Olsen, Henriksen, Halvorsen, Pettersen, T. Olsen (F. Olsen).

| Strömgodset (0) 0 | Liverpool (1) 1 |
|---|---|
|  | *Kennedy* |

*Strömgodset:* Thun; Wroelner, Karlsen, Nostdahl, Wibe, Halvorsen, A. Olsen, Amundsen, Henriksen, B. Olsen, Pettersen.
*Liverpool:* Clemence; Smith, Lindsay, Lawler, Hughes, Hall, Callaghan, Boersma, Keegan, Kennedy, Heighway.

Dundee United (2) 3          Jiul Petrosani (0) 0
*Narey, Copland, Gardner*
*Dundee United:* McAlpine; Rolland, Kopel, Copland, Smith D., Narey, Houston (Sturrock), Gardner, Gray, Fleming (McLeod), McDonald.
*Jiul:* Gabriel (I.) (Naste); Nitu, Tonca, Stocher, Dodu, Mustat, Libordi, Gabriel (S.), Multescu, Rosani, Stoichita.

Jiul Petrosani (2) 2          Dundee United (0) 0
*Roznai, Tonca*
*Jiul:* Naste; Rusu, Tonca, Stocher, Dodu, Naghi, Laberdi, Stan, Multescu, Rosznai, Stoichita.
*Dundee United:* McAlpine; Rolland, Kopel, Copland, Smith D., Narey, Knox, Gardner, Gray, Fleming (Traynor), McDonald.

PSV Eindhoven (5) 10          Ards (0) 0
*Van der Kuylen 3, Lubse 3,*
*Kempar, Deykens, Edstroem,*
*Van Kraay*
Ards (1) 1          PSV Eindhoven (1) 4
*Guy*          *Van der Kuylen, Edstroem,*
          *Dahlqvist 2*

Bursapor (1) 4          Finn Harps (1) 2
*Turan 2, Ali, Sinaul (pen)*          *Ferry, Bradley*
Finn Harps (0) 0          Bursapor (0) 0

Ferencvaros (1) 2          Cardiff City (0) 0
*Nyilasi, Szabo*
*Ferencvaros:* Geczi; Viczko, Balint, Mucha, Megyesi, Takacs, Nyilasi, Szabo, Pusztai, Kelemen, Mate.
*Cardiff City:* Healey; Larmour (Impey), Pethard, Villars, Murray, Powell, Farrington, Charles, Showers, McInch, Anderson.

Cardiff City (0) 1          Ferencvaros (0) 4
*Dwyer*          *Takacs, Szabo, Pustzai, Mate*
*Cardiff City:* Healey; Dwyer, Pethard, Villars (Farrington), Murray, Powell, Anderson, Smith, Showers, Reece (Impey), Vincent.
*Ferencvaros:* Geczi; Eipel, Balint, Megyesi, Takacs, Mucha, Pusztai, Szabo, Kelemen, Ebedli (Onhaus), Mate.

Sliema Wanderers (1) 2          Lahten Reipas (0) 0
*Camilleri*
Lahten Reipas (3) 4          Sliema Wanderers (0) 1
*Salonen, Sanberj 2, Letnanen*          *Aqueline*
Malmö FF (1) 1          Sion (0) 0
*Cervin*
Sion (0) 1          Malmö FF (0) 0
*Cucinotte*
*Malmö won on penalties*
34

Dynamo Kiev 1  
*Blokhin*  
CSKA Sofia (0) 0

CSKA Sofia (0) 0

Dynamo Kiev (0) 1  
*Blokhin*

Waregem (1) 2  
*Deleoie 2*  
FK Austria (2) 4  
*Porkner 2, Weigl, Fiala*  
Eintracht Frankfurt (2) 3  
*Holzenbein 2, Rohrbach*  
Monaco (0) 2  
*Onnis, Petit*  
Fram Reykjavik (0) 0

FK Austria (1) 1  
*Siala*  
Waregem (0) 1  
*Kondijzer*  
Monaco (0) 0

Eintracht Frankfurt (2) 2  
*Beverungen, Nickel*  
Real Madrid (1) 2  
*Martinez 2*  
Fram Reykjavik (0) 0

Real Madrid (3) 6  
*Pirri 2, Santillana, Netzer,*  
*Macanas, Aquilar*  
PAOK Salonica (0) 1  
*Terzanidis*  
Red Star Belgrade (0) 2  
*V. Petrovic, Savic*  
*after extra time*  
Benfica (2) 4  
*Voelko, Nene, Jordao 2*  
Vanlose (1) 1  
*Petersen*  
Slavia Prague (0) 1  
*Henda*  
Carl Zeiss Jena (1) 1  
*Stein*  
*Carl Zeiss won on penalties*  
Gwardia Warsaw (0) 2  
*Zroka (pen), Kraska*  
Bologna (2) 2  
*Savoldi 2*  
*Gwardia won on penalties*

Red Star Belgrade (0) 0

PAOK (0) 0

Vanlose (Denmark) (0) 0

Benfica (3) 4  
*Bene, Jordao 2, Banos*  
Carl Zeiss Jena (0) 0

Slavia Prague (0) 0

Bologna (1) 1  
*Savoldi*  
Gwardia (1) 1  
*Terlecki*

**Second Round**  
Dundee United (0) 0      Bursaspor (0) 0  
*Dundee United:* McAlpine; Rolland, Kopel, Copland, Smith D., Houston, Traynor, Narey, Gray, Knox (Payne), McDonald.  
*Bursaspor:* Rasim; Kemal, Orhan, Jurol, Ismail, Hayreitin, Cemil, Ali, Sinan, Baykul, Vahit.  
Bursaspor (1) 1      Dundee United (0) 0  
*Vahit*  
*Bursaspor:* Rasim; Kemal, Ismail, Hayreitin, Orhan, Gurol, Cemil, Vahit, Ali, Sinan, Baykul.  
*Dundee United:* McAlpine; Rolland, Copland, D. Smith, Kopel, Houston, W. Smith, Fleming, Payne, Gray, Traynor.

Liverpool (1) 1                         Ferencvaros (0) 1
  *Keegan*                                  *Mate*
*Liverpool:* Clemence; Smith, Lindsay, Lawler, Hughes, Boersma,
Keegan, Hall (Toshack), Heighway, Kennedy (Cormack), Callaghan.
*Ferencvaros:* Geczi; Pataki, Balint, Megyesi, Takacs, Mucha, Pusztai,
Szabo (Magyar), Kelemen, Rab (Ohnhaus), Mate.


Ferencvaros (0) 0                       Liverpool (0) 0
*Ferencvaros:* Geczi; Martos, Balint, Mucha, Megyesi, Rab, Nyilasi,
Pusztai (Ebedli), Kelemen, Nagyar (Szabo), Mate.
*Liverpool:* Clemence; Smith, Lindsay, Lawler, Hughes, Keegan,
Boersma, Hall, Heighway (Cormack), Kennedy (Toshack), Callaghan.


Gwardia (0) 1                           PSV Eindhoven (3) 5
                                          *Keykers, Subse,*
                                          *W. Van de Kerkhof,*
                                          *Van der Kuylen, Kielak*
PSV Eindhoven (2) 3                     Gwardia (0) 0
*Van der Kuylen* 2  (1 *pen*)
*Lubse*
Carl Zeiss Jena (0) 1                   Benfica (1) 1
*Vogel*                                    *Nene*
Benfica (0) 0                           Carl Zeiss Jena (0) 0
Malmö FF (1) 3                          Lakolen Reipas (1) 1
*Larsson* 2, *Skoberg*                     *Jukka*
Lakolen Reipas (0) 0                    Malmö FF (0) 0
Eintracht (1) 2                         Dynamo Kiev (1) 3
*Nickel, Koerbel*                          *Kolotov, Blokhin, Muntijan*
Dynamo Kiev (2) 2                       Eintracht (0) 1
*Onishenko* 2                              *Rohrbach*
Avenir (0) 1                            Red Star Belgrade (3) 6
*Sinner*                                   *Sestic* 3, *Filipovic* 2, *Rajkovic*
Red Star Belgrade (3) 5                 Avenir (0) 1
*Rajkovic* 2, *Filipovic,*                 *Dresch*
*Sestic, Savic*
Real Madrid (3) 3                       FK Austria (0) 0
*Kreiger (o.g.), Santillana,*
*Roberto Martinez*
FK Austria (1) 2                        Real Madrid (1) 2
*Pirkner, Fiala*                           *Roberto Martinez, Netzer*


**Quarter-Finals**
Real Madrid (1) 2                       Red Star Belgrade (0) 0
*Santillana, Netzer (pen)*
Red Star Belgrade (1) 2                 Real Madrid (0) 0
*Dzajic, O. Petrovic (pen)*
*Red Star won on penalties*
Malmö FF (0) 1                          Ferencvaros (1) 3
*Sjoberg*                                  *Nyilesi, Magyar, Mata*

Ferencvaros (0) 1          Malmö FF (1) 1
*Mate*                      *Sjoberg*
Bursaspor (0) 0            Dynamo Kiev (1) 1
                           *Onishenko*

Dynamo Kiev (0) 2         Bursaspor (0) 0
*Kolotov, Muntijan*
PSV Eindhoven (0) 0       Benfica (0) 0
Benfica (1) 1             PSV Eindhoven (1) 2
*Coelho*                   *W. Van Der Kerkhof, Quars*

**Semi-Finals**
Dynamo Kiev (2) 3        PSV Eindhoven (0) 0
*Kolotov, Onishenko, Blokhin*
PSV Eindhoven (1) 2      Dynamo Kiev (0) 1
*Edstroem 2*             *Burjak*
Ferencvaros (1) 2        Red Star Belgrade (0) 1
*Magyar, Branikovits*    *Savic*
Red Star Belgrade (0) 2  Ferencvaros (1) 2
*Keri, Filipovic*        *Pustal, Mate (pen)*

**Final**   Basel, 14 May 1975
Dynamo Kiev (2) 3        Ferencvaros (0) 0
*Onishenko 2, Blokhin*

*Dynamo Kiev:* Rudakov; Konkov, Matvienko, Fomenko, Reshko, Muntijan, Troschkin, Kolotov, Onishenko, Burjak, Blokhin.
*Ferencvaros:* Geczi; Martos, Pataki, Megyesi, Juhasz, Rab, Szabo, Nyilasi, Mate, Mucha, Magyar (Ohnhaus).


CHAPTER FOUR

# UEFA Cup 1974–75

A stunning victory in the second leg of the final in Enschede gave Borussia Münchengladbach the UEFA Cup which had eluded them two years before when Liverpool defeated them. Their passage to the final was an impressive one, their victims including fellow West Germans, FC Cologne, and though they faltered in the home leg of the final, the return of Jupp Heynckes galvanised them in the second leg.

Leading scorer in the Bundesliga, Heynckes made one goal, scored three, and Twente, whose victims included Ipswich Town and Juventus, were thrashed 5–1. For once in a while it was a bleak tournament for English clubs. Derby alone getting as far as the Third Round, where they were eliminated by Velez Mostar. Their subsequent appeal, alleging that fireworks and missiles had been thrown in Mostar, was vigorously opposed by the impressive Italian 'observer', Adami, and very properly thrown out.

It was a pity that two such good young teams as Twente and Ipswich should meet as early as the First Round, a pity Ipswich should go out without losing either game, But the writing was on the wall when Twente held them to a 2–2 draw at Portman Road, away goals counting double, in the event that teams finish level on goals, as these did.

At Ipswich, Twente's defence, built around the huge de Vries, the quick, strong Oranen, the subtle Drost, was resilient, while the attack broke well, scoring the first goal after 20 minutes when Zuidema concluded a splendid combination with the German, Pahlplatz. With five minutes left, Zuidema returned the compliment and Pahlplatz ran on for the equaliser. Meantime, Ipswich had got two. The magnificent young Kevin Beattie, with a fine interception, began the movement for the first, Whymark leaping typically high and heading down for Hamilton to shoot in. Five minutes later, Whymark neatly slipped his man and crossed for Talbot to score; but Twente's late revival was impressive.

In Enschede, it was only a wonderful, point blank save by Ardesch from Talbot, three minutes from time, which kept Twente in the Cup. Twente had taken the lead after only eight minutes when Notten split the Ipswich defence and Bos had scored. Ipswich soon equalised, Whymark again making the goal for Hamilton, this time with a right wing cross; but it wasn't enough.

Wolves went out, too, paying the penalty for presumption. They didn't bother to look at the lively Porto side, which included the Peruvian 1970 World Cup star, Cubillas, before they played them in Portugal, and they lost 4–1. It was another story at Molineux, where the veteran Derek Dougan returned to form a vigorous spearhead with Richards. A deeply defensive Porto would have succumbed, but for a weird goal after 38 minutes, when Parkes made a hash of Cubillas' low cross, and the ball bounced off him, then Palmer, into the net. Wolves thus won only by 3–1 with Porto reduced by the end to pulling injured players back on to the pitch to gain time.

Stoke City, unfamiliar figures in European football, were unlucky enough to draw Ajax; not the Ajax of old, deprived now of Neeskens as well as Cruyff, but still a difficult opponent. Both matches were drawn, but Rudi Krol's first half goal at Stoke – equalised by another defender in Denis Smith – took Ajax through on the away goals rule.

Hibernian flooded Rosenborg Trondheim with goals, as Liverpool had inundated another Norwegian team in the Cup-Winners' Cup, but Dundee were knocked out by Racing White, a greatly improved team, setting a hot pace at the top of the Belgian League. Dundee held Racing White to 1–0 in Belgium, but collapsed 4–2 at home.

Derby County qualified comfortably enough against Servette of Geneva, without showing exceptional form. They were too fast and strong for Servette at the Baseball Ground, exploiting de Blaireville's weakness on crosses, though the best goal of the game came from a sinuous dribble by Kevin Hector. In Geneva, Servette took a first half lead, but Lee equalised when de Blairville dropped Rioch's shot, and Hector got the winner 18 minutes from time.

So Derby and Hibs went on to the Second Round as Britain's sole representatives, Derby knocking out Atlético Madrid, but Hibernian floundering and foundering against Juventus.

Both the Derby-Atlético games ended in 2–2 draws, Derby keeping cool heads to win in Madrid after extra time, on penalties. Atlético, villains of the piece at Celtic Park the previous season, showed skill, bite, and resource at Derby. The long-haired Argentinian, Ayala, was never subdued, and he it was who put Atlético ahead with a remarkable goal from 30 yards. Two minutes later David Nish equalised after Hector nodded on Gemmill's corner. In the second half, a dubious penalty each, the 37-year-old Luis coming on as substitute expressly to score for Atlético, Rioch doing the same for Derby, made it 2–2.

In Madrid, where Atlético might have been expected to finish the job, Derby surpassed themselves. Their morale was evident when they would not repine after going 1 - 0 down after only four minutes to a rather soft goal headed by Luis. Attacking forcefully, Derby scored twice within ten minutes of the second half, Rioch smashing home Davies' centre, Hector volleying in another.

Derby had enough chances to win the game outright, missed them, and thus allowed Luis to equalise with one of his celebrated, bending free kicks. So to extra time, and then the ordeal by penalties. Doubtful it may be as a resort, but in this case it was highly dramatic. After the first set of five penalties, each side had scored four. Finally Colin Boulton jumped to save Eusebio's kick, high to his left, and a jubilant Derby were through.

It was a pity that Derby should go out ultimately, in Mostar, to a highly controversial penalty, awarded when the ball seemed to hit Colin Todd on the shoulder, rather than the hand, after Hadziabdic crossed. Bajevic, back after a long absence through injury, and a decisive influence on the game, scored from the kick.

An earlier penalty, when Gemmill tripped Vukoje, was scored by Primorac. It was arguably the goal that turned the tie.

Before half-time Pecely made it 2–0 when Boulton punched a corner straight out to him and Vladic, after 51 minutes, shot a spectacular third with the outside of his right foot. Derby, flagging in midfield, substituted the injured Bourne with Davies, who made a goal for Hector, and fought back well; but the second penalty did it for them. Though they protested to UEFA, it was in vain.

In the same round, Ajax and Juventus, the 1973 European Cup finalists, met, and this time it was the Italians who won; on Damiani's away goal (a penalty) in Amsterdam.

In Turin, a 60,000 crowd paid nearly £140,000 to see Juventus win 1–0 through Damiani's goal after 19 minutes. Already without strikers Johnny Rep, suspended, and the injured Geels, Ajax had a further blow when their German sweeper, Blankenburg, went off with concussion after 20 minutes. Damiani not only scored, heading in Causio's corner, he also hit the bar, while in the last minute Altafini's shot struck a post and whimsically ran along the line.

In Amsterdam, Ajax hammered the Juventus defence. Blankenburg, back again, gave them the lead when a free kick rebounded to him after

15 minutes, Muhren hit a post after 43, Zoff was left stranded after 58. Yet it was Juventus, through Damiani's penalty, who were next to score, in the 67th minute, and not till the last minute of all could Gerry Muhren give Ajax a victory which availed them nothing. They'd missed Rep, but smothered Altafini, Bettega being much the best Juventus forward.

Meanwhile the West Germans, Cologne and Borussia Münchengladbach, had been coming through strongly; till they were drawn to meet one another in the semi-final. This was the more intriguing, as Cologne were one of Borussia's challengers for the Bundesliga title. Borussia had played especially well at Lyon in the second leg of the Second Round, the powerful World Cup star Rainer Bonhof scoring two of their five goals, and they had put nine altogether past Real Saragossa in the next round. Cologne, in that same round, had thrashed Partizan of Yugoslavia 5–1 after losing 1–0 in Belgrade, and scored another five at home to Amsterdam in the quarter-finals.

Jan Jongbloed, the Dutch World Cup goalkeeper, had an untypically fallible match. Previously, Amsterdam had done well to knock out Inter and Fortuna Dusseldorf; whom they beat both home and away. Müller scored three of the Cologne goals at home to Amsterdam, and another in Holland, where Cologne were three up at half-time.

Juventus, meanwhile, defeated Hamburg in the quarter-finals, winning 2–0 in Turin through first-half goals by Capello and Viola, drawing 0–0 in Hamburg thanks largely to a magnificent goalkeeping display by Dino Zoff. At the end of the game the German goalkeeper, Kargus, ran the length of the field to shake his hand.

Not even Zoff, however, could keep out an inspired Twente attack in the semi-final at Enschede. When he blocked but could not hold a shot, Jeuring gave Twente the lead. In the second half, the lively Zuidema scored twice, while in between these goals the ageless Altafini ran through to get one for Juventus, keeping their hopes alive. Dino Zoff had predicted that if Juve did not buckle down to it, they would give away three goals.

The following day, Borussia Münchengladbach also had a 3–1 victory; but in Cologne, which put the tie beyond any reasonable doubt. Two of the goals went to the Danish winger, Simonsen.

If Dino Zoff blamed the mud for the defeat in Holland, there was no such excuse in Turin, where Zuidema's tenth minute goal beat Juventus again; sweet revenge for Twente, four years after the malodorous affair of the team's last meeting.

Zuidema took his goal very well, receiving from Van der Vall, dribbling past two men, then beating Zoff. Thereafter Juventus, wildly daring in their use of no fewer than three attackers, regained the initiative, attacked constantly, made several good chances, but foundered on the saves of Gross.

Gross, Twente's West German goalkeeper, will particularly remember the first leg of the final, in Dusseldorf. On arrival, he was threatened with arrest by the German police if he did not pay 28,600 marks alimoney, in cash, to his wife. With immense difficulty, this was raised, and Gross proceeded to play the game of his life. He needed the bonus, he said. Stielike hit his bar in the first half, Bonhof his post, early in the second, but Heynckes, the Bundesliga's top scorer, was absent, hurt, and Twente held out for a 0–0 draw.

Then Heynckes returned, and in Enschede it was a different ball game. His superb individual display enabled Borussia to win 5–1, and not even Gross could deny him. He made a goal for the Dane, Simonsen, in the second minute, got one himself in the ninth, two more in the 48th and 57th minutes. Drost came upfield to get the solitary goal for Twente, but Simonsen scored a fifth four minutes from time.

## ROUND BY ROUND RESULTS

**First Round**

Valur (Iceland) (0) 0      Portadown (0) 0
Portadown (0) 2      Valur (0) 1
*McFaull, Morrison (pen)*      *Albertson*

Derby County (3) 4      Servette (0) 1
*Hector 2, Daniel, Lee*      *Petrovic*
*Derby County:* Boulton; Webster, Nish, Rioch, Daniel, Todd, Newton (Hinton), Gemmill, Bourne, Hector, Lee.
*Servette:* De Blaireville; Schnyder, Morgenegg (Martin), Guyot, Marchi, Pfister, Castella (Sundermann), Andrey, Riner, Wegmann, Petrovic.

Servette (1) 1      Derby County (0) 2
*Martin*      *Lee, Hector*
*Servette:* De Blaireville; Schnyder, Morgenegg, Guyot, Martin, Sundermann (Barriquand), Andrey (Marti), Wegmann, Pfister, Riner, Petrovic.
*Derby County:* Boulton; Webster, Nish, Rioch, Daniel, Todd, Newton, Gemmill, Bourne, Hector, Lee.

Ipswich Town (2) 2      Twente (1) 2
*Hamilton, Talbot*      *Zuidema, Pahlplatz*
*Ipswich Town:* Sivell; Burley, Hunter, Beattie, Harper, Hamilton (Collard), Talbot, Viljoen, Johnson (Gates), Whymark, Woods
*Twente:* Ardesch; Van Ierssel, Drost, de Vries, Oranen, Thilssen (Overweg), van der Vall, Notten, Bes, Zuidema (Jevring), Pahletz.

Twente (1) 1      Ipswich Town (1) 1
*Bos*      *Hamilton*
*Twente:* Ardesch; Van Ierssel, de Vries, Drost, Oranen, Thilssen, van der Vall, Notten, Bos (Jeuring), Zuidema, Pahlplatz.
*Ipswich Town:* Sivell; Burley, Harper, Talbot, Hunter, Beattie, Hamilton, Viljoen, Whymark, Johnson, Woods.

Stoke City (0) 1      Ajax (1) 1
*Smith*      *Krol*

*Stoke City:* Farmer; Marsh, Pejic, Mahoney, Smith, Dodd, Hasel-
grave, Greenhoff, Conroy, Hudson, Salmons.
*Ajax:* Schrijvers; Van Dord, Blankenburg, Dusbaba, Krol, Van Santen, Haan, Geels, Muhren, Rep, Keizer.

Ajax (0) 0                              Stoke City (0) 0
*Ajax:* Schrijvers; Van Santen, Blankenburg, Dusbaba, Krol, Haan,
G. Muhren, Keizer (A. Muhren), Rep, Geels (Steffenhagen), Mulder.
*Stoke City:* Farmer; Marsh, Pejic, Mahoney, Smith, Dodd, Hasel-
grave (Robertson), Greenhoff (Conroy), Hurst, Hudson, Salmons.

Porto (3) 4                             Wolverhampton W. (0) 1
*McAlle (o.g.), Cubillas,*               *Bailey*
*Flavio, Gomes*
*Porto:* Tibi; Murca, Teixeira, Rolando (Marco Aurelio), Simoes,
Rodolfo, Vieira Nunes, Cubillas, Abel (Lemos), Flavio, Gomes.
*Wolves:* Parkes; Palmer, Parkin, Bailey, Munro, McAlle, Hibbitt,
Powell (Daley), Sunderland, Dougan (Kindon), Farley.

Wolverhampton W. (1) 3                  Porto (1) 1
*Bailey, Daley, Dougan*                  *Palmer (o.g.)*
*Wolves:* Parkes; Palmer, Parkin, Bailey, Munro, McAlle, Hibbitt, Dal-
ey, Richards, Dougan, Sunderland.
*Porto:* Tibi; Murca, Rolando, Gabriel, Leopoldo, Simoes, Rodolfo,
Laurindo (Oliveira), Gomes (Lemos), Cubillas, Viera Nunes.

Rosenberg Trondheim (0) 2               Hibernian (2) 3
*Iversen* 2                              *Stanton, Gordon, Cropley*
*Rosenborg:* Thunshelle; Meirik, Ronnes, Rime, Wormdahl, Christian-
sen, Farstad, Naess, Iversen, Sunde, Garberg.
*Hibernian:* McArthur; Brownlie, Schaedler, Stanton, Spalding,
Blackley, Edwards, Cropley, Harper, Gordon, Munro.

Hibernian (5) 9                         Rosenberg Trondheim (1) 1
*Harper* 2, *Munro* 2, *Stanton* 2,      *Iversen*
*Cropley* (2 *pens*), *Gordon*
*Hibernian:* McArthur; Brownlie, Schaedler, Stanton, Spalding,
Blackley, Edwards, Cropley, Harper, Gordon, Munro.
*Rosenborg:* Thunshelle; Meirik, Ronnes, Rime, Wormdahl, Didritsen,
Christiansen, Farsyad, Garberg, Iversen, Sunde.

Racing White (0) 1                      Dundee (0) 0
*Wellens*
*Racing:* De Bree; Dumon (La Font), Bjerre, De Sanghere, Martens,
Nielsen, Boskamp, Polleunis, Koens, Wellens, Teugel.
*Dundee:* Allan; Wilson (R.), Gemmell, Caldwell (Anderson), Stewart,
Phillip, Scott (I.), Robinson, Hutchinson, Scott (J.), Johnston.

Dundee (1) 2                            Racing White (2) 4
*Duncan, Scott*                          *Teugel, Boskamp, Wellens* 2

*Dundee:* Allan; Wilson, R. (Wilson, J.), Gemmell, Ford, Caldwell, Phillip, Robinson, Duncan, Hutchinson, Scott, J., Johnston.
*Racing:* De Bree; Dumon, Bjerre, De Sanghere, Martens, Boskamp, Nielsen, Polleunis, Koens, Wellens, Teugel.

Boluspor Bolu (Turkey) (0) 0

Dynamo Bucharest (1) 3
*Dinu, Dumitrache, Lucescu*
Randers Freja (0) 1
*Nielsen*
Dynamo Dresden (0) 0
Eter (Bulgaria) (0) 0
Internazionale (1) 3
*Oriali, Boninsegna* 2 (1 *pen*)
Gornik (0) 2
*Kurzeja, Kvasny*
Partizan (1) 3
*Dordevic, Vukotic, Todozevic*
Naples (0) 2
*Massa, Pogliana*
Videoton (1) 1
*Wollek*
Vorwaerts (1) 2
*Schuth, Krautzig*
Juventus (2) 3
*Anastasi, Hause* (o.g.), *Altafini*
Torino (1) 1
*Pulici*
Fortuna (2) 3
*Zimmerman, Seel, Geye* (*pen*)
Rapid Vienna (0) 3
*Pajenk, Ritter, Krankl*
Aris Salonica (0) 1
*Alexiadis*
BK Copenhagen (1) 3
*Soerensen, Holmstrom, Bemburg*
Atlético Madrid (1) 4
*Lea , Irureta* 2, *Garate*
Nantes (0) 2
*Cmikiewicz* (o.g.), *Michel* (*pen*)
Legia Warsaw (0) 0

Olympique Lyon (4) 7
*Lacombe* 3, *Miallard* 3, *Maneiro*
Red Boys Differdange (1) 1
*Christophe*

Dynamo Bucharest (1) 1
*Deleanu*
Boluspor (0) 0

Dynamo Dresden (1) 1
*Dorner*
Randers Freja (0) 0
Internazionale (0) 0
Eter (0) 0

Partizan (0) 2
*Zavisic, Yukotic*
Gornik (0) 0

Videoton (0) 0

Naples (1) 1
*Braglia*
Juventus (1) 1
*Capello*
Vorwaerts (0) 0

Fortuna (0) 1
*Zewe*
Torino (1) 1
*Kriegler* (o.g.)
Aris Salonica (0) 1
*Alexiadis*
Rapid Vienna (0) 0

Atlético Madrid (1) 2
*Ayala, Salcedo*

BK Copenhagen (0) 0

Legia Warsaw (1) 2
*Bialas, Vendrely* (o.g.)
Nantes (0) 1
*Rampillon*
Red Boys Differdange (0) 0

Olympique Lyon (3) 4
*R. Domenech* 2, *Maneiro, Lacombe*

43

Grasshoppers (1) 2
*Elsener, Grahn*
Panathinaikos (0) 2
*Antoniadis* 2
FC Amsterdam (1) 5
*Husens, Jansen* 2,
*Koopman, Otto*
FC Amsterdam (2) 7
*Karte* 2, *Jensen* 2, *Franz,*
*Husens, Dekkers*
Vitoria Setubal (1) 1
*Vicente*
Real Saragossa (1) 4
*Arrua, Duarte, Garcia, Leiros*
Besiktas (0) 2
*Sinan, Tezcan*
Steagul Brasov (0) 3
*Serbaniou* 3
Spartak Moscow (2) 3
*Piskarev, Gladilin, Lovchev*
Velez Mostar (0) 2
*Colic, Popic*
Lokomotiv Plovdiv (2) 3
*Kourbanov, Bonev, Staboliev*
Vasas Györ (3) 3
*Sebuek, Penzes, Poizik*
*Vasas won on penalties*
IK Start Kristiansand (0) 1
*Mathiesen*
Djurgaarden (0) 5
*Karlsson* 2, *Samuelsson,*
*Stenbaeck, Skotte.*
Oester (Sweden) (2) 3
*Matsson* 2, *Nordenburg*
Moscow Dynamo (1) 2
*Evruzhikin, Petrushin*
Real Sociedad (0) 0

Bahik Ostrava (2) 4
*Vojacek, Slany, Albrecht,*
*Kolecko*
Wacker Innsbruck (0) 2
*Flindt* 2
Borussia Münchengladbach (1) 3
*Vogts, Heynckes, Jensen*
Sturm Graz (1) 2
*Stendal, Kulmer*
Royal Antwerp (1) 1
*Kodat*

Panathinaikos (0) 0

Grasshoppers (1) 1
*Sandrac*
Hibernians Malta (0) 0

Hibernians Malta (0) 0
(*both games in Amsterdam*)

Real Saragossa (0) 1
*Arrua*
Vitoria Setubal (0) 0

Steagul Brasov (0) 0

Besiktas (0) 0

Velez Mostar (1) 1
*Bajevic*
Spartak Moscow (0) 0

Vasas Györ (1) 1
*Glazer*
Lokomotiv Plovdiv (1) 1
*Kichekov*

Djurgaarden (1) 2
*Svensson, Skote*
IK Start (0) 0

Moscow Dynamo (2) 2
*Ksokov, Paslenorov*
Oester (0) 1
*Svensson*
Banik Ostrava (0) 1
*Micla*
Real Sociedad (0) 0

Borussia Münchengladbach (0) 1
*Heynckes*
Wacker Innsbruck (0) 0

Royal Antwerp (0) 1
*Heylijen*
Sturm Graz (0) 0

Cologne (4) 5
*Lohr, Müller 2,*
*Overath, Flohe*
Kokkolan (0) 1
*Lamberg*

Kokkolan (Finland) (0) 1
*Makela*

Cologne (0) 4
*Flohe, Lohr, Simmet 2*

## Second Round

Derby County (1) 2
*Nish, Rioch (pen)*

Atlético Madrid (1) 2
*Ayala, Luis (pen)*

*Derby County:* Boulton; Webster, Nish, Rioch, Daniel, Todd, Newton, Gemmill, Bourne (Hinton), Hector, Lee.
*Atlético Madrid:* Reina; Capon, Diaz, Marcellino (Bermejo), Benegas, Eusebio, Leal (Luis), Adelardo, Garate, Irureta, Ayala.

Atlético Madrid (1) 2
*Luis 2*

Derby County (0) 2
*Rioch, Hector*

*Atletico Madrid:* Reina; Capon, Benegas, Diaz, Adelardo, Eusebio, Fernandez, Aragones, Garate, Irureta, Ayala.
*Derby County:* Boulton; Webster, Daniel, Nish, Rioch, Powell, Newton, Gemmill, Davies, Hector, Lee.
*Derby won on penalties*

Hibernian (0) 2
*Stanton, Cropley*

Juventus (1) 4
*Gentile, Altafini 2, Cuccureddu*

*Hibernian:* McArthur; Brownlie, Schaedler, Stanton, Spalding, Blackley, Edwards, Cropley, Harper, Gordon, Duncan.
*Juventus:* Zoff; Spinosi, Longobucco, Furino, Morini, Scirea, Damiani (Altafini), Cuccureddu, Anastasi, Gentile, Bettega (Viola).

Juventus (1) 4
*Bettega, Anastasi 2, Altafini*

Hibernian (0) 0

*Juventus:* Zoff; Gentile, Longobuocco, Cuccureddu, Morini, Scirea, Damiani, Causio, Anastasi, Capello, Bettega.
*Hibernian:* McArthur; Bremner, Schaedler, Stanton, Spalding, Blackley, Duncan, Gordon, Harper, Cropley, Munro.

Partizan Belgrade (2) 5
*Zozic 2, Zavisic,*
*Nikolic, Vukotic*
Portadown (1) 1
*Malcolmson*
Dynamo Bucharest (0) 1
*Dinu*
Cologne (1) 3
*Overath, Müller, Neumann*
Rapid Vienna (0) 1
*Ritter*
Velez Mostar (1) 1
*Halaldiz*

Portadown (0) 0

Partizan (0) 1
*Tordevic*
Cologne (1) 1
*Lauscher*
Dynamo Bucharest (2) 2
*Custov, Georgescu*
Velez Mostar (0) 1
*Halaldiz*
Rapid Vienna (0) 0

Vasas Györ (1) 2        Fortuna (0) 0
*Varsanyi, Stolcz*
Fortuna (3) 3        Vasas Gyor (0) 0
*Herzog, Szernotzky, Brucken*
Dynamo Dresden (1) 1        Moscow Dynamo (0) 0
*Sasche*
Moscow Dynamo (1) 1        Dynamo Dresden (0) 0
*Korneev*
*Dresden won on penalties*
Twente Enschede (1) 2        Racing White (1) 1
*Thijssen, Van Der Vall*        *Koens*
Racing White (0) 0        Twente Enschede (0) 1
       *Zuidema*

Ajax (0) 1        Royal Antwerp (0) 0
*G. Muhren*
Royal Antwerp (1) 2        Ajax (1) 1
*Kodat, Riedl(pen)*        *Geels*
Hamburg (2) 8        Steagul Brasov (0) 0
*Volkert 2, Bertl,Zaczyk,*
*Memering, Nogly, Ripp (o.g.),*
*Krobach (o.g.)*
Steagul Brasov (1) 1        Hamburg (1) 2
*Curbaniou*        *Kaltz, Bjornmose*
Djurgarden (0) 0        Dukla (0) 2
       *Nehoda, Gajdusek*

Dukla (1) 3        Djurgarden (1) 1
*Nehoda 2, Macela*        *Svensson*
Grasshoppers (1) 2        Real Saragossa (0) 1
*Grahn, Santrac*        *Arrua*
Real Saragossa (2) 5        Grasshoppers (0) 0
*Rubial 2, Soto, Ohlhauser (o.g.),*
*Niggl (o.g.)*
Naples (0) 1        Porto (0) 0
*Orlandini*
Porto (0) 0        Naples (0) 1
       *Juliano*

Internazionale (0) 1        Amsterdam (2) 2
*Boninsegna*        *Jansen 2*
Amsterdam (0) 0        Internazionale (0) 0
Borussia Münchengladbach (1) 1        Lyon (0) 0
*Simonsen*
Lyon (1) 2        Borussia Münchengladbach (2) 5
*Valette, R. Domenech*        *Bonhof 2, Simonsen 2, Kulik*
Nantes (1) 1        Banik Ostrava (0) 0
*Bossis*
Banik Ostrava (0) 2        Nantes (0) 0
*Klement 2*
*after extra time*

**Third Round**

Derby County (0) 3      Velez Mostar (1) 1
*Bourne* 2, *Hinton*      *Vladic*

*Derby County:* Boulton; Webster, Nish, Rioch, Daniel, Todd, Newton, Gemmill, Davies (Bourne), Hector, Lee (Hinton).
*Velez:* Mrgan; Colic, Hadziabdic, Prizmorac, Gladovic, Pecelj, Topic, Vladic (Okuka), Vukoje, Ledic, Hodzic.

Velez Mostar (2) 4      Derby County (0) 1
*Primorac* (*pen*), *Pecelj*, *Vladic*,      *Hector*
*Bajevic* (*pen*)

*Velez:* Mrgan; Meter, Hadziabdic, Colic, Primorac, Pecelj, Topic, Halihodic, Bajevic, Vladic, Vukoje.
*Derby County:* Boulton; Webster, Thomas, Rioch, Daniel, Todd, Newton, Gemmill, Bourne (Davies), Hector, Lee (Hinton).

Juventus (1) 1      Ajax (0) 0
*Damiani*

Ajax (1) 2      Juventus (0) 1
*Blankenburg, G. Muhren*      *Damiani* (*pen*)

Partizan, 1      Cologne (0) 0
*Vukotic*

Cologne 5      Partizan 1
*Overath, Lohr, Müller,*      *Pavlovic*
*Growocz, Flohe*

Borussia Münchengladbach (4) 5      Real Saragossa (0) 0
*Simonsen* 2 (1 *pen*), *Heynckes* 2,
*Bonhof*

Real Saragossa 2      Borussia Münchengladbach 4
*Violeta, Galdos*      *Simonsen, Jensen, Strelike,*
     *Heynckes*

Naples (0) 0      Banik Ostrava (0) 2
     *Albrecht, Klement*

Banik Ostrava (0) 1      Naples (1) 1
*Slamy*      *Ferradini*

Hamburg (4) 4      Dynamo Dresden (1) 1
*Bjornmose* 2, *Volkert, Nogly*      *Schmuck*

Dynamo Dresden 2      Hamburg 2
*Doerner, Haefner*

Amsterdam (1) 3      Fortuna (0) 0
*Husers* 2, *Kriegler*

Fortuna 1      Amsterdam 2
*Seel*      *Husens, Jansen*

Dukla 3      Twente Enschede 1
*Dvorak, Krumich, Nehoda*      *Jeuring*

Twente Enschede 5      Dukla (0) 0
*Zuidema* 3, *Notten* 2

## Quarter-Finals

Velez Mostar (1) 1
*Kvesic*
Twente Enschede (1) 2
*Zuidema, Overweg*
Juventus (2) 2
*Capello, Viola*
Hamburg (0) 0
Banik Ostrava (0) 0

Borussia Münchengladbach (1) 3
*Micka (o.g.), Heynckes, Vogts*
Cologne (1) 5
*Flohe 2 (1 pen), Müller 3*
Amsterdam (0) 2
*Jansen 2*

Twente Enschede (0) 0

Velez Mostar (0) 0

Hamburg (0) 0

Juventus (0) 0
Borussia Münchengladbach (0) 1
*Heynckes*
Banik Ostrava (0) 1
*Hudecek*
Amsterdam (1) 1
*Visser*
Cologne (3) 3
*Strack, Müller, Lohr*

## Semi-Finals

Twente Enschede (1) 3
*Jeuring, Zuidema 2*
Juventus (0) 0

Cologne (0) 1
*Lohr*
Borussia Münchengladbach (0) 1
*Danner*

Juventus (0) 1
*Altafini*
Twente Enschede (1) 1
*Zuidema*
Borussia Münchengladbach (2) 3
*Simonsen 2, Danner*
Cologne (0) 0

**Final**   Dusseldorf, 7 May, 1975
Borussia Münchengladbach (0) 0   Twente Enschede (0) 0
*Borussia:* Kleff; Stielike, Vogts, Wittkamp, Surau, Bonhof, Wimmer, Danner, (Del Haye), Kulik (Schaffer), Simonsen, Jensen.
*Twente:* Gross; Van Ierssel, Overweg, Drost, Oranen, Thissen, Pahlplatz, Van der Vall, Bos, Jeuring (Achterberg), Zuidema.
**Second Leg**   Enschede, 21 May, 1975
Twente (0) 1   Borussia Münchengladbach (2) 5
*Drost*   *Simonsen 2, Heynckes 3*
*Twente:* Gross; Van Ierssel, Overweg, Drost, Oranen, Thissen, Van Der Vall, Pahlplatz (Achterberg), Bosh (Muhren), Jeuring, Zuidema.
*Borussia:* Kleff; Vogts, Surau (Shaeffer), Wittkamp, Bonhof, Linhammer, Simonsen, Wimmer (Oeppel), Jensen, Danner, Heynckes.

# CHAPTER FIVE

# British International Championship 1974–75

Again the Championship, the oldest of its kind, was stuck contemptuously at the end of a long, hard season. Worse still, Leeds United were involved in the European Cup final, which deprived Scotland of half-a-dozen stars, and Wales, after the first game, of Terry Yorath. That Gordon McQueen was allowed to play for Scotland was simply because, having been sent off in the European Cup semi-final in Barcelona, he was suspended from the final.

England won the tournament by crushing Scotland in their last, decisive game at Wembley, despite the presence of a huge, vociferous throng of Scots. Tube and rail services to Wembley were suspended in protest against a vicious attack on a railwayman by Scots supporters two years previously at Wembley Park Station. He had been disabled ever since.

For England and Don Revie, the 5-1 victory might best be seen as a reprieve rather than an affirmation. Performances against Northern Ireland and Wales had been abysmal, players such as Viljoen, Macdonald, Tueart, Gillard looking far short of international class, and only the happy emergence of Villa's Brian Little, against Wales, had given hope for the future. But with Beattie, Whitworth, and Gerry Francis digging in against Scotland, Trevor Francis waiting in the wings, things looked rosier, despite the manifest need for a true wing-half-back (Martin Dobson?) in midfield.

The tournament opened in Cardiff – and Belfast, where no British team had played since 1971. The success of the Northern Ireland – Yugoslavia match the previous month, the agreement of Wales to play there, finally moved a reluctant Football Association to accept. Fortunately, there was no adverse incident of any kind. The sun shone, the crowd was large and appreciative. Only the performance of the England team was lacking.

The attempt to integrate Colin Viljoen, Ipswich Town's South African 'general', with Ball and Bell was an utter failure; Derek Spence, a blond 22-year-old centre-forward from Third Division Bury, gave Todd and Watson an alarming time. On several occasions he might have won the match for the Irish.

For England, Kevin Keegan, in the first half, struck the bar with a near post header from Tueart's left wing corner, almost identical to that with which he'd scored six days earlier in Cyprus, and Macdonald, substituted ultimately by Mike Channon, might have had a penalty. But the big Irish stoppers, Chris Nicholl and Alan Hunter, thereafter took control, and victory in the second half would not have flattered the Irish.

Cardiff, despite the Scots manager, Willie Ormond's, bitter com-

49

plaints about the pitch, saw an immeasurably better game, with four notable goals, vast excitement, a fine recovery by Scotland.

The first half belonged to Wales, with tiny Brian Flynn of Burnley replacing the injured Arfon Griffiths and playing extremely well. He was concerned in both goals. For the first, he beat Stewart Kennedy, the excellent Scottish goalkeeper, to Toshack's header, and though his shot was kicked off the line by Jackson, Toshack banged it in. Six minutes later, he was involved in a dazzling move, exchanging one-twos with Mahoney and Toshack and completing the second with a shot past Kennedy.

Scotland revived in the second half. From Parlane's right flank cross after 52 minutes, Jackson out-jumped Davies to head in, and a pulverising left footer from Bruce Rioch, the Anglo-Scot, playing his second international, tore into the top left-hand corner to equalise. Thereafter, Kennedy made a glorious double save from Toshack and Mahoney, while for Scotland, Parlane hit the bar, McQueen a post. A rousing draw.

Scotland did better still the following Tuesday, when a hearteningly large 64,000 crowd applauded their solid victory over the Irish, still without the vital Hamilton. Though Derek Spence had another lively game and three fine headers, one of which forced Kennedy to a single handed save, Scotland dominated the first half and took their chances well.

Two up by the interval, they had opened the score when Munro, playing well at second stopper, headed Duncan's left wing corner back across goal for Ted MacDougall to glance it, on the bounce, past Jennings. A quick throw on the right by Rioch, a burst by Dalglish past a sleepy Irish defence, brought the second. The third was set up by Dalglish with an admirable through pass to the lively Parlane. Alfie Conn came on to vast applause as a late, successful substitute for Robinson, thus winning his first cap and crowning what transpired, after an unhappy start, to be a splendid season.

Splendid was hardly the word for England's inept display the following evening against a Welsh team which came close to winning at Wembley for the first time ever. Dreadful errors by the English defence gave them two second-half goals and a 2-1 lead. It was only the arrival of Brian Little, the 22-year-old Villa centre-forward, that galvanised the limp English attack and saved the game, the day, England, and Don Revie's face. Wales, moreover, were without Terry Yorath, a key player now.

England took the lead when Colin Viljoen drove into the Welsh goalmouth from the left. The ball hit the unlucky Phillips, looped over Davies, and was headed into the empty goal by David Johnson, making his debut for England.

Wales equalised early in the second half. David Smallman got his head to a corner from the right by the elegant Leighton James, Clemence parried the ball but could not hold it, and lay stranded, Griffiths tried again, and the ball curled to the far post where Toshack, like Johnson, scored: the first goal against Revie's England team.

Wales scored again in the 65th minute from what seemed a wholly unpromising situation; a throw-in by Thomas from the right, nodded on by Toshack, the ball looping over a static English defence, off Gillard's thigh, to be put in point blank by Griffiths on the left hand post.

England's inept midfield was making no bullets for a disappointing attack to fire; but now on came Little, wonderfully full of enterprise and dash. A player with less temperament might have wilted under the double burden of making his international debut in such oppressive circumstances. Not Little, who six minutes from time twisted past Page on the right, and crossed for Johnson to head a spectacular and somewhat fortuitous equaliser. Meanwhile Kevin Keegan, dropped from the team, had gone home in a huff.

On the Friday evening, Windsor Park loudly applauded the Welsh, grateful for their decision to come to Belfast; and then applauded an easy Irish victory. Easy, even though the margin was but one scrambled goal before half-time. Dave Clements took an inswinging corner from the right, Dai Davies came out for the ball and didn't get it, the irrepressible Spence headed over him, and Tom Finney forced the ball in.

Subsequently, Spence had a goal disallowed, after again beating Davies in the air, Sammy McIlroy several times threatened to score, Showers hit the bar for Wales, and Jennings saved splendidly from Griffiths' fine overhead kick. By and large, however, the Irish midfield, steadied by Clements, was too good for a Welsh team which lacked Toshack, Yorath, and John Roberts.

This meant that Scotland had only to draw at Wembley on the Saturday to win the Championship. In the event, they were thrashed, exposed as a sadly inadequate team, desperately in need of the absent Leeds United contingent; above all in the shape of a decent goalkeeper.

For Stewart Kennedy, excellent in Wales a week before, had a dreadful game, reminiscent of the ineptitude of Celtic's Frank Haffey, who had let in nine goals, years before. In the fifth and seventh minutes, Gerry Francis, with a long shot, and Kevin Beattie, with a header, beat him in the top, left-hand corner; goals which he or any decent keeper must have saved in other circumstances. He seemed equally to blame when Colin Bell later swept past Frank Munro to score with a low right footer into the bottom left-hand corner.

Scotland, who had missed a fine chance when Parlane wasted Dalglish's glorious through pass, did get back a goal a minute after Bell's, Rioch scoring from a penalty after Todd handled. But early in the first half Duncan, a deep disappointment, hit the side netting when Todd's careless back pass presented him with a fine opportunity, and England scored twice more. Gerry Francis, a far more authoritative figure than in previous games, got another after Alan Ball's free kick, when his right footer was deflected; Johnson, who also played far better than against Wales, left-footed the other, after Kennedy had deflected Keegan's header on to the bar, Watson had hit the post.

Scotland's defence had been porous, despite the presence of two unquestionably talented backs, their front runners limp, their midfield ineffective; though Conn had his moments of grace, Dalglish some fine first-half passes. With a different goalkeeper, perhaps it would have been a different story. England won well, but should not fall to delusions of grandeur. There would be harder tests that Autumn, in Bratislava and in Lisbon.

Belfast, May 17 1975.
Northern Ireland (0) 0          England (0) 0
*Northern Ireland:* Jennings (Spurs); Rice (Arsenal), Hunter (Ipswich T.), Nicholl (Aston Villa), O'Kane; Jackson, O'Neill (all Nottingham F.), Clements (Everton); Hamilton (Ipswich T.), Finney (Sunderland), Spence (Bury), McIlroy (Manchester U.).
*England:* Clemence (Liverpool); Whitworth (Leicester C.), Todd (Derby Co.), Watson (Sunderland), Hughes (Liverpool); Ball (Arsenal), Viljoen (Ipswich T.), Bell (Manchester C.); Tueart (Manchester C.), Macdonald (Newcastle U.), [Channon (Southampton)], Keegan (Liverpool).

Cardiff, May 17 1975.
Wales (2) 2          Scotland (0) 2
*Wales:* Davies (Everton); Thomas (Derby Co.), Roberts (Birmingham C.), Yorath (Leeds U.), Page (Birmingham C.); Mahoney (Stoke C.), Flynn (Burnley), Phillips (Aston Villa); Reece (Cardiff C.), Toshack (Liverpool), James (Burnley).
*Scotland:* Kennedy; Jardine, Jackson (all Rangers), [Munro (Wolverhampton W.)], McQueen (Leeds U.), McGrain (Celtic); Dalglish (Celtic), Rioch (Derby Co.), Duncan (Hibernian); Macari (Manchester U.), Parlane (Rangers), MacDougall (Norwich C.).
*Scorers:* Toshack, Flynn for Wales; Jackson, Rioch for Scotland.

Hampden Park, May 20 1975.
Scotland (2) 3          Northern Ireland (0) 0
*Scotland:* Kennedy; Jardine (Rangers) [Forsyth (Manchester U.)], Munro (Wolverhampton W.), McQueen (Leeds U.), McGrain (Rangers); Dalglish (Celtic), Robinson (Dundee), [Conn (Tottenham H.)], Rioch (Derby Co.); MacDougall (Norwich C.), Parlane (Rangers), Duncan (Hibernian).
*Northern Ireland:* Jennings (Tottenham H.); Rice (Arsenal), Hunter (Ipswich T.), [Blair (Oldham Ath.)], Nicholl (Aston Villa), O'Kane; Jackson, O'Neill (all Nottingham F.), [Anderson (Swindon T.)], Clements (Everton); Finney (Sunderland), Spence (Bury), McIlroy (Manchester U.).
*Scorers:* MacDougall, Dalglish, Parlane for Scotland.

Wembley, May 21 1975.
England (1) 2          Wales (0) 2
*England:* Clemence (Liverpool); Whitworth (Leicester C.), Todd (Derby Co.), Watson (Sunderland), Gillard (Q.P.R.); Viljoen (Ipswich

T.), Francis (Q.P.R.), Ball (Arsenal); Channon (Southampton) [Little (Aston Villa)], Johnson (Ipswich T.), Thomas (Q.P.R.).
*Wales:* Davies (Everton); Thomas (Derby Co.), Phillips, Roberts, Page (Birmingham C.); Mahoney (Stoke C.), Griffiths (Wrexham), Flynn (Burnley); James (Burnley), Smallman (Wrexham) [Showers (Cardiff C.)], Toshack (Liverpool).
*Scorers:* Johnson 2 for England; Toshack, Griffiths for Wales.

Belfast, May 23 1975.
Northern Ireland (1) 1          Wales (0) 0
*Northern Ireland:* Jennings (Tottenham H.); Scott (Everton), Hunter (Ipswich T.), Nicholl (Aston Villa), Rice (Arsenal); Clements (Everton), Blair (Oldham Ath.), Jackson (Nottingham F.); Finney (Sunderland), McIlroy (Manchester U.), Spence (Bury).
*Wales:* Davies (Everton); Thomas (Derby Co.), D. Roberts (Hull C.), Phillips (Aston Villa), Page (Birmingham C.); Mahoney (Stoke C.), Griffiths (Wrexham), Flynn (Burnley); Reece (Cardiff C.), [Smallman (Everton)], Showers (Cardiff C.), James (Burnley).
*Scorer:* Finney for Northern Ireland.

Wembley, May 24 1975.
England (3) 5          Scotland (1) 1
*England:* Clemence (Liverpool); Whitworth (Leicester C.), Todd (Derby Co.), Watson (Sunderland), Beattie (Ipswich T.); Bell (Manchester C.), Francis (Q. P. R.); Channon (Southampton), Johnson (Ipswich T.), Keegan (Liverpool), [Thomas (Q.P.R.)].
*Scotland:* Kennedy (Rangers); Jardine (Rangers), McQueen (Leeds U.), Munro (Wolverhampton W.), McGrain (Celtic); Dalglish (Celtic), Conn (Tottenham H.), Rioch (Derby Co.); Parlane (Rangers), MacDougall (Norwich C.), [Macari (Manchester U.)], Duncan (Hibernian) [Hutchison (Coventry C.)].
*Scorers:* Francis 2, Beattie, Bell, Johnson for England; Rioch (pen) for Scotland.

**Final Table**

|                  | P | W | D | L | F | A | Pts |
|------------------|---|---|---|---|---|---|-----|
| England          | 3 | 1 | 2 | 0 | 7 | 3 | 4   |
| Scotland         | 3 | 1 | 1 | 1 | 6 | 7 | 3   |
| Northern Ireland | 3 | 1 | 1 | 1 | 1 | 3 | 3   |
| Wales            | 3 | 0 | 2 | 1 | 4 | 5 | 2   |

# CHAPTER SIX

# Friendly Internationals Against Foreign Teams

Scotland made a most spirited beginning, thrashing 3–0 an East German team full of World Cup men, which had just failed to beat Iceland in the Nations Cup. Though without Billy Bremner, and opposed by a ruthless, reckless German defence, the Scots shrugged off a missed penalty and won well. Weise, who chopped Deans down after 12 seconds without incurring a penalty, later rammed into Holton, who had to leave the field and give way to Kenny Burns.

Jardine missed the penalty after 17 minutes, but when Jordan was brought down, Hutchison scored from the spot. Burns got the second after Jordan's free kick, and in the second half Dixie Deans, winning his first cap, made the third for his Celtic colleague, Dalglish.

Not till March did England play a friendly match, Don Revie's third as manager, and the third in which England did not concede a goal. It was a promising victory in a somewhat *ersatz* match. Injury, retirement, and absence abroad reduced West Germany to a spectre of their World Cup winning side, and one with little heart for the conflict. England were without their Leeds and Ipswich players, engaged in a Cup replay.

On a rain-soaked, slippery pitch, Alan Hudson displayed his wide range of skills, Todd was impeccable, Watson dominant, while the much-indulged Macdonald had his first good game for England. Bell volleyed Hudson's well flighted free kick in off Bonhof for the first goal. In the second half, Channon's quick free kick enabled Ball to cross over the head of the groping Maier, for Macdonald to head the second, while another error by Maier allowed Keegan's shot to hit the bar.

There was some controversy over the fact that Alan Ball was not only surprisingly recalled but actually made captain, two weeks after being sent off the field at Derby. Like Hudson, Whitworth and Gillard, the young backs, won their first caps. A huge crowd delighted in a somewhat illusory victory.

In Gothenburg, a considerably weakened Scottish team, without, *inter alia*, its powerful Leeds United contingent, nevertheless got a late draw against Sweden, the goal being scored two minutes from time by the controversial Ted MacDougall, winning his first cap. In the 11th minute he had shot wide with only the keeper to beat when sent clear by Kenny Dalglish. Now, when Dalglish found him again, MacDougall chested the ball down and spun to score.

The Swedish goal, scored by Sjoeberg a minute from half-time, had looked suspiciously offside. Ten minutes after the interval, Scotland brought on Hughes, of Sunderland, another debutant, and Johnstone for Macari and Souness.

In an earlier match, two goals by Newcastle United's Tommy Craig, the captain, gave the Scottish Under-23 team victory over Young Sweden.

Only thirteen days after their humiliating 5–0 defeat by Czechoslovakia in the Nations Cup, Portugal went to Hampden Park and lost by the margin of a single own goal. Two minutes from half-time, McQueen headed in Charlie Cooke's corner, Damas pushed the ball out and it rebounded past him off Artur. It was a tedious and uninspiring game, in which Scotland gave a first cap to the Aldershot-born Bruce Rioch of Derby County; qualified, as his name suggests, by a Scottish father. Of the Leeds players, Gordon McQueen alone was available, having been suspended from the European Cup Final. For Portugal, Fraguito hit the post in the second half.

Hampden Park, 30 October
  Scotland (2) 3               East Germany (0) 0
  *Hutchison (pen), Burns, Dalglish*
*Scotland:* Harvey (Leeds U.); Jardine (Rangers), Forsyth (Manchester U.), Souness (Middlesbrough), Holton (Manchester U.) (Burns (Birmingham C.)), Buchan (Manchester U.) J. Johnstone, Dalglish (Celtic) (D. Johnstone (Rangers)), Deans (Celtic), Jordan (Leeds U.), Hutchison (Coventry C.).
*East Germany:* Croy; Kische, Bransch (Zapf), Weise, Watzlich, Kurjuweit (Irmscher), Lauck (Streich), Haefner, Kreische, Sparwasser, Hoffmann.

Wembley, 12 March 1975
  England (1) 2               West Germany (0) 0
  *Bell, Macdonald*
*England:* Clemence (Liverpool); Whitworth (Leicester C.), Gillard (Q.P.R.), Bell (Manchester C.), Watson (Sunderland), Todd (Derby Co.); Ball (Arsenal), Channon (Southampton), Macdonald (Newcastle U.), Hudson (Stoke C.), Keegan (Liverpool).
*West Germany:* Maier; Beckenbauer, Bonhof, Koerbel, Vogts, Wimmer, Cullmann, Flohe, Ritschel, Kostedde, Holzenbein.

Gothenburg, 16 April
  Sweden (1) 1               Scotland (0) 1
  *Sjoeberg*                  *MacDougall*
*Sweden:* Ahlstroem (Nordahl); Andersson, Augustsson, Fredriksson, Hagerg, Karlsson, Matsson, Nordqvist, B., Sjoeberg, Edstroem, Torstensson.
*Scotland:* Kennedy (Rangers); Jardine (Rangers), Munro (Wolverhampton W.), Jackson (Rangers), McGrain (Celtic), Souness (Middlesbrough) (Johnstone (Rangers)), Robinson (Dundee), Dalglish (Celtic), Parlane (Rangers, MacDougall (Norwich C.), Macari (Manchester U.) (Hughes (Sunderland)).

  Sweden Under-23 (0) 1          Scotland Under-23 (1) 2
  *Sjoestroem*                    *Craig 2*

Hampden Park, May 13, 1975
Scotland (1) 1                    Portugal (0) 0
*Artur (o g)*
*Scotland:* Kennedy (Rangers); Jardine (Rangers), Buchan (Manchester U.) (Jackson (Rangers)), McQueen (Leeds U.), McGrain (Celtic); Rioch (Derby Co.) (Macari (Manchester U.)), Cooke (Chelsea), (Duncan (Hibernian)), Dalglish (Celtic); Parlane (Rangers), MacDougall (Norwich C.), Hutchison (Coventry C.).
*Portugal:* Damas; Artur, Humberto, Alhinho, Barros, Octavio, Alves (Gento), Toni, Nene (Pietro), Fraguito (Gomes), Moinhos (Pereira).

Rumania Under-23 1            Scotland Under-23 2

# CHAPTER SEVEN

# Other Internationals Between Foreign Teams

**1974**

| | | |
|---|---|---|
| 4 September: | Switzerland (1) 1 | West Germany (1) 2 |
| | *Muller* | *Cullmann, Geye* |
| | Poland (1) 1 | East Germany (2) 3 |
| | *Lato* | *Kurbjuweit, Vogel, Doerner* |
| | Sweden (0) 1 | Holland (2) 5 |
| | *Larsson (pen)* | *Cruyff, Haan, Neeskens 2 (1 pen), Rensenbrink* |
| 5 September: | Mexico (0) 3 | USA (0) 1 |
| | *De La Torre, Lopez 2* | *Vaninger* |
| 7 September: | Poland (0) 0 | France (2) 2 |
| | | *Coste, Jodar* |
| 8 September: | USA (0) 0 | Mexico (1) 1 |
| | | *Trujillo* |

**ASIAN GAMES FOOTBALL TOURNAMENT Teheran**
Won by Iran, managed by Frank O'Farrell, formerly manager of Leicester, Manchester United, and Cardiff.
**Group A** Kuwait 3, Thailand 2; South Korea 1, Thailand 0; Kuwait 0, South Korea 0.
**Group B** China 7, India 0; Iraq 1, North Korea 0; Iraq 3, India 0; North Korea 2, China 0; North Korea 4, India 1.
**Group C** Israel 8, Malaysia 3; Japan 4, Philippines 0; Israel 6, Philippines 0; Malaysia 1, Japan 1; Malaysia 11, Philippines 0; Israel 3, Japan 0.
**Group D** Iran 7, Pakistan 0; Burma 4, Bahrein 0; Pakistan 5, Bahrein 1; Iran 2, Burma 1; Burma 5, Pakistan 1; Iran 6, Bahrein 0.

**FINAL POOLS**

**Group 1**  Iran 1, Malaysia 0; Iraq 2, South Korea 0; Iraq 0, Malaysia 0; Iran 1, Iraq 0. **Winner:** Iraq.

**Group 2**  Israel 3, Burma 0; North Korea 2, Kuwait 0; Israel 2, Kuwait 0. **Winner:** Israel.

**FINAL**

| | | |
|---|---|---|
| 15 September: | Iran (1) 1 *Adelkhani* | Israel (0) 0 |
| 25 September: | Czechoslovakia (3) 3 *Bicovsky 2, Ondrus* | East Germany (1) 1 *Hoffmann* |
| 28 September: | Yugoslavia (1) 1 *Surjak* | Italy (0) 0 |
| | Austria (1) 1 *Krankl* | Hungary (0) 0 |
| 10 October: | Holland (1) 1 *Geels* | Switzerland (0) 0 |
| | East Germany (1) 2 *Hoffmann, Doerner* | Canada (0) 0 |
| | Denmark (1) 2 *Lund, Lefevre* | Iceland (1) 1 *Hallgrimsson* |
| | Morocco 1 | Syria 1 |
| | *Morocco won on penalties (Kuneitra Cup Final)* | |
| 12 October: | Argentina (0) 1 *Rogel* | Spain (0) 1 *Pirri* |
| 13 October: | Czechoslovakia (3) 4 *Svehlik 2, Masny, Bicovsky* | Sweden (0) 0 |
| 17 October: | Russia (0) 1 *Onishenko* | Bulgaria (0) 1 *Vetkov* |
| 27 October: | Poland (2) 2 *Kasalik, Jakobczak* | Canada (0) 0 |
| 7 November: | Chile (0) 0 | Argentina (0) 2 *Lopez, Ferrero* |
| 13 November: | Turkey (0) 0 | Austria (1) 1 *Stering* |
| | Switzerland (2) 3 *Jeandeupeux, Pfister, Schild (pen)* | Portugal (0) 0 |
| | Czechoslovakia (0) 2 *Svehlik, Masny* | Poland (1) 2 *Gadocha, Szarmach* |
| 15 November: | Greece (2) 3 *Papoiannou, Sarafis, Tersanidis* | Cyprus (0) 1 *Papadopoulos* |
| 20 November: | Argentina (1) 1 *Galletti (pen)* | Chile (1) 1 *Mendez* |
| 4 December: | Rumania (0) 1 *Samas* | Israel (0) 0 |
| | Hungary (1) 1 *Fazekas (pen)* | Switzerland (0) 0 |

| 19 February: | Italy (2) 4 | Norway (0) 1 |
| | *Graziani, Chinaglia,* | *Flugeseth (pen)* |
| | *Savoldi, Cordova* | |
| 2 March: | Japan (0) 0 | Sweden (0) 1 |
| | | *Werner* |
| 5 March: | Japan Olympic XI (0) 1 | Sweden (2) 4 |
| | *Mori* | *Svensson, Grönhagen* 3 |
| 8 March: | Japan Olympic XI (0) 0 | Sweden (0) 2 |
| | | *Grönhagen, Linderoth* |
| 11 March: | Eire (0) 1 | West Germany (0) 0 |
| | *Conway* | |
| 26 March: | France (0) 2 | Hungary (0) 0 |
| | *Michel, Parizon* | |
| | Poland (4) 7 | USA (0) 0 |
| | *Deyna* 3, *Lato* 2, | |
| | *Szarmach* 2 | |
| | East Germany (0) 0 | Bulgaria (0) 0 |
| | Cyprus (1) 1 | Greece (1) 2 |
| 2 April: | Italy (5) 10 | USA (0) 0 |
| | *Rocca* 2, *Cordova,* | |
| | *Chinaglia* 2, *Graziani* 3, | |
| | *Savoldi* 2 | |
| 27 April: | France (0) 0 | Portugal (1) 2 |
| | | *Nene, Marinho* |
| 30 April: | Belgium (0) 1 | Holland (0) 0 |
| | *Lambert* | |
| 17 May: | West Germany (1) 1 | Holland (0) 1 |
| | *Wimmer* | *Van Hanegem* |

CHAPTER EIGHT

# F.A. Cup 1974–75

West Ham won the Cup for the second time in their history, though it might be more accurate to say that Fulham lost it, conceding the final with two dreadful errors in the second half, after playing the better football. Both goals were scored by Alan Taylor, bought a few months previously for only £45,000 from Rochdale, and a reserve till Keith Robson was injured.

It was the first all-London final since 1967, and only the second this century. West Ham's presence, though they faltered in the semi-final and were lucky to survive at Villa Park against an Ipswich team severely reduced by injuries to Beattie and Hunter, was not surprising. Buying new, committed, strikers in Billy Jennings and Keith Robson, they had added bite to their traditional skills; though a thigh injury to

Robson at Birmingham denied them his services for semi-final and final.

Fulham's progress, however, was astounding. No more than a moderate Second Division team, despite the distinguished presence of Alan Mullery and Bobby Moore, they made heavy weather of eliminating Hull and Forest, then suddenly sprang to life to beat three First Division teams; Everton away, thanks to the opportunism of Viv Busby; Carlisle away, where a keeper's error was punished; Birmingham City in a semi-final replay. Here, the hero was the 23–year-old centre-forward John Mitchell, called up belatedly to score in each match.

Fulham were much the better team in the first, and won the replay nine seconds from the end of extra time when Mitchell's close-in shot rebounded on to him from Latchford, and thence into the net.

West Ham were somewhat fortunate in their replay with Ipswich at Stamford Bridge. The East Anglians had put out Leeds in a third replay, thanks to a remarkable, swerving right foot shot by Clive Woods, a reserve *de luxe*. West Ham's two goals against them were both scored by little Alan Taylor, bought from Rochdale, while Jennings sliced bizarrely into his own goal. Bobby Robson, Ipswich's resourceful young manager, complained with some justice about the refereeing. There seemed nothing wrong with Bryan Hamilton's seventh minute goal, mysteriously given offside.

It was a great Cup for giant-killers. Wimbledon of the Southern League did best of all with a magnificent win 1–0 at Burnley, a glorious draw at Leeds, a gallant display in the replay at Crystal Palace, when only a lucky, deflected goal by Giles put them out. Leatherhead won at Brighton, and only just went down at Leicester, inspired by a puckish forward called Chris Kelly, who went – very briefly – to Millwall. Walsall put out Newcastle United.

Fulham had much the better of the opening 20 minutes at Wembley against West Ham, and the best shot of the half when Busby, on the left, provoked a good save from his narrow angled shot by Day. Indeed Day was the true hero of West Ham, making magnificent saves in the second half from John Mitchell, who once left Lock marooned on the right, later took advantage of an error by Tommy Taylor to beat Lock again, through the middle.

The West Ham goals came in a five minute spell, the first on the hour when Cutbush twice carelessly lost the ball to Holland, Mellor could only parry Jennings' shot, and Alan Taylor scored from a sharp angle; the second when Mellor made a dreadful hash of a shot by Paddon, Alan Taylor scoring again.

Bobby Moore had a fine match against his old club, Trevor Brooking did his considerable best to lift West Ham out of the doldrums, but they were unquestionably a fortunate team.

**Final** Wembley, 3 May, 1975

West Ham United (0) 2          Fulham (0) 0
*A. Taylor* (2)

*West Ham United:* Day; McDowell, T. Taylor, Lock, Lampard, Bonds, Paddon, Brooking, Jennings, A. Taylor, Holland.
*Fulham:* Mellor: Cutbush, Lacy, Moore, Fraser, Mullery, Conway, Slough, Mitchell, Busby, Barrett.

## FOOTBALL LEAGUE CUP 1974-75

The atmosphere of unreality which has long surrounded the League Cup became a positive miasma when the 1975 finalists turned out to be two Second Division teams, Aston Villa and Norwich City. The match itself, though watched by a deluded 100,000 and blown up out of all proportion by the sheep-like media, turned out to be appropriately drab. Norwich, managed by John Bond, who had talked a good game all week failed dismally when it came to the crunch. Ron Saunders, the former Norwich manager whom Bond had publicly criticised, had the satisfaction of seeing Villa dominate play, with Jim Cumbes virtually inactive in goal; even if the only goal came when Ray Graydon scored, after the gallant Kevin Keelan stopped his penalty.

On the way to the final, the distinguished giantkillers were little Chester, only team in the League never to have gained promotion, who hung the scalps of Leeds United and Newcastle United on their belts, before Villa dismissed them.

**Final** Wembley, March 1 1975

Aston Villa (0) 1                   Norwich City (0) 0
*Graydon*

*Aston Villa:* Cumbes; Robson, Aitken, Ross, Nicholl, McDonald, Graydon, Little, Leonard, Hamilton, Carrodus.
*Norwich City:* Keelan; Machin, Sullivan, Morris, Forbes, Stringer, Miller, MacDougall, Boyer, Suggett. Powell.

## SCOTTISH CUP 1974-5

Celtic consoled themselves for an unhappy League season by taking the Scottish Cup, beating part-time Airdrieonians convincingly in the final.

Ironically, it was a mistake by their former back, Tommy Gemmell, which allowed Celtic to win a difficult semi-final against Dundee; thus repeating the score of the previous year's semi-final, and enabling Celtic to beat Dundee at this stage for the third year in a row. Gemmell, on the edge of his own penalty box, tried to beat a man instead of clear, Ronnie Glavin snapped the ball up, and powerfully scored.

Airdrie, meanwhile, were making their first appearance in the final since 1924, when they won, beating Hibs 2–0 at Ibrox.

In the final, Lennox, Dalglish, and Wilson were too good for Airdrie. On the quarter hour Celtic led when McGrain found Dalglish, from whose cross Paul Wilson headed an easy goal. But Airdrie fought back with spirit, McCann equalising after a couple of shots had been blocked, only for Wilson to head another just before the break.

Eight minutes into the second half, McCluskey's penalty after Black tripped the speedy Lennox made the game sure for Celtic.

**Final** Hampden Park, 3 May, 1975

| Celtic (2) 3 | Airdrieonians (1) 1 |
|---|---|
| *P. Wilson* (2), | *McCann* |
| *McCluskey* (*pen.*) | |

*Celtic:* Latchford; McGrain, Lynch, Murray, McNeill, McCluskey, Hood, Glavin, Dalglish, Lennox, P. Wilson.

*Airdrieonians:* McWilliams; Jonquin, Cowen, Menzies, Black, Whiteford, McCann, Walker, McCulloch (March), Lapsley (Reynolds), W. Wilson.

---

## SCOTTISH LEAGUE CUP 1974

After struggling painfully to beat Airdrieonians in the semi-final, Celtic comprehensively thrashed Hibernian in the Final at the same Hampden Park, playing vigorous attacking football. Sympathy must go to Joe Harper, the little Hibs centre-forward, who scored three goals but finished on the losing side.

Three goals also went to Dixie Deans of Celtic, one a spectacular diving header, another a splendid turn and powerful shot, while he was also involved in the build up to the well worked opening goal, scored by Jimmy Johnstone.

Harper's hook shot made it only 2–1 at half-time, but when Deans beat John Blackley then drove past McArthur, the floodgates opened. It was Celtic's best performance for weeks.

**Final** Hampden Park, 26 October 1974

| Celtic (2) 6 | Hibernian (1) 3 |
|---|---|
| *Johnstone, Deans* (3), | *Harper* (3) |
| *Wilson, Murray* | |

*Celtic:* Hunter; McGrain, McNeill, McCluskey, Brogan, Hood, Murray, Dalglish; Johnstone, Deans, Wilson.

*Hibernian:* McArthur; Brownlie (Smith), Bremner, Stanton, Spalding, Blackley, Edwards, Cropley, Harper, Munro, Duncan (Murray).

CHAPTER NINE

# Football League 1974–75

What the season lacked in quality – which was much – it partly compensated for in sheer drama. By contrast with the previous Championship, which Leeds dominated for so long, this was democratic to a degree; a degree of mediocrity. At various times Liverpool, Everton,

Stoke City, and Ipswich Town threatened to take a title virtually lost by Leeds in the hectic upheaval of Brian Clough's 44 Days; which left them panting almost at the bottom of the table. Jimmy Armfield arrived from Bolton to take cool and healing charge, after Clough had departed with an alleged £92,000 'golden handshake', but though Leeds vastly improved, and Clough's £250,000 transfer from Forest, Duncan McKenzie, proved an inspired one, it was too late.

Derby, whose appallingly heavy pitch caused bitter comment during the season, emerged, Harry Wragg-like, from the back of the field, taking advantage of the fact that such teams as Ipswich were beset by injuries and the colossal demands of the Cup.

Derby's opportunity to go out with a fine flourish was pitifully lost when, in their last match of the season at the Baseball Ground, the title won, all pressure lifted, they could not even beat Carlisle, the bottom team, drawing drearily, 0–0.

In these last matches, Roy McFarland at last returned to the defence after missing nearly the whole season with tendon trouble. Colin Todd was a defender of world class, Archie Gemmill (the last player to relish such a tiring pitch) toiled mightily in midfield, Francis Lee, though he missed vital, late weeks through injury, brought new life to the attack.

Everton, far too cautious away from home, though much strengthened by the £300,000 purchase of Martin Dobson from Burnley – who had to pay for their new stand – blew up in their last home match when Sheffield United wiped out a 2–0 deficit to beat them. Liverpool got away to a fine start but predictably missed the irreplaceable drive of Bill Shankly. Ipswich played much pleasing football, showed occasional lacunae in defence, but might still have turned the trick had David Johnson, their fine centre-forward, not missed the last weeks of a season in which Kevin Beattie was outstanding.

It was, on the whole, a bleak season for London clubs, and one in which managers fell like autumn leaves. Chelsea sacked Dave Sexton, who promptly succeeded Gordon Jago (resigned) at Queens Park Rangers. Spurs sacked Bill Nicholson and his coach, Eddie Baily, installing the Hull and Northern Ireland manager, Terry Neill. West Ham United successfully appointed Ron Greenwood their general manager, John Lyall, his able young protégé, the team manager. Arsenal bored everyone severely but survived, thanks in no small measure to two transfers from Manchester United, the goalkeeper Jimmy Rimmer and the goal scorer Brian Kidd.

Chelsea, beaten 2–0 by Spurs at White Hart Lane in an all or nothing game (in which, bewilderingly, they gave 17–year-old Teddy Maybank his debut at centre-forward) went down. Making Eddie McCreadie team manager at the last gasp availed them nothing – they couldn't even win their last two home matches, and their £2½ million grandstand now graces the Second Division. With Osgood gone, there was no one to score goals. Spurs scrambled clear with little credit, beating an uninterested Leeds team 4–2 in their final game. That sent down a

Luton Town side which performed bravely in the final weeks. Carlisle, though bottom, were not remotely disgraced.

Manchester United bounced straight back from the Second Division, which they won comfortably, Pearson giving them new thrust at centre-forward, Willy Morgan surprisingly falling out of the team after a successful World Cup and a good beginning. Their hooligan, nihilist fans were the terror of the country. Aston Villa, appointing Ron Saunders, sacked by Manchester City, to manage them, had a very good season, excellent players like Brian Little, a free scoring forward, and McDonald emerging from their youth scheme. Norwich bought Martin Peters from Spurs, reconstituted the Boyer-Mac-Dougall, ex-Bournemouth, partnership in attack, but were a little lucky to scramble home ahead of Sunderland. Southampton, despite the expensive presence of Osgood and Channon, never looked like coming up.

Blackburn Rovers authoritatively won Division III, followed by Plymouth Argyle, and a Charlton team which slipped badly in the final stages. Mansfield Town were easy winners of the Fourth Division.

Overall, alas, it was a picture of tactical conservatism and technical insufficiency. Outstanding individuals were at a premium.

| DIVISION 1 | | Home | | | | | Away | | | | | |
|---|---|---|---|---|---|---|---|---|---|---|---|---|
| | P | W | D | L | F | A | W | D | L | F | A | pts |
| Derby Co. | 42 | 14 | 4 | 3 | 41 | 18 | 7 | 7 | 7 | 26 | 31 | 53 |
| Liverpool | 42 | 14 | 5 | 2 | 44 | 17 | 6 | 6 | 9 | 16 | 22 | 51 |
| Ipswich T. | 42 | 17 | 2 | 2 | 47 | 14 | 6 | 3 | 12 | 19 | 30 | 51 |
| Everton | 42 | 10 | 9 | 2 | 33 | 19 | 6 | 9 | 6 | 23 | 23 | 50 |
| Stoke C. | 42 | 12 | 7 | 2 | 40 | 18 | 5 | 8 | 8 | 24 | 30 | 49 |
| Sheffield U. | 42 | 12 | 7 | 2 | 35 | 20 | 6 | 6 | 9 | 23 | 31 | 49 |
| Middlesbrough | 42 | 11 | 7 | 3 | 33 | 14 | 7 | 5 | 9 | 21 | 26 | 48 |
| Manchester C. | 42 | 16 | 3 | 2 | 40 | 15 | 2 | 7 | 12 | 14 | 39 | 46 |
| Leeds U. | 42 | 10 | 8 | 3 | 34 | 20 | 6 | 5 | 10 | 23 | 29 | 45 |
| Burnley | 42 | 11 | 6 | 4 | 40 | 29 | 6 | 5 | 10 | 28 | 38 | 45 |
| Q. P. R. | 42 | 10 | 4 | 7 | 25 | 17 | 6 | 6 | 9 | 29 | 37 | 42 |
| Wolverhampton W. | 42 | 12 | 5 | 4 | 43 | 21 | 2 | 6 | 13 | 14 | 33 | 39 |
| West Ham U. | 42 | 10 | 6 | 5 | 38 | 22 | 3 | 7 | 11 | 20 | 37 | 39 |
| Coventry C. | 42 | 8 | 9 | 4 | 31 | 27 | 4 | 6 | 11 | 20 | 35 | 39 |
| Newcastle U. | 42 | 12 | 4 | 5 | 39 | 23 | 5 | 5 | 13 | 20 | 49 | 39 |
| Arsenal | 42 | 10 | 6 | 5 | 31 | 16 | 3 | 5 | 13 | 16 | 33 | 37 |
| Birmingham C. | 42 | 10 | 4 | 7 | 34 | 28 | 4 | 5 | 12 | 19 | 33 | 37 |
| Leicester C. | 42 | 8 | 7 | 6 | 25 | 17 | 4 | 5 | 12 | 21 | 43 | 36 |
| Tottenham H. | 42 | 8 | 4 | 9 | 29 | 27 | 5 | 4 | 12 | 23 | 36 | 34 |
| Luton T. | 42 | 8 | 6 | 7 | 27 | 26 | 3 | 5 | 13 | 20 | 39 | 33 |
| Chelsea | 42 | 4 | 9 | 8 | 22 | 31 | 5 | 6 | 10 | 20 | 41 | 33 |
| Carlisle U. | 42 | 8 | 2 | 11 | 22 | 21 | 4 | 3 | 14 | 21 | 38 | 29 |

| DIVISION 2 | | Home | | | | | Away | | | | | |
|---|---|---|---|---|---|---|---|---|---|---|---|---|
| | P | W | D | L | F | A | W | D | L | F | A | pts |
| Manchester U. | 42 | 17 | 3 | 1 | 45 | 12 | 9 | 6 | 6 | 21 | 18 | 61 |
| Aston Villa | 42 | 16 | 4 | 1 | 47 | 6 | 9 | 4 | 8 | 32 | 26 | 58 |
| Norwich C. | 42 | 14 | 3 | 4 | 34 | 17 | 6 | 10 | 5 | 24 | 20 | 53 |
| Sunderland | 42 | 14 | 6 | 1 | 41 | 8 | 5 | 7 | 9 | 24 | 27 | 51 |
| Bristol C. | 42 | 14 | 5 | 2 | 31 | 10 | 7 | 3 | 11 | 16 | 23 | 50 |
| W.B.A. | 42 | 13 | 4 | 4 | 33 | 15 | 5 | 5 | 11 | 21 | 27 | 45 |
| Blackpool | 42 | 12 | 6 | 3 | 31 | 17 | 2 | 11 | 8 | 7 | 16 | 45 |
| Hull C. | 42 | 12 | 8 | 1 | 25 | 10 | 3 | 6 | 12 | 15 | 43 | 44 |
| Fulham | 42 | 9 | 8 | 4 | 29 | 17 | 4 | 8 | 9 | 15 | 22 | 42 |
| Bolton W. | 42 | 9 | 7 | 5 | 27 | 16 | 6 | 5 | 10 | 18 | 25 | 42 |
| Oxford U. | 42 | 14 | 3 | 4 | 30 | 19 | 1 | 9 | 11 | 11 | 32 | 42 |
| Orient | 42 | 8 | 9 | 4 | 17 | 16 | 3 | 11 | 7 | 11 | 23 | 42 |
| Southampton | 42 | 10 | 6 | 5 | 29 | 20 | 5 | 5 | 11 | 24 | 34 | 41 |
| Notts Co. | 42 | 7 | 11 | 3 | 34 | 26 | 5 | 5 | 11 | 15 | 33 | 40 |
| York C. | 42 | 9 | 7 | 5 | 28 | 18 | 5 | 3 | 13 | 23 | 37 | 38 |
| Nottingham F. | 42 | 7 | 7 | 7 | 24 | 23 | 5 | 7 | 9 | 19 | 32 | 38 |
| Portsmouth | 42 | 9 | 7 | 5 | 28 | 20 | 3 | 6 | 12 | 16 | 34 | 37 |
| Oldham Ath. | 42 | 10 | 7 | 4 | 28 | 16 | 0 | 8 | 13 | 12 | 32 | 35 |
| Bristol R. | 42 | 10 | 4 | 7 | 25 | 23 | 2 | 7 | 12 | 17 | 41 | 35 |
| Millwall | 42 | 8 | 9 | 4 | 31 | 19 | 2 | 3 | 16 | 13 | 37 | 32 |
| Cardiff C. | 42 | 7 | 8 | 6 | 24 | 21 | 2 | 6 | 13 | 12 | 41 | 32 |
| Sheffield W. | 42 | 3 | 7 | 11 | 17 | 29 | 2 | 4 | 15 | 12 | 35 | 21 |

| DIVISION 3 | | | | | | | | | | | | |
|---|---|---|---|---|---|---|---|---|---|---|---|---|
| | P | W | D | L | F | A | W | D | L | F | A | Pts |
| Blackburn R. | 46 | 15 | 7 | 1 | 40 | 16 | 7 | 9 | 7 | 28 | 29 | 60 |
| Plymouth Arg. | 46 | 16 | 5 | 2 | 38 | 19 | 8 | 6 | 9 | 41 | 39 | 59 |
| Charlton Ath. | 46 | 15 | 5 | 3 | 51 | 29 | 7 | 6 | 10 | 25 | 32 | 55 |
| Swindon T. | 46 | 18 | 3 | 2 | 43 | 17 | 3 | 8 | 12 | 21 | 41 | 53 |
| Crystal Palace | 46 | 14 | 8 | 1 | 48 | 22 | 4 | 7 | 12 | 18 | 35 | 51 |
| Port Vale | 46 | 15 | 6 | 2 | 37 | 19 | 3 | 9 | 11 | 24 | 35 | 51 |
| Peterborough U. | 46 | 10 | 9 | 4 | 24 | 17 | 9 | 3 | 11 | 23 | 36 | 50 |
| Walsall | 46 | 15 | 5 | 3 | 46 | 13 | 3 | 8 | 12 | 21 | 39 | 49 |
| Preston N.E. | 46 | 16 | 5 | 2 | 42 | 19 | 3 | 6 | 14 | 21 | 37 | 49 |
| Gillingham | 46 | 14 | 6 | 3 | 43 | 23 | 3 | 8 | 12 | 22 | 37 | 48 |
| Colchester U. | 46 | 13 | 7 | 3 | 45 | 22 | 4 | 6 | 13 | 25 | 41 | 47 |
| Hereford U. | 46 | 14 | 6 | 3 | 42 | 21 | 2 | 8 | 13 | 22 | 45 | 46 |
| Wrexham | 46 | 10 | 8 | 5 | 41 | 23 | 5 | 7 | 11 | 24 | 32 | 45 |
| Bury | 46 | 13 | 6 | 4 | 38 | 17 | 3 | 6 | 14 | 15 | 33 | 44 |
| Chesterfield | 46 | 11 | 7 | 5 | 37 | 25 | 5 | 5 | 13 | 25 | 41 | 44 |
| Grimsby T. | 46 | 12 | 8 | 3 | 35 | 19 | 3 | 5 | 15 | 20 | 45 | 43 |
| Halifax T. | 46 | 11 | 10 | 2 | 33 | 20 | 2 | 7 | 14 | 16 | 45 | 43 |
| Southend U. | 46 | 11 | 9 | 3 | 32 | 17 | 2 | 7 | 14 | 14 | 34 | 42 |
| Brighton & H. A. | 46 | 14 | 7 | 2 | 38 | 21 | 2 | 3 | 18 | 18 | 43 | 42 |
| Aldershot* | 46 | 13 | 5 | 5 | 40 | 21 | 1 | 6 | 16 | 13 | 42 | 38 |
| AFC Bournemouth | 46 | 9 | 6 | 8 | 27 | 25 | 4 | 6 | 13 | 17 | 33 | 38 |
| Tranmere R. | 46 | 12 | 4 | 7 | 39 | 21 | 2 | 5 | 16 | 16 | 36 | 37 |
| Watford | 46 | 9 | 7 | 7 | 30 | 31 | 1 | 10 | 12 | 22 | 44 | 37 |
| Huddersfield T. | 46 | 9 | 6 | 8 | 32 | 29 | 2 | 4 | 17 | 15 | 47 | 32 |

*One point deducted for playing an unregistered player.

| | | Home | | | | | Away | | | | | |
|---|---|---|---|---|---|---|---|---|---|---|---|---|
| | P | W | D | L | F | A | W | D | L | F | A | Pts |
| Mansfield T. | 46 | 17 | 6 | 0 | 55 | 15 | 11 | 6 | 6 | 35 | 25 | 63 |
| Shrewsbury T. | 46 | 16 | 3 | 4 | 46 | 18 | 10 | 7 | 6 | 34 | 25 | 62 |
| Rotherham U. | 46 | 13 | 7 | 3 | 40 | 19 | 9 | 8 | 6 | 31 | 22 | 59 |
| Chester | 46 | 17 | 5 | 1 | 48 | 9 | 6 | 6 | 11 | 16 | 29 | 57 |
| Lincoln C. | 46 | 14 | 8 | 1 | 47 | 14 | 7 | 7 | 9 | 32 | 34 | 57 |
| Cambridge U. | 46 | 15 | 5 | 3 | 43 | 16 | 5 | 9 | 9 | 19 | 28 | 54 |
| Reading | 46 | 13 | 6 | 4 | 38 | 20 | 8 | 4 | 11 | 25 | 27 | 52 |
| Brentford | 46 | 15 | 6 | 2 | 38 | 14 | 3 | 7 | 13 | 15 | 31 | 49 |
| Exeter C. | 46 | 14 | 3 | 8 | 33 | 24 | 5 | 8 | 10 | 27 | 39 | 49 |
| Bradford C. | 46 | 10 | 5 | 8 | 32 | 21 | 7 | 8 | 8 | 24 | 30 | 47 |
| Southport | 46 | 13 | 7 | 3 | 36 | 19 | 2 | 10 | 11 | 20 | 37 | 47 |
| Newport Co. | 46 | 13 | 5 | 5 | 43 | 30 | 6 | 4 | 13 | 25 | 45 | 47 |
| Hartlepool | 46 | 13 | 6 | 4 | 40 | 24 | 3 | 5 | 15 | 12 | 36 | 43 |
| Torquay U. | 46 | 10 | 7 | 6 | 30 | 25 | 4 | 7 | 12 | 16 | 36 | 42 |
| Barnsley | 46 | 10 | 7 | 6 | 34 | 24 | 5 | 4 | 14 | 28 | 41 | 41 |
| Northampton T. | 46 | 12 | 6 | 5 | 43 | 22 | 3 | 5 | 15 | 24 | 51 | 41 |
| Doncaster R. | 46 | 10 | 9 | 4 | 41 | 29 | 4 | 3 | 16 | 24 | 50 | 40 |
| Crewe Alex. | 46 | 9 | 9 | 5 | 22 | 16 | 2 | 9 | 12 | 12 | 31 | 40 |
| Rochdale | 46 | 9 | 9 | 5 | 35 | 22 | 4 | 4 | 15 | 24 | 53 | 39 |
| Stockport Co. | 46 | 10 | 8 | 5 | 26 | 27 | 2 | 6 | 15 | 17 | 43 | 38 |
| Darlington | 46 | 11 | 4 | 8 | 38 | 27 | 2 | 6 | 15 | 16 | 40 | 36 |
| Swansea C. | 46 | 9 | 4 | 10 | 25 | 31 | 6 | 2 | 15 | 21 | 42 | 36 |
| Workington | 46 | 7 | 5 | 11 | 23 | 29 | 3 | 6 | 14 | 13 | 37 | 31 |
| Scunthorpe U. | 46 | 7 | 8 | 8 | 27 | 29 | 0 | 7 | 16 | 14 | 49 | 29 |

# Scottish League 1974–75

Celtic did not carry off their 10th successive Championship. Rangers, their eternal rivals, took the title for the first time since 1964, as much thanks to Celtic's failings as their own Spartan virtues.

Under the driving management of Jock Wallace, Rangers forced their way into the lead, in the exact sense of the word, with a 3–0 win over Celtic on their escutcheon. It was highly physical football, plenty of high balls to three big strikers in the versatile Derek Johnstone, the promising young Derek Parlane, and to Colin Stein brought back after long absence, late in the season, from Coventry. Two particularly successful signings were of Second Division men in Stewart Kennedy, the goalkeeper who arrived the previous season from Stenhousemuir, and in 1974–75 ousted McCloy and became the Scotland keeper, and the midfield player, Bobby McKean, from St Mirren.

Celtic laboured, no longer the irresistible force. There were strong rumours through the season that Jock Stein would leave the club whose success he had forced to become team manager of Scotland. A particular irony was that Bobby Murdoch, given a free transfer, should be playing so successfully for Middlesbrough, while Celtic laboured in midfield. Nor were they too happy in defence, with

Billy McNeill a veteran now, and the goalkeeping problem persisting to such an extent that Peter Latchford was imported from West Bromwich Albion.

## DIVISION 1

| | | | Home | | | | Away | | | | |
|---|---|---|---|---|---|---|---|---|---|---|---|
| | P | W | D | L | F | A | W | D | L | F | A Pts |
| Rangers | 34 | 14 | 1 | 2 | 39 | 15 | 11 | 5 | 1 | 47 | 18 56 |
| Hibernian | 34 | 12 | 2 | 3 | 41 | 16 | 8 | 7 | 2 | 28 | 21 49 |
| Celtic | 34 | 11 | 2 | 4 | 47 | 20 | 9 | 3 | 5 | 34 | 21 45 |
| Dundee U. | 34 | 10 | 5 | 2 | 41 | 19 | 9 | 2 | 6 | 31 | 24 45 |
| Aberdeen | 34 | 9 | 6 | 2 | 42 | 20 | 7 | 3 | 7 | 24 | 23 41 |
| Dundee | 34 | 11 | 1 | 5 | 32 | 17 | 5 | 5 | 7 | 16 | 25 36 |
| Ayr U. | 34 | 9 | 5 | 3 | 29 | 27 | 5 | 3 | 9 | 21 | 34 36 |
| Hearts | 34 | 8 | 6 | 3 | 24 | 16 | 3 | 7 | 7 | 23 | 36 35 |
| St Johnstone | 34 | 8 | 4 | 5 | 27 | 20 | 3 | 6 | 6 | 14 | 24 34 |
| Motherwell | 34 | 8 | 2 | 7 | 30 | 23 | 6 | 3 | 8 | 22 | 34 33 |
| Airdrieonians | 34 | 7 | 7 | 3 | 26 | 20 | 4 | 2 | 11 | 17 | 35 31 |
| Kilmarnock | 34 | 5 | 7 | 5 | 26 | 29 | 3 | 8 | 6 | 26 | 39 31 |
| Partick Th. | 34 | 7 | 5 | 5 | 27 | 31 | 3 | 5 | 9 | 21 | 31 30 |
| Dumbarton | 34 | 3 | 5 | 9 | 19 | 24 | 4 | 5 | 8 | 25 | 31 24 |
| Dunfermline Ath. | 34 | 3 | 6 | 8 | 24 | 32 | 4 | 3 | 10 | 22 | 34 23 |
| Clyde | 34 | 4 | 6 | 7 | 25 | 30 | 2 | 4 | 11 | 15 | 33 22 |
| Morton | 34 | 4 | 5 | 8 | 17 | 28 | 2 | 5 | 10 | 14 | 34 22 |
| Arbroath | 34 | 4 | 5 | 8 | 20 | 27 | 1 | 2 | 14 | 14 | 39 17 |

## DIVISION 2

| | | | Home | | | | Away | | | | |
|---|---|---|---|---|---|---|---|---|---|---|---|
| | P | W | D | L | F | A | W | D | L | F | A Pts |
| Falkirk | 38 | 16 | 0 | 3 | 52 | 12 | 10 | 2 | 7 | 24 | 17 54 |
| Queen of the S. | 38 | 12 | 4 | 3 | 37 | 13 | 11 | 3 | 5 | 40 | 20 53 |
| Montrose | 38 | 13 | 4 | 2 | 34 | 14 | 10 | 3 | 6 | 36 | 23 53 |
| Hamilton A. | 38 | 10 | 3 | 6 | 38 | 17 | 11 | 4 | 4 | 31 | 13 49 |
| East Fife | 38 | 11 | 6 | 2 | 35 | 19 | 9 | 1 | 9 | 22 | 23 47 |
| St Mirren | 38 | 10 | 3 | 6 | 36 | 20 | 9 | 5 | 5 | 38 | 32 46 |
| Clydebank | 38 | 11 | 5 | 3 | 31 | 19 | 7 | 3 | 9 | 19 | 21 44 |
| Stirling A. | 38 | 10 | 4 | 5 | 37 | 22 | 7 | 5 | 7 | 30 | 33 43 |
| Berwick R. | 38 | 12 | 2 | 5 | 35 | 22 | 5 | 4 | 10 | 18 | 27 40 |
| East Stirling | 38 | 11 | 3 | 5 | 32 | 18 | 5 | 5 | 9 | 24 | 34 40 |
| Stenhousemuir | 38 | 9 | 4 | 6 | 29 | 17 | 5 | 7 | 7 | 23 | 25 39 |
| Albion R. | 38 | 11 | 2 | 6 | 44 | 29 | 5 | 5 | 9 | 28 | 35 39 |
| Raith R. | 38 | 11 | 3 | 5 | 33 | 22 | 3 | 6 | 10 | 15 | 22 37 |
| Stranraer | 38 | 7 | 8 | 4 | 24 | 25 | 5 | 3 | 11 | 23 | 40 35 |
| Alloa | 38 | 7 | 6 | 6 | 25 | 20 | 4 | 5 | 10 | 24 | 36 33 |
| Queen's Park | 38 | 4 | 6 | 9 | 19 | 27 | 6 | 4 | 9 | 22 | 27 30 |
| Brechin C. | 38 | 6 | 4 | 9 | 30 | 39 | 3 | 3 | 13 | 14 | 46 25 |
| Meadowbank Th. | 38 | 6 | 4 | 9 | 15 | 30 | 3 | 1 | 15 | 11 | 57 23 |
| Cowdenbeath | 38 | 4 | 5 | 10 | 21 | 36 | 1 | 6 | 12 | 18 | 40 21 |
| Forfar Ath. | 38 | 1 | 3 | 15 | 16 | 50 | 0 | 4 | 15 | 11 | 52 9 |

The lines indicate the division of the Scottish League into the Premier Division, Division 1, and Division 2 for 1975–76.

CHAPTER TEN

# Fifty World Stars

**ACIMOVIC, Jovan** (Red Star Belgrade and Yugoslavia). A midfield inside-left of great skill, both in control and strategy, Acimovic made his League debut for Red Star at 17, and was married a year later. Dark and compactly built – a love of confectionery causes weight problems – he became known to Europe in 1968 when he was a prominent figure in the Yugoslav team which reached, and most debatably lost, the European Nations final against Italy in Rome. Six years later, he helped Yugoslavia to get to the finals of the World Cup in West Germany, where he played in all six games. By way of anti-climax, he then had to serve his conscription in the Yugoslav Army.

**AYALA, Ruben** (Atlético Madrid and Argentina). A dashing and spectacular striker whose goals did much to qualify Argentina for the World Cup, and who did not miss a match for them in West Germany. Between these appearances for Argentina, Ayala, an unusual figure with shoulder length hair, drooping moustache, and thick, solid legs, had moved from San Lorenzo de Almagro to Atlético Madrid. Played a vital part in their 1973-74 European Cup run, but missed the final, being suspended after expulsion from the notorious Celtic – Atlético semi-final in Glasgow. Explosively fast, with superb ball control.

**BABINGTON, Carlos** (Wattenscheid 09 and Argentina). This blond, curly headed inside-left was one of the outstanding midfield players of the 1974 World Cup, when his fine control and beautifully judged passing showed the Argentinian game at its most fetching. Surprisingly, his club, Huracan of Buenos Aires, sold him a few months later for £80,000 to a mere West German Second Division club. But Babington is used to ups and downs. He was added to the Argentinian World Cup party only as an afterthought, when they were already in Europe; and he would have joined Stoke City a few years earlier, had his father – of English descent – not relinquished his British passport. Born September 20 1949, he played for River Plate's ninth team. Made League debut for Deportivo Colon, 1969.

**BECKENBAUER, Franz** (Bayern Munich and West Germany). Not only a great but a greatly influential player, whose concept of the mobile, attacking sweeper has transformed football. Has now captained West Germany to the Nations Cup of 1972 and the World Cup of 1974, and Bayern to the 1974 European Cup. A wonderfully elegant foot-baller, he was a schoolboy and youth international at right-half, winning his first full cap at 20, in 1965. He was outstanding in the 1966 and 1970 World Cups, and his shoulder injury probably cost West Germany the 1970 semi-final against Italy. A beautiful striker and passer of the ball, a superb strategist and the possessor of unusual acceleration, he was European Footballer of the Year in 1972.

**BLOKHIN, Oleg** (Kiev Dynamo and Russia). One of the sadly few outstanding individual players to emerge from Russia in recent years. A blond, natural left winger with speed and a fine left-footed shot. He emerged in 1972 as a member of the Russian Olympic football team in West Germany, then played for the World Cup team which was eventually eliminated by Chile. In 1974, he helped Dynamo Kiev to regain the Russian Championship.

**BONEV, Christo** (Lokomotiv Plovdiv and Bulgaria). Though not as popular in Bulgaria as some heroes of the past, Bonev is outstandingly their best contemporary player, and one of the finest they've ever had; an inside-right of superb gifts, subtlety and effectiveness. His right foot is among the best and most adroit in the game, whether he be passing, or swerving in his remarkable free kicks. Did more than anybody to qualify Bulgaria for the 1974 World Cup, when he was the outstanding player in an unsuccessful team and scored his team's goal, a fine one, against Uruguay. First capped in 1967 against West Germany in Hanover, he was born February 3 1947. Surprisingly dropped by Bulgaria last season, but remains their outstanding player.

**BONHOF, Rainer** (Borussia Münchengladbach and West Germany). When the 1974 World Cup began, Bonhof had made a mere four appearances for West Germany and wasn't in the team. By the time it was over, he was acknowledged one of the chief engineers of their victory, an immensely powerful, driving midfield player whose forays on the right brought vital goals and gave new dynamism to the team. He was chosen for the last four matches, immediately after the defeat in Hamburg by East Germany, and he scored in the second of them, against Sweden. Best of all, his splendid burst past Haan and cross from the right set up the winning goal of the World Cup final. Born 29 March 1952.

**BREITNER, Paul** (Real Madrid and West Germany). Having played superbly in the World Cup for West Germany as an attacking full back, scoring three goals, Breitner promptly began a brilliant 'new' career as a midfield player for Real Madrid. Although he'd also won a 1974 European Cup medal with Bayern Munich, till then his only club, he'd long been uneasy there. A convinced Maoist who has adopted a Vietnamese orphan and plans on retirement to open a school for handicapped children, he was a fish out of water in Munich. Born in Bavaria on 5 September 1951, he made his name as a 20-year-old left-back in the splendid West German team which won the 1972 Nations Cup.

**BREMNER, Billy** (Leeds United and Scotland). A splendidly resourceful 1974 World Cup as captain of Scotland crowned Bremner's fine career, which began when he joined Leeds as a 15-year-old schoolboy outside-right. He metamorphosed to inside-right then midfield right-half. A tiny, red haired, indefatigable player who combined strength in the tackle with strength of shot, unbounded energy with close control and clever distribution. Helped Leeds to win the F.A. Cup, the Championship, the League Cup and the Fairs Cup. First capped against England at Hampden Park in 1966, he was born at Stirling on 9 December 1942.

**CASZELY, Carlos** (Levante and Chile). Though he was controversially sent off for retaliation in the opening match against West Germany in the World Cup of 1974, little Caszely did well enough to justify his reputation. He is a front runner of courage, strength, and fine control, exceedingly quick and persistent. Made his name in 1973 when his goal-scoring helped Colo Colo of Santiago to reach the South American Cup Final, and Chile to qualify for the World Cup at the expense of Peru. Then Levante signed him and brought him to Spain. Born 5 July 1950.

CHANNON, Mike (Southampton and England). Essentially a 'striking' inside-right though he can, as he says, hit the line on either side, with his glorious acceleration. A splendidly rhythmic mover, Channon is a Wiltshire country man, a breeder of horses, whose career was fashioned at Southampton. In October 1972 England picked him for the first time against Yugoslavia at Wembley, but though he played well he was promptly dropped, as he was, with dire results, the following year in Katowice in the World Cup match with Poland. A fine right-footed shot, strong in the air, he made himself an inevitable choice for England a few days after Katowice, when he routed the Russian defence in Moscow.

CLEMENCE, Ray (Liverpool and England). A goalkeeper immensely quick to come off his line, whose career is a triumph of perseverance. He was actually working as a deckchair attendant in Scunthorpe when the local club took him on. From there he moved to Liverpool where he understudied Tommy Lawrence, won caps for England in their two 1973 World Cup qualifying matches against Wales, but had to wait till May 1974 for an extended and distinguished run in the England team. Has won Cup and League Championship medals for Liverpool. Born Skegness.

CRUYFF, Johan (Barcelona and Holland). After an outstanding 1974 World Cup and a remarkable season with Barcelona, whom he inspired to win the Spanish Championship, Johan Cruyff was voted European Footballer of the Year for the third time in four seasons. Since he also won three European Cup medals with his original club, Ajax of Amsterdam – where his mother once cleaned the floors – there is reason to call him the outstanding player of the day. A slender, tall, galvanic player, with astonishing control, fierce acceleration, a strong shot, and remarkable tactical flair, Cruyff is a little reminiscent of a Dutch player he himself admired – Faas Wilkes. Ajax had him from boyhood, but in 1973 he insisted on following his former manager, Rinus Michels, to Barcelona, where he is thought to earn, all told, some £300,000 a year. He is, among other things, an excellent linguist, fluent in English and Spanish. Born 25 April 1947.

DZAJIC, Dragan (Bastia and Yugoslavia). One of the finest outside-lefts of his time, a player of grace, poise, skill, and incision, Dzajic became a major star at 22 when, in the European Nations Cup of 1968, he knocked out England with a semi-final goal in Florence, then scored in the drawn final against Italy in Rome. Born in Belgrade on 30 May 1946, he made his debut for his only club, Red Star, on 4 June 1963. His career was severely affected when in 1973 he first broke a leg, then had to serve his conscription, but he came back to help Yugoslavia reach and then compete in the 1974 World Cup finals. Has always said that his idol was Josip Skoblar, the Yugoslav left winger who eventually joined Marseille.

**EDSTROEM, Ralf** (PSV Eindhoven and Sweden). There was no more elegant striker in the 1974 World Cup than Edstroem, with his tall, slim figure, his splendid jumping for the ball, his cool control, and good left foot. Nor did anybody score a more spectacular goal than the one he volleyed against West Germany in Dusseldorf. Born on 7 October 1952, he came to European attention in August 1972 when, still 19, he scored three goals against Russia. With Degerfors until 1971, he went on to score 16 goals for Atvidaberg, who won the Swedish Championship. Sandberg, his admirable partner there and in the Swedish World Cup team, also scored 16 goals. In the summer of 1973, Edstroem joined PSV in Holland, but continued to play for Sweden, helping them to qualify for West Germany after an eventful play-off against Austria, in Gelsenkirchen.

**FIGUEROA, Elias** (Internacional Porto Alegre and Chile). Figueroa very nearly missed the 1974 World Cup, as he had missed the eliminators of the 1970 World Cup, because his club would not release him. In 1970 it was Penarol of Uruguay – Chile's opponents. In 1974 it was Internacional of Brazil. Luckily Figueroa, who had done much to help Chile qualify, did play, and play splendidly, in West Germany. A strong, athletic, mobile, confident centre-half whose first World Cup for Chile had been 1966, in England. Born 25 October 1946.

**GADOCHA, Robert** (Nantes and Poland). An outside-left who had a superb World Cup in 1974, even though, surprisingly, he didn't score a goal. But his devastating running, his clever crossing from either wing, the skilled use of his powerful left foot, made him one of the most admired forwards of the tournament. Afterwards, he was greatly put out when the Poles wouldn't let him join Bayern Munich, but at the turn of the year, he signed for Nantes of France; having previously helped his club Legia Warsaw knock them out of the UEFA Cup. Bald, strong stockily built, very fast, he was a star of the Polish team which eliminated Wales and England from the 1974 World Cup. Born Cracow 10 January 1946. Played for Poland's 1972 Olympic gold medallists.

**GORGON, Jerzy** (Gornik and Poland). Huge, blond centre-half, formidable in the air, who was a leading figure in Poland's path to the 1974 World Cup finals, and in their fine performance in West Germany. Playing as cover to the young Zmuda, he redeemed many dangerous situations, and even scored a goal against Haiti. Born 19 July 1949, he'd already had considerable European experience with Gornik, for whom he played against Manchester City in the Cup-Winners' Cup final of 1970 in Vienna. Two years later, he was a member of the Olympic title-winning team.

**GUILLOU, Jean-Marc** (Nice and France). Angers knew in the summer of 1974, when they hung on to Guillou by the skin of their teeth that he wouldn't be with them much longer, but none could blame them for wanting to keep the most gifted player in France – a shrewd, composed, elegant midfield player who had become a star of the national team. Born at Bouaye on 20 December 1945, he has been something of a late developer. His first cap came only in March 1974 against Rumania, when he had an outstanding game, and it took him five years to win a regular place with Angers. Has been described by a French critic as 'a sort of knight of football, a player full of fair play and courtesy'. Not to mention a refined technique.

**HAAN, Arie** (Anderlecht and Holland). Injury to Hulshoff forced this outstanding, dynamic midfield player to become a stopper cum sweeper for the World Cup; a transformation clearly ungrateful to him, though he had fine matches and moments. Essentially a right-sided player, he came on as substitute for Ajax in the European Cup final of 1971 at Wembley against Panathinaikos, scoring his team's second goal. By the 1972 Final, he was a major force in the team, adding a second medal against Inter and a third against Juventus in Belgrade a year later. Born 16 November 1948, he joined Ajax as a schoolboy. Has a teacher's diploma and speaks both French and English.

**HELLSTROEM, Ronnie** (Kaiserslautern and Sweden). A blond goalkeeper who played admirably for Sweden in the 1974 World Cup; some felt him to be the best keeper of all. It must have been particularly pleasing to him as his mistake in the 1970 World Cup in Mexico had cost the game and the match against Italy; galling, because he had already signed for Kaiserslautern of the Bundesliga at a far inferior sum to what he would have commanded after the World Cup. A brave, alert, athletic keeper who did so much to take Sweden into the last eight, Hellstroem previously played for Hammerby, had won 42 caps by the end of the World Cup, and was born on 21 February 1949.

**HOENESS, Uli** (Bayern Munich and West Germany). After an uncertain beginning, the young Hoeness became one of the principal stars of West Germany's victory in the 1974 World Cup, above all with his marvellous, long, sustained bursts. Originally a right winger, his runs down the flank are still remarkable, but he has become an all-round player, eminently right for Total Football; as effective in midfield as in defence. He was a European star as a 20-year-old, helping West Germany to win the 1972 European Nations Cup, after which, still an amateur, he played for their Olympic team. He has won Championship medals for Bayern, and played a spectacular part in their 1974 European Cup final victory over Atlético Madrid, scoring twice in the replay at Brussels. Born 5 January 1952.

**HOUSEMAN, René** (Huracan and Argentina). One of the dazzling surprises of the 1974 World Cup, when his classical wing play on either flank did so much to take Argentina into the last eight. He was particularly devastating in Stuttgart against Italy, who never began to master him, and against whom he scored a fine goal. A tiny, seemingly fragile figure, stockings round his ankles, Houseman is in fact durable, enterprising, fast and brave, with admirable control. Plays for Huracan of Buenos Aires, where Babington and Brindisi were his colleagues. Born 19 July 1953.

**JAMES, Leighton** (Burnley and Wales). One of the very few orthodox wingers in the First Division, and an immensely successful one. A very fast, very skilful player with immaculate ball control, the ability to score goals and to set them up. The red headed James was a Welsh grammar school boy when Burnley persuaded him to leave at 15 and come to them; one case in which the gamble has proved successful. Has been a regular choice for the Welsh international team since 1972, and played for them in the World Cup eliminating tournament when Poland both lost to them and beat them.

**JENNINGS, Pat** (Tottenham Hotspur and Northern Ireland). Many think him the best of Britain's many fine goalkeepers. Born in Newry, he took to football surprisingly late, after working as a forester, but he was good enough to play for his country in England in the 1963 European Youth Championship, after which Watford signed him. From there he moved to Tottenham, first as deputy to Bill Brown, whom he then succeeded. Won his first Irish cap with Watford against Wales, in 1964; helped Spurs win the Cup in 1967, the UEFA Cup in 1972. Powerfully built with huge hands, a tremendous kick, vast courage, and agility.

**KRANKL, Hans** (Rapid Vienna and Austria). The best centre-forward Austria has produced for many years. Born in 1953 in Vienna, in season 1973–74 his 36 League goals equalled the 23-year-old record of Robert Dienst. A great many of them were headed, but a hat trick in the derby against FK Austria, beaten 3–1, was scored wholly with the feet. Rapid signed him, lent him to Wacker, took him back after he had scored eight goals in a game. His first cap for Austria came against Brazil in Vienna in June 1973. Since he watched the 1974 World Cup tournament, he has become a convert to 'Total Football', more mobile on the field. But it is his headed goals which have made him the most popular player in Austria.

**KROL, Rudi** (Ajax and Holland). An attacking, enterprising left-back who can attack equally well down the right, Krol has won two European Cups and a world club Championship with Ajax, was a remarkable member of the Dutch team which reached the 1974 World Cup final. Fast, strongly built, a firm tackler, born on 24 March 1949, his first club was Rood Wit, whence he joined Ajax in 1968. He missed the 1971 European Cup final with a broken leg, but played in those of 1972 and 1973.

**LATO, Grzegorz** (Stal Mielec and Poland). When Lubanski dropped out of Poland's World Cup team the blow seemed fatal. Instead, the stocky young Lato took the chance to emerge as one of the most dangerous forwards in international football. Having helped Stal to win the Polish Championship, he helped Poland to qualify for the World Cup, his fine individual run bringing their goal against England at Wembley. In the World Cup itself he was formidably effective, his pace, incision, and strong right foot making him leading scorer, with seven goals; one of which gave Poland third place. Born 8 April 1950.

**MARIC, Enver** (Velez Mostar and Yugoslavia). Fair-haired goalkeeper whose resourcefulness had much to do with Yugoslavia's qualification for the 1974 World Cup, and their passage to the last eight. Following which, he, like so many Yugoslav stars, disappeared into the Army to serve his conscription. Born on 16 April 1948, he played for his country in the Brazilian Independence Cup of 1972, perhaps had his best game in the World Cup eliminator against Spain in Zagreb in October 1973, when his astonishing saves allowed Yugoslavia to draw. They eventually beat Spain in a play-off.

**MARINHO, Francisco** (Botafogo and Brazil). The best, most exciting, enterprising left-back Brazil have had since Nilton Santos, though he is as fair as Nilton was dark. Had a magnificent 1974 World Cup, when his thundering free kicks, famous in Brazil, were much in evidence, as were his fast, powerful breaks down the left flank. Born on 8 February 1952 in Natal, in the North of Brazil, where he began with the local ABC club. Thence he moved to Nautico of Recife, where his manager, Gradim, encouraged him to practise his free kicks. Botafogo brought him to Rio in late 1962, and he was an instant success.

**MULLER, Gerd** (Bayern Munich and West Germany). If ever a great player quit when he was ahead it was Gerd Müller, who announced his retirement immediately after scoring the winning goal for West Germany in the World Cup final of 1974. It was his 62nd match for West Germany, and he had the astonishing total of 68 goals; a record which left even Uwe Seeler far behind. Squat, dark, thick-thighed, Müller has been ludicrously criticised for 'only' scoring goals, as though this were easy at a time when defences have never been so packed and powerful. His formidable, low slung balance, his flair for being in the right place, his resilience, have made him so amazingly prolific. Yet Bayern Munich's then manager, the Yugoslav Cjaicowski, had to be persuaded by Bayern's President to sign him, after two other clubs had turned him down. Born at Noerdlingen on 3 November1945 he made his debut for West Germany against Turkey in Ankara in October 1966, was leading World Cup scorer of 1970 with ten goals, won a Nations Cup medal in 1972, getting two goals in the final, became European Footballer of the Year the following December. In May 1974, he scored twice for Bayern when they won the European Cup final against Atlético Madrid

**NEESKENS, Johan** (Barcelona and Holland). After a spectacular World Cup for Holland, whose penalty goal he scored in the Final, Neeskens left Ajax for Barcelona, to resume his brilliant partnership with Cruyff. A midfield player of total versatility, hard in the tackle, fast, a ferocious right-footed shot, Neeskens was actually at right-back in the 1971 European Cup final against Panathinaikos. He joined Ajax from Haarlem, enjoys baseball, basketball, and playing in goal. Born 15 September 1951. Scored five goals in the 1974 World Cup, three of them penalties.

**OBLAK, Branko** (Hajduk and Yugoslavia). Sadly, a grave tendon injury put Oblak out of the game in late 1974, a year in which he had established himself as one of the most versatile and effective players in Central Europe. Having played in the World Cup tournament as midfield half-back, he returned to Yugoslavia to be moved successfully into the attack, where his strength and remarkable shooting made him just as successful. Fair haired and compactly built, Oblak was born on 27 May 1947, and has won more than 30 caps, not to mention a Championship medal with Hajduk in 1974.

**OCTAVIO, Machado** (Atlético Madrid and Portugal). A clever, compactly built midfield player who makes devastatingly well judged use of the through pass, as he showed particularly when playing against England at Wembley in 1974. He was 25 then, and it was only his fifth cap for Portugal. Born in Setubal, lack of height has been no handicap to his career.

**OVERATH Wolfgang** (Cologne and West Germany). Schoolboy, youth, and full international, Overath crowned his career by helping West Germany to win the World Cup final of 1974, whereupon he retired from international football. It had been his third World Cup, his second World Cup final; yet in 1972, Netzer's superb form had kept him out of the West German team which won the Nations Cup, and his international career seemed in peril. Overath is less spectacular but perhaps more durable than Netzer. A fine user of the long ball, with his excellent left foot. He was outstandingly good in Mexico in 1970, winning a Third Place medal, and did much to knit the 1974 team together. Born 29 September 1943, he won eighty caps for West Germany, the first in November 1963, against Sweden. Joined Cologne from local Siegburg 04; League debut at 19.

**PEREIRA Luis** (Palmeiras and Brazil). A fine 1974 World Cup confirmed Pereira as probably the best centre-half Brazil have produced— a compound of power, technique, and aplomb. His old nickname, 'Chevrolet', conferred for his enthusiastic dashes upfield, would now be a misnomer. Born at Juazeiro, Bahia, on 21 June 1949, he began with Salvador de Bahia, went to Palmeira in Sao Paolo in 1968, but had a hard time establishing himself in a team which already had two fine centre-halves. Played impressively for Brazil on their 1973 European tour, and again in 1974. Splendid in the air, and now carefully selective, and effective, in his forays from defence.

**PIVARNIK Jan** (Slovan Bratislava and Czechoslovakia). This blond adventurous right-back succeeded Dobias in the Czech international team in 1973. Had a particularly fine, attacking game against England that May and played well against them again at Wembley in October, the following year. Born in November 1947, he was a youth international, made his name with SS Kosice, and from there was transferred to Slovan, where he has won Championship honours. A fast, strong, versatile footballer.

**POKOU, Laurent** (Rennes and Ivory Coast). A vastly gifted African centre-forward, coveted by French clubs for years, and at last persuaded to leave Abidjan for Rennes in January 1974, with instant success. Pokou is a player of great subtlety, flexibility, and skill, capable of scoring spectacular individual goals. He has also developed into a splendid constructive forward, adept in the one-two of the clever pass to a colleague; one more example of the colossal reservoir of footballing talent to be found in Africa. Born August 10 1947, at Abidjan, where he played for Asec, he was top scorer in the African Nations Cup of 1968 and 1970 for the Ivory Coast.

**SANDBERG, Roland** (Kaiserslautern and Sweden). A striking inside-forward who had a fine 1974 World Cup for Sweden, renewing his admirable partnership with Edstroem. Initially they had played together for Atvidaberg, each scoring 16 goals when they won the 1973 Swedish Championship, after which each went abroad, Sandberg to West Germany's Kaiserslautern; though each helped Sweden to qualify for the World Cup. Very fast and mobile, Sandberg is quick to exploit the flicks and touches of Edstroem in the Swedish team. He scored twice in the World Cup, including a particularly fine goal against West Germany. Born 16 December 1946.

**SHILTON, Peter** (Stoke City and England). Became the most expensive goalkeeper in the history of British football when Stoke paid some £325,000 for him in 1974. The whole of his previous career had been spent with his local club, Leicester City, who had first found him when he was an 11-year-old schoolboy. Powerfully built, remarkably agile, immensely dedicated, Shilton was a protégé of Gordon Banks, whom he has followed into the Leicester, Stoke, and England goals. First capped against East Germany at Wembley in 1971 but, established himself as an international with a series of splendid performances in the 1972–73 season. Since then, has played Box and Cox with Liverpool's Clemence. Height 6ft. weight 14st.

**SPARWASSER, Jurgen** (Magdeburg and East Germany). A strong, fast-striking inside-forward who had a splendid 1974, first helping Magdeburg to win both the East German Championship and the European Cup-Winners' Cup, then scoring the fine goal whereby East Germany beat West Germany in Hamburg in the World Cup. A player of acceleration and initiative, he was born on 4 June 1948.

**SUURBIER, Wim** (Ajax and Holland). A notable attacking right-back, fast and resilient, who in fact played on the left when Ajax first won the European Cup in 1971, but figured on the right when they won it in 1972 and 1973; as he did in the 1974 World Cup final, for Holland. He also played for Ajax when Milan beat them in the 1969 European Cup final, and in 1972 when they won the Intercontinental Cup. Kovacs, his ex-manager, described him as 'the fastest in the team; a razor blade'. Born January 16 1945, he played for Amstel as an amateur, then DWS Amsterdam, before joining Ajax. First capped 1966 versus Czechoslovakia.

**SZARMACH, Andrzej** (Gornik and Poland). Few young centre-forwards have had a rapid a rise as Szarmach. When the 1974 World Cup began he was virtually unknown, had five caps to his name, had played as recently as the previous April for the Under-23 team in Haiti. Indeed, it was only in the current season that Gornik had brought him from an obscure professional club into First Division football. In the event, this tall, blond, well built player, so immensely dangerous in the air, proved the very ace in the hole the Poles had needed, making up, with Lato, for the sad loss of Lubanski. 23 years old – he was born on December 3 1950 – he proceeded to score five goals, which made him second highest scorer of the World Cup.

**TODD, Colin** (Derby County and England). Suspended, cruelly and controversially, for two years from international football when he would not go on the England Under-23 tour of 1972, Todd has emphatically had the last laugh, establishing himself in the England team as a splendid successor to Bobby Moore. First capped, out of position at right-back, against Northern Ireland at Wembley in 1972, it was another two years before he was recalled to the England team, giving a series of brilliant performances at home and on tour. A player of admirable temperament, with a usefully low centre of gravity, fine anticipation, a strong tackle, abundant enterprise, he was a Sunderland product who cost Derby a large fee. He helped them win the Second then the First Division Championship. Born Chester-le-Street. Height 5ft 8in., Weight 11st 5lb.

**TOMASZEWSKI, Jan** (LKS Lodz and Poland). The goalkeeper who was called 'a clown' by Brian Clough when, with luck, courage, and varying virtuosity, he was defying the England attack at Wembley in October 1973, had the last laugh the following summer. He was unquestionably one of the best goalkeepers in the World Cup, saving two penalties, and generally distinguishing himself. Born in 1948, he won his first cap for Poland in October 1971 against West Germany. Stands 6ft. 3ins. and won an Olympic gold medal at Munich in 1972. Matured tremendously between that celebrated game at Wembley and the World Cup tournament, in which he looked immensely more reliable.

**VAN HANEGEM, Wim** (Feyenoord and Holland). Inside-left; a tall, powerful, unhurried player of exceptional technique, a glorious left foot, great strategy. A man for the great occasion, he was at his best both in the 1970 European Cup final in Milan, when Feyenoord beat Celtic, and in the 1974 World Cup Final in Munich, when he played so well for Holland against West Germany. 1969–70 was actually his first season with Feyenoord, whom he had joined from the other Rotterdam club, Xerces, just about to expire. It was also the season which he won his first cap for Holland. He added a UEFA Cup medal to his bag in 1974. scoring against Spurs at White Hart Lane in the first leg of the final. Suspension kept him out of the second. Born February 20 1944.

**VAN HIMST, Paul** (Racing White and Belgium). Still one of the finest players in Europe and the best in Belgium, after over a decade at the top, during which he has become his country's most capped player. He was first picked for Belgium as a 17-year-old centre-forward; now, this tall, strong but graceful player has dropped back into midfield. Born on October 2 1943, he was Belgian Footballer of the Year at 17 and 18, helped them to reach the World Cup finals of 1970, the European Nations Cup finals of 1972, playing below his best in Mexico but well up to it two years later, in Belgium, where his team took third place.

**VOGTS, Berti** (Borussia Münchengladbach and West Germany). This blond, resourceful full-back had much the better of his duel with Cruyff, after a disastrous first minute, in the World Cup final of 1974; thus repeating the success he'd once had when they clashed as youth internationals. It must have been all the more satisfying for Vogts in that, like Overath, he'd lost his international place in the fine 1972 European Nations Cup-winning West German team. He had certainly been one of the best backs of the 1970 World Cup, when West Germany reached the semi-final, forceful alike in attack and defence. Born December 20 1946, in Buttgen, he played for VfR Buttgen, then joined Borussia in 1965. Was first capped against Rumania on November 22 1967.

**ZE MARIA, Jose Maria** (Corinthians and Brazil). Large, strongly built right-back who, in physique and enterprising style, recalls the splendid Djalma Santos. Had an excellent 1974 World Cup, making a memorable goal with his run and centre against Argentina. Born at Botucatu on May 18 1949, he established himself in the international team as successor to Carlos Alberto in 1972, playing for the side which won the Independence Cup in Rio. The following year he successfully toured Europe with Brazil, and returned to give an impressive account of himself in 1974.

**ZOFF, Dino** (Juventus and Italy). When Sanon scored against Italy in Munich in June 1974, it was the first goal Dino Zoff had conceded in the Italian goal for 1,143 minutes; an astounding record which testifies to his cool professionalism, courage, and splendid reflexes. Zoff is indeed a born goalkeeper; has played there since earliest schooldays in the North East of Italy. He was born at Mariano del Friuli on February 28 1942 and turned pro. with Udinese, making his Serie A debut in 1961. Thence to Mantova in 1963, Naples in 1967 and Juventus at a huge fee in 1972. Played for Italy when they won the 1968 Nations Cup, but Albertosi displaced him in the 1970 World Cup in Mexico. By 1974 he had magisterially regained his place, in the meantime winning Championship honours and playing in the 1973 European Cup final for Juventus.

Note: One of the game's most brilliant midfield inside-forwards, KAZIMIERZ DEYNA (Legia Warsaw and Poland) announced his intention of retiring at the end of the season, at 28. It remained to be seen whether he would stick to this decision.

CHAPTER ELEVEN

# World Club Championship History

**1960 Montevideo, 3 July**
Peñarol (0) 0, Real Madrid (0) 0
*Peñarol:* Maidana; Martinez, Aguerre; Pino, Salvador, Goncalvez; Cubilla, Linazza, Hohberg, Spencer, Borges.

*Real Madrid:* Dominguez; Marquitos, Pachin; Vidal, Santamaria, Zarraga; Canario, Del Sol, Di Stefano, Puskas, Bueno.

**Madrid, 4 September**

Real Madrid (4) 5           Peñarol (0) 1

*Real Madrid:* Dominguez; Marquitos, Pachin; Vidal, Santamaria, Zarraga; Herrera, Del Sol, Di Stefano, Puskas, Gento.

*Peñarol:* Maidana; Pino, Mayewki, Martinez; Aguerre, Salvador; Cubilla, Linazza, Hohberg, Spencer, Borges.

*Scorers:* Puskas (2), Di Stefano, Herrera, Gento for Real; Borges for Peñarol.


**1961 Lisbon, 4 September**

Benfica (0) 1, Peñarol (0) 0

*Benfica:* Costa Pereira; Angelo, Joao; Neto, Saraiva, Cruz; Augusto, Santana, Aguas, Coluña, Cavem.

*Peñarol:* Maidana; Gonzales, Martinez, Aguerre; Cano, Gonçalvez; Cubilla, Spencer, Cabrera, Sasia, Ledesma.

*Scorer:* Coluña for Benfica.

**Montevideo, 17 September**

Peñarol (4) 5, Benfica (0) 0

*Penarol:* Maidana; Gonzales, Martinez, Aguerre; Cano, Gonçalvez; Cubilla, Ledesma, Sasia, Spencer, Joya.

*Benfica:* Costa Pereira; Angelo, Joao; Neto, Saraiva, Cruz; Augusto, Santana, Mendes, Coluña, Cavem.

*Scorers:* Sasia (pen), Joya (2), Spencer (2) for Peñarol.

**Montevideo 19 September**

Peñarol (2) 2, Benfica (1) 1

*Peñarol:* Maidana; Gonzales, Martinez, Aguerre; Cano, Gonçalvez; Cubilla, Ledesma, Sasia, Spencer, Joya.

*Benfica:* Costa Pereira; Angelo, Cruz; Neto, Humberto, Coluña; Augusto, Eusebio, Aguas, Cavem, Simões.

*Scorers:* Sasia (2) (1 pen) for Peñarol; Eusebio for Benfica.


**1962 Rio, 19 September**

Santos (1) 3, Benfica (0) 2

*Santos:* Gilmar; Lima, Calvet; Zito, Mauro, Dalmo; Dorval, Mengalvio, Coutinho, Pelé, Pepe.

*Benfica:* Costa Pereira; Jacinto, Raul, Humberto, Cruz; Cavem, Coluña, Augusto, Santana, Eusebio, Simões.

*Scorers:* Pelé (2), Coutinho for Santos; Santana (2) for Benfica.

**Lisbon, 11 October**

Benfica (0) 2, Santos (2) 5

*Benfica:* Costa Pereira; Jacinto, Raul, Humberto, Cruz; Cavem, Coluña; Augusto, Santana, Eusebio, Simões.

*Santos:* Gilmar; Olavo, Calvet; Dalmo, Mauro, Lima; Dorval, Zito, Coutinho, Pelé, Pepe.

*Scorers:* Pelé (3), Coutinho, Pepe for Santos; Eusebio, Santana for Benfica.

**1963 Milan, 16 October**
Milan (2) 4, Santos (0) 2
*Milan:* Ghezzi; David, Trebbi; Pelagalli, Maldini, Trapattoni; Mora Lodetti, Altafini, Rivera, Amarildo.
*Santos:* Gilmar; Lima, Haroldo, Calvet, Geraldion; Zito, Mengalvio; Dorval, Coutinho, Pelé, Pepe.
*Scorers:* Trapattoni, Amarildo (2), Mora for Milan; Pelé (2) (1 pen) for Santos.

**Rio, 14 November**
Santos (0) 4, Milan (2) 2
*Santos:* Gilmar; Ismael, Dalmo, Mauro, Haroldo; Lima, Mengalvio; Dorval, Coutinho, Almir, Pepe.
*Milan:* Ghezzi; David, Trebbi; Pelagalli, Maldini, Trapattoni; Mora, Lodetti, Altafini, Rivera, Amarildo.
*Scorers:* Pepe (2), Almira, Lima for Santos; Altafini, Mora for Milan.

**Rio, 16 November**
Santos (1) 1, Milan (0) 0
*Santos:* Gilmar; Ismael, Dalmo, Mauro, Haroldo; Lima, Mengalvio; Dorval, Coutinho, Almir, Pepe.
*Milan:* Balzarini (Barluzzi); Pelagalli, Trebbi; Benitez, Maldini, Trapattoni; Mora, Lodetti, Altafini, Amarildo, Fortunato.
*Scorer:* Dalmo (pen) for Santos.


**1964 Buenos Aires, 9 September**
Independiente (0) 1, Internazionale (0) 0
*Independiente:* Santoro; Ferreiro, Rolan; Acevedo, Guzman, Maldonado; Bernao, Mura, Prospitti, Rodriguez, Savoy.
*Internazionale:* Sarti; Burgnich, Facchetti; Tagnin, Guarneri, Picchi; Jair, Mazzola, Peiró, Suarez, Corso.
*Scorer:* Rodriguez for Independiente.

**Milan, 23 September**
Internazionale (2) 2, Independiente (0) 0
*Internazionale:* Sarti; Burgnich, Facchetti; Malatrasi, Guarneri, Picchi; Jair, Mazzola, Milani, Suarez, Corso.
*Independiente:* Santoro; Acevedo, Decaria; Maldonado, Ferreiro Paflik; Suarez, Mura, Prospitti, Rodriguez, Savoy.
*Scorers:* Mazzola, Corso for Inter.

**Madrid, 26 September**
Internazionale (0) 1, Independiente (0) 0 after extra time
*Internazionale:* Sarti; Malatrasi, Facchetti; Tagnin, Guarneri, Picchi; Domenghini, Peiró, Milani, Suarez, Corso.
*Independiente:* Santoro; Guzman, Decaria; Acevedo, Paflik, Maldonado; Bernao, Prospitti, Suarez, Rodriguez, Savoy.
*Scorer:* Corso for Inter.


**1965 Milan, 8 September**
Internazionale (2) 3, Independiente (0) 0
*Internazionale:* Sarti; Burgnich, Facchetti; Bedin, Guarneri, Picchi; Jair, Mazzola, Peiró, Suarez, Corso.

*Independiente:* Santoro; Pavoni, Navarro; Acevedo, Guzman, Ferreiro; Bernao, De La Mata, Avallay, Rodriguez, Savoy.
*Scorers:* Peiró, Mazzola (2) for Internazionale.
**Buenos Aires, 15 September**
Independiente (0) 0, Internazionale (0) 0
*Independiente:* Santoro; Navarro, Pavoni; Rolan, Guzman, Ferreiro; Bernao, Mura, Avallay, Mori, Savoy.
*Internazionale:* Sarti; Burgnich, Facchetti; Bedin, Guarneri, Picchi; Jair, Mazzola, Peiró, Suarez, Corso.


**1966 Montevideo, 12 October**
Peñarol (1) 2, Real Madrid (0) 0
*Peñarol:* Mazurkiewicz; Forlan, Gonzales; Gonçalvez, Lezcano Varela; Abbadie, Cortes, Spencer, Rocha, Joya.
*Real Madrid:* Betancort; Calpe, Sanchis; Pirri, De Felipe, Zoco; Serena, Amancio, Pirri, Velázquez, Bueno.
*Scorer:* Spencer (2) for Peñarol.
**Madrid, 26 October**
Real Madrid (0) 0, Peñarol (2) 2
*Real Madrid:* Betancort; Calpe, Sanchis; Pirri, De Felipe, Zoco; Serena, Amancio, Grosso, Velázquez, Gento.
*Peñarol:* Mazurkiewicz; Gonzales, Caetano; Gonçalvez, Lezcano, Varela; Abbadie, Cortes, Spencer, Rocha, Joya.
*Scorers:* Rocha (pen), Spencer for Peñarol.


**1967 Glasgow, 18 October**
Celtic (0) 1, Racing Club (0) 0
*Celtic:* Simpson; Craig, Gemmell; Murdoch, McNeill, Clark; Johnstone, Lennox, Wallace, Auld, Hughes.
*Racing:* Cejas; Perfumo, Diaz; Martin, Mori, Basile; Raffo, Rulli, Cardenas, Rodriguez, Maschio.
*Scorer:* McNeill for Celtic.
**Buenos Aires, 1 November**
Racing Club (1) 2, Celtic (1) 1
*Racing:* Cejas; Perfumo, Chabay; Martin, Rulli, Basile; Raffo, Cardoso, Cardenas, Rodriguez, Maschio.
*Celtic:* Fallon; Craig, Gemmell; Murdoch, McNeill, Clark; Johnstone, Wallace, Chalmers, O'Neill, Lennox.
*Scorers:* Raffo, Cardenas for Racing; Gemmell (pen) for Celtic.
**Montevideo, 4 November**
Racing Club (0) 1, Celtic (0) 0
*Racing:* Cejas; Perfumo, Chabay; Martin, Rulli, Basile; Raffo, Cardoso, Cardenas, Rodriguez, Maschio.
*Celtic:* Fallon; Craig, Gemmell; Murdoch, McNeill, Clark; Johnstone, Lennox, Wallace, Auld, Hughes.
*Scorer:* Cardenas for Racing.

**1968 Buenos Aires, 25 September**
Estudiantes (1) 1, Manchester United (0) 0
*Estudiantes:* Poletti; Malbernat, Suarez, Madero, Medina; Bilardo, Pachame, Togneri; Ribaudo, Conigliaro, Veron.
*Manchester United:* Stepney; Dunne, Burns; Crerand, Foulkes, Stiles; Morgan, Sadler, Law, Charlton, Best.
*Scorer:* Conigliaro for Estudiantes.
**Manchester, 16 October**
Manchester United (0) 1, Estudiantes (1) 1
*Manchester United:* Stepney; Dunne, Brennan; Crerand, Foulkes, Sadler; Morgan, Kidd, Charlton, Law (Sartori), Best.
*Estudiantes:* Poletti; Malbernat, Suarez, Madero, Medina; Bilardo, Pachame, Togneri; Ribaudo, Conigliaro, Veron (Echecopar).
*Scorers:* Morgan for Manchester United; Veron for Estudiantes.

**1969 Milan, 8 October**
Milan (2) 3, Estudiantes (0) 0
*Milan:* Cudicini; Malatrasi; Anquilletti, Rosato, Schnellinger; Lodett, Rivera, Fogli; Sormani, Combin (Rognoni), Prati.
*Estudiantes:* Poletti; Aguirre Suarez, Manera, Madero, Malbernat; Bilardo, Togneri, Echecopar; Flores, Conigliaro, Veron.
*Scorers:* Sormani, (2), Combin for Milan.
**Buenos Aires, 22 October**
Estudiantes (2) 2, Milan (1) 1
*Estudiantes:* Poletti; Manera, Aguirre Suarez, Madero, Malbernat; Bilardo (Echecopar), Romeo, Togneri; Conigliaro, Taverna, Veron.
*Milan:* Cudicini; Malatrasi (Fogli); Anquilletti, Maldera, Rosato, Schnellinger; Lodetti, Rivera; Sormani, Combin, Prati (Rognoni).
*Scorers:* Aguirre Suarez, Conigliaro for Estudiantes; Rivera for Milan.
Milan won 4–2 on goal aggregate.

**1970 Buenos Aires, 26 August**
Estudiantes (2) 2, Feyenoord (1) 2
*Estudiantes:* Errea; Pagnanini, Spadaro, Togneri, Malbernat, Bilardo, (Solari), Pachame, Echecopar (Rudzki), Conigliaro, Flores, Veron.
*Feyenoord:* Treytel; Romeyn, Israel, Laseroms, Van Duivenbode, Hasil, Jansen, Van Hanegem (Boskamp), Wery, Kindvall, Moulijn.
*Scorers:* Echecopar, Veron for Estudiantes; Kindvall, Van Hanegem for Feyenoord.
**Rotterdam, 9 September**
Feyenoord (0) 1, Estudiantes (0) 0
*Feyenoord:* Treytel; Romeyn, Israel, Laseroms, Van Duivenbode, Hasil (Boskamp), Van Hanegem, Jansen, Wery, Kindvall, Moulijn (Van Deale).
*Estudientes:* Pezzano; Malbernat, Spadaro, Togneri, Medina (Pagnanini), Bilardo, Pachame, Romeo, Conigliaro (Rudzki), Flores, Veron.
*Scorer:* Van Deale for Feyenoord.

**1971 Athens, 15 December**
Panathinaikos (0) 1, Nacional (1) 1
*Panathinaikos:* Ikonomopoulos; Tomaras (Vlahos), Kapsis, Sourpis, Athanassopoulos, Eleftherakiss, Filakouris, Dimitrou, Kouvos, Antoniadis, Domazos.
*Nacional:* Manga; Masnik, Maneiro, Montero Castillo, Blanco, Ubinas Esparrago, Cubilla, Artime, Brunel, Morales.
*Scorers:* Filakouris for Panathinaikos; Artime for Nacional.
**Montevideo, 29 December**
Nacional (1) 2, Panathinaikos (0) 1
*Nacional:* Manga; Ubinas, Brunel, Masnik, Blanco, Montero Castillo, Maneiro, Esparrago, Cubilla (Mujica), Artime, Manelli (Bareno)
*Panathinaikos:* Ikonomopoulos; Mitropoulos, Kapsis, Sourpis, Athanassopoulos, Kamaras (Filakouris), Domazos, Eleftherakis, Dimitrou, Antoniadis, Koudas.
*Scorers:* Artime (2) for Nacional; Filakouris for Panathinaikos.

**1972 Buenos Aires, 6 September**
Independiente (0) 1, Ajax (1) 1
*Independiente:* Santoro; Commisso, Lopez, Sa, Pavoni, Semenewiecz, Pastoriza, Raimundo (Bulla), Balbuena, Maglioni, Mircoli.
*Ajax:* Stuy; Suurbier, Hulshoff, Blankenburg, Krol, Neeskens, Haan, G. Muhren, Swart, Cruyff, (A. Muhren), Keizer.
*Scorers:* Sa for Independiente; Cruyff for Ajax.
**Amsterdam, 28 September**
Ajax (1) 3, Independiente (0) 0
*Ajax:* Stuy; Suurbier, Hulshoff, Blankenburg, Krol, Neeskens, Haan, G. Muhren, Swart (Rep), Cruyff, Keizer.
*Independiente:* Santoro; Commisso, Lopez, Sa, Pavoni, Pastoriza, Garisto (Magan), Semenewiecz, Balbuena, Maglioni, Mircoli (Bulla).
*Scorers:* Neeskens, Rep (2) for Ajax.

**1973 Rome, 28 November**
Juventus (0) 0, Independiente (0) 1
*Juventus:* Zoff; Spinosi (Longobucco), Marchetti, Gentile, Morini, Salvadore, Causio, Cuccureddu, Anastasi, Altafini, Bettega (Viola).
* *Independiente:* Santoro; Lopez, Pavoni, Comisso, Raimondo, Sa, Balbuena, Galvan, Maglione, Bocchini, Bertone (Semenewicz).
*Scorer:* Bocchini for Independiente.

**1975 Buenos Aires, 11 March**
   Independiente (1) 1 *Balbueno*     Atlético Madrid (0) 0
*Independiente:* Perez; Commisso, Lopez, Sa, Pavoni, Rodriguez, Galvan, Bocchini, Balbuena, Percy-Rojas, Bertoni.
*Atlético Madrid:* Reina; Melo, Heredia, Benegas, Capon, Eusebio, Alberto, Adelardo, Irrureta, Garate, Ayala.
**Madrid, 10 April**
   Atlético Madrid (1) 2 *Irureta, Ayala*    Independiente (0) 0

*Atlético Madrid:* Pacheco; Melo, Heredia, Eusebio, Capon, Adelardo, Irureta, Albertos (Salcedo), Aguilar, Garate, Ayala.
*Independiente:* Perez; Commisso, Lopez, Carrico, Pavoni, Saggiorato, Galvan, Bocchini, Balbuena, Rojas (Rodriguez), Bertoni.


CHAPTER TWELVE

# World Cup History

The World Cup – or to give it its proper name, the Jules Rimet Trophy – was first played in Montevideo in 1930, but the principle of it was agreed by FIFA, the Federation of International Football Associations, at their Antwerp Congress of 1920. No man did more to further the idea than Jules Rimet, President of the French Football Federation, who was elected FIFA president in Antwerp, and it was thus that the attractive gold cup came to be given his name.

By 1930 the four British associations had withdrawn from FIFA, and it was not for another 20 years that British teams competed for a World Cup. Whether they would have won it between the wars is open to question. The fact that they did not undergo the test allowed the myth of British superiority in football to last a generation longer than it might otherwise have done. In 1934, just before the Italian version of the World Cup, Hugo Meisl, the brilliant manager of the Austrians, expressed the view that England, had they competed, would not even have reached the semi-final.

Four years later, England were invited to compete in the finals without qualifying, to take the place of Austria, overrun by the Nazis. But the invitation was refused.

In 1930 the competing countries were divided into four pools, the qualifiers going into the semi-finals, which were played on the normal cup-tie basis of 'sudden death'. In 1934 and 1938 the World Cup finals were played as a straight knock-out tournament, but in 1950 the four pools were reconstituted, with one main difference. The four winners went into a further pool to contest the title. It was thus only a matter of chance that the last match between Brazil and Uruguay, one of the most passionate and exciting in the history of the tournament, should also turn out to be the decider.

In 1958 and 1962 four groups were again constituted, but on these occasions, two teams from each went into the quarter-finals after which, as in 1930, the tournament followed the pattern of a straight knock-out contest. In 1966, when the World Cup was played in England, the same dubious formula applied. In 1970, goal 'difference' replaced goal average. In 1974, two further qualifying groups replaced the quarter and semi-finals, and produced the finalists.

## WORLD CUP 1930 – Montevideo

Though the tournament was won by a very fine team – Uruguay had previously come to Europe to take the Olympic titles of 1924 and 1928 – it hardly drew a representative entry.

In the 1926 FIFA Congress Henri Delaunay, the French Federation's excellent secretary, expressed the view that football could no longer be confined to the Olympics: 'Many countries where professionalism is now recognised and organised cannot any longer be represented there by their best players.' In 1928, FIFA passed his resolution to hold a World Cup tournament at once. Only the Scandinavian block, and Estonia, voted against it! Odd that Sweden should eventually stage a World Cup and play in the final.

Uruguay got the competition for a variety of reasons: their Olympic success, their promise to pay every competing team's full expenses and to build a new stadium, and the fact that 1930 was their centenary.

But distance and the need to pay their players for a couple of months led to most of the big European powers withdrawing: Italy, Spain, Austria, Hungary, Germany, Switzerland, Czechoslovakia, Britain, of course, were out of FIFA. It was only thanks to King Carol himself that Romania entered; he not only picked the team but got time off for the players from their firms. France, Belgium, and Yugoslavia were the other three: lower middle-class European teams of that era. The stage was set for South American domination.

It was the United States who provided the surprise. Their team, made up largely of ex-British professionals jokingly christened 'the shot putters' by the French, because of their massive physique, showed great stamina and drive and actually qualified for the semi-finals. There, an excellent Argentinian eleven – beaten 2–1 in the replayed 1928 Olympic final by Uruguay – brushed them aside.

Uruguay, however, again proved irresistible. They prepared with the dedication one has come to expect over the past fifteen years from leading South American teams; but then, it was quite new. For two months, their players were 'in concentration' at an expensive hotel in the middle of the Prado park. When Mazzali, the brilliant goalkeeper, sneaked home late one night, he was thrown out of the team.

A splendid half-back line (playing in the old attacking centre-half-back style) was Uruguay's strength: José Andrade, Lorenzo Fernandez and Alvaro Gestido. José Nasazzi, the captain and right-back, was a great force, and in the forward-line Scarone and Petrone (now slightly over the hill) were superb technicians and dangerous goalscorers.

The tournament began on 13 July 1930. France surprised Argentina in an early match, losing only 1–0 after the crowd had invaded the pitch, when the referee blew for time six minutes early – then had to clear the pitch and restart the game. The Argentinians, who had the ruthless but effective Monti at centre-half, and the clever Stabile at centre-forward, duly won that group. Their match with Chile included a violent free-for-all, provoked by Monti.

Yugoslavia, beating Brazil 2–1 in their first match, also qualified.

The brave Americans won their pool without conceding a goal, while Uruguay, too, kept their defence intact, though Peru ran them very close. This was the first match to be played at the new Centenary Stadium, which still wasn't ready when the competition started.

In the semi-finals, Argentina and Uruguay both had 6–1 wins, against the USA and Yugoslavia respectively. In the final, Uruguay had to take the field without their new star, the young centre-forward Anselmo, who was unfit. But Argentina's new man, Stabile, first capped in their opening game, was able to lead their attack.

The match took place on 30 July 1930. Uruguay deservedly won, but their team seemed to lack the confidence it had shown in the two Olympic successes. An argument about the ball led to each side playing one half with a ball of native manufacture. Argentina survived an early goal by Pablo Dorado, the Uruguayan outside-right, to lead 2–1 at half-time, through Peucelle and Stabile. But a splendid dribble by Pedro Cea was crowned by the equaliser, after which Iriarte and Castro made it 4–2. Montevideo went wild – the following day was a national holiday.

## POOL 1
France (3) 4, Mexico (0) 1
*France:* Thépot; Mattler, Capelle; Villaplane (capt), Pinel, Chantrel; Liberati, Delfour, Maschinot, Laurent, Langiller.
*Mexico:* Bonfiglio; R. Guitierrez (capt), M. Rosas; F. Rosas, Sanchez, Amezcua; Perez, Carreno, Mejia, Ruiz, Lopez.
*Scorers:* Laurent, Langiller, Maschinot (2) for France; Carreno for Mexico.

Argentina (0) 1, France (0) 0
*Argentina:* Bossio; Della Torre, Muttis; Suarez, Monti, J. Evaristo; Perinetti, Varallo, Ferreira, (capt), Cierra, M. Evaristo.
*France:* Thépot; Mattler, Capelle; Villaplane (capt), Pinel, Chantrel; Liberati, Delfour, Maschinot, Laurent, Langiller.
*Scorer:* Monti for Argentina.

Chile (1) 3, Mexico (0) 0
*Chile:* Cortes; Morales, Poirer; A. Torres, Saavedra, Helgueta; Ojeda, Subiabre, Villalobos, Vidal, Schneeberger (capt).
*Mexico:* Sota; R. Guitierrez (capt) M. Rosas; F. Rosas; Sanchez, Amezcua; Perez, Carreno, Ruiz, Gayon, Lopez.
*Scorers:* Vidal, Subiabre (2) for Chile.

Chile (0) 1, France (0) 0
*Chile:* Cortes; Ciaparro, Morales; A. Torres, Saavedra, C. Torres; Ojeda, Subiabre, Villalobos, Vidal, Schneeberger (capt).
*France:* Thepot; Mattler, Capella; Chantrel, Delmer, Villaplane (capt); Liberati, Delfour, Pinel, Veinantie, Langiller.
*Scorer:* Subiabre for Chile.

Argentina (3) 6, Mexico (0) 3
*Argentina:* Bossio; Della Torre, Paternoster; Cividini, Zumelzu (capt),
Orlandini; Peucelle, Varallo, Stabile, Demeria, Spadaro.
*Mexico:* Bonfiglio; R. Guitierrez (capt), F. Guiterrez; M. Rosas,
Sanchez, Rodriguez; F. Rosas, Lopez, Gayon, Carreno, Olivares.
*Scorers:* Stabile (3), Varallo (2), Zumelzu for Argentina; Lopez, F.
Rosas, M. Rosas for Mexico.

Argentina (2) 3, Chile (1) 1
*Argentina:* Bossio; Della Torre, Paternoster: J. Evaristo, Monti,
Orlandini; Peucelle, Varallo, Stabile, Ferreira, M. Evaristo.
*Chile:* Cortes; Ciaparro, Morales; A. Torres, Saavedra, C. Torres;
Arellanc, Subiabre (capt), Villalobos, Vidal, Aguilera.
*Scorers:* Stabile (2), M. Evaristo for Argentina; Subiabre for Chile.

|           | P | W | D | L | F  | A  | Pts |
|-----------|---|---|---|---|----|----|-----|
| Argentina | 3 | 3 | 0 | 0 | 10 | 4  | 6   |
| Chile     | 3 | 2 | 0 | 1 | 5  | 3  | 4   |
| France    | 3 | 1 | 0 | 2 | 4  | 3  | 2   |
| Mexico    | 3 | 0 | 0 | 3 | 4  | 13 | 0   |

## POOL 2

Yugoslavia (2) 2, Brazil (0) 1
*Yugoslavia:* Yavocic; Ivkovic (capt), Milhailovic; Arsenievic, Stefan-
ovic, Djokic; Tirnanic, Marianovic, Beck, Vujadinovic, Seculic.
*Brazil:* Montiero; Costa, Gervasoni; Fonseca, Santos, Guidicelli;
Ribeiro, Braga, Patsuca, Neto, Pereira.
*Scorers:* Tirnanic. Beck for Yugoslavia; Neto for Brazil.

Yugoslavia (0) 4, Bolivia (0) 0
*Yugoslavia:* Yavocic; Ivkovic (capt), Milhailovic; Arsenievic, Stefan-
ovic, Djokic; Tirnanic, Marianovic, Beck, Vujadinovic, Naidanovic.
*Bolivia:* Bermudez; Durandal, Civarria; Argote, Lara, Valderama;
Gomez, Bustamante, Mendez (capt), Alborta, Fernandez.
*Scorers:* Beck (2), Marianovic, Vujadinovic for Yugoslavia.

Brazil (1) 4, Bolivia (0) 0
*Brazil:* Velloso; Gervasoni, Oliveira; Fonseca, Santos, Guidicelli;
Meneses, Quieroz, Leite, Neto (capt), Visintainer.
*Bolivia:* Bermudez; Durandal, Civarria; Sainz, Lara, Valderama;
Oritiz, Bustamante, Mendez (capt), Alborta, Fernandez.
*Scorers:* Visintainer (2), Neto (2) for Brazil.

|            | P | W | D | L | F | A | Pts |
|------------|---|---|---|---|---|---|-----|
| Yugoslavia | 2 | 2 | 0 | 0 | 6 | 1 | 4   |
| Brazil     | 2 | 1 | 0 | 1 | 5 | 2 | 2   |
| Bolivia    | 2 | 0 | 0 | 2 | 0 | 8 | 0   |

## POOL 3

Romania (1) 3, Peru (0) 1

*Romania:* Lapuseanu; Steiner, Burger; Rafinski, Vogl (capt), Eisembeisser; Covaci, Desu, Wetzer, Staucin, Barbu.

*Peru:* Valdivieso; De las Casas (capt), Soria; Galindo, Garcia, Valle; Flores, Villanueva, Denegri, Neira, Souza.

*Scorers:* Staucin (2), Barbu for Romania; Souza for Peru.


Uruguay (0) 1, Peru (0) 0

*Uruguay:* Ballesteros; Nasazzi (capt), Tejera; Andrade, Fernandez, Gestido; Urdinaran, Castro, Petrone, Cea, Iriarte.

*Peru:* Pardon; De las Casas, Maquilon (capt); Denegri, Galindo, Astengo; Lavalle, Flores, Villanueva, Neira, Souza.

*Scorer:* Castro for Uruguay.


Uruguay (4) 4, Romania (0) 0

*Uruguay:* Ballesteros; Nasazzi (capt), Mascheroni; Andrade, Fernandez, Gestido; Dorado, Scarone, Anselmo, Cea, Iriarte.

*Romania:* Lapuseanu; Burger, Tacu; Robe, Vogl (capt), Eisembeisser Covaci, Desu, Wetzer, Rafinski, Barbu.

*Scorers:* Dorado, Scarone, Anselmo, Cea for Uruguay.

|         | P | W | D | L | F | A | Pts |
|---------|---|---|---|---|---|---|-----|
| Uruguay | 2 | 2 | 0 | 0 | 5 | 0 | 4   |
| Romania | 2 | 1 | 0 | 1 | 3 | 5 | 2   |
| Peru    | 2 | 0 | 0 | 2 | 1 | 4 | 0   |


## POOL 4

United States (2) 3, Belgium (0) 0

*United States:* Douglas; Wood, Moorhouse; Gallacher, Tracey, Brown; Gonsalvez, Florie (capt), Patenaude, Auld, McGhee.

*Belgium:* Badjou; Nouwens, Hoydonckx; Braine (capt), Hellemans, De Clercq; Diddens, Moeschal, Adams, Voorhoof, Versijp.

*Scorers:* McGhee (2), Patenaude for United States.


United States (2) 3, Paraguay (0) 0

*United States:* Douglas; Wood, Moorhouse; Gallacher, Tracey, Auld; Brown, Gonsalvez, Patenaude, Florie (capt), McGhee.

*Paraguay:* Denis; Olmedo, Miracca; Etcheverri, Diaz, Aguirre; Nessi, Romero, Dominguez, Gonzales, Carceres, Pena (capt).

*Scorers:* Patenaude (2), Florie for United States.


Paraguay (1) 1, Belgium (0) 0

*Paraguay:* P. Benitez; Olmedo, Flores; S. Benitez, Diaz, Garcete; Nessi, Romero, Gonzales, Carceres, Pena (capt).

*Belgium:* Badjou; De Deken, Hoydonckx; Braine (capt), Hellemans, Moeschal; Versijp, Delbeke, Adams, Nouwens, Diddens.

*Scorer:* Pena for Paraguay.

| | P | W | D | L | F | A | Pts |
|---|---|---|---|---|---|---|---|
| United States | 2 | 2 | 0 | 0 | 6 | 0 | 4 |
| Paraguay | 2 | 1 | 0 | 1 | 1 | 3 | 2 |
| Belgium | 2 | 0 | 0 | 2 | 0 | 4 | 0 |

## SEMI-FINALS
Argentina (1) 6, United States (0) 1
*Argentina:* Botasso; Della Torre, Paternoster; J. Evaristo, Monti, Orlandini; Peucelle, Scopelli, Stabile, Ferreira (capt), M. Evaristo.
*United States:* Douglas; Wood, Moorhouse; Gallacher, Tracey, Auld; Brown, Gonsalvez, Patenaude, Florie (capt), McGhee.
*Scorers:* Monti; Scopelli, Stabile (2), Peucelle (2) for Argentina; Brown for United States.

Uruguay (3) 6, Yugoslavia (1) 1
*Uruguay:* Ballesteros; Nasazzi (capt), Mascheroni; Andrade, Fernandez, Gestido; Dorado, Scarone, Anselmo, Cea, Iriarte.
*Yugoslavia:* Yavocic; Ivkovic (capt), Milhailovic; Arsenievic, Stefanovic, Djokic; Tirnanic, Marianovic, Beck, Vujadinovic, Seculic.
*Scorers:* Cea (3), Anselmo (2), Iriarte for Uruguay; Seculic for Yugoslavia.

## FINAL
Uruguay (1) 4, Argentina (2) 2
*Uruguay:* Ballesteros; Nasazzi (capt), Mascheroni; Andrade, Fernandez, Gestido; Dorado, Scarone, Castro, Cea, Iriarte.
*Argentina:* Botasso; Della Torre, Paternoster; J. Evaristo, Monti, Suarez; Peucelle, Varallo, Stabile, Ferreira (capt), M. Evaristo.
*Scorers:* Dorado, Cea, Iriarte, Castro for Uruguay; Peucelle, Stabile for Argentina.
**Leading Scorer:** Stabile (Argentina) 8.

## WORLD CUP 1934 – Italy
The 1934 World Cup was altogether more representative and better attended, even though Uruguay, piqued by the way the European powers had snubbed them, stayed away and Argentina, fearful to lose more of their stars to Italian clubs, did not take part at full strength. Eight FIFA conferences were needed before Italy was chosen as the host. It had been realised that future World Cups could no longer be played in a single city nor could they be put on by any but a wealthy football federation. Italy, whose Fascist government looked on the powerful national team as a fine instrument of propaganda, eagerly put forward her claims. 'The ultimate purpose of the tournament', said General Vaccaro, a political appointment as president of the Italian Federation (FIGC), 'was to show that Fascist sport partakes of a great quality of the ideal'.

'Italy wanted to win', wrote the Belgian referee, John Langenus, 'it was natural. But they allowed it to be seen too clearly.'

Italy's remarkable team manager Vittorio Pozzo drew from the inflated, martial spirit of the times the authority and inspiration to build a fine team. It contained three Argentinians – Monti, Guaita, and Orsi – of Italian extraction, whose inclusion Pozzo justified on the grounds that they would have been eligible to fight for Italy in the first world war. 'If they were able to die for Italy, they could certainly play for Italy.'

His team pivoted round a strong, attacking centre-half in Monti; had a splendid goalkeeper in Combi; a powerful defence, and a clever attack in which Meazza, one of the most gifted Italian forwards of all time, figured as a 'striking' inside-right.

Austria, Italy's great rivals, were a tired team, and their equally gifted manager, Hugo Meisl, was convinced they could not win the tournament. Nevertheless in Seszta, their rugged left-back, Smistik, the roving centre-half, and Sindelar, the brilliantly elusive, ball-playing centre-forward, they had players of world class. The previous February Austria's *wunderteam* had beaten Italy 4–2, in Turin.

Hungary and Spain were the strongest 'outsiders'. Hungary had a fine centre-forward in Dr Georges Sarosi, later to become an attacking centre-half. Their technique was brilliant, but their finishing poor. Both they and the Czechs had beaten England 2–1 on England's May tour of Europe. Spain had their great veteran, Ricardo Zamora, in goal, and the excellent Quincoces at left-back. The Czechs had an equally famous and experienced goalkeeper in Planicka and a smooth, clever forward-line.

Then there was Germany, playing a rigid third-back game, captained by the blond and versatile Franz Szepan.

Italy kicked off in Rome with an easy win against the United States, fielding only three of their 1930 team. The surprise of the first round was France's excellent performance against Austria in Turin. As in 1930, the French rose to the occasion. They nearly scored in the first minute when Seszta's mistake was brilliantly retrieved by Peter Platzer, Austria's goalkeeper, and would probably have won had it not been for an injury to Nicolas, their captain and centre-forward, who had to go on the wing. He scored almost at once, but that was virtually his last contribution. Despite the handicap, France dominated the second half, and it was only a doubtful goal by Schall in extra-time – he looked offside – that really beat them. In later years, Schall himself said it was offside.

Germany, beating Belgium in Florence, looked uninspired; only Szepan, at centre-half, rose above mediocrity. The Czechs were another disappointment, needing two fine saves by Planicka to survive against the Romanians in Trieste; Egypt gave Hungary a fright at Naples, going down 4–2; and both South American challengers went out at once, Brazil to Spain, Argentina to Sweden.

In the second round in Florence, a marvellous exhibition of goal-keeping by Zamora enabled Spain to hold Italy to a 1–1 draw, but so roughly was he handled in a feebly refereed match that he could not take part in the replay. This was still more lamentably refereed, so much so that the Swiss official, Mercet, was suspended by his own Federation. Italy got through, thanks to a goal by Meazza, in a game that left a very nasty aftertaste.

The other match of the second round was that which opposed the classical Danubian rivals, Hungary and Austria. 'It was a brawl', said Meisl, 'not an exhibition of football'. He brought the lively Horwath into his attack, and Horwath rewarded him with a goal after only seven minutes. Markos, Hungary's outside-right, was sent off, soon after Sarosi (on a poor day) had got Hungary's only goal from a penalty. The Austrians just about deserved their 2–1 win. Germany beat a Swedish team reduced for most of the match to 10 men, and the Czechs beat Switzerland 3–2 in Turin in the most thrilling match of the round. Nejedly got the winning goal seven minutes from the end.

The semi-finals pitted Italy against Austria in Milan, Germany against Czechoslovakia in Rome. Italy deservedly got through, on a muddy ground thanks to a goal by Guaita after 18 minutes, showing amazing stamina after their hard replay against Spain only two days before. Austria did not have a shot until the 42nd minute.

The Czechs, surviving the trauma of a ridiculous equalising goal, when Planicka inexplicably let the ball sail over his head, were much too clever for the Germans and beat them 3–1. Thus, they would meet Italy in the final.

Meanwhile, in the third place match, a dejected Austrian team surprisingly went down 3–2 at Naples to the plodding Germans, who scored in 24 seconds.

Fortified by gargantuan presents of food, the Czechs gave Italy a tremendous run for their money in the final. Short passing cleverly, making use of Puc's thrust on the left wing, with Planicka at his best in goal, they had slightly the better of the first half. Twenty minutes from time, Puc took a corner, and when the ball came back to him, drove it past Combi for the first goal.

Czechoslovakia should have clinched it then. Sobotka missed a fine chance, Svoboda hit the post. Then Guaita and Schiavio switched, the Italian attack began to move better, and a freak goal by Orsi equalised. His curling, right-foot shot swerved in the air, and went over Planicka's hands. Next day in practice he tried 20 times, without success, to repeat it.

In the seventh minute of extra time, the injured Meazza got the ball on the wing, centred to Guaita, and the ball was moved on to Schiavio, who scored. Italy had done it, with little to spare. Neutral experts believed that home ground, frenzied support, the consequent intimidation of referees, may have been decisive. Nevertheless, theirs was a fine, splendidly fit and dedicated team.

## FIRST ROUND

Italy (3) 7, United States (0) 1 (Rome)
*Italy:* Combi; Rosetta (capt), Allemandi; Pizziolo, Monti, Bertolini; Guarisi, Meazza, Schiavio, Ferrari, Orsi.

*United States:* Hjulian; Czerchiewicz, Moorhouse (capt); Pietras, Gonsalvez, Florie, Ryan, Nilsen, Donelli, Dick, Maclean.
*Scorers:* Schiavio (3), Orsi (2), Meazza, Ferrari for Italy; Donelli for United States.

Czechoslovakia (0) 2, Romania (1) 1 (Trieste)
*Czechoslovakia:* Planicka (capt); Zenisek, Ctyroky; Kostalek, Cambal, Krcil; Junek, Silny, Sobotka, Nejedly, Puc.
*Romania:* Zambori; Vogl, Albu; Deheleanu, Cotormani (capt), Moravet; Bindea, Covaci, Depi, Bodola, Dobai.
*Scorers:* Puc, Nejedly for Czechoslovakia; Dobai for Romania.

Germany (1) 5, Belgium (2) 2 (Florence)
*Germany:* Kress; Haringer, Schwarz; Janes, Szepan (capt), Zielinksi; Lehner, Hohmann, Conen, Siffling, Kovierski.
*Belgium:* Van de Weyer; Smellinckx, Joacim; Peeraer, Welkenhuyzen (capt), Klaessens; Devries, Voorhoof, Capelle, Grimmonprez, Herremans
*Scorers:* Voorhoof (2) for Belgium; Conen (3), Kovierski (2) for Germany.

Austria (1) 3, France (1) 2 (1–1) after extra time (Turin)
*Austria:* Platzer; Cisar, Seszta; Wagner, Smistik (capt), Urbanek; Zischek, Bican, Sindelar, Schall, Viertel.

*France:* Thépot; Mairesse, Mattler; Delflour, Verriest, Llense; Keller Alcazar, Nicolas (capt), Rio, Aston.
*Scorers:* Nicolas, Verriest (pen) for France; Sindelar, Schall, Bican for Austria.

Spain (3) 3, Brazil (1) 1 (Genoa)
*Spain:* Zamora (capt); Ciriaco, Quincoces; Cillauren, Muguerza, Marculeta; Lafuente, Iraragorri, Langara, Lecue, Gorostiza.
*Brazil:* Pedrosa; Mazzi, Luz; Tinoco, Zaccone, Canilli; Oliviera, De Britto, Leonidas, Silva, Bartesko.
*Scorers:* Iraragorri (pen), Langara (2) for Spain; Silva for Brazil.

Switzerland (2) 3, Netherlands (1) 2 (Milan)
*Switzerland:* Sechehaye; Minelli, Weiler (capt); Guinchard, Jaccard, Hufschmid; Von Kaenel, Passello, Kielholz, Abegglen III, Bossi.
*Netherlands:* Van der Meulen; Weber, Van Run; Rellikaan, Andeniesen (capt), Van Heel; Wels, Vente, Bakhuijs, Smit, Van Nellen.
*Scorers:* Kleilholz (2), Abegglen III for Switzerland; Smit, Vente for Netherlands.

Sweden (1) 3, Argentina (1) 2 (Bologna)
*Sweden:* Rydberg; Axelsson, S. Andersson; Carlsson, Rosen (capt), E. Andersson; Dunker, Gustafsson, Jonasson, Keller, Kroon.

*Argentina:* Freschi; Pedevilla, Belis; Nehin, Sosa-Urbieta, Lopez; Rua, Wilde, De Vincenzi (capt), Galateo, Iraneta.
*Scorers:* Bellis, Galateo for Argentina; Jonasson (2), Kroon for Sweden.

Hungary (2) 4, Egypt (1) 2 (Naples)
*Hungary:* A. Szabo; Futo, Sternberg; Palotas, Szucs, Lazar; Markos, Vincze, Teleky, Toldi, F. Szabo.
*Egypt:* Moustafa Kamel; Ali Caf, Hamitu; El Far, Refaat, Rayab; Latif, Fawzi, Muktar (capt), Masoud Kamel, Hassan.
*Scorers:* Teleky, Toldi (2), Vincze for Hungary; Fawzi (2) for Egypt.

## SECOND ROUND
Germany (1) 2, Sweden (0) 1 (Milan)
*Germany:* Kress; Haringer, Busch; Gramlich, Szepan (capt), Zielinski; Lehner, Hohmann, Conen, Siffling, Kobierski.
*Sweden:* Rydberg; Axelsson, S. Andersson; Carlsson, Rosen (capt), E. Andersson; Dunker, Jonasson, Gustafsson, Keller, Kroon.
*Scorers:* Hohmann (2) for Germany; Dunker for Sweden.

Austria (1) 2, Hungary (0) 1 (Bologna)
*Austria:* Platzer; Disar, Seszta; Wagner, Smistik (capt), Urbanek; Zischek, Bican, Sindelar, Horwath, Viertel.
*Hungary:* A. Szabo; Vago, Sternberg; Palotas, Szucs, Szalay; Markos, Avar, Sarosi, Toldi, Kemeny.
*Scorers:* Horwarth, Zischek for Austria; Sarosi (pen) for Hungary.

Italy (0) 1, Spain (1) 1 after extra time (Florence)
*Italy:* Combi (capt); Monzeglio, Allemandi; Pizziolo, Monti, Castellazzi; Guaita, Meazza, Schiavio, Ferrari, Orsi.
*Spain:* Zamora (capt); Ciriaco, Quincoces; Cillauren, Muguerza, Fede; Lafuente, Iraragorri, Langara, Regueiro, Gorostiza.
*Scorers:* Regueiro for Spain; Ferrari for Italy.

Italy (1) 1, Spain (0) 0. Replay (Florence)
*Italy:* Combi (capt); Monzeglio, Allemandi; Ferraris IV, Monti, Bertolini; Guaita, Meazza, Borel, De Maria, Orsi.
*Spain:* Noguet; Zabalo, Quincoces (capt); Cillauren, Muguerza Lecue, Ventolra, Regueiro, Campanal, Chacho, Bosch.
*Scorer:* Meazza for Italy.

Czechoslovakia (1) 3, Switzerland (1) 2 (Turin)
*Czechoslovakia:* Planicka; Zenisek, Ctyroky; Kostalek, Cambal, Krcil; Junek, Svoboda, Sobotka, Nejedly, Puc.
*Switzerland:* Sechehaye; Minelli, Weiler; Guinchard, Jaccard, Hufschmid; Von Kaenel, Jaeggi IV, Kielholz, Abegglen III, Jaeck.
*Scorers:* Kielholz, Abegglen III for Switzerland; Svoboda, Sobotka, Nejedly for Czechoslovakia.

## SEMI-FINALS
Czechoslovakia (1) 3, Germany (0) 1 (Rome)
*Czechoslovakia:* Planicka (capt); Burger, Ctyroky; Kostalek, Cambal, Krcil; Junek, Svoboda, Sobotka, Nejedly, Puc.
*Germany:* Kress; Haringer, Busch; Zielinski, Szepan (capt), Bender; Lehner, Siffling, Conen, Noack, Kobierski.
*Scorers:* Nejedly (2) Krcil for Czechoslovakia; Noack for Germany.

Italy (1) 1, Austria (0) 0 (Milan)
*Italy:* Combi (capt); Monzeglio, Allemandi; Ferraris IV, Monti, Bertolini; Guaita, Meazza, Schiavio, Ferrari, Orsi.
*Austria:* Platzer; Disar, Seszta; Wagner, Smistik (capt), Urbanek; Zischek, Bican, Sindelar, Schall, Viertel.
*Scorer:* Guaita for Italy.

## THIRD PLACE MATCH
Germany (3) 3, Austria (1) 2 (Naples)
*Germany:* Jakob; Janes, Busch; Zielinski, Muenzenberg, Bender; Lehner, Siffling, Conen, Szepan (capt), Heidemann.
*Austria:* Platzer; Disar, Seszta; Wagner, Smistik (capt), Urbanek; Zischek, Braun, Horwath, Viertel.
*Scorers:* Lehner (2), Conen for Germany; Horwath, Seszta for Austria.

## FINAL
Italy (0) 2, Czechoslovakia (0) 1 after extra time (Rome)
*Italy:* Combi (capt); Monzeglio, Allemandi; Ferraris IV, Monti, Bertolini; Guaita, Meazza, Schiavio, Ferrari, Orsi.
*Czechoslovakia:* Planicka (capt); Zenisek, Ctyroky; Kostalek, Cambal, Krcil; Junek, Svoboda, Sobotka, Nejedly, Puc.
*Scorers:* Orsi, Schiavio for Italy; Puc for Czechoslovakia.
**Leading Scorers:** Schiavio (Italy), Nejedly (Czechoslovakia), Conen (Germany) each 4.

## WORLD CUP 1938 – France
Italy were the winners again, but this time their win was more convincing. For the first time, indeed, a host nation failed to take the World Cup. Pozzo himself has said that on grounds of pure football, his 1938 side was superior to the team of 1934. Only the inside-forwards Meazza and Ferrari survived from that eleven. Monti's place at centre-half had been taken by another South American, Andreolo from Uruguay. Foni and Rava, fullbacks in the successful Italian Olympic side of 1936, were now in the full national side. Olivieri, an excellent goalkeeper, was a fitting successor to Combi. At centre-forward, the tall, powerful Silvio Piola rivalled Meazza (and overhauled him in 1951!) as the most prolific Italian goalscorer of all time.

Argentina wanted to stage this World Cup, but the claims of France were preferred. Austria and Spain had to withdraw for political reasons, Uruguay, still worried by the crisis of professionalism (another factor in their refusal to compete in 1934) refused again to take part. So did Argentina – whose fans demonstrated their displeasure outside the offices of the Federation.

But Brazil, a much improved side, were there again, with the great Leonidas at centre-forward and Da Guia at fullback. Sarosi was in great form for Hungary, who had not long since beaten the Czechs 8–3, and he had fine support from Szengeller, the 22-year-old inside-left. Planicka, Nejedly, and Puc survived from the Czechs' 1934 team, and Germany, now under Sepp Herberger, was still recovering from a 6–3 home defeat by England. The Swiss, who had beaten England 2–1 a few days later in Zurich, looked strong.

In the first round, the hardest fought tie was that between Germany and Switzerland. The Germans fielded four Austrians in the first match, one of whom, the outside-left, Pesser, was sent off in extra time. Gauchel gave Germany the lead from Pesser's centre. Abegglen headed an equaliser, and extra time brought no more goals. The teams had a good five days to gird themselves for the replay. This time, Germany fielded three Austrians and brought back their talented 1934 captain, Szepan, to play at inside-left. They went into a 2–0 lead – one from Hahnemann, an unlucky own goal by Loertscher, the Swiss left-half – at half-time. Wallaschek made it 1–2 early in the second half, but when the Swiss left-winger Aebi went off injured, the die seemed cast.

Not a bit of it. The Swiss held out till Aebi came back, Bickel equalised and Abegglen, the star of the match, rounded it off with two fine goals.

The greatest surprise was Cuba's defeat of Romania, after a 3–3 draw in Toulouse. Half the Romanian side had previous World Cup experience, three having played in Uruguay. But the Cubans played with great speed and *brio* and were 3–2 ahead in extra time when the Romanians equalised. In the replay, they surprisingly dropped their star goalkeeper, Carvajales, who was brilliantly replaced by Ayra, and won, after being a goal down. The winner, according to the French linesman, was offside, but the German referee allowed it. What has happened to Cuban football since 1938? Obscurely, it has sunk without trace.

The Czechs, with four 1934 men, beat the Netherlands 3–0 in Le Havre, but needed extra time to do it and were fortunate that the Dutch lacked Bakhuijs, their leading scorer. Two of the Czech goals came from their half-backs; the celebrated Nejedly got the other.

At Strasbourg, a marvellous match between Brazil and Poland saw the score at 4–4 after 90 minutes. Poland had had a fine season, culminating with a 6–1 win over Ireland and victory by 4–1 aggregate over Yugoslavia in the eliminators for the World Cup. Their inside-forward, Ernest Willimowski, was one of the most talented in Europe and a notable goalscorer. Brazil had six players making their international debut. Their magnificent centre-forward Leonidas, the Black Diamond, did the hat-trick for them in the first half, but in the second the Polish half-backs took control. In extra time, Leonidas and Willimowski each scored his fourth goal, but another by Romeu for Brazil was decisive – 6–5.

In Marseilles, Italy got the shock of their lives from little Norway. Within two minutes, Ferrari had given Italy the lead, but Norway tightened their grip on Piola and their own centre-forward, the powerful Brunyldsen, gave Andreolo a terrible time of it. Three times the Italian posts and bar were hit; at others Olivieri saved them. In the second half, Brustad, an excellent left-winger, made it 1–1, but Piola eventually got the winner from a rebound.

Pozzo, however, revived his team's morale, and in the next round they won comfortably, 3–1 against France in Paris before 58,000 spectators, the biggest crowd of that World Cup. Foni replaced Monzeglio at right-back, and Biavati, the winger with the fluttering foot, took over from Paserati. For France, Delfour and Mattler were playing their third World Cup. The star was Piola. His two goals in the second half won the game, after France had rashly thrown themselves into attack.

Sweden, exempt from the first round, managed by Nagy, a Hungarian, and smarting from their humiliation by Japan in the last Olympiad, put an end to the Cuban illusion, winning 8–0. Torre Keller, their 35-year-old right-half and captain, was celebrating 14 years of international competition. The fair-haired right-winger, Gustav Wetterstroem, was, however, the chief destroyer. Four of the goals were his.

In Lille, a tired Swiss team lost 2–0 to a technically superior Hungary; the Swiss felt the lack of Minelli and Aebi.

In Bordeaux, where the new municipal stadium was inaugurated, Czechoslovakia, 1934 finalists, played Brazil, the now joint favourites with Italy. It was a holocaust; three players sent off, two Brazilians and a Czech, while Planicka with a broken arm and Nejedly with a broken leg finished in hospital. Zeze, violently kicking Nejedly for no apparent reason – and getting himself sent off – began it. Leonidas gave Brazil the lead, Nejedly equalised from a penalty in the second half, and the depleted Czechs held out against the nine-man Brazilians in extra time.

Curiously enough, the replay was conducted in the mildest of climates. The Brazilians made nine changes, the Czechs six. The Czechs led at half-time through the energetic Kopecky, moved up to the attack, but they badly missed the passing of Nejedly. Worse, Kopecky had to leave the field injured, a shot by Senecky seemed to be over the line before the Brazilian 'keeper cleared it – and Leonidas was at his best. He it was who equalised and Roberto got the winning goal.

In the semi-finals, Brazil paid the penalty for over-confidence, inexplicably omitting Leonidas and the brilliant Tim, against the Italians at Marseilles. Colaussi scored the opening goal and Meazza clinched the game from a penalty after Domingas had rashly fouled Piola. Thus it was 2–0, and Romeu's goal for Brazil had no real significance. For all his folly, Domingas had impressed Pozzo as 'one of the greatest defenders one is likely to meet'.

In the other semi-final, Hungary thrashed Sweden 5–1 in Paris. Nyberg got a 35-second goal for Sweden, but the Hungarians took it in their stride. They were 3–1 up by half-time – two for Szengeller – and he and Sarosi added goals in the second half. There could have been many more.

Sweden again took the lead in the third place match, at Bordeaux, and led 2–1 against Brazil at half-time. Then Leonidas turned it on, scored two goals, and Brazil won 4–2.

On 19 June, at the Stade Colombes, the Hungarians played graceful, short-passing football, the Italians showed rhythm and bite. Again, Colaussi got the first goal. Titkos equalised within a minute – he was Hungary's great hope – but Meazza, getting too much room all the while, made one for Piola, and Italy led 2–1. By half-time Colaussi, put through by Meazza, had scored again – 3–1.

In the second half, Sarosi added Hungary's second in a scramble, but the Italian defence was in control. Colaussi was too fast for Polgar, while Biavati and Piola were too quick for the whole defence when Piola scored from Biavati's ultimate back-heel. A swift, strong, ruthless team had kept the World Cup in Italy.

## FIRST ROUND

Switzerland (1) 1, Germany (1) 1 after extra time (Paris)
*Switzerland:* Huber Minelli (capt), Lehmann; Springer, Vernati, Loertscher; Amado, Wallaschek, Bickel, Abegglen III, Abei.
*Germany:* Raftl; Janes, Schnaus; Kupfer, Mock (capt), Kitzinger; Lehner, Gellesch, Gauchel, Hahnemann, Pesser.
*Scorers:* Gauchel for Germany, Abegglen III for Switzerland.

Switzerland (0) 4, Germany (2) 2 Replay (Parc des Princes, Paris)
*Switzerland:* Huber; Minelli (capt), Lehmann; Springer, Vernati, Loertscher; Amado, Abegglen III, Bickel, Wallaschek, Abei.
*Germany:* Raftl; Janes, Strietel; Kupfer, Goldbrunner, Skoumal; Lehner, Stroh, Hahnemann, Szepan (capt), Haumer.
*Scorers:* Hahnemann, Loertscher o.g. for Germany; Wallaschek, Bickel, Abegglen III (2) for Switzerland.

Cuba (0) 3, Romania (1) 3 after extra time (Toulouse)
*Cuba:* Cavajeles; Barquin, Chorens (capt); Arias, Rodriguez, Berges; Maquina, Fernandez, Socorro, Tunas, Sosa.
*Romania:* Palovici; Burger, Chiroiu; Vintila, Rasinaru (capt), Rafinski; Bindea, Covaci, Baratki, Bodola, Dobai.
*Scorers:* Covaci, Baratki, Dobai for Romania; Tunas, Maquina, Sosa for Cuba.

Cuba (0) 2, Romania (1) 1 Replay (Toulouse)
*Cuba:* Ayra; Barquin, Chorens (capt); Arias, Rodriguez, Berges; Maquina, Fernandez, Socorro, Tunas, Sosa.

*Romania:* Sadowski; Berger, Felecan; Barbulescu, Rasinaru, Rafinski; Bogden, Moldoveanu, Baratki, Pranzler, Dobai.
*Scorers:* Socorro, Maquina for Cuba; Dobai for Romania.

Hungary (4) 6, Dutch East Indies (0) 0 (Reims)
*Hungary:* Hada; Koranyi, Biro; Lazar, Turai, Balogh; Sas, Szengeller, Sarosi (capt), Toldi, Kohut.
*Dutch East Indies:* Mo Heng; Hu Kom, Sameuls; Nawir, Meng (capt), Anwar; Hang Djin, Soedarmadji, Sommers, Pattiwael, Taihuttu.
*Scorers:* Kohut, Toldi, Sarosi (2), Szengeller (2) for Hungary.

France (2) 3, Belgium (1) 1 (Colombes, Paris)
*France:* Di Lorto, Czenave, Mattler (capt); Bastien, Jordan, Diagne; Aston, Heisserer, Nicolas, Delfour, Veinante.
*Belgium:* Badjou; Pavrick (capt), Sayes; Van Alphen, Stynen, De Winter; Van de Wouwer, Voorhoof, Isemborghs, R., Braine, Byle.
*Scorers:* Vienante, Nicolas (2) for France, Isemborghs for Belgium.

Czechoslovakia (0) 3, Netherlands (0) 0 after extra time (Le Havre)
*Czechoslovakia:* Planicka; Berger, Daucik; Kostalek, Boucek (capt), Kopecky; Riha, Simunek, Zeman, Nejedly, Puc.
*Netherlands:* Van Male; Weber, Caldenhove; Pawae, Anderiesen (capt), Van Heel; Wels, Van der Veen, Smit, Vente, De Harder.
*Scorers:* Kostalek, Boucek, Nejedly for Czechoslovakia.

Brail (3) 6, Poland (1) 5 after extra time (Strasbourg)
*Brazil:* Batatoes; Domingas Da Guia, Machados; Zeze, Martin (capt), Alfonsinho; Lopez, Romeu, Leonidas, Peracio, Hercules.
*Poland:* Madejski; Szczepaniak, Galecki; Gora, Nytz (capt), Dytko; Piec I, Piontek, Szerfke, Willimowski, Wodarz.
*Scorers:* Leonidas (4), Peracio, Romeu for Brazil; Willimowski (4), Piontek for Poland.

Italy (1) 2, Norway (0) 1 after extra time (Marseilles)
*Italy:* Olivieri; Monzeglio, Rava; Serantoni, Andreolo, Locatelli; Paserati, Meazza (capt), Piola, Ferrari, Ferraris.
*Norway:* H. Johansen; R. Johansen (capt), Holmsen; Henriksen, Eriksen, Homberg; Frantzen, Kwammen, Brunylden, Isaksen, Brustad.
*Scorers:* Ferrari, Piola for Italy; Brustad for Norway.

**SECOND ROUND**
Sweden (4) 8, Cuba (0) 0 (Antibes)
*Sweden:* Abrahamson; Eriksson, Kjellgren; Almgren, Jacobsson. Svanstroem; Wetterstroem, Keller, H. Andersson, Jonasson, Nyberg.
*Cuba:* Carvajeles; Barquin, Chorens; Arias, Rodriquez, Berges; Ferrer, Fernandez, Socorro, Tunas, Alonzo.
*Scorers:* Andersson, Jonasson, Wetterstroem (4), Nyberg, Keller for Sweden.

Hungary (1) 2, Switzerland (0) 0 (Lille)
*Hungary:* Szabo; Koranyi, Biro; Szalay, Turai, Lazar; Sas, Vincze, Sarosi (capt), Szengeller, Kohut.
*Switzerland:* Huber; Stelzer, Lehmann (capt); Springer, Vernati, Loertscher; Amado, Wallaschek, Bickel, Abegglen III, Grassi.
*Scorers:* Szengeller (2) for Hungary.

Italy (1) 3, France (1) 1 (Colombes, Paris)
*Italy:* Olivieri; Foni, Rava; Serantoni, Andreolo, Locatelli; Biavati, Meazza (capt), Piola, Ferrari, Colaussi.
*France:* Di Lorto; Czenave, Mattler (capt); Bastien, Jordan, Diagne; Aston, Heisserer, Nicolas, Delfour, Veinante.
*Scorers:* Colaussi, Piola (2) for Italy; Heisserer for France.

Brazil (1) 1, Czechoslovakia (1) 1 after extra time (Bordeaux)
*Brazil:* Walter; Domingas Da Guia, Machados; Zeze, Martin (capt), Alfonsinho; Lopez, Romeu, Leonidas, Peracio, Hercules.
*Czechoslovakia:* Planicka; Berger, Daucik; Kostalek, Bocek (capt), Kopecky; Riha, Simunek, Ludl, Nejedly, Puc.
*Scorers:* Leonidas for Brazil; Nejedly (pen) for Czechoslovakia.

Brazil (0) 2, Czechoslovakia (1) 1 Replay (Bordeaux)
*Brazil:* Walter; Jahu, Nariz; Britto, Brandao (capt), Algemiro; Roberto, Luisinho, Leonidas, Tim, Patesko.
*Czechoslovakia:* Burket; Berger, Daucik; Kostalek, Bocek (capt), Ludl; Horak, Senecky, Kreutz, Kopecky, Rulc.
*Scorers:* Leonidas, Roberto for Brazil; Kopecky for Czechoslovakia.

**SEMI-FINALS**
Italy (2) 2, Brazil (0) 1 (Marseilles)
*Italy:* Olivieri; Foni, Rava; Serantoni, Andreolo, Locatelli; Biavati, Meazza (capt), Piola, Ferrari, Colaussi.
*Brazil:* Walter; Domingas, Da Guia, Machados; Zeze, Martin (capt), Alfonsinho; Lopez, Luisinho, Peracio, Romeu, Patesko.
*Scorers:* Colaussi, Meazza (pen) for Italy, Romeu for Brazil.

Hungary (3) 5, Sweden (1) 1 (Colombes, Paris)
*Hungary:* Szabo; Koranyi, Biro; Szalay, Turai, Lazar; Sas, Szengeller, Sarosi (capt), Toldi, Titkos.
*Sweden:* Abrahamson; Eriksson, Kjellgren; Almgren, Jacobsson, Svanstroem; Wetterstroem, Keller (capt), H. Andersson, Johanasson, Nyberg.
*Scorers:* Szengeller (3), Titkos, Sarosi for Hungary; Nyberg for Seden.

**THIRD PLACE MATCH**
Brazil (1) 4, Sweden (2) 2 (Bordeaux)
*Brazil:* Batatoes; Domingas Da Guia, Machados; Zeze, Brandao, Alfonsinho; Roberto, Romeu, Leonidas (capt), Peracio, Patesko.

*Sweden:* Abrahamson; Eriksson, Nilssen; Almgren, Linderholm, Svanstroem (capt); Berssen, H. Andersson, Jonasson, A. Andersson, Nyberg.
*Scorers:* Romeu, Leonidas (2), Peracio for Brazil; Jonasson, Nyberg for Sweden.


## FINAL

Italy (3) 4, Hungary (1) 2 (Colombes, Paris)
*Italy:* Olivieri; Foni, Rava; Serantoni, Andreolo, Locatelli; Biavati, Meazza (capt), Piola, Ferrari, Colaussi.
*Hungary:* Szabo; Polgar, Biro; Szalay, Szucs, Lazar; Sas, Vincze, Sarosi (capt), Szengeller, Titkos.
*Scorers:* Colaussi (2), Piola (2) for Italy; Titkos, Sarosi for Hungary.


## WORLD CUP 1950 – Brazil

The first World Cup for 12 years, the first since the outbreak of war, was in many ways the most vivid and impassioned yet. If Brazil were the moral victors, Uruguay's success was a marvellous anti-climax, emphasising the uncertainties of the game. Certainly the Uruguayans were most fortunate to have their qualifying pool reduced to a single, ludicrous match against Bolivia – but in the final the defensive prowess of Varela, Andrade, and Maspoli, and the counter-attacking of Schiaffino and Ghiggia, were worthy of success.

For the first – and so far last – time the competition was organised on the curious basis of four qualifying pools and a final pool. Again, there were several distinguished absentees; Austria, Hungary, Czecho-slovakia, Argentina. The Austrians, who seem to suffer from a periodic inferiority complex (they were to withdraw again in 1962) said quaintly that their team was too inexperienced – and then proceeded to beat Italy in Vienna. Russia stayed out, and Germany were still excluded from FIFA. But the British countries took part for the first time, their own International Championship charitably being recognised as a qualifying group, in which the first two would go through to the finals. Scotland, with baffling insularity and pique, decided that if they did not win the title they would not go to Brazil. England beat them 1–0 at Hampden – and they stayed at home to sulk.

England and Brazil were the favourites; Brazil as talented hosts, England for, presumably, historical reasons. Their chances were diminished by the withdrawal of Neil Franklin, their gifted centre-half, who flew off to play in Bogota, Colombia, then unregistered with FIFA. Injuries had blunted the edge of the gallant Mortensen, a splendid opportunist, but there were still such giants as Matthews, Finney, Williams, Ramsey, Mannion. In retrospect, the team looks better than one felt it to be in prospect.

Brazil approached the tournament with all the intense dedication shown by Uruguay in 1930 – and Italy in 1934. Managed by Flavio Costa, a lean, intense man with the inevitable South American mous-tache, they took up monastic residence in a house just outside Rio, with vitamin drinks, 10 o'clock curfew, and a ban on wives. Local firms accoutred the house for nothing. There were two doctors, two masseurs, three chefs.

The massive Maraçana Stadium – shades of Uruguay in 1930 – was still being completed (capacity 200,000) when the teams arrived – and when they left. Its seats had been painted blue; allegedly a pacifying colour.

France, angered by the amount of travelling they would have to do, withdrew at the last moment; this, after having been eliminated, then invited to take the place of Turkey, another country that withdrew. Though the French attitude was hardly defensible, there's no doubt that the travelling arrangements strongly favoured Brazil. So did the thin air of Rio.

Brazil kicked off against Mexico in a stadium that was still no more than an ambitious shambles. Brazil won 4–0, two of the goals coming from their lithe and brilliant centre-forward, Ademir. In São Paulo, a brave Swedish team sprang the first surprise of the competition by beating Italy. George Raynor, their clever little Yorkshire coach, had brilliantly rebuilt an Olympic-winning team pillaged of its stars by – the Italians. In Nacka Skoglund and Kalle Palmer, he had unearthed two delicate and subtle inside-forwards, flanking a powerful leader in the fair-haired Hasse Jeppson who completely mastered the great Carlo Parola. Italy had picked a strange team with Campatelli, a veteran left-half, at inside-left – after three years out of the national side. Carapallese, the Italian captain and outside-left, gave them the lead before a crowd that was full of Italo-Brazilians, but the hefty Knud Nordahl dominated Gino Cappello, their centre-forward. Jeppson equalised, Andersson gave Sweden the lead with a long shot, and a mistake in the second half by Sentimenti in goal allowed Jeppson to clinch it. Muccinelli pulled back a goal, Carapallese hit the bar – but that was as near as Italy could get.

In the other matches, the United States roused echoes of 1930 by leading Spain at half-time, fighting gallantly, and going down only by 3–1. Spain, with fine wingers in Basora and Gainza, and a tough centre-forward in Zarra, were greatly surprised. At the hard little Belo Horizonte ground, Yugoslavia easily beat Switzerland. Cjaicowski at right-half and Mitic and Bobek at inside-forward stood out for their skill.

England's win against Chile in Rio was laboured, but in their next match they suffered one of the greatest humiliations in world football history; they were beaten 1–0 by the United States in Belo Horizonte. So casually did the Americans take the game that most of them were up till the small hours. Everything seemed set for England: crisp mountain air; a British mining firm to put them up; a forward line of stars. But gallant defence by Borghi in goal, Colombo at centre-half, and Eddie McIlvenny, a Scotsman discarded 18 months earlier by Third Division Wrexham on a free transfer, held them out; and after 37 minutes America scored. Gaetjens got his head to a cross by Bahr to beat Williams; and all England's pressure could not bring an equaliser. Did Mullen's header from Ramsey's free kick cross Borghi's line? Perhaps; but America deserved their win for their courage.

In São Paulo, Brazil, too, faltered; held to a 2–2 draw by little Switzerland, who equalised two minutes from the end. Costa had picked a team full of *paulistas*, to flatter São Paulo, and the gesture had very nearly been expensive.

Italy beat Paraguay, who had drawn with Sweden, but the die was cast. Brazil, who had to beat Yugoslavia, conquerors of Mexico, in Rio, to qualify, got through by the skin of their teeth. Indeed, had it not been for a wretchedly unlucky head injury to Mitic on a steel girder outside the dressing-room, who knows what might have happened?

In the third minute, Ademir took a pass from the splendid right-half Bauer and opened the score. Yugoslavia, however, gave as good as they got. Cjaicowski II missed a fine chance to equalise, Bauer found the inimitable Zizinho – playing his first game of the tournament – and the inside-right wriggled through to clinch a difficult game. The Brazilians, playing 'diagonal' defence with a wandering centre-half and half-backs on the flanks, had made heavy weather of qualifying. Uruguay, 8–0 conquerors of Bolivia, had no trouble at all.

As for England, they went down 1–0 to Spain (a goal headed by Zarra) in Rio, and that was the end of them. Changes brought in Eddie Baily of Spurs at inside-left, Stanley Matthews on the right wing, Jackie Milburn at centre-forward, but the forward-line was still dogged by bad luck, and when Milburn did get the ball in the net, he was very dubiously given offside. Chile, winning 5–2 against the United States, emphasised England's shame.

In their first matches of the final pool, Brazil played some of the finest football that has ever graced the World Cup. Their inside-forward trio of Zizinho, Ademir, and Jair, with its pyrotechnical ball play, its marvellous understanding, was practically unstoppable, and Bauer gave it marvellous support. Raynor planned for Sweden to get an early goal, but two early chances went begging, and after that Brazil swept them aside. It was sheer execution. A second-half penalty by Andersson was the most Sweden could do against seven Brazilian goals, four of them Ademir's.

Spain went the same way, giving one goal less away. This time Jair and Chico got two each, Ademir did not score. Meanwhile Spain had held Uruguay to a bad-tempered 2–2 draw, Basora getting two more goals, despite the markings of Andrade. It seemed doubtful indeed whether the Uruguayans, bogeys of Brazil though they were, could hold them this time when they were under full sail.

Against Sweden, in São Paulo, the Uruguayans scraped through 3–2, after being a goal down at half-time. Skogland's off day and a bad foul by M. Gonzales on Johnsson – not to mention Uruguay's far easier programme – weighed against Sweden in the second half.

Thus to the deciding match, played before 200,000 impassioned fans at the Maracaña; a match which Brazil had only to draw to take the

World Cup. For three quarters of an hour they pounded a superb Uruguayan defence, brilliantly marshalled by their veteran centre-half, Obdulio Varela. Not till two minutes after half-time did Friaça meet a cross from the left to beat the astonishing Maspoli. Then Uruguay began to hit back, Varela turned to the attack, and after 20 minutes sent the fragile Ghiggia away on the right. Tall, pale, slender Juan Schiaffino controlled his centre unmarked, advanced, shot – and scored. Eleven minutes from time, Ghiggia took a return from Perez, ran on, and scored the winner.

Sweden, beating Spain 3–1 with a sudden late show of life, bravely took third place. And Brazil had to wait another eight years for ultimate satisfaction.


## POOL 1

Brazil (1) 4, Mexico (0) 0 (Rio)
*Brazil:* Barbosa; Augusto (capt), Juvenal; Eli, Danilo, Bigode; Meneca, Ademir, Baltazar, Jair, Friaça.
*Mexico:* Carbajal; Zetter, Montemajor; Ruiz, Ochoa, Roca; Septien, Ortis, Casarin, Perez, Velasquez (capt).
*Scorers:* Ademir (2), Jair, Baltazar for Brazil.


Yugoslavia (3) 3, Switzerland (0) 0 (Belo Horizonte)
*Yugoslavia:* Mrkusic; Horvat, Stankovic; Cjaicowski I (capt), Jovanovic, Djaic; Ognanov, Mitic, Tomasevic, Bobek, Vukas.
*Switzerland:* Corrodi; Gyger, Rey; Bocquet, Eggimann, Neury; Bickel (capt), Antenen, Tamini, Bader, Fatton.
*Scorers:* Tomasevic (2), Ognanov for Yugoslavia.


Yugoslavia (2) 4, Mexico (0) 1 (Porto Alegre)
*Yugoslavia:* Mrkusic; Horvat, Stankovic; Cjaicowski I (capt), Jovanovic, Djaic; Milhailovic, Mitic, Tomasevic, Bobek, Cjaicowski II.
*Mexico:* Carbajal; Gutierrez, Ruiz; Gomez, Ochoa, Ortiz; Flores, Naranjo, Casarin, Perez, Velasquez (capt).
*Scorers:* Bobek, Cjaicowski II (2), Tomasevic for Yugoslavia; Casarin for Mexico.


Brazil (2) 2, Switzerland (1) 2 (São Paulo)
*Brazil:* Barbosa; Augusto (capt), Juvenal; Bauer, Ruy, Noronha; Alfredo, Maneca, Baltazar, Ademir, Friaço.
*Switzerland:* Stuber; Neury, Bocquet; Lasenti, Eggimann, Quinche; Tamini, Bickel (capt), Antenen, Bader, Fatton.
*Scorers:* Alfredo, Baltazar for Brazil; Fatton, Tamini for Switzerland.


Brazil (1) 2, Yugoslavia (0) 0 (Rio)
*Brazil:* Barbosa; Augusto (capt), Juvenal; Bauer, Danilo, Bigode; Maneca, Zizinho, Ademir, Jair, Chico.

*Yugoslavia:* Mrkusic; Horvat, Brokela; Cjaicowski I (capt), Jovanovic, Djaic; Vukas, Mitic, Tomasevic, Bobek, Cjaicowski II.
*Scorers:* Ademir, Zizinho for Brazil.

Switzerland (2) 2, Mexico (0) 1 (Porto Alegre)
*Switzerland:* Hug; Neury, Bocquet; Lusenti, Eggimann (capt),
Kerner; Tamini, Antenen, Friedlander, Bader, Fatton.
*Mexico:* Carbajal; Gutierrez, Gomez; Roca, Ortiz, Vuburu; Flores,
Naranjo, Casarin, Borbolla, Velasquez (capt).
*Scorers:* Bader, Fatton for Switzerland; Velasquez for Mexico.

|            | P | W | D | L | F | A  | Pts |
|------------|---|---|---|---|---|----|-----|
| Brazil     | 3 | 2 | 1 | 0 | 8 | 2  | 5   |
| Yugoslavia | 3 | 2 | 0 | 1 | 7 | 3  | 4   |
| Switzerland| 3 | 1 | 1 | 1 | 4 | 6  | 3   |
| Mexico     | 3 | 0 | 0 | 3 | 2 | 10 | 0   |

## POOL 2
Spain (0) 3, United States (1) 1. (Curitiba)
*Spain:* Eizaguirre; Asensi, Alonzo; Gonzalvo III, Gonzalvo II,
Puchades; Basora, Hernandez, Zarra, Igoa, Gainza.
*United States:* Borghi; Keough, Maca; McIlvenny (capt), Colombo,
Bahr; Craddock, J. Souza, Gaetjens, Pariani, Valentini.
*Scorers:* Basora (2), Zarra for Spain. J. Souza for United States.

England (1) 2, Chile (0) 0 (Rio)
*England:* Williams; Ramsey, Aston; Wright (capt), Hughes, Dickin-
son; Finney, Mortensen, Bentley, Mannion, Mullen.
*Chile:* Livingstone; Faerias, Rolden; Alvarez, Busquez (capt) Carvalho;
Malanej, Cremaschi, Robledo, Munoz, Dias.
*Scorers:* Mortensen, Mannion for England.

United States (1) 1, England (0) 0 (Belo Horizonte)
*United States:* Borghi; Keough, Maca; McIlvenny (capt), Colombo,
Bahr; Wallace, Pariani, Gaetjens, J. Souza, E. Souza.
*England:* Williams; Ramsey, Aston; Wright (capt), Hughes, Dickin-
son; Finney, Mortensen, Bentley, Mannion, Mullen.
*Scorer:* Gaetjens for United States.

Spain (2) 2, Chile (0) 0 (Rio)
*Spain:* Eizaguirre; Alonzo, Pana; Gonzalvo III, Antunez, Puchades;
Basora, Igoa, Zarra, Panizo, Gainza.
*Chile:* Livingstone; Faerias, Roldon; Alvarez, Brusquez (capt),
Valho, Prieto, Cremaschi, Robledo, Munoz, Dias.
*Scorers:* Basora, Zarra for Spain.

Spain (0) 1, England (0) 0 (Rio)
*Spain:* Ramallets; Asensi, Alonzo; Gonzalvo III, Antunez, Puchades,
Basora, Igoa, Zarra, Panizo, Gainza.

*England:* Williams; Ramsey, Eckersley; Wright (capt), Hughes, Dickinson; Matthews, Mortensen, Milburn, Baily, Finney.
*Scorer:* Zarra for Spain.

Chile (2) 5, United States (0) 2 (Recife)
*Chile:* Livingstone; Machuca, Roldon; Alvarez, Busquez (capt), Faerias; Munoz, Cremaschi, Robledo, Prieto, Ibanez.
*United States:* Borghi; Keough, Maca; McIlvenny (capt), Colombo, Bahr; Wallace, Pariani, Gaetjens, J. Souza, E. Souza.
*Scorers:* Robledo, Cremaschi, (3), Prieto for Chile; Pariani, J. Souza (pen.) for United States.

|               | P | W | D | L | F | A | Pts |
|---------------|---|---|---|---|---|---|-----|
| Spain         | 3 | 3 | 0 | 0 | 6 | 1 | 6   |
| England       | 3 | 1 | 0 | 2 | 2 | 2 | 2   |
| Chile         | 3 | 1 | 0 | 2 | 5 | 6 | 2   |
| United States | 3 | 1 | 0 | 2 | 4 | 8 | 2   |

## POOL 3

Sweden (2) 3, Italy (1) 2 (São Paulo)
*Sweden:* Svensson; Samuelsson, G. Nilsson (capt); Andersson, K. Nordahl, Gard; Sundqvist, Palmer, Jeppson, Skoglund, S. Nilsson.
*Italy:* Sentiment IV; Giovannini, Furiassi; Annovazzi, Parola, Magli; Muccinelli, Boniperti, Cappello, Campatelli, Carapallese (capt).
*Scorers:* Jeppson (2), Andersson for Sweden; Carapellese, Muccinelli for Italy.

Sweden (2) 2, Paraguay (1) 2 (Curitiba)
*Sweden:* Svensson; Samuelsson, E. Nilsson (capt); Andersson, K. Nordahl; Gard; Johnsson, Palmer, Jeppson, Skoglund, Sundqvist.
*Paraguay:* Vargas; Gonzalito, Cespedes; Gavilan, Lequizamon, Cantero; Avalos, A. Lopez, Jara, F. Lopez, Unzaim.
*Scorers:* Sundqvist, Palmer for Sweden; A. Lopez, F. Lopez, for Paraguay.

Italy (1) 2, Paraguay (0) 0 (São Paulo)
*Italy:* Moro; Blason, Furiassi; Fattori, Remondini, Mari; Muccinelli, Pandolfini, Amadei, Cappello, Carapellese.
*Paraguay:* Vargas; Gonzalito, Cespedes; Gavilan, Lequizamon, Cantero; Avalos, A. Lopez, Jara, F. Lopez, Unzaim.
*Scorers:* Carapellese, Pandolfini for Italy.

|          | P | W | D | L | F | A | Pts |
|----------|---|---|---|---|---|---|-----|
| Sweden   | 2 | 1 | 1 | 0 | 5 | 4 | 3   |
| Italy    | 2 | 1 | 0 | 1 | 4 | 3 | 2   |
| Paraguay | 2 | 0 | 1 | 1 | 1 | 4 | 1   |

## POOL 4

Uruguay (4) 8, Bolivia (0) 0 (Recife)

*Uruguay:* Maspoli; M. Gonzales, Tejera; W. Gonzales, Varela (capt), Andrade; Ghiggia, Perez, Miguez, Schiaffino, Vidal.
*Bolivia:* Gutierrez I; Achs, Bustamente; Greco, Valencia, Ferrel; Alganaraz, Ugarte, Caparelli, Gutierrez II, Maldonado.
*Scorers:* Schiaffino (4), Miguez (2), Vidal, Ghiggia for Uruguay.


## FINAL POOL

Uruguay (1) 2, Spain (2) 2 (São Paulo)
*Uruguay:* Maspoli; M. Gonzales, Tejera; W. Gonzales, Varela (capt), Andrade; Ghiggia, Perez, Miguez, Schiaffino, Vidal.
*Spain:* Ramallets; Alonzo, Gonzalvo II; Gonzalvo III, Parra, Puchades; Basora, Igoa, Zarra, Molowny, Gainza.
*Scorers:* Ghiggia, Varela for Uruguay; Basora (2) for Spain.


Brazil (3) 7, Sweden (0) 1 (Rio)
*Brazil:* Barbosa; Augusto (capt), Juvenal; Bauer, Danilo, Bigode; Maneca, Zizinho, Ademir, Jair, Chico.
*Sweden:* Svensson; Samuelsson, E. Nilsson; Andersson, K. Nordahl, Gard; Sunqvist, Palmer, Jeppson, Skoglund, S. Nilsson.
*Scorers:* Ademir (4), Chico (2), Maneca for Brazil; Andersson (pen) for Sweden.


Uruguay (1) 3, Sweden (2) 2 (São Paulo)
*Uruguay:* Paz; M. Gonzales, Tejera; Gambetta, Varela (capt), Andrade; Ghiggia, Perez, Miguez, Schiaffino, Vidal.
*Sweden:* Svensson; Samuelsson, E. Nilsson; Andersson, Johansson, Gard, Johnsson, Palmer, Melberg, Skoglund, Sunqvist.
*Scorers:* Ghiggia, Miguez (2) for Uruguay; Palmer, Sunqvist for Sweden,


Brazil (3) 6, Spain (0) 1 (Rio)
*Brazil:* Barbosa; Augusto (capt), Juvenal; Bauer, Danilo, Bigode; Friaça, Zizinho, Ademir, Jair, Chico.
*Spain:* Eizaguirre; Alonzo, Gonzalvo II; Gonzalvo III, Parra, Puchades; Basora, Igoa, Zarra, Panizo, Gainza.
*Scorers:* Jair (2), Chico (2), Zizinho, Parra (o.g.) for Brazil; Igoa for Spain.


Sweden (2) 3, Spain (0) 1 (São Paulo)
*Sweden:* Svensson; Samuelsson, E. Nilsson; Andersson, Johansson, Gard; Sunqvist, Mellberg, Rydell, Palmer, Johnsson.
*Spain:* Eizaguirre; Asensi, Alonzo; Silva, Parra, Puchades; Basora, Fernandez, Zarra, Panizo, Juncosa.
*Scorers:* Johansson, Mellberg, Palmer for Sweden; Zarra for Spain.


Uruguay (0) 2, Brazil (0) 1 (Rio)
*Uruguay:* Maspoli; M. Gonzales, Tejera; Gambetta, Varela (capt), Andrade; Ghiggia, Perez, Miguez, Schiaffino, Moran.

*Brazil:* Barbosa; Augusto (capt), Juvenal; Bauer, Danilo, Bigode; Friaça, Zizinho, Ademir, Jair, Chico.
*Scorers:* Schiaffino, Ghiggia for Uruguay; Friaça for Brazil.

|         | P | W | D | L | F  | A  | Pts |
|---------|---|---|---|---|----|----|-----|
| Uruguay | 3 | 2 | 1 | 0 | 7  | 5  | 5   |
| Brazil  | 3 | 2 | 0 | 1 | 14 | 4  | 4   |
| Sweden  | 3 | 1 | 0 | 2 | 6  | 11 | 2   |
| Spain   | 3 | 0 | 1 | 2 | 4  | 11 | 1   |

**Leading Scorers:** Ademir (Brazil) 7, Schiaffino (Uruguay), Basora (Spain) 5.

## WORLD CUP 1954 – Switzerland

The 1954 World Cup, which rolled over little, under-organised Switzerland like a tidal wave over some peaceful village, was another instance of the Cup being won, at the last gasp, by the 'wrong' team. This time, the 'wrong' team was Sepp Herberger's cunningly managed Germany, the 'wronged' team, the brilliant Hungarians.

Hungary, who had smashed England's unbeaten home record against foreign teams 6–3 at Wembley the previous November, then beaten them again 7–1 in Budapest, as an aperitif to the World Cup, had the finest team the world had seen since the 1950 Brazilians; and probably the best Europe has ever seen.

The organisation of the tournament settled down into the somewhat hybrid and equally unsatisfactory form it retained until 1970. Four qualifying groups provided two qualifiers each, which then met in the quarter-finals, those finishing first playing those finishing second. Again, the British Championship was charitably designated as a qualifying group, and this time Scotland, again runner-up to England, deigned to enter. Their team paid a heavy penalty for the insularity of their Association in 1950.

Uruguay at last entered a European World Cup; they had yet to lose a match in the competition. Of the victorious 1950 team, still playing with a roving centre-half and 'bolt' defence, Maspoli, Andrade, Varela, Miguez, and Schiaffino all remained. There were splendid new wingers in Abbadie and Borges, and a powerful stopper in the fair-haired Santamaria, later to become a bulwark of Real Madrid.

Even so, Hungary remained favourites with their marvellous attack, pivoting on Boszik, the right-half, and Nandor Hidegkuti, the deeply-lying centre-forward; most of their goals scored from the remarkable head of Sandor Kocsis or the matchlessly powerful left foot of the captain, Ferenc Puskas, whose injury was probably to decide the series.

Austria, whose European dominance was ended by Hungary, had the remains of a fine team, a superb half-back in the tall, dark, strong Ernst Ocwirk, formerly their roving centre-half, now a wing-half. Austria had at last abandoned the classic Vienna School for the third back game which Meisl would have loathed.

Sweden, robbed of their stars by Italian clubs and eliminated by Belgium, were not there. Italy, under the management of the Hungarian Lajos Czeizler, basing their defence on the Inter (Milan) block, had a good recent record. Brazil had largely rebuilt their side. The great inside-forward trio had disappeared *en bloc*. Only Bauer and Baltazar remained, but the black Djalma Santos and his elegant namesake Nilton were fine backs, and Julinho came with a forbidding reputation for power and brilliance on the right wing. The defence still clung to the old 'diagonal' system and had not mastered the third-back game. Costa had given way to Zeze Moreira as the manager.

Yugoslavia, with the experience of Mitic, Bobek, and Cjaicowski I, the acrobatic goalkeeping of Beara, the skill and finishing power of the excellent Zebec and Vukas, were obviously good outsiders. One should add that an absurd omission in the rules made it necessary for extra time to be played *whenever* two teams were level at full-time. Each pool included two 'seeded' teams.

The tournament began with France losing by a single goal to Yugoslavia – a goal scored by the young Milutinovic, who was later to play for Racing Club de Paris. Brazil, with Didi directing operations, gobbled up Mexico. Hungary had an even easier task against little Korea in Pool 2. Germany disposed of Turkey without trouble.

Scotland played well against the talented Austrian side in Zürich, and their remodelled defence, with new backs in Willy Cunningham and Aird, looked promisingly solid. In attack, they missed the punch of Lawrie Reilly, who had been ill. Scotland gave Schmied in the Austrian goal much more to do than had their own goalkeeper; their half-backs were excellent, and it was only Schmied's late, daring save from centre-forward Mochan that allowed the Austrians to hang on to Probst's first-half goal.

England, still tottering from the travesty of Budapest, threw away all Matthews' brilliant work in a 4–4 draw with Belgium. Pol Anoul, the fair-haired inside-forward, gave Belgium the lead after only five minutes. Fifteen minutes from time England were 3–1 in the lead thanks to the finishing of Ivor Broadis and Nat Lofthouse but, over-complacent, they allowed Belgium to wipe out the lead through Anoul again and the talented compact centre-forward, the unpredictable Rik Coppens. That meant – under the farcical rules of the competition – extra time.

For half an hour, England were dominant, but Matthews, the inspiration of the side – here, there and everywhere – pulled a muscle, and two minutes after Lofthouse had crowned a fine inter-passing movement between Broadis and Manchester United's Tommy Taylor, Dickinson headed Dries' free kick past Merrick for the Belgian equaliser.

In the meantime, Italy surprisingly came a cropper at Lausanne against Switzerland. The days of Pozzo, present only in his capacity of journalist, were distant indeed. Bad refereeing by Viana of Brazil unsettled the players and led to a holocaust of fouls and bad temper. Italy had the play, Switzerland got the goals, Hugi, who had switched to outside-right, scoring the winner 12 minutes from time. Two Swiss players were kicked in the stomach, and the Italians chased Viana off the field after he had dubiously ruled out a goal by Benito Lorenzi, who had persistently argued with him. Not for nothing was Lorenzi nicknamed '*Veleno*' – Poison.

The next round of matches included what was perhaps the decisive moment of the competition; the kick, accidental perhaps, with which Germany's centre-half Werner Liebrich injured Ferenc Puskas and put him out of action till a final in which he should not really have taken part. Sepp Herberger cleverly decided to throw away this match, fielding a team which consisted largely of reserves, convinced that Germany would easily dispose of Turkey in the play-off. The Hungarians tore Germany apart, getting eight goals, four of them by Kocsis, whose heading was remarkable. The fact that a team could be thus overwhelmed and still come back to win a *cup* competition was as good a comment on the organisation of this World Cup as one could require. Three of Hungary's goals came in the last 15 minutes, when Puskas was off the field.

Uruguay, who had conquered the mud in Berne to beat an uninspired Czech team, now exploited the firmer going in Basle to humiliate Scotland 7–0. Schiaffino, tall, pale, lean, a wonderful ball-player and strategist with a splendid understanding with his centre-forward, Miguez, tore Scotland's defence to pieces. Borges and Abbadie, the wingers, got five of the goals between them against a wretched Scottish team, which had not been helped by dissension among its officials. Andy Beattie, the team manager, had resigned after the Austrian game.

Austria, meanwhile, showed dazzling form in thrashing the Czechs 5–0, Ocwirk and the polished Gerhard Hanappi cleverly supporting an attack in which inside-forwards Probst and Stojaspal shared the goals.

But the finest match of all, perhaps the best of the whole tournament, with the exception of the Hungary–Uruguay semi-final, was Brazil's draw with Yugoslavia in Pool 1.

On the pretty Lausanne ground overlooking Lake Geneva, the Yugoslavs gave a splendid exhibition, Cjaicowski and Boskov dominating midfields with Beara superb in goal. But the only goal was by Zebec three minutes from half-time. In the second half Brazil came to life and Didi, after sustained pressure, scored the equaliser with a spectacular drive. There were no more goals in extra time.

In the play-offs, Germany, with a full team again, swamped Turkey while Italy, who had revived to beat Belgium 4–1, lost by the same score to Switzerland; a bafflingly inconsistent team. England, who had beaten the Swiss 2–0 in a dull game in Berne, were already through. They had strengthened their defence by moving Wright to centre-half in place of the injured Owen, a move which would bear abundant fruit in the years to come.

In the quarter-finals, England's 4–2 defeat by Uruguay has subsequently been put down to the goalkeeping of Merrick, as though England really deserved to win. In fact, the Uruguayans did remarkably well to defeat England, with both Varela and Andrade pulling muscles and Abbadie limping for much of the game.

England, with Matthews back in the side and shining again, did well, Lofthouse rubbing out Borges' fifth-minute goal. Varela's long-distance volley gave Uruguay a lead they did not deserve on the play – Merrick might have saved it; then after Varela had taken a free kick 'from hand', Schiaffino made it 3–1; again with a shot that could have been saved. Schiaffino's later excellence at left-half saw to it that England did not save the game. Finney's goal made it 2–3, Matthews hit the post, but at last Ambois slipped through for the fourth, and England were eliminated.

In Lausanne, Austria, again on form, won an astonishing 12-goal match with the Swiss; a score unthinkable two World Cups later! Using the speed of the Koerners down the wings and shooting, untypically, from long range, Austria had the star of the match in the classical Ocwirk. The best Swiss player was their dark inside-right, Roger Vonlanthen, who was behind most of their goals.

Meanwhile, the Brazilians met the Hungarians in what has come to be known as the Battle of Berne; a potentially great match that degenerated into a shocking display of violence.

Hungary made one of their spectacular starts, Hidegkuti scoring from a corner in the third minute, and getting his shorts ripped off for his pains. Then, five minutes later, he centred for Kocsis to head in. As the rain poured down, tackling grew ferocious. Buzansky knocked Indio down, big Djalma Santos scored from the penalty, and Hungary, without Puskas, were faltering.

A quarter of an hour after half-time, they too scored from a penalty – by Lantos, after Pinheiro had handled – but a marvellous run and shot by Julinho made it 3–2. Nilton Santos and Bozsik came to blows, and Arthur Ellis, the Halifax referee, sent both off the field. Hostilities were well and truly open. Four minutes from time, when the field resembled a boxing ring, Ellis sent off Humberto Tozzi, Brazil's inside-left, for kicking at an opponent, and in the last minute, Koscis headed the fourth for Hungary. Then the battle was transferred to the dressing-rooms ...

In Geneva, Yugoslavia dominated Germany for an hour without being able to score. But the towering Horvat put past his own goalkeeper. The Slav forwards again finished poorly; Kohlmeyer kicked off the German line three times, and at last a breakaway goal by the bull-like Helmut Rahn, Germany's splendid outside-right, settled matters.

The Lausanne Hungary-Uruguay semi-final was unforgettable. Though Hungary missed Puskas, Czibor gave Hungary a 15-minute lead, from Kocsis' header, and Hidegkuti's head made it 2–0 just before half-time.

That seemed to be that, but with only a quarter of an hour left

Schiaffino put the Argentinian-born Hohberg through to make it 2–1 – and repeated the move three minutes from the end.

In the first half of extra time Hohberg was through a third time, but his shot hit the post and Hungary survived. Two splendid headers from Kocsis in the last 15 minutes gave them a wonderful match.

Germany, meanwhile, to the general astonishment, routed Austria, not least because goalkeeper Walter Zeman had a tragic game. The Germans, splendidly marshalled by their captain, Fritz Walter, backed up by his Kaiserslautern 'block', scored twice from corners, twice from centres, twice from penalties. Germany's switching, Walter's scheming and his cunning corners gave Austria a nightmare second-half, in which they conceded five goals.

In the third place match, in Zurich, Austria gained consolation. Unlike the equivalent game of 1934, they started underdogs, yet won – against a tired, demoralised Uruguay. A first-half injury to Schiaffino put the lid on it; Stojaspal emerged as the game's cleverest forward, and Ocwirk was magisterial. It was Ocwirk who shot the third goal from 25 yards in a tepid second-half.

And so to Berne, and the dramatic, unexpected final.

Hungary, with Puskas insisting that he play, might have demoralised Germany with their opening attack. After six minutes Boszik put Kocsis through, his shot was blocked, but Puskas followed up to score. Two minutes more and Czibor, on the right wing, made it 2–0.

What saved Germany was their swift reply – Morlock putting in Fritz Walter's fast centre. Rahn scored from a corner – and the game was open again. Turek, in Germany's goal, made save after dazzling save, Hidegkuti hit a post, Kocsis the bar, and Kohlemeyer kicked off the line. Then Eckel and Mai got a tighter grip on the Hungarian inside-forwards, Fritz Walter brought his wingers into the game and at last Boszik mispassed. Schaefer found Fritz Walter, the cross was pushed out – and Rahn smashed the ball in. Germany had won. When Puskas, coming to life again, raced on to Toth's pass to score, the goal was flagged offside. And when Czibor shot, Turek made another marvellous save.

Hungary, tired in body and spirit by their battles with the South Americans, may have been the moral victors, but Germany's success was none the less a memorable one.

## POOL 1

Yugoslavia (1) 1, France (0) 0 (Lausanne)
*Yugoslavia:* Beara; Stankovic, Crnkovic; Cjaicowski I (capt), Horvat, Boskov; Milutinovic, Mitic, Vukas, Bobek, Zebec.
*France:* Remetter; Gianessi, Kaelbel; Penverne, Jonquet (capt), Marcel; Kopa, Glovacki, Strappe, Dereuddre, Vincent.
*Scorer:* Milutinovic for Yugoslavia.

Brazil (4) 5, Mexico (0) 0 (Geneva)
*Brazil:* Castilho; D. Santos, N. Santos; Brandaozinho, Pinheiro

(capt), Bauer; Julinho, Didi, Baltazar, Pinga, Rodriguez.
*Mexico:* Mota; Lopez, Gomez; Gardenas, Romo, Avalos; Torres,
Naranjo (capt), Lamadrid, Balcazar, Arellano.
*Scorers:* Baltazar, Didi, Pinga (2), Julinho for Brazil.


France (1) 3, Mexico (0) 2 (Geneva)
*France:* Remetter; Gianessi, Marche (capt); Marcel, Kaelbel, Mah-
joub; Kopa, Dereuddre, Strappe, Ben Tifour, Vincent.
*Mexico:* Carbajal; Lopez, Romo; Cardenas, Avalos, Martinez;
Torres, Naranjo (capt), Lamadrid, Balcazar, Arellano.
*Scorers:* Vincent, Cardenas (o.g.), Kopa (pen) for France; Naranjo,
Balcazar for Mexico.


Brazil (0) 1, Yugoslavia (0) 1 after extra time (Lausanne)
*Brazil:* Castilho; D. Santos, N. Santos; Brandaozinho, Pinheiro
(capt), Bauer; Julinho, Didi, Baltazar, Pinga, Rodriguez.
*Yugoslavia:* Beara; Stankovic, Crnkovic; Cjaicowski I (capt), Horvat,
Boskov; Milutinovic, Mitic, Zebec, Vukas, Dvornic.
*Scorers:* Zebec for Yugoslavia; Didi for Brazil.

|  | P | W | D | L | F | A | Pts |
|---|---|---|---|---|---|---|---|
| Brazil | 2 | 1 | 1 | 0 | 6 | 1 | 3 |
| Yugoslavia | 2 | 1 | 1 | 0 | 2 | 1 | 3 |
| France | 2 | 1 | 0 | 1 | 3 | 3 | 2 |
| Mexico | 2 | 0 | 0 | 2 | 2 | 8 | 0 |

## POOL 2
Hungary (4) 9, South Korea (0) 0 (Zurich)
*Hungary:* Grosics; Buzansky, Lantos; Bozsik, Lorant, Szojka; Budai,
Kocsis, Palotas, Puskas (capt), Czibor.
*South Korea:* Hong; K. Park, Kang; Min (capt), Y. Park, Chu;
Chung, I. Park, Sung, Woo, Choi.
*Scorers:* Czibor, Kocsis (3), Puskas (2), Lantos, Palotas (2) for Hun-
gary.


West Germany (1) 4, Turkey (1) 1 (Berne)
*West Germany:* Turek; Laband, Kohlmeyer; Eckel, Posipal, Mai;
Klodt, Morlock, O. Walter, F. Walter (capt), Schaefer.
*Turkey:* Turgay (capt); Ridvan, Basti; Mustafa, Cetin, Rober; Erol,
Suat, Feridun, Burhan, Lefter.
*Scorers:* Klodt, Morlock, Schaefer, O. Walter for West Germany;
Suat for Turkey.


Hungary (3) 8, West Germany (1) 3 (Basle)
*Hungary:* Grosics; Buzansky, Lantos; Bozsik, Lorant, Zakarias;
J. Toth, Kocsis, Hidegkuti, Paskas (capt), Czibor.
*West Germany:* Kwiatowski; Bauer, Kohlmeyer; Posipal, Liebrich,
Mebus; Rahn, Eckel, F. Walter (capt), Pfaff, Herrmann.

111

*Scorers:* Hidegkuti (2), Kocsis (4), Puskas, Toth for Hungary; Pfaff, Herrmann, Rahn for Germany.

Turkey (4) 7, South Korea (0) 0 (Geneva)
*Turkey:* Turgay (capt); Ridvan, Basri; Mustafa, Cetin, Rober; Erol, Suat, Necmettin, Lefter, Burhan.
*South Korea:* Hong; K. Park (Capt), Kang; Han, C. K. Lee, Kim, Choi, S. Lee, G. C. Lee, Woo, Chung.
*Scorers:* Burham (3), Erol, Lefter, Suat (2) for Turkey.

| | P | W | D | L | F | A | Pts |
|---|---|---|---|---|---|---|---|
| Hungary | 2 | 2 | 0 | 0 | 17 | 3 | 4 |
| Germany | 2 | 1 | 0 | 1 | 7 | 9 | 2 |
| Turkey | 2 | 1 | 0 | 1 | 8 | 4 | 2 |
| Korea | 2 | 0 | 0 | 2 | 0 | 16 | 0 |

**Play-off**
West Germany (3) 7, Turkey (1) 2 (Zurich)
*West Germany:* Turek; Laband, Bauer; Eckel, Posipal, Mai; Klodt, Morlock, O. Walter, F. Walter (capt), Schaefer.
*Turkey:* Sukru; Ridvan, Basri; Mehmet, Cetin (capt), Rober; Erol, Mustafa, Necmettin, Soskun, Lefter.
*Scorers:* Morlock (3), O. Walter, Schaefer (2), F. Walter for West Germany; Mustafa, Lefter for Turkey.

## POOL 3
Austria (1) 1, Scotland (0) 0 (Zurich)
*Austria:* Schmied; Hanappi, Barschandt; Ocwirk (capt), Happel, Koller; R. Koerner, Schleger, Dienst, Probst, A. Koerner.
*Scotland:* Martin; Cunningham (capt), Aird; Docherty, Davidson, Cowie; McKenzie, Fernie, Mochan, Brown, Ormond.
*Scorer:* Probst for Austria.

Uruguay (0) 2, Czechoslovakia (0) 0 (Berne)
*Uruguay:* Maspoli; Santamaría, Martinez; Andrade, Varela (capt), Cruz; Abbadie, Ambrois, Miguez, Schiaffino, Borges.
*Czechoslovakia:* Reiman; Safranek, Novak (capt); Trnka, Hledik, Hertl; Hlavacek, Hemele, Kacani, Pazicky, Krauss.
*Scorers:* Miguez, Schiaffino for Uruguay.

Austria (4) 5, Czechoslovakia (0) 0, (Zurich)
*Austria:* Schmied; Hanappi, Barschandt; Ocwirk (capt), Happel, Koller; R. Koerner, Wagner, Stojaspal, Probst, A. Koerner.
*Czechoslovakia:* Stacho; Safranek, Novak (capt); Trnka, Pluskal, Hertl; Hlavacek, Hemele, Kacani, Pazicky, Krauss.
*Scorers:* Stojaspal (2), Probst (3) for Austria.

Uruguay (2) 7, Scotland (0) 0 (Basle)

*Uruguay:* Maspoli; Santamaría, Martinez; Andrade, Varela (capt),
Cruz; Abbadie, Ambrois, Miguez, Schiaffino, Borges.
*Scotland:* Martin; Cunningham (capt), Aird; Docherty, Davidson,
Cowie; McKenzie, Fernie, Mochan, Brown, Ormond.
*Scorers:* Borges (3), Miguez (2), Abbadie (2) for Uruguay.

|  | P | W | D | L | F | A | Pts |
|---|---|---|---|---|---|---|---|
| Uruguay | 2 | 2 | 0 | 0 | 9 | 0 | 4 |
| Austria | 2 | 2 | 0 | 0 | 6 | 0 | 4 |
| Czechoslovakia | 2 | 0 | 0 | 2 | 0 | 7 | 0 |
| Scotland | 2 | 0 | 0 | 2 | 0 | 8 | 0 |

## POOL 4

England (2) 4, Belgium (1) 4 after extra time (Basle)
*England:* Merrick; Staniforth, Byrne; Wright (capt), Owen, Dickinson;
Matthews, Broadis, Lofthouse, Taylor, Finney.
*Belgium:* Gerneay; Dries (capt), Van Brandt; Huysmans, Carré, Mees;
Mermans, Houf, Coppens, Anoul, P. Van den Bosch.
*Scorers:* Anoul (2), Coppens, Dickinson (o.g.) for Belgium: Broadis
(2), Lofthouse (2) for England.

England (1) 2, Switzerland (0) 0 (Berne)
*England:* Merrick; Staniforth, Byrne; McGarry, Wright (capt),
Dickinson; Finney, Broadis, Wilshaw, Taylor, Mullen.
*Switzerland:* Parlier; Neury, Kernen; Eggimann, Bocquet (capt),
Bigler; Antenen, Vonlanthen, Meier, Ballaman, Fatton.
*Scorers:* Mullen, Wilshaw for England.

Switzerland (1) 2, Italy (1) 1 (Lausanne)
*Switzerland:* Parlier; Neury, Kernen; Flueckiger, Bocquet (capt),
Casali; Ballaman, Vonlanthen, Hugi, Meier, Fatton.
*Italy:* Ghezzi; Vincenzi, Giacomazzi; Neri, Tognon, Nesti; Muccinell
Boniperti (capt), Galli, Pandolfini, Lorenzi.
*Scorers:* Ballaman, Hugi for Switzerland; Boniperti for Italy.

Italy (1) 4, Belgium (0) 1 (Lugano)
*Italy:* Ghezzi; Magnini, Giacomazzi (capt); Neri, Tognon, Nesti;
Frignani, Cappello, Galli, Pandolfini, Lorenzi.
*Belgium:* Gernaey; Dries (capt), Van Brandt; Huysmans, Carré,
Mees; Mermans, H. Van den Bosch, Coppens, Anoul, P. Van den
Bosch.
*Scorers:* Pandolfini (pen), Galli, Frignani, Lorenzi for Italy; Anoul
for Belgium.

|  | P | W | D | L | F | A | Pts. |
|---|---|---|---|---|---|---|---|
| England | 2 | 1 | 1 | 0 | 6 | 4 | 3 |
| Italy | 2 | 1 | 0 | 1 | 5 | 3 | 2 |
| Switzerland | 2 | 1 | 0 | 1 | 2 | 3 | 2 |
| Belgium | 2 | 0 | 1 | 1 | 5 | 8 | 1 |

**Play-off**

Switzerland (1) 4, Italy (0) 1 (Basle)

*Switzerland:* Parlier, Neury, Kernen; Eggimann, Bocquet (capt), Casali; Antenen, Vonlanthen, Hugi, Ballaman, Fatton.

*Italy:* Viola; Vincenzi, Giacomazzi (capt), Neri, Tognon, Nesti; Muccinelli, Pandolfini, Lorenzi, Segato, Frignani.

*Scorers:* Hugi (2), Ballaman, Fatton for Switzerland; Nesti for Italy.

## QUARTER FINALS

West Germany (1) 2, Yugoslavia (0) 0 (Geneva)

*West Germany:* Turek; Laband, Kohlmeyer; Eckel, Liebrich, Mai; Rahn, Morlock, O. Walter, F. Walter (capt), Schaefer.

*Yugoslavia:* Beara; Stankovic, Crnkovic; Cjaicowski I, Horvat, Boskov; Milutinovic, Mitic (capt), Vukas, Bobek, Zebec.

*Scorers:* Horvat (o.g.), Rahn for West Germany.

Hungary (2) 4, Brazil (1) 2 (Berne)

*Hungary:* Grosics; Buzansky, Lantos; Bozsik (capt), Lorant, Zakarias; M. Toth, Kocsis, Hidegkuti, Czibor, J. Toth.

*Brazil:* Castilho; D. Santos, N. Santos; Brandaozinho, Pinheiro (capt), Bauer; Julinho, Didi, Indio, Tozzi, Maurinho.

*Scorers:* Hidegkuti (2), Kocsis, Lantos (penalty) for Hungary; D. Santos, (pen), Julinho for Brazil.

Austria (5) 7, Switzerland (4) 5 (Lausanne)

*Austria:* Schmied; Hanappi, Barschandt; Ocwirk (capt), Happel, Koller; R. Koerner, Wagner, Stojaspal, Probst, A. Koerner.

*Switzerland:* Parlier; Neury, Kernen, Eggimann, Bocquet (capt), Casali; Antenen, Vonlanthen, Hugi, Ballaman, Fatton.

*Scorers:* Ballaman (2), Hugi (2), Hanappi (o.g.) for Switzerland; A. Koerner (2), Ocwirk, Wagner (3), Probst for Austria.

Uruguay (2) 4, England (1) 2 (Basle)

*Uruguay:* Maspoli; Santamaría, Martinez; Andrade, Varela (capt), Cruz; Abbadie, Ambrois, Miguez, Schiaffino, Borges.

*England:* Merrick, Staniforth, Byrne; McGarry, Wright (capt), Dickinson; Matthews, Broadis, Lofthouse, Wilshaw, Finney.

*Scorers:* Borges, Varela, Schiaffino, Ambrois for Uruguay; Lofthouse, Finney for England.

## SEMI-FINALS

West Germany (1) 6, Austria (0) 1 (Basle)

*West Germany:* Turek; Posipal, Kohlmeyer; Eckel, Liebrich, Mal; Rahn, Morlock, O. Walter, F. Walter (capt), Schaefer.

*Austria:* Zeman; Hanappi, Schleger; Ocwirk (capt), Happel, Koller; R. Koerner, Wagner, Stojaspal, Probst, A. Koerner.

*Scorers:* Schaefer, Morlock, F. Walter, (2 pen), O. Walter (2) for West Germany; Probst for Austria.

Hungary (1) 4, Uruguay (0) 2, after extra time (Lausanne)
*Hungary:* Grosics; Buzansky, Lantos; Bozsik (capt), Lorant, Zakarias; Budai, Kocsis, Palotas, Hidegkuti, Czibor.
*Uruguay:* Maspoli; Santamaría, Martinez; Andrade (capt), Carballo, Cruz; Souto, Ambrois, Schiaffino, Hohberg, Borges.
*Scorers:* Czibor, Hidegkuti, Kocsis (2) for Hungary; Hohberg (2) for Uruguay.


## THIRD PLACE MATCH

Austria (1) 3, Uruguay (1) 1 (Zurich)
*Austria:* Schmied; Hanappi, Barschandt; Ocwirk (capt), Kollmann, Koller; R. Koerner, Wagner, Dienst, Stojaspal, Probst.
*Uruguay:* Mospoli; Santamaría, Martinez; Andrade (capt), Carballo, Cruz; Abbadie, Hohberg, Mendez, Schiaffino, Borges.
*Scorers:* Stojaspal (pen), Cruz (o.g.), Ocwirk for Austria; Hohberg for Uruguay.


## FINAL

West Germany (2) 3, Hungary (2) 2 (Berne)
*West Germany:* Turek; Posipal, Kohlmeyer; Eckel, Liebrich, Mai; Rahn, Morlock, O. Walter, F. Walter, Schaefer.
*Hungary:* Groscis; Buzansky, Lantos; Bozsik, Lorant, Zakarias; Czibor, Kocsis, Hidegkuti, Puskas, J. Toth.
*Scorers:* Morlock, Rahn (2) for West Germany; Puskas, Czibor for Hungary.
**Leading Scorer:** Kocsis (Hungary) 11.


## WORLD CUP 1958 – Sweden

At long last, after the disappointment of 1950 and the violent elimination of 1954, Brazil carried off the World Cup in spectacular fashion, with a performance in the final against Sweden which rivalled the greatest ever seen. There, on the rain-soaked stadium of Rasunda, the Brazilian forwards juggled, gyrated and, above all finished with marvellous, gymnastic skill. There, Garrincha, the outside-right, and Pelé, the 17-year-old inside left, together with the incomparable Didi, wrote themselves indelibly into the history of the game.

It was a World Cup which began greyly, and built up to an ultimate crescendo; a World Cup heavy with nostalgia, thanks to the return of Sweden's stars. Professionals now, the Swedes could recall Nacka Skoglund, a hero of their 1950 World Cup team, and Nils Liedholm and Gunnar Gren from their great 1948 Olympic team. They could also bring back from Italy Julli Gustavsson, their splended centre-half, and Kurt Hamrin, a dazzling little outside-right. To begin with, their supporters were pessimistic, but as round succeeded round and George Raynor's elderly team marched on to the final, nationalist feeling mounted alarmingly, culminating in the Gothenburg semi-final.

Brazil had toured Europe in 1956 without much success, but they had learned from their tour. Now they brought with them the 4–2–4 formation that was soon to sweep the world. Four defenders in line, two pivotal players in midfield, four forwards up to strike. They were established, if a little precariously, as the favourites.

England's chances had been gravely affected by the tragic air disaster at Munich, in which their Manchester United stars, Tommy Taylor, Roger Byrne, and the mighty Duncan Edwards, had perished.

The Russians, included with England, Brazil, and Austria in quite the most powerful qualifying group of all (this time, all three teams would play one another), had just drawn 1–1 with England in Moscow. This was their first World Cup, but they had won the Olympic tournament in Australia two years before, while in Lev Yachin they had one of the finest goalkeepers in the game.

Italy and Uruguay were out; Uruguay thrashed 5–0 in Asuncion by Paraguay, Italy eliminated by brave little Northern Ireland. The Irish brilliantly captained by their elegant right-half Danny Blanchflower, generalled in attack by Jimmy McIlroy, were the surprise of the eliminators. After a black game of violence in Belfast, when the referee, Hungary's Zsolt, was fog bound and the World Cup game was turned into a friendly, Chiappella of Italy was sent off and the crowd swarmed on to the pitch. The rematch saw Ireland victorious 2–1. But the Munich crash deprived them of Jackie Blanchflower, a key man at centre-half.

Wales was there on the most fragile grounds. Already eliminated, they were given a second chance when FIFA decided Israel could not qualify by forfeit alone after Uruguay had refused to come back into the competition. So Wales had the fairly easy task of eliminating Israel, which they did surprisingly well.

Scotland, who had eliminated Spain, were in mediocre form, and had been humiliated by England in Glasgow 4–0. West Germany, the holders, captained again by Fritz Walter, had the burly Helmut Rahn on the right wing, but had turned Hans Schaefer into an inside-forward. A new star was the powerful, ruthless wing-half, Horst Szymaniak. Clearly they would take some beating.

Sweden opened the tournament on 8 June in Stockholm, with an easy 3–0 win over Mexico. Two of the goals were scored by their strong, fair-haired centre-forward, Ange Simonsson, while Liedholme got the other goal from a penalty. Bror Mellberg, a 1950 World Cup man, played at inside-right.

In the same group, Hungary, shorn of Puskas, Kocsis, and Czibor, who had stayed in the West after the 1956 Revolution, were held to a 1–1 draw by Wales. Jack Kelsey, Wales' calm, strong goalkeeper, a hero of the tournament, was dazzled by the sun when Bozsik scored after four minutes, but the massive John Charles, recalled from Italy, headed the equaliser from a corner.

In Gothenburg, England and Russia had an exciting battle in which England rallied for a somewhat lucky draw. The power of Voinov and Tsarev (left-half and captain Igor Netto was injured) plus the skill of Salnikov, in midfield, the goalkeeping of Yachin and the domination of

116

Krijevski, enabled Russia to take a 2–0 lead. But Kevan headed in a free kick and at last Tom Finney, injured in a ruthless tackle and destined to take no further part in the competition, equalised with a penalty.

The Brazilians accounted for Austria 3–0 in Boras, but their team was still in the melting-pot. Pelé, canvassed as their *wunderkind*, was injured, and some wanted the unorthodox Garrincha on the right wing. Team manager Feola himself preferred Vavá to Mazzola at centre-forward, despite the fact that Mazzola (real name José Altafini) scored two of the three goals.

In Group 1, the brave Irish at once showed their quality by defeating the Czechs 1–0 at Halmstad, tough little Wilbur Cush, their versatile inside-right, getting the goal. Harry Gregg had a fine game in goal, but the absence of Jackie Blanchflower forced his brother Danny much deeper into defence.

At Malmö, West Germany were too strong and efficient for an Argentina side which, having brilliantly won the South American Championship the previous year, at once lost its chief stars to Italy. Their style looked old-fashioned, and they had no answer to Rahn, who added two more to his tally of World Cup goals.

No one had expected anything from the French, yet here they were in Norrköping, thrashing Paraguay 7–3, their inside-forward trio of Fontaine (who had expected to be a reserve), Kopa, back from Real Madrid and playing deep, and Piantoni doing remarkable things. Three of the goals were from Kopa. In fact the weeks in training camp at Kopparberg, under Paul Nicolas, had transformed the French morale.

Scotland, meanwhile, undeterred by the fact that Yugoslavia had recently beaten England 5–0, held them to a 1–1 draw at Vasteras. Stamina and determination saved the game after an anxious first half and a seven-minute goal by Petakovic. At right-half, the 35-year-old Eddie Turnbull was in splendid form for the Scots.

The second 'round' was full of surprises. In Gothenburg, an English defence cleverly organised to the prescription of Bill Nicholson, the team coach, held up Brazil's forwards. Howe, the right-back, played in the middle, Clamp, the right half, on the flank, while Slater marked Didi out of the game. Brazil were rather lucky not to give away a penalty in the second half when Bellini felled Kevan, but England, on the other hand, owed much to the cool elegance in goal of Colin McDonald of Burnley. There was no score.

At Boras, Russia, too, accounted for an ageing Austria.

In Group 1, Ireland had a shock 3–1 defeat by the Argentinians, who brought back 40-year-old Angel Labruna at inside-left and gave them a casual lesson in the skills of the game. The stars were Labruna and another veteran, the roving-centre-half Nestor Rossi.

West Germany, two down, rallied to draw with the Czechs, a goal going to the rejuvenated Helmut Rahn, who'd been written off between the two World Cups.

Yugoslavia, who had Branko Zebec, their Rest of Europe left-winger, at centre-half, surprised France to win with a breakaway goal three minutes from time. At Norrköping, a tired-looking Scottish team went down to Paraguay, inspired by Silvio Parodi from inside-forward. Bobby Evans, the red-haired Celtic centre-half, laboured in vain against a thrustful Paraguayan attack.

Wales, feeble in attack, were held to a draw by Mexico in Stockholm, and the following day, again at Rasunda, the Swedes rather unconvincingly beat Hungary. Hungary, with Bozsik of all people at deep centre-forward, were laboured in attack, with only the ferocious shooting of Tichy to keep them in the game. Did Tichy score in the 55th minute with a shot that beat Svensson and hit the underside of the bar? The referee thought not, and half a minute later Hamrin's lob was deflected past Grosics to make it 2–0. Tichy's goal, when it did come, was irrelevant.

The shock of the final round was Czechoslovakia's 6–1 crushing of Argentina at Halsingborg, the sequel to which was a bombardment of rubbish for the Argentina players when they got back to Buenos Aires airport. The Czechs were altogether too fast, with Borovicka and Molnar unstoppable.

Northern Ireland and West Germany drew 2–2 in one of the best matches of the competition, with Gregg superb in goal and Rahn having a superb first half but fading in the second. Peter McParland, Ireland's tough outside-left, twice gave them the lead, but Uwe Seeler, a new young star at centre-forward, equalised 11 minutes from time; so Ireland had to play off against the Czechs.

England, in Boras, stubbornly unchanged by their manager Walter Winterbottom, toiled to a mediocre draw with Austria, so they too had to replay. Haynes, the general, and Douglas, on the right wing, were plainly exhausted after the effort they had made to drag their respective clubs out of Division II; Kevan remained a blunt instrument; Finney was still injured. In Gothenburg, meanwhile, Brazil, at the plea of their own players, at last gave a chance to Garrincha, who mesmerised the Russian defence. Pelé had his first game, and the clever Zito replaced Dino as linking right-half. Russia used Netto to shadow Didi, but Didi was the dominant player of the match. Vivá, replacing Mazzola at centre-forward, scored in the third and 77th minutes, but the 2–0 score flattered Russia. Brazil had found their team, and their form.

In Group 2, France just got home against a Scottish team well served by Bill Brown, making his debut in goal, while Paraguay held the Yugoslavs to a draw. Sweden, fielding five reserves, were satisfied with a goalless draw with Wales, who thus had to meet Hungary (easy conquerors of Mexico) in the play-off.

This they bravely and surprisingly won 2–1 with John Charles back in defence. Tichy opened the score; Ivor Allchurch equalised with a superb 40-yard volley, and, five minutes later Terry Medwin intercepted Grosics' short goal kick to win the game. Sipos was sent off for kicking Hewitt, and Wales hung on to win and to qualify. A famous victory.

Equally famous was Northern Ireland's defeat of the Czechs. Peter

Doherty, once a great Irish inside-forward, now an inspirational team manager, had expressed his confidence that what they had done once, they could do again; and so they did. Injuries to Uprichard, in goal, and to Bertie Peacock did not hold them back. A goal down and forced to play half an hour's extra time, they won in the 100th minute when McParland converted Blanchflower's free kick. Again, the winger scored both goals.

England, at last making changes, throwing Peter Broadbent and Peter Brabrook in the deep end, unluckily went down to Russia in Gothenburg. Twice Brabrook hit the post, but when Russia's Ilyin hit the post, the ball went in. England were eliminated.

In the quarter-finals, the weary, depleted Irish went down 4–0 to France at Norrköping, Casey playing despite just having had four stitches in his shin and Gregg keeping goal on one leg. But theirs had been a glorious achievement.

Wales too went out, defending superbly against Brazil but falling at last to a goal by Pelé, deflected past the splendid Kelsey by the equally splendid Williams. John Charles was unfit to play, but his brother Mel was a superb centre-half and Hopkins cleverly contained Garrincha.

Sweden, with Hamrin irresistible, knocked out the Russians. The little winger headed the first goal, and made the second for Simonsson Finally, a ruthless German team knocked out the Yugoslavs in Malmö with Rahn inevitably getting the goal. As in Switzerland four years earlier, the Slavs dominated the game but just could not score.

In the semi-finals, France's luck deserted them. For 37 minutes, at the Rasunda, they held Brazil, but with the score 1–1, Jonquet, their elegant centre-half, was hurt, and that was that. Didi's 30-yard swerver gave Brazil the lead, and Pelé, at last showing his quality, got three more in the second half.

In Gothenburg, a chanting, nationalistic crowd mustered by official cheer leaders was urging Sweden on to victory against the West Germans. It was rather an unsatisfactory match in many ways. Schaefer brilliantly volleyed Germany into the lead – but Sweden equalised after Liedholm had handled with impunity. In the second half, the game turned on Juskowiak's flash of temper. He kicked Hamrin, was sent off, and the way was clear for Gren, nine minutes from time, and Hemrin himself – a wonderfully impertinent, dribbling goal – to take Sweden into the final.

France thrashed Germany 6–3 on that same ground, in the third-place match, four of the goals going to the rampant Fontaine brilliantly combining with Kopa. This was one of the finest partnerships the World Cup has seen, giving Fontaine a new scoring record for the competition.

It rained in Stockholm on the day of the final, but the crowd, its cheer leaders now properly banned, was quiet, and even Liedholm's fine, early goal, as he picked his way through the Brazilian penalty area, did not decide the game. The Brazilians, scornful of George

Raynor's forecast that if they gave away an early goal, 'they'd panic all over the show', stubbornly held on. Six minutes later, Garrincha, with marvellous swerve and acceleration, left Axbom and Parling standing and made the equaliser for Vavá. Pelé hit a post; Zagalo, always ready to drop deep, cleared from under his own bar; but it was clear that the two fullbacks Santos (with Djalma playing his first game of the tournament) had the measure of Sweden's little wingers.

After 32 minutes Garrincha repeated his astonishing *tour de force*, and Vavá scored again. In the second half, he gave way to the incredible Pelé, who coolly juggled the ball to smash in a third. Zito and Didi were immaculate now in midfield, while Zagalo had sandwiched a goal of his own between Pelé's and the Swedes' second, making it 4–2. Then came the final goal, a brilliant header from Pelé, with the Brazilian fans shouting '*Samba, samba!*' It had been a dazzling exhibition of the arts of the game, and victory at last for the team that morally deserved it.


## POOL 1

West Germany (2) 3, Argentina (1) 1 (Malmö)
*West Germany:* Herkenrath; Stollenwerk, Juskowiak; Eckel, Erhardt, Szymaniak; Rahn, Walter, Seeler, Schmidt, Schaefer.
*Argentina:* Carrizo; Lombardo, Vairo; Rossi, Dellacha, Varacka; Corbatta, Prado, Menendez, Rojas, Cruz.
*Scorers:* Rahn (2), Schmidt for West Germany; Corbatta for Argentina.

Northern Ireland (1) 1, Czechoslovakia (0) 0 (Halmstad)
*Ireland:* Gregg; Keith, McMichael; Blanchflower, Cunningham, Peacock; Bingham, Cush, Dougan, McIlroy, McParland.
*Czechoslovakia:* Dolejsi; Mraz, Novak; Pluskal, Cadek, Masopust; Hovorka, Dvorak, Borovicka, Hartl, Kraus.
*Scorer:* Cush for Northern Ireland.

West Germany (1) 2, Czechoslovakia (0) 2 (Halsingborg)
*West Germany:* Herkenrath; Stollenwerk, Juskowiak; Schnellinger, Erhardt, Szymaniak; Rahn, Walter, Seeler, Schaefer, Klodt.
*Czechoslovakia:* Dolejsi; Mraz, Novak; Pluskal, Popluhar, Masopust; Hovorka, Dvorak, Molnar, Feureisl, Zikan.
*Scorers:* Rahn, Schaefer for West Germany; Dvorak (pen) Zikan for Czechoslovakia.

Argentina (1) 3, Northern Ireland (1) 1 (Halmstad)
*Argentina:* Carrizo; Lombardo, Vario; Rossi, Dellacha, Varacka; Corbatta, Avio, Menendez, Labruna, Boggio.
*Northern Ireland:* Gregg; Keith, McMichael; Blanchflower, Cunnham, Peacock; Bingham, Cush, Casey, McIlroy, McParland.
*Scorers:* Corbatta (2) (one pen), Menendez for Argentina; McParland for Northern Ireland.

120

West Germany (1) 2, Northern Ireland (1) 2 (Malmö)
*West Germany:* Herkenrath; Stollenwerk, Juskowiak; Eckel, Erhardt, Szymaniak; Rahn, Walter, Seeler, Schaefer, Klodt.
*Northern Ireland:* Gregg; Keith, McMichael; Blanchflower, Cunningham, Peacock; Bingham, Cush, Casey, McIlroy, McParland.
*Scorers:* Rahn, Seeler for West Germany; McParland (2) for Northern Ireland.


Czechoslovakia (3) 6, Argentina (1) 1 (Halsingborg)
*Czechoslovakia:* Dolejsi; Mraz, Novak; Dvorak, Popluhar, Masopust; Hovorka, Borovicka, Molnar, Feureisl, Zikan.
*Argentina:* Carrizo; Lombardo, Vario; Rossi, Dellacha, Varacka; Corbatta, Avio, Menendez, Labruna, Cruz.
*Scorers:* Dvorak, Zikan (2), Feureisl, Hovorka (2) for Czechoslovakia; Corbatta for Argentina.

|                  | P | W | D | L | F | A  | Pts |
|------------------|---|---|---|---|---|----|-----|
| West Germany     | 3 | 1 | 2 | 0 | 7 | 5  | 4   |
| Czechoslovakia   | 3 | 1 | 1 | 1 | 8 | 4  | 3   |
| Northern Ireland | 3 | 1 | 1 | 1 | 4 | 5  | 3   |
| Argentina        | 3 | 1 | 0 | 2 | 5 | 10 | 2   |


**Play-off**
Northern Ireland (1) 2, Czechoslovakia (1) 1 after extra time (Malmö)
*Northern Ireland:* Uprichard; Keith, McMichael; Blanchflower, Cunningham, Peacock; Bingham, Cush, Scott, McIlroy, McParland.
*Czechoslovakia:* Dolejsi; Mraz, Novak; Bubernik, Popluhar, Masopust; Dvorak, Borovicka, Feureisl, Molnar, Zikan.
*Scorers:* McParland (2) for Northern Ireland; Zikan for Czechoslovakia.


**POOL 2**
France (2) 7, Paraguay (2) 3 (Norrköping)
*France:* Lemetter; Kaelbel, Lerond; Penverne, Jonquet, Marcel; Wisnieski, Fontaine, Kopa, Piantoni, Vincent.
*Paraguay:* Mayeregger; Arevalo, Miranda; Achucarro, Lezcano, Villalba; Aguero, Parodi, Romero, Re, Amarilla.
*Scorers:* Fontaine (3), Piantoni, Wisnieski, Kopa, Vincent for France; Amarilla (2) (1 pen), Romero for Paraguay.


Yugoslavia (1) 1, Scotland (0) 1 (Vasteras)
*Yugoslavia:* Beara; Sijakovic, Crnkovic; Krstic, Zebec, Boskov; Petakovic, Veselinovic, Milutinovic, Sekularac, Rajkov.
*Scotland:* Younger; Caldow, Hewie; Turnbull, Evans, Cowie; Leggat, Murray, Mudie, Collins, Imlach.
*Scorers:* Petakovic for Yugoslavia; Murray for Scotland.

Yugoslavia (1) 3, France (1) 2 (Vasteras)
*Yugoslavia:* Beara; Tomic, Crnkovic; Krstic, Zebec, Boskov; Petakovic, Veselinovic, Milutinovic, Sekularac, Rajkov.
*France:* Remetter; Kaelbel, Marche; Penverne, Jonquet, Lerond; Wisnieski, Fontaine, Kopa, Piantoni, Vincent.
*Scorers:* Petakovic, Veselinovic (2) for Yugoslavia; Fontaine (2) for France.

Paraguay (2) 3, Scotland (1) 2 (Norrköping)
*Paraguay:* Aguilar; Arevalo, Enhague; Achucarro, Lezcano, Villalba; Aguero, Parodi, Romero, Re, Amarilla.
*Scotland:* Younger; Parker, Caldow; Turnbull, Evans, Cowie; Leggat, Collins, Mudie, Robertson, Fernie.
*Scorers:* Aguero, Re, Parodi for Paraguay; Mudie, Collins for Scotland.

France (2) 2, Scotland (0) 1 (Cerebro)
*France:* Abbes; Kaelbel, Lerond; Penverne, Jonquet, Marcel; Wisnieski, Fontaine, Kopa, Piantoni, Vincent.
*Scotland:* Brown; Caldow, Hewie; Turnbull, Evans, Mackay; Collins, Murray, Mudie, Baird, Imlach.
*Scorers:* Kopa, Fontaine for France; Baird for Scotland.

Yugoslavia (2) 3, Paraguay (1) 3 (Ekilstuna)
*Yugoslavia:* Beara; Tomic, Crnkovic; Boskov, Zebec, Krstic; Petakovic, Velesinovic, Ognjanovic, Sekularac, Rajkov.
*Paraguay;* Aguilar; Arevalo, Echague; Villalba, Lezcano, Achucarro; Aguero, Parodi, Romero, Re, Amarilla.
*Scorers:* Ognjanovic, Veselinovic, Rajkov for Yugoslavia; Parodi, Aguero, Romero for Paraguay.

|  | P | W | D | L | F | A | Pts |
|---|---|---|---|---|---|---|---|
| France | 3 | 2 | 0 | 1 | 11 | 7 | 4 |
| Yugoslavia | 3 | 1 | 2 | 0 | 7 | 6 | 4 |
| Paraguay | 3 | 1 | 1 | 1 | 9 | 12 | 3 |
| Scotland | 3 | 0 | 1 | 2 | 4 | 6 | 1 |

## POOL 3
Sweden (1) 3, Mexico (0) 0 (Stockholm)
*Sweden:* Svensson; Bergmark, Axbom; Liedholm, Gustavsson, Parling; Hamrin, Melberg, Simonsson, Gren, Skoglund.
*Mexico:* Carbajal; Del Muro, Gutierrez; Cardenas, Romo, Flores; Hernandez, Reyes, Calderon, Gutierrez, Sesma.
*Scorers:* Simonsson (2), Liedholm (pen) for Sweden.

Hungary (1) 1, Wales (1) 1 (Sandviken)
*Hungary:* Grosics; Matray, Sarosi; Bozsik, Sipos, Berendi; Sandor, Tichy, Hidegkuti, Bundzsak, Fenyvesi.
*Wales:* Kelsey; Williams, Hopkins; Sullivan, M. Charles, Bowen; Webster, Medwin, J. Charles, Allchurch, Jones.
*Scorers:* Bozsik for Hungary; J. Charles, for Wales.

Wales (1) 1, Mexico (1) 1 (Stockholm)
*Wales:* Kelsey; Williams, Hopkins; Baker, M. Charles, Bowen; Webster, Medwin, J. Charles, Allchurch, Jones.
*Mexico:* Carbajal: Del Muro, Gutierrez; Cardenas, Romo, Flores; Belmonte, Reyes, Blanco, Gonzales, Sesma.
*Scorers:* Allchurch for Wales; Belmonte for Mexico.


Sweden (1) 2, Hungary (0) 1 (Stockholm)
*Sweden:* Svensson; Bergmark, Axbom; Liedholm, Gustavsson, Parling; ling; Berndtsson, Selmosson, Kaelgren, Lofgren, Skoglund.
*Hungary:* Grosics; Matray, Sarosi; Szojka, Sipos, Berendi; Sandor, Tichy, Bozsik, Bundzsak, Fenyvesi.
*Scorers:* Hamrin (2) for Sweden; Tichy for Hungary.


Sweden (0) 0, Wales (0) 0 (Stockholm)
*Sweden:* Svensson; Bergmark, Axbom; Boerjesson, Gustavsson, Parling; Berndtsson, Kaelgren, Lofgren, Skoglund.
*Wales:* Kelsey; Williams, Hopkins; Sullivan, M. Charles, Bowen; Vernon, Hewitt, J. Charles, Allchurch, Jones.


Hungary (1) 4, Mexico (0) 0 (Sandviken)
*Hungary:* Ilku; Matray, Sarosi; Bozsik, Sipos, Kotasz; Budai, Bencsics, Tichy, Bundzsak, Fenyvesi.
*Mexico:* Carbajal; Del Muro, Gutierrez; Cardenas, Sepulvedo, Flores; Belmonte, Reyes, Blanco, Gonzales, Sesma.
*Scorers:* Tichy (2), Sandor, Bencsics for Hungary.

|         | P | W | D | L | F | A | Pts |
|---------|---|---|---|---|---|---|-----|
| Sweden  | 3 | 2 | 1 | 0 | 5 | 1 | 5 |
| Hungary | 3 | 1 | 1 | 1 | 6 | 3 | 3 |
| Wales   | 3 | 0 | 3 | 0 | 2 | 2 | 3 |
| Mexico  | 3 | 0 | 1 | 2 | 1 | 8 | 1 |

**Play-off**
Wales (0) 2, Hungary (1) 1 (Stockholm)
*Wales:* Kelsey; Williams, Hopkins; Sullivan, M. Charles, Bowen; Medwin, Hewitt, J. Charles, Allchurch, Jones.
*Hungary:* Grosics; Matray, Sarosi; Bozsik, Sipos, Kotasz; Budai, Bencsics, Tichy, Bundzsak, Fenyvesi.
*Scorers:* Allchurch, Medwin for Wales; Tichy for Hungary.


# POOL 4
England (0) 2, Russia (1) 2 (Gothenburg)
*England:* McDonald; Howe, Banks; Clamp, Wright, Slater; Douglas, Robson, Kevan, Haynes, Finney.
*Russia:* Yachin; Kessarev, Kuznetsov; Voinov, Krijevski, Tsarev; A. Ivanov, V. Ivanov, Simonian, Salnikov, Ilyin.
*Scorers:* Simonian, A. Ivanov, for Russia; Kevan, Finney (pen) for England.

Brazil (1) 3, Austria (0) 0 (Boras)
*Brazil:* Gilmar; De Sordi, N. Santos; Dino, Bellini, Orlando; Joel, Didi, Mazzola, Dida, Zagalo.
*Austria:* Szanwald; Halla, Swoboda; Hanappi, Happel, Koller; Horak, Senekowitsch, Buzek, Koerner, Schleger.
*Scorers:* Mazzola (2), Santos for Brazil.


England (0) 0, Brazil (0) 0 (Gothenburg)
*England:* McDonald; Howe, Banks; Clamp, Wright, Slater; Douglas, Robson, Kevan, Haynes, A'Court.
*Brazil:* Gilmar; De Sordi, N. Santos; Dino, Bellini, Orlando; Joel, Didi, Mazzola, Vavá, Zagalo.


Russia (1) 2, Austria (0) 0 (Boras)
*Russia:* Yachin; Kessarev, Kuznetsov; Voinov, Krijevski, Tsarev; A. Ivanov, V. Ivanov, Simonian, Salnikov, Ilyin.
*Austria:* Schmied; E. Kozlicek, Swoboda; Hanappi, Stotz, Koller; Horak, P. Hozlicek, Buzek, Koerner, Senekowitsch.
*Scorers:* Ilyin, V. Ivanov for Russia.


Brazil (1) 2, Russia (0) 0 (Gothenburg)
*Brazil:* Gilmar; De Sordi, N. Santos; Zito, Bellini, Orlando; Garrincha, Didi, Vavá, Pelé, Zagalo.
*Russia:* Yachin; Kessarev, Kuznetsov; Voinov, Krijevski, Tsarev; A. Ivanov, V. Ivanov, Simonian, Netto, Ilyin.
*Scorer:* Vavá (2) for Brazil.


England (0) 2, Austria (1) 2 (Boras)
*England:* McDonald; Howe, Banks; Clamp, Wright, Slater; Douglas, Robson, Kevan, Haynes, A'Court.
*Austria:* Szanwald; Kollmann, Swoboda; Hanappi, Happel, Koller; E. Kozlicek, P. Kozlicek, Buzek, Koerner, Senekowitsch.
*Scorers:* Haynes, Kevan for England; Koller, Koerner for Austria.


|         | P | W | D | L | F | A | Pts |
|---------|---|---|---|---|---|---|-----|
| Brazil  | 3 | 2 | 1 | 0 | 5 | 0 | 5   |
| England | 3 | 0 | 3 | 0 | 4 | 4 | 3   |
| Russia  | 3 | 1 | 1 | 1 | 4 | 4 | 3   |
| Austria | 3 | 0 | 1 | 2 | 2 | 7 | 1   |

**Play-off**
Russia (0) 1, England (0) 0 (Gothenburg)
*Russia:* Yachin; Kessarev, Kuznetsov; Voinov, Krijevski, Tsarev; Apoukhtin, V. Ivanov, Simonian, Falin, Ilyin.
*England:* McDonald; Howe, Banks; Clayton, Wright, Slater; Brabrook, Broadbent, Kevan, Haynes, A'Court.
*Scorer:* Ilyin for Russia.

## QUARTER-FINALS
France (1) 4, Ireland (0) 0 (Norrköping)
*France:* Abbes; Kaelbel, Lerond; Penverne, Jonquet, Marcel; Wisnieski, Fontaine, Kopa, Piantoni, Vincent.
*Northern Ireland:* Gregg; Keith, McMichael; Blanchflower, Cunningham, Cush; Bingham, Casey, Scott, McIlroy, McParland.
*Scorers:* Wisnieski, Fontaine (2), Piantoni for France.

West Germany (1) 1, Yugoslavia (0) 0 (Malmö)
*West Germany:* Herkenrath; Stollenwerk, Juskowiak; Eckel, Erhardt, Szymaniak; Rahn, Walter, Seeler, Schmidt, Schaefer.
*Yugoslavia:* Krivocuka; Sijakovic, Crnkovic; Kristic, Zebec, Boskov; Petakovic; Veselinovic, Milutinovic, Ognjanovic, Rajkov.
*Scorer:* Rahn for West Germany.

Sweden (0) 2, Russia (0) 0 (Stockholm)
*Sweden:* Svensson; Bergmark, Axbom; Boerjesson, Gustavsson, Parling; Hamrin, Gren, Simonsson, Liedholm, Skoglund.
*Russia:* Yachin; Kessarev, Kuznetsov; Voinov, Krijevski Tsarev; A. Ivanov, V. Ivanov, Simonian, Salnikov, Ilyin.
*Scorers:* Hamrin, Simonsson for Sweden

Brazil (0) 1, Wales (0) 0 (Gothenburg)
*Brazil:* Gilmar; De Sordi, N. Santos; Zito, Bellini, Orlando; Garrincha, Didi, Mazzola, Pelé, Zagalo.
*Wales:* Kelsey; Williams, Hopkins; Sullivan, M. Charles, Bowen; Medwin, Hewitt, Webster, Allchurch, Jones.
*Scorer:* Pelé for Brazil.

## SEMI-FINALS
Brazil (2) 5, France (1) 2 (Stockholm)
*Brazil:* Gilmar; De Sordi, N. Santos; Zito, Bellini, Orlando; Garrincha, Didi, Vavá, Pelé, Zagalo.
*France:* Abbes; Kaelbel, Lerond; Penverne, Jonquet, Marcel; Wisnieski, Fontaine, Kopa, Piantoni, Vincent.
*Scorers:* Vavá, Didi, Pelé (3) for Brazil; Fontaine, Piantoni for France.

Sweden (1) 3, West Germany (1) 1 (Gothenburg)
*Sweden:* Svensson; Bergmark, Axbom; Boerjesson, Gustavsson, Parling; Hamrin, Gren, Simonsson, Liedholm, Skoglund.
*West Germany:* Herkenrath; Stollenwerk, Juskowiak; Eckel, Erhardt, Szymaniak; Rahn, Walter, Seeler, Schaefer, Cieslarczyk.
*Scorers:* Skoglund, Gren, Hamrin for Sweden; Schaefer for West Germany.

## THIRD PLACE MATCH
France (0) 6, West Germany (0) 3 (Gothenburg)
*France:* Abbes; Kaelbel, Lerond; Penverne, Lafont, Marcel; Wisnieski, Douis, Kopa, Fontaine, Vincent.

*West Germany:* Kwiatowski; Stollenwerk, Erhardt; Schnellinger, Wewers, Szymaniak; Rahn, Sturm, Kelbassa, Schaefer, Cieslarzcyk.
*Scorers:* Fontaine (4) Kopa (pen), Douis for France; Cieslarczyk, Rahn, Schaefer for West Germany.

## FINAL

Brazil (2) 5, Sweden (1) 2 (Stockholm)
*Brazil:* Gilmar; D. Santos, N. Santos; Zito, Bellini, Orlando; Garrincha, Didi, Vavá, Pelé, Zagalo.
*Sweden:* Svensson; Bergmark, Axbom; Boerjesson, Gustavsson, Parling; Hamrin, Gren, Simonsson, Liedholm, Skoglund.
*Scorers:* Vavá (2), Pelé (2), Zagalo for Brazil; Liedholm, Simonsson for Sweden.
**Leading Scorer:** Fontaine (France )13 (present record total).

## WORLD CUP 1962 – Chile

The selection of Chile as host to the 1962 World Cup was a surprising one, determined largely by sentiment and by the pressures of Chile's representative to FIFA, the late Carlos Dittborn: 'We have nothing, that is why we must have the World Cup.' Chile had recently suffered a disastrous earthquake, but Dittborn promised all would be ready in time. Argentina, the logical choice, had a poor record in terms of loyalty to the tournament and, in fact, Chile made a good enough job of the organisation, though the insanely high prices kept out an impoverished working class and there was flagrant profiteering by hotels and agencies.

Once again, the four-pool qualifying system was employed, this time with such disastrous effects (goal average was counted) as to cast doubt not only on the system but on the whole future of the game. Manic defence, eight men in the penalty box, reduced many of the qualifying matches to farce.

Brazil and Russia were the favourites, Russia because, on their recent South American tour, they had beaten Argentina, Uruguay, and Chile. Otherwise, the field looked a mediocre one. England had just lost to Scotland in Glasgow for the first time for 25 years; Hungary, Argentina, and Italy were in decline; West Germany as tough as ever, but lacking a Fritz Walter. Chile had the great advantage of playing at home, and the experienced managership of Fernando Riera, but nobody much favoured them.

The Brazilians, after various experiments, fell back on almost exactly the team that won in 1958. Vavá and Didi had returned from Madrid, and Mauro, Bellini's understudy in Sweden, replaced him at centre-half. Zagalo, when Pelé dropped out injured after the second game, played a still deeper left wing role, turning 4–2–4 into a definite 4–3–3. The one 'revelation' was Pelé's 24-year-old replacement, Amarildo. The outstanding figure was Garrincha, adding remarkable finishing power with both feet and his head to his known gifts of swerve and acceleration.

Playing in the delightful seaside *cancha* of Viña del Mar, they

126

began with a laborious 2–0 win over the resilient Mexicans, drew 0–0 with the well organised Czechs, losing Pelé with a severely pulled muscle, and were given a bad fright by Spain. Helenio Herrera, recalled from Milan to manage the Spaniards, made four changes and nearly did the trick. Spain led by Adelardo's goal at half-time, and only Garrincha's brilliance, making two goals for Adelardo, turned the trick for Brazil. The Czechs, though beaten by Mexico, were runners-up.

England, in the Rancagua group played on the stadium owned by the Braden Copper Company (they themselves had a remote mountain camp at Coya) came second to Hungary; their conquerors in the first match. A team based on the crossfield and through passing of Johnny Haynes was too predictable. The 21-year-old Bobby Moore, first capped in Lima on the way to Chile, did well at wing-half, but too closely resembled the other halfback Flowers for a 4–2–4 to be workable. Haynes hadn't enough creative support. These problems were compounded by Ron Springett's strange vulnerability in goal to long shots. The powerful Tichy beat him with one in the opening match, Albert brilliantly scoring the other after Flowers had equalised from a penalty. A halfback like the admirable Solymosi of Hungary was just what England needed.

They did much better against Argentina, who had won a dull, dour match 1–0 against Bulgaria. Alan Peacock of Middlesbrough made an excellent debut at centre-forward, despite the brutal attentions of Navarro. Again Flowers scored from a penalty, Bobby Charlton, admirable on the left wing, made it 2–0 before half-time, Greaves scored at third, and Sanfilippo's goal came too late to count.

Hungary overwhelmed Bulgaria then went through the motions in a draw with Argentina. England also drew 0–0 against Bulgaria in a game of unspeakable tedium, and they nearly lost when Kolev broke clear.

The Chileans, with Toro and Rojas a forceful pair in midfield, were the surprise of Group 1, which produced their notorious match against Italy. The Italians, stuffed with South Americans, were unpopular because two of their correspondents had criticised life in Santiago. At the imposing new stadium – not yet a camp for political prisoners, as it became 11 years later – Chile were provocative from the first. The Italians responded in kind and Ken Aston, the referee, much criticised for his performance, found it 'uncontrollable'. In the event, the Chileans did better. Two Italians, Ferrini and David, were sent off, while Leonel Sanchez broke the Italo-Argentinian Maschio's nose with impunity. Chile won 2–0, but lost by the same score to the parsimonious, counter-attacking Germans, themselves conquerors of the Swiss after breaking Eschmann's leg. Italy and Germany had drawn 0–0; Germany and Chile qualified.

Far up in the North, at Arica, Russia were the disappointment, Colombia the surprise. When the two met, Lev Yachin for once was out of form and the result was a remarkable 4–4 draw, Klinger, the little black Colombian inside-left, being the best man afield. The Colombians, who had held Uruguay to 2–1 in their opening match, then ran out of steam and were thrashed 5–0 by Yugoslavia.

Yachin had his only good game of the tournament in the opening match against Yugoslavia, a vicious but skilful affair in which Dubinski, the Russian fullback, had his leg broken by Mujic, who was sent home. Victor Ponedelnik engineered both goals, in the second half, scoring the second himself after hitting the bar with a free kick for Ivanov to score the first.

Dragoslav Sekularac, who had a magnificent tournament, was irrepressible, while he was better still against the Uruguayans, who carried him off the field after they'd lost 3–1. Russia, lucky to beat Uruguay, won the group, with the Yugoslavs second. But it was Yugoslavia who survived the quarter-finals.

In Santiago, they at long last beat their eternal 'bogeys', the West Germans, with a late goal by their little midfield halfback, Radakovic, playing with a bandaged head. They were much the more creative.

Brazil 'at home' in Viña del Mar, won a curious match against England, who had to take the field without the injured Peacock. Garrincha was in unstoppable form, his swerve and acceleration as irresistible as in Sweden. After 31 minutes, he showed another talent, getting up splendidly to head in a corner. England should have been two down when Flowers unaccountably passed across his own goal to Amarildo, but Springett saved brilliantly, and Hitchens equalised after Greaves' header came back from the bar.

Alas for Springett, however, he allowed Garrincha's second-half free kick to come back off his chest for Vavá to score easily, and later he was tricked by Garrincha's clever swerving long shot. Brazil were through, but they had been a little lucky.

In Arica, Chile, whose fans were growing more and more crazily excited, put out Russia. Again, Yachin had a poor game, badly placed for Leonel Sanchez's goal straight from a free kick after 10 minutes; still more at fault with Eladio Rojas' 35-yard second. Chislenko replied a couple of minutes later, but the 4–2–4 Chilean team held on to a narrow success.

Surprisingly, the Czechs beat the Hungarians 1–0 in Rancagua. For 80 minutes they were penned in their own half, while Hungary beat a tattoo on their goalposts. Schroiff, in goal, was unbeatable, and Scherer's breakaway goal in the 13th minute won the match. Tichy's 'equaliser' was ruled, disputably, offside.

In the semi-finals, Garrincha dashed Chile's hopes with another marvellous display. A magnificent 20-yard left-footer after nine minutes put Brazil ahead; a header from a corner doubled the lead. Toro, with a mighty free kick, made it 2–1, but just after half-time Vavá headed a vital goal from Garrincha's dropping corner-kick: 3–1. Leonel Sanchez made it 3–2, from a penalty, but Vavá tied up the match, heading in Zagalo's centre. Zagalo had worked with boundless stamina and decisive effect.

In a displeasing finale, Landa, Chile's centre-forward, and Garrincha were in turn sent off the field. Garrincha for kicking Rojas, Landa for a foul on Zito. As he made his way round the track, Garrincha had his head cut by a missile thrown from a frantically partisan crowd.

The Czechs, to everyone's amazement, prevailed again – over the talented Yugoslavs. At Viña del Mar, watched by a mere and miserable 5000, Schroiff was again the determining player. The Slavs had most of the game but, weak on the wings, could not turn their domination into more than Jerkovic's equalising goal. A breakaway allowed Scherer to give the Czechs the lead again; a silly handling offence by Markovic allowed the same player to decide the match from the penalty spot.

A tired Yugoslav team, with Sekularac even so the best player on the field, lost 1–0 to Chile in the third place game. Rojas' long shot, deflected, beat an excellent Soskic for the only goal of a dreary match.

In the final, Brazil once more had to play without Pelé. Playing at a slow, steady rhythm, with Kvasniak tireless and long-legged in midfield, the Czechs cleverly took the lead when Masopust ran on to Scherer's through pass. But alas for the Czechs, this was not to be a good day for Schroiff. He should have stopped Amarildo's equaliser from the narrowest of angles. In the second half, Amarildo whiplashed past his man to make a headed goal, under the bar, for Zito, and, 13 minutes from time, poor Schroiff dropped high lob into the sun by Djalma Santos and that was number three. Not a Brazilian victory to be compared with Stockholm; this was an older, more cautious team, without Pelé, with a slower Didi, with Garrincha well controlled by the experienced Czech defence. The Czechs had been distinguished losers.

**GROUP 1** (Arica)
Uruguay (0) 2, Colombia (1) 1
*Uruguay:* Sosa; Troche, Em. Alvarez; El. Alvarez, Mendez, Gonçalves; Rocha, Perez, Langon, Sasia, Cubilla.
*Colombia:* Sanchez; Zaluaga, Gonzalez, Lopez, Etcheverri; Silva, Coll; Aceros, Klinger, Gamboa, Arias.
*Scorers:* Cubilla, Sasia for Uruguay; Zaluaga for Colombia.

Russia (0) 2, Yugoslavia (0) 0
*Russia:* Yachin; Dubinski, Ostrovski; Voronin, Maslenkin, Netto; Metreveli, Ivanov, Ponedelnik, Kanevski, Meschki.
*Yugoslavia:* Soskic; Durkovic, Jusufi; Matus, Markovic, Popovic; Mujic, Sekularac, Jerkovic, Galic, Skoblar.
*Scorers:* Ivanov, Ponedelnik for Russia.

Yugoslavia (2) 3, Uruguay (1) 1
*Yugoslavia:* Soskic; Durkovic, Jusufi; Radakovic, Markovic, Popovic; Melic, Sekularac, Jerkovic, Galic, Skoblar.
*Uruguay:* Sosa; Troche, Em. Alvarez, El. Alvarez, Mendez; Gonçalves, Rocha; Cubilla, Cabrera, Sasia, Perez.
*Scorers:* Skoblar, Galic, Jerkovic for Yugoslavia; Cabrera for Uruguay.

Russia (3) 4, Colombia (1) 4
*Russia:* Yachin; Tchokelli, Ostrovski; Netto, Maslenkin, Voronin; Chislenko, Ivanov, Ponedelnik, Kanevski, Meschki.
*Colombia:* Sanchez; L. Gonzalez, Lopez, Alzate, Etcheverri; Serrano, Coll; Aceros, Rada, Klinger, C. Gonzalez.
*Scorers:* Ivanov (2), Chislenko, Ponedelnik for Russia; Aceros, Coll, Rada, Klinger for Colombia.

Russia (1) 2, Uruguay (0) 1
*Russia:* Yachin; Tchokelli, Ostrovski; Netto, Maslenkin, Voronin; Chislenko, Ivanov, Ponedelnik, Mamikin, Hussainov.
*Uruguay:* Sosa; Troche, El. Alvarez, Em. Alvarez, Mendez; Gonçalves, Cortes; Cubilla, Cabrera, Sasia, Perez.
*Scorers:* Mamikin, Ivanov for Russia; Sasia for Uruguay.

Yugoslavia (2) 5, Colombia (0) 0
*Yugoslavia:* Soskic; Durkovic, Yusufi; Radakovic, Markovic, Popovic; Ankovic, Sekularac, Jerkovic, Galic, Melic.
*Colombia:* Sanchez; Alzate, O. Gonzalez, Lopez, Etcheverri; Serrano, Coll; Aceros, Klinger, Rada, C. Gonzalez.
*Scorers:* Galic, Jerkovic (3), Melic for Yugoslavia.

|            | P | W | D | L | F | A  | Pts |
|------------|---|---|---|---|---|----|-----|
| Russia     | 3 | 2 | 1 | 0 | 8 | 5  | 5   |
| Yugoslavia | 3 | 2 | 0 | 1 | 8 | 3  | 4   |
| Uruguay    | 3 | 1 | 0 | 2 | 4 | 6  | 2   |
| Colombia   | 3 | 0 | 1 | 2 | 5 | 11 | 1   |

## GROUP 2 (Santiago)
Chile (1) 3, Switzerland (1) 1
*Chile:* Escuti; Eyzaguirre, R. Sanchez, Contreras, Navarro; Toro, Rojas; Ramirez, Landa, Fouilloux, L. Sanchez.
*Switzerland:* Elsener; Morf, Schneiter, Tacchella; Grobety, Weber; Allemann, Pottier, Eschmann, Wuthrich, Antenen.
*Scorers:* L. Sanchez (2), Ramirez for Chile; Wuthrich for Switzerland.

West Germany (0) 0, Italy (0) 0
*West Germany:* Fahrian; Novak, Schnellinger; Schulz, Erhardt, Szymaniak; Sturm, Haller, Seeler, Brülls, Schaefer.
*Italy:* Buffon; Losi, Robotti; Salvadore, Maldini, Radice; Ferrini, Rivera, Altafino, Sivori, Menichelli.

Chile (0) 2, Italy (0) 0
*Chile:* Escuti; Eyzaguirre, Contreras, R. Sanchez, Navarro; Toro, Rojas; Ramirez, Landa, Fouilloux, L. Sanchez.
*Italy:* Mattrel; David, Robotti; Salvadore, Janich, Tumburus; Mora, Maschio, Altafini, Ferrini, Menichelli.
*Scorers:* Ramirez, Toro for Chile.

West Germany (1) 2, Switzerland (0) 1
*West Germany:* Fahrian; Novak, Schnellinger; Schulz, Erhardt,
Szymaniak; Koslowski, Haller, Seeler, Brülls, Schaefer.
*Switzerland:* Elsener; Schneiter, Tacchella, Grobety; Wuthrich,
Weber; Antenen, Vonlanthen, Allemann, Eschmann, Durr.
*Scorers:* Brülls, Seeler for West Germany; Schneiter for Switzerland

West Germany (1) 2, Chile (0) 0
*West Germany:* Fahrian; Novak, Schnellinger; Schulz, Erhardt,
Giesemann; Krauss, Szymaniak, Seeler, Schaefer, Brülls.
*Chile:* Escuti; Eyzaguirre, Contreras, R. Sanchez, Navarro; Tobar,
Rojas; Moreno, Landa, L. Sanchez, Ramirez.
*Scorers:* Szymaniak (pen), Seeler for West Germany.

Italy (1) 3, Switzerland (0) 0
*Italy:* Buffon; Losi, Robotti; Salvadore, Maldini, Radice; Mora,
Bulgarelli, Sormani, Sivori, Pascutti.
*Switzerland:* Elsener; Schneiter, Meier, Tacchella; Grobety, Weber;
Antenen, Vonlanthen, Wuthrich, Allemann, Durr.
*Scorers:* Mora, Bulgarelli (2) for Italy.

|  | P | W | D | L | F | A | Pts |
|---|---|---|---|---|---|---|---|
| West Germany | 3 | 2 | 1 | 0 | 4 | 1 | 5 |
| Chile | 3 | 2 | 0 | 1 | 5 | 3 | 4 |
| Italy | 3 | 1 | 1 | 1 | 3 | 2 | 3 |
| Switzerland | 3 | 0 | 0 | 3 | 2 | 8 | 0 |

**GROUP 3** (Viña del Mar)
Brazil (0) 2, Mexico (0) 0
*Brazil:* Gilmar; D. Santos, Mauro, Zozimo, N. Santos; Zito, Didi;
Garrincha, Vavá, Pelé, Zagalo.
*Mexico:* Carbajal; Del Muro, Cardenas, Sepulveda, Villegas; Reyes,
Najera; Del Aguila, Hernandez, Jasso, Diaz.
*Scorers:* Zagalo, Pelé for Brazil.

Czechoslovakia (0) 1, Spain (0) 0
*Czechoslovakia:* Schroiff; Lala, Novak; Pluskal, Popluhar, Masopust;
Stibranyi, Scherer, Kvasniak, Adamec, Jelinck.
*Spain:* Carmelo; Rivilla, Reija; Segarra, Santamaría, Garay; Del Sol,
Martinez, Puskas, Suarez, Gento.
*Scorer:* Stibranyi for Czechoslovakia.

Brazil (0) 0, Czechoslovakia (0) 0
*Brazil:* Gilmar; D. Santos, Mauro, Zozimo, N. Santos; Zito, Didi;
Garrincha, Vavá, Pelé, Zagalo.
*Czechoslovakia:* Schroiff; Lala, Novak; Pluskal, Popluhar, Masopust;
Stibranyi, Scherer, Kvasniak, Adamec, Jelinck.

Spain (0) 1, Mexico (0) 0
*Spain:* Carmelo; Rodri, Garcia; Verges, Santamaria, Pachin; Del Sol, Peiró, Puskas, Suarez, Gento.
*Mexico:* Carbajal; Del Muro, Cardenas, Sepulveda, Jauregui; Reyes, Najera; Del Aguila, H. Hernandez, Jasso, Diaz.
*Scorer:* Peiró for Spain.

Brazil (0) 2, Spain (1) 1
*Brazil:* Gilmar; D. Santos, Mauro, Zozimo, N. Santos, Zito, Didi; Garrincha, Vavá, Amarildo, Zagalo.
*Spain:* Araguistain; Rodri, Gracia; Verges, Echevarria, Pachin; Collar, Adelardo, Puskas, Peiró, Gento.
*Scorers:* Amarildo (2) for Brazil; Adelardo for Spain.

Mexico (2) 3, Czechoslovakia (1) 1
*Mexico:* Carbajal; Del Muro, Cardenas, Sepulveda, Jauregui; Reyes, Najera; Del Aguila, A. Hernandez, H. Hernandez, Diaz.
*Czechoslovakia:* Schroiff; Lala, Novak; Pluskal, Popluhar, Masopust; Stibranyi, Scherer, Kvasniak, Adamec, Masek.
*Scorers:* Diaz, Del Aguila, H. Hernandez (pen) for Mexico; Masek for Czechoslovakia.

|  | P | W | D | L | F | A | Pts |
|---|---|---|---|---|---|---|---|
| Brazil | 3 | 2 | 1 | 0 | 4 | 1 | 5 |
| Czechoslovakia | 3 | 1 | 1 | 1 | 2 | 3 | 3 |
| Mexico | 3 | 1 | 0 | 2 | 3 | 4 | 2 |
| Spain | 3 | 1 | 0 | 2 | 2 | 3 | 2 |

**GROUP 4** (Rancagua)
Argentina (1) 1, Bulgaria (0) 0
*Argentina:* Roma; Navarro, Baez, Sainz, Marzolini; Sacchi, Rossi; Facundo, Pagani, Sanfilippo, Belen.
*Bulgaria:* Naidenov; Rakarov, Kotov; Kostov, Dimitrov, Kovatchev; Diev, Velitchkov, Iliev, Yakimov, Kolev.
*Scorer:* Facundo for Argentina.

Hungary (1) 2, England (0) 1
*Hungary:* Grosics; Matrai, Sarosi; Solymosi, Meszoly, Sipos; Sandor, Rakosi, Albert, Tichy, Fenyvesi.
*England:* Springett; Armfield, Wilson; Moore, Norman, Flowers; Douglas, Greaves, Hitchens, Haynes, Charlton.
*Scorers:* Tichy, Albert for Hungary; Flowers (pen) for England.

England (2) 3, Argentina (0) 1
*England:* Springett; Armfield, Wilson; Moore, Norman, Flowers; Douglas, Greaves, Peacock, Haynes, Charlton.
*Argentina:* Roma; Capp, Baez, Navarro, Marzolini; Sacchi, Rattin; Oleniak, Sosa, Sanfilippo, Belen.
*Scorers:* Flowers (pen), Charlton, Greaves for England; Sanfilippo for Argentina.

Hungary (4) 6, Bulgaria (0) 1
*Hungary:* Ilku; Matrai, Sarosi; Solymosi, Meszoly, Sipos, Sandor, Rakosi, Alberr, Tichy, Fenyvesi.
*Bulgaria:* Naidenov; Rakarov, Kotov; Kostov, Dimitrov, Kovatchev; Sokolov, Velitchkov, Asparoukhov, Kolev, Dermendiev.
*Scorers:* Albert (3), Tichy (2), Solymosi for Hungary; Sokolov for Bulgaria.

Argentina (0) 0, Hungary (0) 0
*Argentina:* Dominguez; Capp, Sainz, Delgado, Marzolini; Sacchi, Pando; Facundo, Pagani, Oleniak, Gonzales.
*Hungary:* Grosics; Matrai, Sarosi; Solymosi, Meszoly, Sipos; Kuharszki, Gorocs, Monostroi, Tichy, Rakosi.

England (0) 0, Bulgaria (0) 0
*England:* Springett; Armfield, Wilson; Moore, Norman, Flowers; Douglas, Greaves, Peacock, Haynes, Charlton.
*Bulgaria:* Naidenov; Rakarov, Jetchev; D. Kostov, Dimitrov, Kovatchev; A. Kostov, Velitchkov, Iliev, Kolev, Yakimov.

|           | P | W | D | L | F | A | Pts |
|-----------|---|---|---|---|---|---|-----|
| Hungary   | 3 | 2 | 1 | 0 | 8 | 2 | 5   |
| England   | 3 | 1 | 1 | 1 | 4 | 3 | 3   |
| Argentina | 3 | 1 | 1 | 1 | 2 | 3 | 3   |
| Bulgaria  | 3 | 0 | 1 | 2 | 1 | 7 | 1   |

## QUARTER-FINALS
Yugoslavia (0) 1, West Germany (0) 0 (Santiago)
*Yugoslavia:* Soskic; Durkovic, Jusufi; Radakovic, Markovic, Popovic; Kovacevic, Sekularac, Jerkovic, Galic, Skoblar.
*West Germany:* Fahrian; Novak, Schnellinger; Schulz, Erhardt, Giesemann; Haller, Szymaniak, Seeler, Brülls, Schaefer.
*Scorer:* Radakovic for Yugoslavia.

Brazil (1) 3, England (1) 1 (Viña del Mar)
*Brazil:* Gilmar; D. Santos, Mauro, Zozimo, N. Santos; Zito, Didi; Garrincha, Vavá, Amarildo, Zagalo.
*England:* Springett; Armfield, Wilson; Moore, Norman, Flowers; Douglas, Greaves, Hitchens, Haynes, Charlton.
*Scorers:* Garrincha (2), Vavá for Brazil; Hitchens for England.

Chile (2) 2, Russia (1) 1 (Arica)
*Chile:* Escutti; Eyzaguirre, Contreras, R. Sanchez, Navarro; Toro, Rojas; Ramirez, Landa, Tobar, L. Sanchez.
*Russia:* Yachin; Tchokelli, Ostrovski; Voronin, Maslenkin, Netto; Chislenko, Ivanov, Ponedelnik, Mamikin, Meshki.
*Scorers:* L. Sanchez, Rojas for Chile; Chislenko for Russia.

Czechoslovakia (1) 1, Hungary (0) 0 (Rancagua)
*Czechoslovakia:* Schroiff; Lala, Novak; Pluskal, Popluhar, Masopust; Pospichal, Scherer, Kvasniak, Kadraba, Jelinek.
*Hungary:* Grosics; Matrai, Sorisi; Solymosi, Meszoly, Sipos; Sandor, Rakosi, Albert, Tichy, Fenyvesi.
*Scorer:* Scherer for Czechoslovakia.

**SEMI-FINALS**
Brazil (2) 4, Chile (1) 2 (Santiago)
*Brazil:* Gilmar; D. Santos, Mauro, Zozimo, N. Santos; Zito, Didì; Garrincha, Vavá, Amarildo, Zagalo.
*Chile:* Escutti; Eyzaguirre, Contreras, R. Sanchez, Rodriguez; Toro, Rojas; Ramirez, Landa, Tobar, L. Sanchez.
*Scorers:* Garrincha (2), Vavá (2) for Brazil; Toro, L. Sanchez (pen) for Chile.

Czechoslovakia (0) 3, Yugoslavia (0) 1 (Viña del Mar)
*Czechoslovakia:* Schroiff; Lala, Novak; Pluskal, Popluhar, Masupust; Pospichal, Scherer, Kvasniak, Kadraba, Jelinek.
*Yugoslavia:* Soskic; Durkovic, Jusufi; Radakovic, Markovic, Popovic; Sujakovic, Sekularac, Jerkovic, Galic, Skoblar.
*Scorers:* Kadraba, Scherer (2), for Czechoslovakia; Jerkovic for Yugoslavia.

**THIRD PLACE MATCH**
Chile (0) 1, Yugoslavia (0) 0 (Santiago)
*Chile:* Godoy; Eyzaguirre, Cruz, R. Sanchez, Rodriguez; Toro, Rojas; Ramirez, Campos, Tobar, L. Sanchez.
*Yugoslavia:* Soskic; Durkovic, Svinjarevic; Radakovic, Markovic, Popovic; Kovacevic, Sekularac, Jerkovic, Galic, Skoblar.
*Scorer:* Rojas for Chile.

**FINAL**
Brazil (1) 3, Czechoslovakia (1) 1 (Santiago)
*Brazil:* Gilmar; D. Santos, Mauro, Zozimo, N. Santos; Zito, Didì; Garrincha, Vavá, Amarildo, Zagalo.
*Czechoslovakia;* Schroiff; Tichy, Novak; Pluskal, Popluhar, Masopust; Pospichal, Scherer, Kvasniak, Kadraba, Jelinek.
*Scorers:* Amarildo, Zito, Vavá for Brazil; Masopust for Czechoslovakia.

**Leading Scorers:** Albert (Hungary, Ivanov (Russia), L. Sanchez (Chile), Garrincha, Vavá (Brazil), Jerkovic (Yugoslavia) each 4.

**WORLD CUP 1966 – England**
England, as Alf Ramsey had promised, won the World Cup. They won it, in the end, deservedly, with two fine performances in semi-final and

final, won it without Jimmy Greaves, won it despite a brutal setback in the last minute of the final itself.

Starting painfully and laboriously, their attack terribly unimpressive in the three qualifying games, England 'came good' when it was most necessary – in the ill-tempered quarter-final against Argentina (when the Argentinians went virtually berserk in the tunnel at the end). Geoff Hurst, the West Ham United player, who had looked sadly out of form as recently as the tour match against Denmark in Copenhagen, came back into the team against Argentina to become, perhaps, the decisive force in England's success. His three goals in the final established a new record.

In general terms, it was a disappointing World Cup, with no team to match the Brazilians of 1958 and 1962 or the Hungarians of 1954. England had a superb defence, but their 4–3–3 formation, generally without specialised wingers, was by no means as impressive in attack. What saved them was the eruption of Hurst, the sudden blossoming of Bobby Charlton in semi-final and final, the energy of Alan Ball against Portugal followed by his astonishing, all-round performance against the West Germans.

Brazil were shown to be clearly in decline. This time they and their manager, Feola, paid the penalty for an exaggerated reliance on old names, old faces. An injury to Pelé in the first game had an effect on them which it never had in Chile. Good young players had, it's true, been left behind, but obviously a period of retrenchment was needed.

The surprise of the tournament were the lively little North Koreans, who astonished and humiliated the listless Italians. Quick, intelligent, learning from game to game, they were wonderfully popular with the Middlesbrough crowd, and gave Portugal an enormous scare in the quarter-finals.

The Hungarians, with a novel tactical formation, played superbly against Brazil but were betrayed by poor goalkeeping. Portugal, with Eusebio the leading scorer and perhaps the outstanding player of the whole tournament, might have done better still had their defence in any way matched their attack. As for the West Germans, the runners-up, their powerful, well-balanced side, though it never lived up to its opening flourish against Switzerland, was full of talent.

Fittingly, the tournament started with that epitome of modern World Cups, a goalless draw. Uruguay went out to stop England from scoring, massed eight and nine men in defence, and succeeded with little trouble. An ingenuously chosen England team, with Ball as a pseudo-winger and the essentially destructive Stiles at linking wing-half, played into their hands. The strikers and schemers alike were impotent against the tough, rhythmic, immensely professional Uruguayans, responding as always to the challenge of a World Cup.

It was Pelé, appropriately, who scored the first goal of the tournament next day – the player who, above all others, was expected to dominate the tournament. After 14 minutes of Brazil's match at Everton with Bulgaria, he smashed in a pheonomenal right-footed free-kick. In the

135

second half, an equally remarkable free-kick by Garrincha gave Brazil a second, but they were not over impressive. Pelé dazzlingly apart, the team often stuttered. He himself was ruthlessly marked by Zhechev.

This turned out to be the most exciting group of all. Hungary and Portugal, who would each beat Brazil and qualify, met at Old Trafford, Portugal winning thanks to a couple of errors by the Hungarian 'keeper, Szentmihalyi. The Hungarians' formation, three link-men breaking to support two strikers, was promising, however, and they came to fulfilment at Everton three days later against Brazil. Brazil severely felt the loss of Pelé; and the burden of years carried by Djalma Santos, Bellini, and Garrincha. Moreover, they left Florian Albert free to dominate the field. Bene, the little right winger, wriggled through for a lovely individual goal after only three minutes, but Brazil equalised when Tostão, making his World Cup debut, drove in the rebound from Lima's free kick. However, under pouring rain, Hungary took firm hold of the game. Albert and Bene, in the second half, made a spectacularly shot goal for Farkas, Meszöly scored the third from a penalty. It was Brazil's first World Cup defeat since 1954.

Portugal, helped by an own goal and a silly back-pass, easily beat Bulgaria at Old Trafford, then tackled Brazil at Goodison. Desperately, Brazil made nine belated changes, giving a World Cup debut to seven men. But Manga was shaky in goal. After 14 minutes, he weakly pushed out Eusebio's cross for Simões to head in, then the huge Torres nodded Coluna's free kick across for Eusebio to head a second. Pelé was back, but struggling, and a brutal, gratuitous foul by Morais put him definitively out. Late on, Rildo came up to whip home a goal, but the excellent Eusebio drove in Portugal's third after a right wing corner. Brazil were out.

England unimpressively beat Mexico and France 2–0 to win Group 2. The Mexicans staked everything on defence, but were at last breached by a marvellous right-foot goal from Bobby Charlton, Hunt scoring the second after a superb through pass by Charlton had split the defence for Greaves. Hunt scored twice more against a French team reduced to 10 by Herbin's early injury, but both midfield and defence were unconvincing. Uruguay, with minimal enterprise, beat France at the White City, drew 0–0 with Mexico, and came second.

In Group 3, West Germany unmasked the splendid Franz Beckenbauer who scored two goals against a Swiss team that suspended two leading players, Kuhn and Leimgruber, for breaking curfew. The Argentinians, elegant but ruthless, beat Spain, whose use of Suarez was harsh at Villa Park. Argentina scored twice through the opportunism of the gifted Luis Artime, well abetted by Onega. When they and the West Germans met, it was a horrid, goalless affair in which Argentina's fearsome Albrecht was sent off. Argentina then beat Switzerland, West Germany disposed of a lively Spain, and both qualified.

In Group 4, the North Koreans finished poorly, fought bravely, but were physically overwhelmed at Ayresome Park by Russia. Italy beat Chile in a bloodless reprise of the Battle of Santiago, left out Rivera, and surprisingly went down to Russia at Sunderland, Chislenko scoring a fine only goal.

So the cataclysm of a Tuesday that saw North Korea beat Italy; Brazil lose to Portugal and go out. Having drawn with Chile, North Korea ran hard and fast against a flaccid Italy, who lost Bulgarelli after 34 minutes with a damaged knee after he had fouled an opponent. Seven minutes later Pak Doo Ik scored his unforgettable goal and Italy were on their knees. Russia and North Korea went through.

England's quarter-final with Argentina at Wembley remains notorious; the match which after Alf Ramsey expressed the hope that his next opponents would not 'act as animals'. Argentina had the all-round skill to win, but preferred a policy of cynical obstruction and endless petty fouling. Herr Kreitlein, the tiny, bald West German referee, took names with manic zeal, and eventually sent off the towering Argentinian captain, Antonio Rattin, for dissent and 'the look on his face'. Still, England found it hard. Geoff Hurst, brought in to replace the injured Greaves, forced Roma to an incredible save early in the first half and at last beat him with a fine, glided header to Peter's left wing cross.

At Everton, Portugal found themselves 3–0 down to the dazzling North Koreans in 20 minutes. Then Eusebio took the game by the scruff of the neck and scored four goals (two of them penalties); a couple before half-time, a couple after. Running out of steam, the gallant Koreans lost 5–3 – and subsided anew into anonymity.

Russia surprisingly beat Hungary, betrayed again by poor goal-keeping. Gelei, fumbling a shot and failing with a cross, took blame for both Russian goals; Rakosi missed an open goal at the Russian end, and the technically superior Hungarians had to settle for Bene's goal.

At Hillsbrough, more mayhem. Two Uruguayans were sent off and West Germany beat their depleted team 4–0. Uruguay were incensed when Schnellinger seemed to handle on the line with impunity, then Held's shot was freakishly deflected home off Haller. Troche was expelled for kicking Emmerich, Silva for fouling Haller.

In the semi-finals, England took wing at last in a memorable game with Portugal, Bobby Charlton rampant; West Germany won a dismal struggle against Russia at Everton. There were cries of 'conspiracy' when it was known England would play at Wembley, accusations that Sir Stanley Rous had had his way. The truth was that Rous wanted the game played at Everton and was overruled by the World Cup committee!

England, with Stiles playing Eusebio out of the match and galvanising his defence, dominated the match, but found goals hard to score. Bobby Charlton got both. After 30 minutes, Wilson put Hunt through, Pereira couldn't hold the shot, and Charlton followed up. Eleven minutes from time, Hurst forced his way to the right hand goal-line and pulled the ball back for Charlton to score again. Three minutes later, Eusebio converted a penalty after Jackie Charlton punched

Torres' clever header, but Stiles and Banks took England safely through the difficult closing minutes.

At Everton, squalor. Sabo hurt himself early on trying to foul Beckenbauer, Chislenko had himself sent off in the second half for kicking Held soon after being badly hurt when Schnellinger went through to make the second goal. Even against nine fit men, Germany had a hard time of it, and Russia actually scored two minutes from time when Tilkowski dropped a cross. A skilful, swerving shot by Beckenbauer beat the splendid Yachin for Germany's second goal.

The third place match was equally dreary. Portugal won, for what it mattered. Khurtsilava's foolish hand-ball allowed Eusebio to score another penalty and take his total of goals to nine, highest of the tournament. Pereira's error gave Malafeev the equiliser, but Torres scored the winner when Augusto nodded down Simões' cross.

England won the dramatic final, so maintaining a 65-year-old unbeaten record against Germany. Greaves was omitted from their team, Hunt controversially stayed, missing a good chance in the first half, throwing away another with an inept pass in the second; errors that made extra time necessary. For the Germans, seemingly well beaten at 2–1, hit back in the last minute to score through Weber, on the far post, after Emmerich's free-kick; itself dubiously given against Jackie Charlton. They had opened the scoring, after 13 minutes, when Wilson uncharacteristically headed a cross straight to Haller's feet. Hurst headed in Moore's quickly taken free-kick to equalise, and Peters put England ahead in the second half when Weber blocked Hurst's shot after a corner.

At the last, it was Ball's astonishing stamina, his inextinguishable running, that gave England victory in extra time. His was the run and cross which, after 100 minutes, allowed Hurst to smash the ball in off the crossbar. Bakhramov, the Russian linesman, gave a goal that is still contested in West Germany. Perhaps we shall never be quite sure whether the ball crossed the line. In any case, Hurst, with his left foot, scored a fourth goal as England broke away in the closing seconds.

England's morale and resistance were a credit to Alf Ramsey, who unquestionably inspired this team. The Germans must still regret Helmut Schoen's decision to use Beckenbauer so negatively as the guardian of Bobby Charlton. Beckenbauer, nonetheless, was still among the best of his team, with Schultz, Held, and Seeler. But Alan Ball was the true hero of the day.

## GROUP 1
England (0) 0, Uruguay (0) 0 (Wembley)
*England:* Banks (Leicester City); Cohen (Fulham), Wilson (Everton); Stiles (Manchester United), J. Charlton (Leeds United), Moore (West Ham United); Ball (Blackpool), Greaves (Spurs), R. Charlton (Manchester United), Hunt (Liverpool), Connelly (Manchester United).
*Uruguay:* Mazurkiewicz; Troche, Ubinas; Gonçalves, Manicera, Caetano; Cortes, Viera, Silva, Rocha, Perez.

France (0) 1, Mexico (0) 1 (Wembley)
*France:* Aubour; Djorkaeff, Budzinski, Artelesa, De Michele; Bosquier, Herbin, Bonnel; Combin, Gondet, Hausser.
*Mexico:* Calderon; Chaires, Pena, Nunez, Hernandez; Diaz, Mercado, Reyes; Borja, Fragoso, Padilla.
*Scorers:* Borja for Mexico; Hausser for France.

Uruguay (2) 2, France (1) 1 (White City)
*Uruguay:* Mazurkiewicz; Troche, Ubinas; Gonçalves, Manicera, Caetano; Viera, Cortes, Rocha, Sacia, Perez.
*France:* Aubour; Djorkaeff, Artelesa, Budzinski, Bosquier; Bonnel, Simon; Herbet, Gondet, De Bourgoing, Hausser.
*Scorers:* Rocha, Cortes for Uruguay; De Bourgoing (pen) for France.

England (1) 2, Mexico (0) 0 (Wembley)
*England:* Banks (Leicester City); Cohen (Fulham), Wilson (Everton); Stiles (Manchester United), J. Charlton, (Leeds United), Moore (West Ham United); Paine (Southampton), Greaves (Spurs), R. Charlton (Manchester United), Hunt (Liverpool), Peters (West Ham United).
*Mexico:* Calderon; Del Muro; Chaires, Pena Nunez, Hernandez; Diaz, Jauregui, Reyes; Borja, Padilla.
*Scorers:* R. Charlton, Hunt for England.

Uruguay (0) 0, Mexico (0) 0 (Wembley)
*Uruguay:* Mazurkiewicz; Troche; Ubinas, Gonçalves, Manicera, Caetano; Viera, Rocha, Cortes, Sacia, Perez.
*Mexico:* Carbajal; Chaires, Pena, Nunez, Hernandez; Diaz, Mercado; Reyes, Cisneros, Borja, Padilla.

England (1) 2, France (0) 0 (Wembley)
*England:* Banks (Leicester City); Cohen (Fulham), Wilson (Everton); Stiles (Manchester United), J. Charlton (Leeds United), Moore (West Ham United); Callaghan (Liverpool), Greaves (Spurs), R. Charlton (Manchester United), Hunt (Liverpool), Peters (West Ham United).
*France:* Aubour; Djorkaeff, Artelesa, Budzinski, Bosquier; Bonnel, Herbin, Simon; Herbet, Gondet, Hausser.
*Scorer:* Hunt (2) for England.

| | P | W | D | L | F | A | Pts |
|---|---|---|---|---|---|---|---|
| England | 3 | 2 | 1 | 0 | 4 | 0 | 5 |
| Uruguay | 3 | 1 | 2 | 0 | 2 | 1 | 4 |
| Mexico | 3 | 0 | 2 | 1 | 1 | 3 | 2 |
| France | 3 | 0 | 1 | 2 | 2 | 5 | 1 |

## GROUP 2
West Germany (3) 5, Switzerland (0) 0 (Hillsborough, Sheffield)
*West Germany:* Tilkowski; Hottges, Schulz, Weber, Schnellinger; Beckenbauer, Haller; Brülls, Seeler, Overath, Held.

*Switzerland:* Elsener; Grobety, Schneiter; Techella, Fuhrer, Bani; Durr, Odermatt, Kunzli, Hosp, Schindelholz.
*Scorers:* Held, Haller (2) (1 pen), Beckenbauer 2 for West Germany.

Argentina (0) 2, Spain (0) 1 (Villa Park, Birmingham)
*Argentina:* Roma; Perfumo, Marzolini; Ferreiro, Rattin, Albrecht; Solari, Gonzalez, Artime, Onega, Mas.
*Spain:* Iribar; Sanchis, Eladio; Pirri, Gallego, Zoco; Ufarte, Del Sol, Peiro, Suarez, Gento.
*Scorers:* Artime (2) for Argentine; Pirri for Spain.

Spain (0) 2, Switzerland (1) 1 (Hillsborough, Sheffield)
*Spain:* Iribar; Sanchis, Reija; Pirri, Callego, Zoco; Amancio, Del Sol, Peiro, Suarez, Gento.
*Switzerland:* Elsener; Brodmann, Fuhrer; Leimgruber, Armbruster, Stierli; Bani, Kuhn, Gottardi, Hosp, Quentin.
*Scorers:* Sanchis, Amancio for Spain; Quentin for Switzerland.

Argentine (0) 0, West Germany (0) 0 (Villa Park Birmingham)
*Argentina:* Roma; Perfumo, Marzolini; Ferreiro, Rattin, Albrecht; Solari, Gonzalez, Artime, Onega, Mas.
*West Germany:* Tilkowski; Hottges, Schulz, Weber, Schnellinger; Beckenbauer, Haller, Brülls, Seeler, Overath, Held.

Argentina (0) 2, Switzerland (0) 0 (Villa Park, Birmingham)
*Argentina:* Roma; Perfumo, Marzolini; Ferreiro, Rattin, Calics; Solari, Gonzalez, Artime, Onega, Mas.
*Switzerland:* Eichmann; Fuhrer, Brodmann; Kuhn, Armbruster, Stierli; Bani, Kunzli, Gottardi, Hosp, Quentin.
*Scorers:* Artime, Onega for Argentina.

West Germany (1) 2, Spain (1) 1 (Villa Park, Birmingham)
*West Germany:* Tilkowski; Hottges, Schulz, Weber, Schnellinger; Beckenbauer, Overath; Kramer, Seeler, Held, Emmerich.
*Spain:* Iribar; Sanchis, Reija; Glaria, Callego, Zoco; Amancio, Adelardo, Marcelino, Fuste, Lapetra.
*Scorers:* Emmerich and Seeler for West Germany; Fuste for Spain.

|  | P | W | D | L | F | A | Pts |
|---|---|---|---|---|---|---|---|
| West Germany | 3 | 2 | 1 | 0 | 7 | 1 | 5 |
| Argentina | 3 | 2 | 1 | 0 | 4 | 1 | 5 |
| Spain | 3 | 1 | 0 | 2 | 4 | 5 | 2 |
| Switzerland | 3 | 0 | 0 | 3 | 1 | 9 | 0 |

## GROUP 3
Brazil (1) 2, Bulgaria (0) 0 (Goodison Park, Liverpool)
*Brazil:* Gilmar; D. Santos, Bellini, Altair, Paolo Henrique; Edilson, Lima; Garrincha, Pelé, Alcindo, Jairzinho.
140

*Bulgaria:* Neidenov; Chalamanov, Vutzov, Gaganelov, Penev; Kitov, Zhechev, Yakimov; Dermendjiev, Asparoukhov, Kolev.
*Scorers:* Pelé, Garrincha for Brazil.


Portugal (1) 3, Hungary (0) 1 (Old Trafford, Manchester)
*Portugal:* Carvalho; Morais, Baptista, Vicente, Hilario; Graça, Coluna; Augusto, Eusebio, Torres, Simões.
*Hungary:* Szentmihalyi; Matrai, Kaposzta; Sovari, Meszoly, Sipos; Bene, Nagy, Albert, Farkas, Rakosi.
*Scorers:* Augusto (2), Torres for Portugal; Bene for Hungary.


Hungary (1) 3, Brazil (1) 1 (Goodison Park, Liverpool)
*Hungary:* Gelei; Kaposzta, Matrai, Sipos, Szepesi; Mathesz, Meszoly; Bene, Albert, Farkas, Rakosi.
*Brazil:* Gilmar; D. Santos, Bellini, Altair, Paolo Henrique; Lima, Gerson; Garrincha, Alcindo, Tostão, Jairzinho.
*Scorers:* Bene, Farkas, Meszoly (pen) for Hungary; Tostão for Brazil.


Portugal (2) 3, Bulgaria (0) 0 (Old Trafford, Manchester)
*Portugal:* José Pereira; Festa, Germano, Vicente, Hilario; Graça, Coluna; Augusto, Eusebio, Torres, Simões.
*Bulgaria:* Naidenov; Chalamanov, Vutzov, Gaganelov, Penev; Zechev, Yakimov; Dermendjiev, Zhekov, Asparoukhov, Kostov.
*Scorers:* Vutzov (o.g.), Eusebio, Torres for Portugal.


Portugal (2) 3, Brazil (0) 1 (Goodison Park, Liverpool)
*Portugal:* José Pereira; Morais, Baptista, Vicente, Hilario; Graça, Coluna, Augusto; Eusebio, Torres, Simões.
*Brazil:* Manga; Fidelis, Brito, Orlando, Rildo; Denilson, Lima; Jair, Silva, Pelé, Parana.
*Scorers:* Simoes, Eusebio (2) for Portugal; Rildo for Brazil.


Hungary (2) 3, Bulgaria (1) 1 (Old Trafford, Manchester)
*Hungary:* Gelei; Kaposzta, Matrai, Meszoly, Sipos, Szepesi; Mathesz, Albert, Rakosi; Bene, Farkas.
*Bulgaria:* Simenov; Penev, Largov, Vutzov, Gaganelov; Zhechev, Dadidov; Kotkov, Asparoukhov, Yakimov, Kolev.
*Scorers:* Davidov (o.g.), Meszoly, Bene for Hungary; Asparoukhov for Bulgaria.


| | P | W | D | L | F | A | Pts |
|---|---|---|---|---|---|---|---|
| Portugal | 3 | 3 | 0 | 0 | 9 | 2 | 6 |
| Hungary | 3 | 2 | 0 | 1 | 7 | 5 | 4 |
| Brazil | 3 | 1 | 0 | 2 | 4 | 6 | 2 |
| Bulgaria | 3 | 0 | 0 | 3 | 1 | 8 | 0 |

## GROUP 4

Russia (2) 3, North Korea (0) 0 (Middlesbrough)
*Russia:* Kavazashvili; Ponomarev, Chesternjiev, Khurtsilava, Ostrovski; Sabo, Schinava; Chislenko, Malafeev, Banichevski, Khusainov.
*North Korea:* Li Chan Myung; Pak Li Sup, Shin Yung Kyoo, Lim

Zoong Sun, Kang Bong Chil; Pak Seung Din, Im Seung Hwi; Han Bong Jin, Pak Doo Ik, Kang Ryong-Woon, Kim Seung II.
*Scorers:* Malafeev (2), Banichevski for Russia.

Italy (1) 2, Chile (0) 0 (Sunderland)
*Italy:* Albertosi; Burgnich, Facchetti; Rosato, Salvadore, Lodetti; Perani, Bulgarelli, Mazzola, Rivera, Barison,
*Chile:* Olivares; Eyzaguirre, Cruz, Figueroa, Villanueva; Prieto, Marcos; Araya, Tobar, Fouilloux, Sanchez.
*Scorers:* Barison, Mazzola for Italy.

Chile (1) 1, North Korea (0) 1 (Middlesbrough)
*Chile:* Olivares; Valentini, Cruz; Figueroa, Villanueva, Prieto; Marcos, Fouilloux, Landa, Araya, Sanchez.
*North Korea:* Li Chan Myung; Pak Li Sup, Shin Yung Kyoo, Kim Joon Sun, O Yoon Kyung; Pak Seung Jin, Im Seung Hwi; Han Bong Jin, Pak Doo Ik, Ri Dong Woon, Kim Seung II.
*Scorers:* Marcos (pen) for Chile; Pak Sung Jin for North Korea.

Russia (0) 1, Italy (0) 0 (Sunderland)
*Russia:* Yachin; Ponomarev, Chesternjiev, Khurtsilava, Danilov; Sabo, Voronin; Chislenko, Malafeev, Banichevski, Khusainov.
*Italy:* Albertosi; Burgnich, Facchetti; Rosato, Salvadore, Leoncini; Meroni, Lodetti, Mazzola, Bulgarelli, Pascutti.
*Scorer:* Chislenko for Russia.

North Korea (1) 1, Italy (0) 0 (Middlesbrough)
*North Korea:* Li Chan Myung; Lim Zoong Sun, Shin Yung Kyoo; Ha Jung Won, O Yoon Kyung, Im Seung Hwi; Han Bong Jin, Pak Doo Ik, Pak Seung Zin, Kim Bong Hwan, Yan Sung Kook.
*Italy:* Albertosi; Landini, Facchetti; Guarneri, Janich, Fogli; Perani, Bulgarelli, Mazzola, Rivera, Barison.
*Scorer:* Pak Doo Ik for North Korea.

Russia (1) 2, Chile (1) 1 (Sunderland)
*Russia:* Kavazashvili; Getmanov, Chesternjiev, Afonin, Ostrovski; Voronin, Korneev; Metreveli, Serebrianikov, Markarov, Porkujan.
*Chile:* Olivares; Valentini, Cruz, Figueroa, Villaneuva; Marcos, Prieto; Araya, Landa, Yavar, Sanchez.
*Scorers:* Porkujan (2) for Russia; Marcos for Chile.

|          | P | W | D | L | F | A | Pts |
|----------|---|---|---|---|---|---|-----|
| Russia   | 3 | 3 | 0 | 0 | 6 | 1 | 6   |
| North Korea | 3 | 1 | 1 | 1 | 2 | 4 | 3 |
| Italy    | 3 | 1 | 0 | 2 | 2 | 2 | 2   |
| Chile    | 3 | 0 | 1 | 2 | 2 | 5 | 1   |

## QUARTER-FINALS

England (0) 1, Argentina (0) 0 (Wembley)
*England:* Banks (Leicester City); Cohen (Fulham), Wilson (Everton); Stiles (Manchester United), J. Charlton (Leeds United), Moore (West Ham United); Ball (Blackpool), Hurst (West Ham United), R. Charlton, (Manchester United), Hunt (Liverpool), Peters (West Ham United).
*Argentina:* Roma; Ferreiro, Perfumo, Albrecht, Marzolini; Gonzalez, Rattin, Onega; Solari, Artime, Mas.
*Scorer:* Hurst for England.

West Germany (1) 4, Uruguay (0) 0 (Sheffield)
*West Germany:* Tilkowski; Hottges, Weber, Schulz, Schnellinger; Beckenbauer, Haller, Overath, Seeler, Held, Emmerich.
*Uruguay:* Mazurkiewicz; Troche; Ubinas, Gonçalves, Manicera, Caetano; Salva, Rocha; Silva, Cortez, Perez.
*Scorers:* Held, Beckenbauer, Seeler, Haller for West Germany.

*Portugal* (2) 5, *North Korea* (3) 3 (Goodison)
*Portugal:* José Pereira; Morais, Baptista, Vicente, Hilario; Graça, Coluna; Augusto, Eusebio, Torres, Simões.
*North Korea:* Li Chan Myung; Rim Yung Sum, Shin Yung Kyoo, Ha Jung Won, O Yoon Kyung; Pak Seung Jin, Im Seung Hwi; Han Bong Jin, Pak Doo Ik, Li Dong Woon, Yang Sung Kook.
*Scorers:* Eusebio 4 (2 pen), Augusto for Portugal; Pak Seung Jin, Yang Sung Kook, Li Dong Woon for North Korea.

Russia (1) 2, Hungary (0) 1 (Sunderland)
*Russia:* Yachin; Ponomarev, Chesternjiev, Voronin, Danilov; Sabo, Khusainov; Chislenko, Banichevski, Malafeev, Porkujan.
*Hungary:* Gelei; Matrai, Kaposzta, Meszoly, Sipos, Szepesi; Nagy, Albert, Rakosi; Bene, Farkas.
*Scorers:* Chislenko, Portkujan for Russia; Bene for Hungary.

## SEMI-FINALS

West Germany (1) 2, Russia (0) 1 (Goodison)
*West Germany:* Tilkowski; Hottges, Weber, Schulz, Schnellinger; Beckenbauer, Haller, Overath; Seeler, Held, Emmerich.
*Russia:* Yachin; Ponomarev, Chesternjiev, Voronin, Danilov; Sabo, Khusainov; Chislenko, Banichevski, Malafeev, Porkujan.
*Scorers:* Haller, Beckenbauer for West Germany; Porkujan for Russia.

England (1) 2, Portugal (0) 1 (Wembley)
*England:* Banks (Leicester City); Cohen (Fulham), Wilson (Everton); Stiles (Manchester United), J. Charlton (Leeds United), Moore (West Ham United); Ball (Blackpool), Hurst (West Ham United), R. Charlton, (Manchester United), Hunt (Liverpool), Peters (West Ham United).
*Portugal:* José Pereira; Festa, Baptista, Carlos, Hilario; Graça, Coluna, Augusto; Eusebio, Torres, Simões.
*Scorers:* R. Charlton (2) for England; Eusebio (pen) for Portugal.

**THIRD PLACE MATCH**
Portugal (1) 2, Russia (1) 1 (Wembley)
*Portugal:* José Pereira; Festa, Baptista, Carlos, Hilario; Graça, Coluna, Augusto; Eusebio, Torres, Simões.
*Russia:* Yachin; Ponomarev, Khurtsilava, Korneev, Danilov; Voronin, Sichinava; Metreveli, Malafeev, Banichevski, Serebrianikov.
*Scorers:* Eusebio (pen), Torres for Portugal; Malafeev for Russia.

**FINAL**
England (1) 4, West Germany (1) 2 after extra time (Wembley)
*England:* Banks; Cohen, Wilson, Stiles, J. Charlton, Moore; Ball, Hurst, Hunt, R. Charlton, Peters.
*West Germany:* Tilkowski; Hottges, Schulz, Weber, Schnellinger; Haller, Beckenbauer, Overath; Seeler, Held, Emmerich.
*Scorers:* Hurst (3) Peters for England; Haller, Weber for West Germany.
**Leading Scorer:** Eusebio 9.

**WORLD CUP 1970**
For the third time in four tournaments, Brazil won the World Cup, and very properly retained the Jules Rimet Trophy in consequence. There was no doubt at all of the merits of their success, even if the Italian team they crushed 4–1 in the final could scarcely claim to be the competition's second best. Brazil won every one of their matches, including a narrow and slightly fortunate win against England – thus condemned to play their quarter final in León against West Germany.

Most teams seemed to solve the problem of altitude, but that of heat was simply insoluble. Goodness knows how much the temperatures in Guadalajara, which sometimes rose as high as 98° in a match, affected the England players. In the circumstances they acquitted themselves with honour, especially Bobby Moore, rising superbly above the dingy and unfounded charges of theft brought against him in Colombia.

From an objective point of view, the success of a Brazilian team so wholeheartedly committed to attack – and definitely porous in defence – was a splendid sign in a grey footballing world. For the next four years, one was entitled to hope, the future might at long last lie with creative rather than negative football.

Brazil's triumph was the more remarkable in that they had changed horses, or managers, rather further than mid-stream, Zagalo, a hero of

144

their 1958 and 1962 teams, succeeding the controversial João Saldanha.

The Guadalajara group pivoted on the match between Brazil and England; the second for both of them, and one of those played in the roasting heat of noon. England's players were not helped by the fact that a yelling throng of Mexicans, unharassed by the police, laid siege to their hotel, chanting and honking till the small hours.

Without their 'slow sodium' pills, England would have wilted in the 98°F heat, each player as it was losing an average of 10 pounds during the game. Brazil clearly missed Gerson, their general, but only Banks' amazing one-handed save from Pelé's bouncing header, after Jairzinho beat Cooper and crossed from the line, kept the score goalless at half-time. England themselves missed chances through Lee and Hurst, then, after Brazil had scored, through Ball and Astle, whose was the most clamorous miss of all. The only goal came 14 minutes into the second half. Tostão held off three English defenders – literally in the case of the immaculate Moore – crossed from the left, Pelé rolled the ball on, and Jairzinho scored.

Playing with Rivelino as a 'retractable' left winger, Brazil had beaten the Czechs in their opening game, despite an early goal by the powerful Petras and a near miss. Then Brazil's wonderful control and shooting prevailed, the Czechs throwing away their last chance when Kvasniak, so much slower than in 1962, missed. Rivelino's fierce free-kick, Pelé's cool virtuosity as he caught Gerson's long pass on his chest, Jairzinho's irresistible run; these brought memorable goals.

England, their players ill-treated by the brutal Mocanu, beat Romania on merit with a goal by Hurst; but made tediously hard work of defeating the Czechs, thanks to a dubious penalty, in their final game. The Brazilians won only 3–2 against Romania, for whom Dumitrache was an admirable, skilled centre-forward.

Group 1 began with a tiresome 0–0 draw – the curtain raiser – between Mexico and Russia, and produced two scandalous decisions. When Mexico beat El Salvador, they took and exploited a free-kick that had been awarded to the visitors! The penalty by which they beat Belgium had no basis in reality. Belgium, however, were a team without morale, their players bickering over football boot contracts. Russia beat them easily, finishing second on goal average to the Mexicans.

Group 2 saw Italy at their most fearful and defensive, clearly terrified of another North Korean experience A major row over the dropping of Gianni Rivera in favour of Sandro Mazzola did not help. It took Franchi, president of their Federation, to calm the waters. Ferruccio Valcareggi, the uneasy team manager, eventually found the compromise of using both players; Mazzola in the first half, Rivera in the second. All went well, particularly in the quarter- and semi-finals, till the final itself. Mazzola played too well to be replaced; Rivera came on for the last six minutes!

A goalkeeping error gave Italy a narrow win against the Swedes at Toluca. They then drew cravenly, without scoring, against Uruguay

and little Israel who, also boldly forced a draw with the Swedes. Sweden beat the Uruguayans in a game overshadowed by the fact that Sir Stanley Rous took the designated referee, De Moraes, off the match at the 11th hour because of rumours that he might have been corrupted. They were never proved and turned out to have been spread by another Brazilian referee, jealous that De Moraes had been preferred to him. Uruguay made a furious protest, which was rejected. Meanwhile, they scraped through to the quarter finals on goal average.

Peru and the brilliant young black inside-left Teofilo Cubillas were the revelations of the León group, despite the blow to their morale of the appalling Peruvian earthquakes. This probably accounted for their slow start against Bulgaria, two up before Peru overhauled them. West Germany were given a fright by Morocco, who deservedly scored after 20 minutes, but were caught in the second half when Germany scored through Seeler and Müller; the two centre forwards whom Schoen had cleverly integrated by using Seeler 'deep'. The Germans, and the remarkable Müller, then got into their stride, thrashing Bulgaria then beating Peru, Müller scoring five of the eight goals. Müller's opportunism undid Peru, in the first half, and when the Germans flagged in the steamy heat, Sepp Maier's goalkeeping saved them. So they and Peru survived.

It was in León that West Germany beat England in an extraordinary quarter-final, which seemed virtually over when England made it 2–0 early in the second half. The determining factor may well have been the fact that Gordon Banks, England's fine goalkeeper, drank a bottle of beer, upset his stomach, and had to drop out of the game. Peter Bonetti, his replacement, hadn't played a match for a month, and was blamed for at least one and by some for all three of the German goals. Other critics pointed out that Alf Ramsey overworked and exhausted his overlapping fullbacks in the heat, then failed to make intelligent substitutions. Certainly the game turned when the fresh Grabowski came on at outside-right and ran rings round a weary Terry Cooper. England took the lead with a goal beautifully orchestrated then scored by Alan Mullery. Newton made the cross, as he did for Peters' goal after half-time. But Beckenbauer's shot went under Bonetti's body, a remarkable backheader from Seeler made it 2–2, and Gerd Müller volleyed the winner in extra time.

In Mexico City the Uruguayans, who had lost their star midfield player Pedro Rocha in their very first game, unexpectedly beat Russia with a disputed 'over the line' goal in the last minute of extra time, little Cubilla crossing for Esparrago to score.

Mexico's balloon burst in Toluca. They got the first, illusory goal after only 12 minutes, but a deflected shot by Domenghini made it 1–1; and when Rivera came on in the second half and Riva at last found his famous touch, the Mexicans were outclassed 4–1.

Brazil beat Peru 4–2 in an error-ridden match in Guadalajara. Gallardo, Peru's black striker, once with Milan, kept Peru within range, but Brazil, despite the manifest insufficiency of Felix, their

goalkeeper, always had something in hand. Tostão restored the two-goal margin, Cubillas pulled it back to one, then Jairzinho scored the fourth, decisive goal with a fine, individual flourish.

The Italy-West Germany semi-final in Mexico City may be seen either as a classic of excitement or a comedy of errors. As one who was there, I incline towards the second. I also believe that the match was lost and won when the marvellous Beckenbauer was viciously chopped down, on the very edge of the penalty box, as he flowed through Italy's defence. Since Schoen, hoist with his own petard this time, had used both his substitutes, Beckenbauer had to play through extra time with his arm in a sling. Yamasaki was a wretchedly indulgent referee. Italy took an early lead through a left-foot shot by Boninsegna after a lucky rebound from two German defenders, and they held it, despite Germany's strong rally in the second half, till the third minute of injury time. Then the Germans, who had abandoned their *catenaccio* and brought on their 1966 World Cup final star, Held, for Patzke, equalised when Schnellinger banged in Grabowski's cross.

Extra time brought a deluge of goals. First, Poletti clumsily ran the ball away from his own goalkeeper, Müller putting the final touch. Burgnich came up to score after Rivera's free-kick, Gigi Riva pivoted to beat Schnellinger and drive in a fine left-foot cross-shot, Müller equalised in the second period when he nodded in Seeler's headed pass. And finally Boninsegna broke away, pulled the ball back, and Gianni Rivera, who had come on at half-time, scored the winner.

In Guadalajara, Uruguay surprised Brazil with a ludicrous first goal, Cubilla's narrow angled shot literally bouncing past Felix. Would Uruguay reaffirm their old hoodoo over Brazil? It seemed they might till late in the first half when Clodoaldo, growing in stature with every game, came through on the blind side to equalise. After that, Brazil were in charge, though Felix had to make one magnificent save from Cubilla's header. With 14 minutes remaining, a superb run and shot by Jairzinho put Brazil ahead at last, and in the last minute Rivelino's left foot made it 3–1. Uruguay, furious at having to play in Guadalajara rather than Mexico City, had more than justified their prestige as World Cup fighters.

Brazil found the final a much easier affair. Italy's craven tactics played into their hands; and weren't even well calculated. Gerson was given the freedom of midfield, Jairzinho constantly pulled Facchetti into the middle which, as Italy had no left winger, allowed Carlos Alberto to overlap at will and ultimately to score Brazil's fourth, exciting goal.

Pelé, again in glorious form, gave them the lead after 18 minutes, leaping to Rivelino's high left wing cross. A silly backheel by Clodoaldo, seven minutes from half-time, allowed Boninsegna to equalise, and with Mazzola dribbling beautifully there might have been a chance, had Italy been bolder. As it was, Gerson's fine left-foot goal from outside the box, after 66 minutes, stunned them, and the initiative returned to Brazil. The third goal came when Pelé touched Gerson's free-kick

to the onrushing Jairzinho, and Carlos Alberto thumped in the fourth.
Pure, joyous football had triumphed over negativity.


**GROUP 1** (Mexico City)
Mexico (0) 0, Russia (0) 0
*Mexico:* Calderon; Vantolra, Pena, Guzman, Perez; Hernandez
Pulido, Velarde (Munguia); Valdivia, Fragoso, Horacio Lopez.
*Russia:* Kavazashvili; Lovchev, Chesternjief, Kaplichni, Logofet,
Serebrianikov (Pusacs), Muntijan, Asatiani; Nodia (Porkujan), Byche-
vetz, Evriuzhikin.


Belgium (1) 3, El Salvador (0) 0
*Belgium:* Piot; Heylens, Thissen; Dewalque, Dockx, Semmeling, Van
Moer, Devrindt, Van Himst, Lambert, Puis.
*El Salvador:* Magaña; Rivas, Mariona, Osorio, Manzano; Quintanilla,
Vazquez, Cabezas; Rodriguez, Martinez, Aparicio.
*Scorers:* Van Moer (2), Lambert (pen) for Belgium.


Russia (1) 4, Belgium (0) 1
*Russia:* Kavazashvili; Dzodzuashvili (Kiselev), Chesternjiev, Khurtsi-
lava, Afonin, Kaplichni (Lovchev); Asatiani, Muntijan; Bychevetz,
Evriuzhikin, Khmelnitzki.
*Belgium:* Piot; Heylens, Thissen, Dewalque, Jeck, Dockx, Semmeling,
Van Moer, Van Himst, Puis, Lambert.
*Scorers:* Bychevetz (2), Asatiani, Khmelnitzki for Russia; Lambert for
Belgium.


Mexico (1) 4, El Salvador (0) 0
*Mexico:* Calderon; Vantolra, Pena, Guzman, Perez; Gonzalez, Mun-
guia; Valdivia, Borja (Basaguren, then Lopez), Fragoso, Padilla.
*El Salvador:* Magaña; Rivas, Mariona, Osorio, Cortez, (Monge);
Quintanilla, Vazquez, Cabezas; Rodriguez, Martinez, Aparicio (Men-
dez).
*Scorers:* Valdivia (2), Fragoso, Basaguren for Mexico.


Russia (0) 2, El Salvador (0) 0
*Russia:* Kavazashvili; Dzodzuashvili, Khurtsilava, Chesternjiev,
Afonin; Kiselev (Asatiani), Serebrianikov, Muntijan; Pusacs, (Evriuz-
hikin), Bychevetz, Khmelnitzki.
*El Salvador:* Magana; Rivas, Mariona, Castro, Osorio, Vazquez;
Portillo, Cabezas (Aparicio), Rodriguez (Sermeno), Mendez, Monge.
*Scorers:* Bychevetz (2) for Russia.


Mexico (1) 1, Belgium (0) 0
*Mexico:* Calderon; Vantolra, Guzman, Pena, Perez; Gonzalez, Munguia, Pulido; Padilla, Fragoso, Valdivia (Basaguren).
148

*Belgium:* Piot; Heylens, Jeck, Dockx, Thissen, Dewalque, Polleunis, (Devrindt), Semmeling, Van Moer, Van Himst, Puis.
*Scorer:* Pena (pen) for Mexico.

|  | P | W | D | L | F | A | Pts |
|---|---|---|---|---|---|---|---|
| Mexico | 3 | 2 | 1 | 0 | 5 | 0 | 5 |
| Russia | 3 | 2 | 1 | 0 | 6 | 1 | 5 |
| Belgium | 3 | 1 | 0 | 2 | 4 | 5 | 2 |
| El Salvador | 3 | 0 | 0 | 3 | 0 | 9 | 0 |

**GROUP 2** (Puebla, Toluca)
Uruguay (1) 2, Israel (0) 0
*Uruguay:* Mazurkiewicz; Ubinas, Mujica; Montero Castillo, Ancheta, Matosas; Cubilla, Esparrago, Maneiro, Rocha (Cortes), Lozado.
*Israel:* Vissoker; Bello, Rosen, Daniel, Talbi (Bar), Schwager (Vollach), Rosenthal, Shum, Spiegler, Spiegel, Faygenbaum.
*Scorers:* Maneiro, Mujica for Uruguay.

Italy (1) 1, Sweden (0) 0
*Italy:* Albertosi; Burgnich, Facchetti; Cera, Niccolai (Rosato), Bertini; Domenghini, Mazzola, Boninsegna, De Sisti, Riva.
*Sweden:* Hellstrom; Nordqvist, Grip, Svensson, Axelsson, B. Larsson; Grahn, Eriksson (Ejderstedt), Kindvall, Kronqvist, Olsson.
*Scorer:* Domenghini for Italy.

Uruguay (0) 0, Italy (0) 0
*Uruguay:* Mazurkiewicz; Ubinas, Ancheta, Matosas, Mujica; Cortes, Montero Castillo, Maniziro; Cubilla, Esparrago, Bareno (Zubia).
*Italy:* Albertosi; Burgnich, Cera, Rosato, Facchetti; De Sisti, Bertini, Mazzola, Domenghini (Furino), Boninsegna, Riva.

Sweden (0) 1, Israel (0) 1
*Sweden:* G. Larsson; Selander, Axelsson, Grip, Svensson, B. Larsson (Nicklasson), Nordahl, Turesson, Kindvall, Persson, Olsson.
*Israel:* Vissoker; Primo, Rosen, Bar, Rosenthal, Shum, Schwager, Spiegel, Vollach, Spiegler, Faygenbaum.
*Scorers:* Turesson for Sweden; Spiegler for Israel.

Sweden (0) 1, Uruguay (0) 0
*Sweden:* G. Larsson; Selander, Nordqvist, Axelsson, Grip, Svensson, B. Larsson, Eriksson, Kindvall, Nicklasson (Grahn), Persson (Turesson).
*Uruguay:* Mazurkiewicz; Ubinas, Ancheta, Matosas, Mujica; Montero Castillo, Maneiro, Cortes; Esparrago (Fontes), Zubia, Losada.
*Scorer:* Grahn for Sweden.

Italy (0) 0, Israel (0) 0
*Italy:* Albertosi; Burgnich, Facchetti; Cera, Rosato, Bertini; Domenghini (Rivera), Mazzola, Boninsegna, De Sisti, Riva.

*Israel:* Vissoker; Primo, Bello, Bar, Rosenthal, Rosen, Shum, Spiegel, Faygenbaum (Daniel), Spiegler, Schwager.

|  | P | W | D | L | F | A | Pts |
|---|---|---|---|---|---|---|---|
| Italy | 3 | 1 | 2 | 0 | 1 | 0 | 4 |
| Uruguay | 3 | 1 | 1 | 1 | 2 | 1 | 3 |
| Sweden | 3 | 1 | 1 | 1 | 2 | 2 | 3 |
| Israel | 3 | 0 | 2 | 1 | 1 | 3 | 2 |

## GROUP 3 (Guadalajara)

England (0) 1, Romania (0) 0

*England:* Banks (Stoke City); Newton (Everton) [sub. Wright (Everton)], Cooper (Leeds United); Mullery (Spurs), Labone (Everton), Moore (West Ham United); Lee (Manchester City) [sub. Osgood (Chelsea)], Ball (Everton), Charlton (Manchester United), Hurst (West Ham United), Peters (Spurs).

*Romania:* Adamache; Satmareanu, Lupescu, Dinu, Mocanu; Dumitru, Nunweiller VI; Dembrowski, Tataru (sub. Neagu), Dumitrache, Lucescu.

*Scorer:* Hurst for England.

Brazil (1) 4, Czechoslovakia (1) 1

*Brazil:* Felix; Carlos Alberto, Piazza, Brito, Everaldo; Clodaldo, Gerson (Paulo César), Jairzinho, Tostão, Pelé, Rivelino.

*Czechoslovakia:* Viktor; Dobias, Migas, Horvath, Hagara; Hrdlicka (Kvasniak), Kuna; F. Vesely (B. Vesely), Petras, Adamec, Jokl.

*Scorers:* Petras for Czechoslovakia; Rivelino, Pelé, Jairzinho (2) for Brazil.

Romania (0) 2, Czechoslovakia (1) 1

*Romania:* Adamache; Satmareanu, Lupescu, Dinu, Mocanu; Dumitru (Tataru), Nunweiller VI; Dembrowski, Neagu, Dumitrache, Lucescu (Ghergheli).

*Czechoslovakia:* Vencel; Dobias, Migas, Horvath, Zlocha; Kuna, Kvasniak; B. Vesely, Petras, Jurkanin (Adamec), Jokl (F. Vesely).

*Scorers:* Neagu, Dumitrache (pen) for Romania; Petras for Czechoslovakia.

Brazil (0) 1, England (0) 0

*Brazil:* Felix; Carlos Alberto, Brito, Piazza, Everaldo; Clodaldo Rivelino, Paulo César; Jairzinho, Tostão (Roberto), Pelé.

*England:* Banks (Stoke City); Wright (Everton), Cooper (Leeds United), Mullery (Spurs), Labone (Everton), Moore (West Ham United); Lee (Manchester City) [Astle (West Bromwich Albion)], Ball (Everton), Charlton (Manchester United) [Bell (Manchester City)], Hurst (West Ham United), Peters (Spurs).

*Scorer:* Jairzinho for Brazil.

Brazil (2) 3, Romania (1) 2
*Brazil:* Felix; Carlos Alberto, Brito, Fontana, Everaldo (Marco Antonio); Clodoaldo, Piazza; Jairzinho, Tostão, Pelé, Paulo César.
*Romania:* Adamache (Raducanu); Satmareanu, Lupescu, Dumitru, Mocanu; Neagu, Dinu, Nunweiller VI; Dembrowski, Dumitrache (Tataru), Lucescu.
*Scorers:* Jairzinho, Pelé (2) for Brazil; Dumitrache, Dembrowski for Romania.


England (0) 1, Czechoslovakia (0) 0
*England:* Banks (Stoke City); Newton (Everton), Cooper (Leeds United); Mullery (Spurs), J. Charlton (Leeds United), Moore (West Ham United); Bell (Manchester City), Clarke (Leeds United), Astle (West Bromwich Albion) [Osgood (Chelsea)], R. Charlton (Manchester United) [Ball (Everton)], Peters (Spurs).
*Czechoslovakia:* Viktor; Dobias, Migas, Hrivnak, Hagara; Pollak, Kuna; F. Vesely (Jokl), Petras, Adamec, Jan Capkovic.
*Scorer:* Clarke (pen) for England.

| | P | W | D | L | F | A | Pts |
|---|---|---|---|---|---|---|---|
| Brazil | 3 | 3 | 0 | 0 | 8 | 3 | 6 |
| England | 3 | 2 | 0 | 1 | 2 | 1 | 4 |
| Romania | 3 | 1 | 0 | 2 | 4 | 5 | 2 |
| Czechoslovakia | 3 | 0 | 0 | 3 | 2 | 7 | 0 |

## GROUP 4 (León)
Peru (0) 3, Bulgaria (1) 2
*Peru:* Rubiños; Campos (J. Gonzalez), De La Torre, Chumpitaz, Fuentes; Cubillas, Mifflin, Challe, Baylon (Sotil), Perico Leon, Gallardo.
*Bulgaria:* Simeonov; Chalamanov, Dimitrov, Davidov, Aladjiev, Bonev (Asparoukhov), Penev, Yakimov, Popov (Maraschliev), Jekov, Dermendjiev.
*Scorers:* Chumpitaz, Gallardo, Cubillas for Peru; Dermendjiev, Donev for Bulgaria.


West Germany (0) 2, Morocco (1) 1
*West Germany:* Maier; Vogts, Schulz, Fichtel, Hottges (Loehr); Haller (Grabowski), Beckenbauer, Overath; Seeler, Müller, Held.
*Morocco:* Allal Abdallah; Lamrani, Moulay, Slimani; Boujema, Bamous (Faras), Maaroufi, Filali; Said, Houmane, Ghazouani (Abdelkader).
*Scorers:* Seeler, Müller for West Germany; Houmane for Morocco.


Peru (0) 3, Morocco (0) 0
*Peru:* Rubiños; P. Gonzalez, De La Torre, Chumpitaz, Fuentes; Challe, Mifflin (Cruzado), Cubillas; Sotil, Perico Leon, Gallardo (Ramirez).

*Morocco:* Allal Abdallah; Lamrani, Khanoussi, Slimani, Boujema (Gadili); Maaroufi, Bamous, Filali; Ghandi (Allaqui), Houmane, Fhazouani.
*Scorers:* Cubillas (2), Challe for Peru.

West Germany (2) 5, Bulgaria (1) 2
*West Germany:* Maier; Vogts, Schnellinger, Fichtel, Hottges; Beckenbauer (Weber), Overath; Libuda, Seeler, Müller, Loehr (Grabowski).
*Bulgaria:* Simeonov; Gaydarski, Penev, Jetchev, Gaganelov; Kolev, Bonev, Nikodimov; Dermendjiev, Asparoukhov, Maraschliev.
*Scorers:* Libuda, Müller (3) (1 pen), Seeler for West Germany; Nikodimov, Kolev for Bulgaria.

West Germany (3) 3, Peru (1) 1
*West Germany:* Maier; Vogts, Fichtel, Schnellinger, Hottges (Patzke), Beckenbauer, Seeler, Overath; Libuda (Grabowski), Müller, Loehr.
*Peru:* Rubiños; P. Gonzalez, De La Torre, Chumpitaz, Fuentes; Mifflin, Challe (Cruzado); Sotil, Perico Leon (Ramirez), Gallardo.
*Scorers:* Müller (3) for West Germany; Perico Leon for Peru.

Bulgaria (1) 1, Morocco (0) 1
*Bulgaria:* Yordanov; Chalamanov, Gaydarski, Jetchev, Penev (Dimitrov), Popov, T. Kolev, Yakimov (Bonev), Mitkov, Asparoukhov, Nikodimov.
*Morocco:* Hazzaaz; Khanoussi, Slimani, Benkrif, Fadili; Maaroufi, Bamous (Choukhri), Filali; Ghandi, Allaqui (Faras), Ghazouani.
*Scorers:* Jetchev for Bulgaria; Ghazouani for Morocco.

|  | P | W | D | L | F | A | Pts |
|---|---|---|---|---|---|---|---|
| West Germany | 3 | 3 | 0 | 0 | 10 | 4 | 6 |
| Peru | 3 | 2 | 0 | 1 | 7 | 5 | 4 |
| Bulgaria | 3 | 0 | 1 | 2 | 5 | 9 | 1 |
| Morocco | 3 | 0 | 1 | 2 | 2 | 6 | 1 |

## QUARTER-FINALS
West Germany (0) 3, England (1) 2 after extra time (León)
*West Germany:* Maier; Schnellinger, Vogts, Hottges (Schulz); Beckenbauer, Overath, Seeler; Libuda (Grabowski), Müller, Loehr.
*England:* Bonetti (Chelsea); Newton (Everton), Cooper (Leeds United); Mullery (Spurs), Labone (Everton,) Moore (West Ham United); Lee (Manchester City), Ball (Everton), Hurst (West Ham United), Charlton (Manchester United) [Bell (Manchester City)], Peters (Spurs) [Hunter (Leeds United)].
*Scorers:* Beckenbauer, Seeler, Müller for West Germany; Mullery, Peters for England.

Brazil (2) 4, Peru (1) 2 (Guadalajara)
*Brazil:* Felix; Carlos Alberto, Brito, Piazza, Marco Antonio; Clodoaldo, Gerson (Paulo César); Jairzinho (Roberto), Tostão, Pelé, Rivelino.

*Peru:* Rubiños; Campos, Fernandez, Chumpitaz, Fuentes; Mifflin, Challe; Baylon (Sotil), Perico Leon (Eladio Reyes), Cubillas, Gallardo.
*Scorers:* Rivellino, Tostão (2), Jairzinho for Brazil; Gallardo, Cubillas for Peru.

Italy (1) 4, Mexico (1) 1 (Toluca)
*Italy:* Albertosi; Burgnich, Cera, Rossato, Facchetti; Bertini, Mazzola (Rivera), De Sisti; Domenghini (Gori), Boninsegna, Riva.
*Mexico:* Calderon; Vantolra, Pena, Guzman, Perez; Gonzales (Borja), Pulido, Munguia (Diaz); Valdivia, Fragoso, Padilla.
*Scorers:* Domenghini, Riva (2), Rivera for Italy; Gonzalez for Mexico.

Uruguay (0) 1, Russia (0) 0 after extra time (Mexico City)
*Uruguay:* Mazurkiewicz; Ubinas, Ancheta, Matosas, Mujica; Maneiro, Cortes, Montero Castiloo; Cubilla, Fontes (Gomez), Morales (Esparrago).
*Russia:* Kavazashvili; Dzodzuashvili, Afonin, Khurtsilava (Logofet), Chesternjiev; Muntijan, Asatiani (Kiselev), Kaplichni; Evriuzhkinzin, Bychevetz, Khmelnitzki.
*Scorer:* Esparrago for Uruguay.


**SEMI-FINALS**
Italy (1) 4, West Germany (0) 3 after extra time (Mexico City)
*Italy:* Albertosi; Cera; Burgnich, Bertini, Rosato, (Poletti) Facchetti; Domenghini, Mazzola (Rivera), De Sisti; Boninsegna, Riva.
*West Germany:* Maier; Schnellinger; Vogts, Schulz, Beckenbauer Patzke (Held); Seeler, Overath; Grabowski, Müller, Loehr (Libuda).
*Scorers:* Boninsegna, Burgnich, Riva, Rivera for Italy; Schnellinger, Müller (2) for West Germany.

Brazil (1) 3, Uruguay (1) 1 (Guadalajara)
*Brazil:* Felix; Carlos Alberto, Brito, Piazza, Everaldo; Clodoaldo, Gerson; Jairzinho, Tostão, Pelé, Rivelino.
*Uruguay:* Mazurkiewicz; Ubinas, Ancheta, Matosas, Mujica; Montero Castillo, Cortes, Fontes; Cabilla, Maneiro (Esparrago), Morales.
*Scorers:* Clodoaldo, Jairzinho, Rivelino for Brazil; Cubilla for Uruguay.


**THIRD PLACE MATCH**
West Germany (1) 1, Uruguay (0) 0 (Mexico City)
*West Germany:* Wolter; Schnellinger (Lorenz); Patzke, Fichtel, Weber, Vogts; Seeler, Overath; Libuda (Loehr), Müller, Held.
*Uruguay:* Mazurkiewicz; Ubinas, Ancheta, Matosas, Mujica; Montero Castillo, Cortes, Fontes (Sandoval); Cubilla, Maneiro (Esparrago) Morales.
*Scorer:* Overath for West Germany.

**FINAL**

Brazil (1) 4, Italy (1) 1 (Mexico City)

*Brazil:* Felix; Carlos Alberto, Brito, Piazza, Everaldo; Clodoaldo, Gerson; Jairzinho, Tostão, Pelé, Rivelino.

*Italy:* Albertosi; Cera; Burgnich, Bertini, (Juliano), Rosato, Facchetti; Domenghini, Mazzola, De Sisti; Boninsegna (Rivera), Riva.

*Scorers:* Pelé, Gerson, Jairzinho, Carlos Alberto for Brazil; Boninsegna for Italy.

Leading Scorer: Müller (West Germany) 10.


## WORLD CUP 1974

West Germany, after 20 years, regained the World Cup, beating a brilliant but fallible Dutch team 2–1 in the final in Munich. As in 1954 the West Germans lost a match on the way to the title; but this time it could hardly be said that they lightly let it go. Their conquerors were East Germany, in Hamburg; but the defeat may have been a disguised boon. In the first place, it galvanised the West Germans. In the second place, it induced them to make productive changes. In the third, as Franz Beckenbauer himself pointed out, it sent them into the weaker of the two qualifying groups for the final.

The Netherlands might well have won the World Cup had they not lost Barrie Hulshoff, their powerful Ajax centre-half, with a knee injury before the tournament. This led them to pull Arie Haan, one of their best midfield players, into the back four as notional 'sweeper'. Behind these, unexpectedly, they chose the veteran 33-year-old goalkeeper Jongbloed, who had been thought by most to have gone along merely for the ride. Van Beveren, the first-choice 'keeper, and another brilliant midfield player in Gerry Muhren, were also absent. But no one could have played better than did the big inside-left, Wim Van Hanegem, in the final.

The Dutch, who had made heavy weather of their passage to the finals, and whose players till then seemed a bunch of mercenary individualists, were pulled together by a fine manager in Rinus Michels, the former Ajax coach, now with Barcelona. He it was who turned them into the great team their talents suggested they could be. He it was who healed the breach between Cruyff, his protégé, and the rest. But Holland's superb attacking play was not supported by a sound defence. Indeed, it was a tournament full of defensive error, often surprisingly unpunished by the attacks. The most glaring and expensive interest was Johnny Rep's first-half miss in the final, when he and Cruyff were through with only Beckenbauer between them and Sepp Maier. Cruyff passed to Rep, Maier stopped his shot, West Germany went on to score the next, the decisive, goal.

Brazil, the holders, simply could not stand the loss of Gerson, Tostao, Clodoaldo, and the incomparable Pelé. Who could?

Scotland went out with credit, and a large measure of ill fortune. Some insisted that it was their own fault; for playing so cautiously

154

against feeble Zaire. They scored only twice, whereas the Yugoslavs got nine and the Brazilians, in their last match, three. The third goal, the one that knocked Scotland out of the competition on a basis – such a dubious basis – of 'goal difference', came from a shot by Valdomiro that crept between the goalkeeper's body and the near post. Kazadi had previously been injured in a harsh challenge by Mirandinha.

So Scotland went out without losing a game, having drawn a bruising match 0–0 with Brazil, then drawing 1–1 in Frankfurt with Yugoslavia. Billy Bremner, after an indifferent start against Zaire, was Scotland's chief hero, playing with such inspirational fire that Pelé praised him to the skies, calling him 'a true captain'.

Scotland certainly finished the stronger in a bruising match against Brazil and deserved to win in the last stages. The Brazilians, Pereira and Rivelino in particular, were often displeasingly violent. The Scots might also have won against Yugoslavia. After an uneasy beginning, they took a strong grip on events, and Peter Lorimer, in incisive form, almost scored in the second half when he hooked over Maric, only for Buljan to clear from the line. So it was the Yugoslavs, in a breakaway, who took the first goal. Dragan Dzajic, on the right, cleverly pulled the ball inside his man, crossed elegantly with his left foot, and Karasi, the substitute, headed past the excellent Harvey. With Tommy Hutchison on for the disappointing Dalglish, Scotland fought back for a fine equaliser. Hutchison beat his man in classical winger's style on the left, went to the line, pulled the ball back, and after one Scot had swung and missed, Joe Jordan collected it to tuck it inside the far post with his left foot.

The World Cup was opened with the traditional goalless draw; the third in succession. There might, however, have been several goals in the match in Frankfurt between Yugoslavia and Brazil. The Brazilians might have scored in the first half, Yugoslavia should certainly have done so in the second.

After bringing a couple of splendid saves from Harvey, they virtually survived against Scotland, too. Yugoslavia thrashed Zaire, the 'mattress team', 9–0, after which the Zaireans wanted to go straight home and had to be talked out of it by Vidinic, their coach. Their individual talent was as plain as their total lack of organisation. Brazil beat them 3–0 and thus joined Yugoslavia in the next round.

In Group 1, the West Germans played three indifferent games, won the first two, lost the third, There was unrest at their training camp in Malente, outside Hamburg; the regimen was too severe, they complained. Günter Netzer, out of form and hurt into the bargain, the ghost of himself after a bad season in Spain, missed the first two matches, played 20 anonymous minutes against East Germany, and had to yield the palm to the hero of 1970, Wolfgang Overath.

The limited but courageous Australians acquitted themselves well. The East Germans, playing a harsh game, were rather lucky to beat them 2–0. There was a touch of offside about their first goal – diverted past his own 'keeper by Curran – though Streich took the second well. Against the West Germans, in Hamburg, Australia might well have scored twice in the second half, especially when Abonyi hit the post. Tighter marking might have prevented Overath's first goal, from outside the box; Cullmann's, from a right-wing cross; Gerd Müller's, from a near-post header. But the Australians covered themselves with glory when they held Chile 0–0 in their last match.

The East Germans did still better, in Hamburg. Playing West Germany for the first time, they now eschewed an attacking midfield, put only two men up, defended forcefully, broke dangerously. The West Germans might have scored two first-half goals when Müller twice slipped Weise, once to give Grabowski a chance, once to hit the post. But by same token, Kreische missed the simplest of chances bang in front of goal for East Germany, and Lauck too might have scored. Eight minutes from time, after dominating the second half, the West German defence at last paid for its failings. Sparwasser took a good pass from the substitute, Hamann, forced his way past Vogts, and beat Maier to win the day.

In Group 3, the Dutch began brilliantly against Uruguay, stumbled against Sweden, then easily despatched the Bulgarians to establish themselves as favourites. No one had ever doubted their potential. The question was whether they could express it, after their indifferent qualifying form, and the endless bickering about money. But Rinus Michels licked them into shape, and with Johan Cruyff everything was possible.

Playing with sinuous irresistibility, dynamic and even majestic, Cruyff quickly established himself as the best player in the competition. The cynical Uruguayans did their best to kick him, but couldn't. Demanding money for every statement they made, having put Australia's Ray Baartz out of the tournament with a karate chop, they were a wretched crew. The Dutch might have had six against them; probably would, had they not been fearful for their legs. As it was, Johnny Rep scored twice for them, and that was enough. Forlan's display was vicious, but it was Montero Castillo who was sent off; for punching Rensenbrink in the stomach.

Using their midfield star, Arie Haan, in the back four, the Dutch then proceeded to draw 0–0 with the surprising Swedes, who had themselves drawn their first match with Bulgaria. Sweden, discounted by everybody, in fact showed their old World Cup resourcefulness, under the able managership of Eriksson. Ralf Edstroem, so elegent on the ground and splendid in the air, resumed his old Atvidaberg partnership with the busy Sandberg, the defence crystallised solidly around Nordqvist and in front of Ronnie Hellstroem: and after the opening match, a more ambitious style was used.

Italy, among the favourites when the tournament started, went out ignominiously, howling all the way back to Milan. There was abundant trouble in the camp, first with Juliano, then Re Cecconi, and finally and most cataclysmically with Giorgio Chinaglia.

The Haitians, of all people, put an end to Dino Zoff's amazing record, after 1,143 unbeaten minutes. It was the rapid centre-forward, Sanon, who was responsible, and who gave Italy brief nightmares of another North Korea. Taking a pass from Vorbe, he slipped Spinosi with ease, swerved outside Zoff, and scored. The stunned Italians then pulled themselves together, and replied three times, despite the excellence of Francillon, the Haitian 'keeper, who was later signed by Munich 1860.

Haiti lost 7–0 in Munich to the rampant Poles, 4–1 to the Argentinians, and did little more than Zaire to suggest they had any right to be there.

The Poles, grown vastly in stature since beating England, were the revelation of the group, winning all three matches and finally despatching a stunned Italian team. In their first game, they opened furiously against Argentina, who deployed a weird formation, with Perfumo an uneasy sweeper behind a line of three, Bargas floating about in front of them. Only when Houseman and then Telch came on in the second half did they get to grips with things. Yet they might have scored in the third minute when Brindisi's lovely ball sent Kempes clear through; to miss. Two banal errors in the seventh minute then cost them two goals. First Carnevali inexplicably dropped Gadocha's corner for Lato to score. Then Lato's pass utterly breached a slack defence for Szarmach, a fine new centre-forward, to make it 2–0. Heredia came up to reduce the margin, after half-time; but then Carnevali, after a fine save, threw the ball straight out to Lato, who promptly cantered in from the right to make it 3–1. Babington's subsequent goal was not enough.

Against Italy, however, Carlos Babington was one of the two finest players on the field. The other was little René Houseman, who danced rings around the Italians, while Babington coolly and elegantly ran the show from midfield. Obsessed to a bizarre fault by tactics, Valcareggi convinced himself that Houseman, a natural winger, would play in midfield, and marked him with Capello. This cost him a good inside-forward and gave him an indifferent fullback.

Not for a full 25 minutes, in which Houseman had splendidly exploited Babington's pass to score, did the penny drop. Then Valcareggi swopped Benetti for Capello. Houseman continued to run riot, despite Benetti's many and ugly fouls, but Italy survived. A silly own goal by Perfumo, diverting Benetti's cross from the left past Carnevali, lost them a lead they never won back. But Telch played a limp Rivera out of the game, the talismanic Riva did nothing, and both were dropped from the match against Poland.

The Poles, thumping seven past the Haitians, were much too lively for the demoralised Italians. Well judged crosses by Kasperczak gave goals to Szarmach, a glorious header, and Deyna, a glorious volley. Italy might have had an early penalty, and did get a late goal through Capello, but they were simply not in the hunt. They went home, vowing as always that they'd change everything, train their players harder, and turn their backs on negative *catenaccio* with a fixed sweeper.

Hardly had the Italians returned home, however, than they were involved in another sensation. A few days after the World Cup final, the Polish team manager, Gorski, alleged in a newspaper interview that attempts had been made by Italians to bribe his team to allow Italy to draw – and so qualify. Gorski withdrew the allegations, but stories circulating in Warsaw suggested they had strong foundation; that attempts had even been made by Italian Players to bribe the Poles on the field.

Now the tournament divided itself into two final groups of four, and contrived to produce the 'ideal' final. Holland, stronger and more adventurous with every game, won all their matches without conceding a goal; though there were times when their undermanned defence trembled. West Germany, rising from the ashes of the East German defeat, won all three of their matches, too, though Sweden gave them a fright in Dusseldorf.

For the Dutch, Johan Cruyff seemed to reach greater heights with every game. If the Brazilians succeeded in subduing him, by fair means and foul, in the first half of their decisive match in Dortmund, he played havoc with them in the second, making one goal and scoring another.

Holland's first opponents were Argentina, severely weakened by the absence of the immaculate Babington. He had been booked three times, and must bitterly have regretted his idiocy in twice handling the ball in the Italian game. Without him, Argentina had neither the craft nor the pace to withstand a superb Dutch performance. Already 4–1 victors over Argentina in a friendly match, they showed even greater superiority in Gelsenkirchen.

The East Germans played a dourly negative game on the same ground, Weise marking Cruyff diligently. The Dutch, who were rather subdued in the first half after a dazzling first 10 minutes, scored in nine from a left-foot shot by Neeskens, from a chance made by Rensenbrink. Rensenbrink himself scored the second goal, after a movement begun by Cruyff and carried on by Neeskens and Van Hanegem.

So the Dutch needed only a draw in their third match, against Brazil, to qualify on goal difference. A cunning free kick, struck by Rivelino, with Jairzinho ducking in the 'wall', brought Brazil victory against the East Germans. The Argentinians were beaten 2–1 at Hanover in a game that might have gone either way; though at least the Brazilians did score twice in other than dead-ball situations.

Against the Dutch, Brazil's performance was frankly shameful. True, the Dutch defenders fouled frequently, and incurred several bookings, but it was the Brazilians who cynically began it, the Brazilians who cold-bloodedly sustained it till, in the end, Luis Pereira was sent off for chopping Neeskens. Neeskens, previously, had been knocked cold by Mario Marinho of Santos, a foul the unimpressive West German referee, Herr Tschencher, couldn't see.

Yet Brazil might have won. The Dutch defence was incredibly thin and presumptuous in the first half, when Paulo César and Jairzinho missed easy chances. As against that, only a wonderful save by Leao stopped Holland scoring an early goal when Zé Maria pushed the ball straight to Cruyff's feet. In the second half, however, the Brazilians had shot their bolt. Neeskens, working an electric one-two with Cruyff, lobbed over Leao for the first goal, Cruyff himself, with a superb volley, scored the second, from Krol's left-wing cross. The Brazilians, in keeping Rivelino so deep, allowed Neeskens to attack forcefully.

West Germany ploughed on to the final, given a hard run for their money by Poland. Indeed, the decisive third match, in Frankfurt, might have gone the other way had there not been torrential rain, and had Poland not lacked Szarmach. The game was held up for over half an hour, and some thought it should still not have been played. As it was, the drenched conditions favoured West Germany's strength. The Poles were the better team in the first half, when only a marvellous double save by Sepp Maier from Lato and Gadocha, after Beckenbauer's mistake, prevented a goal. In the second half, Maier's opposite number, Jan Tomaszewski, saved a penalty after Holzenbein was brought down. But he had no chance when a shot by Hoeness was deflected to Gerd Müller, who swooped and scored.

Though Lato and Gadocha were superb throughout, Poland had not had an easy passage in their previous two games. In Stuttgart, it was only Sweden's carelessness that prevented them winning. Playing a clever, counter attacking game, with Grahn and Larsson shrewd in midfield, Sandberg and Edstroem a fine spearhead, well supported from behind, they twice split Poland in the first half. First Tapper, then Grahn, missed his chance, while in the second half, Tomaszewski (moving before the kick?) saved Tapper's penalty.

So it was that the Lato and Gadocha combination produced the only goal, in the first half; a cross from Gadocha on the right, a header by Szarmach, another by Lato.

Poland then beat Yugoslavia at Frankfurt, but again were fortunate. A stupid aberration by Karasi, flooring Szarmach, gave Poland a penalty and a goal by Deyna to open the score. Just before half-time, Karasi spun through for a clever equaliser. Poland won with yet another Lato-Gadocha goal; Gadocha's left-wing corner, Lato's shrewd header on the near post, after 63 minutes; just when Yugoslavia seemed to be calling the tune.

This the Yugoslavs never did against West Germany. They were quite simply overplayed, and might have lost by much more than 2–0. A spectacular drive from Paul Breitner, Germany's attacking fullback, produced the first goal, after 38 minutes. Uli Hoeness got to the line and pulled the ball back for Müller to swoop and get the second, 12 minutes from time. Franz Beckenbauer had a majestic game.

Sweden gave the Germans much more trouble, in rainy Dusseldorf, and might have given more, had Larsson not had to go off, injured, in the second half. Edstroem, with a fine volley after Schwarzenbeck's weak header, scored the opening goal. But West Germany, with Bonhof again making a great difference with his powerful midfield play, fought back to win a fine game 4-2.

Sweden went on to beat Yugoslavia 2–1 to take third place. In the other group, the Argentinians and East Germans drew 1–1 in their last match, each ending with a single point, but with the DDR ahead on goal difference.

The third-place match was the usual tired fiasco between two disappointed teams, though it did give Brazil's Ademir Da Guia, son of the famous Domingas, the chance to make his only World Cup appearance; and a pleasing one. Lato won it with a second-half goal, after running the legs off Alfredo; and he missed a much easier chance in the last minutes.

So to the final, and that astonishing first goal. Not a single West German player had touched the ball between the Dutch kick-off and the moment that Cruyff, spurting into the penalty area, was brought down by Hoeness. Neeskens scored from the spot as Maier dived the wrong way.

For 25 minutes, the Netherlands dominated the game but made no more scoring chances. So it was that the West Germans were able to equalise: from another penalty. Young Holzenbein, who played a lively game, cut boldly inside, was brought down by Jansen, and Paul Breitner scored.

Rep missed his chance, and after 43 minutes, West Germany scored their winner. Grabowski cleverly sent the powerful Bonhof, who had given the German midfield new drive, up the right. Bonhof beat Haan for pace, crossed, the Dutch failed to clear, and Gerd Müller shot home. After the final, Müller would announce his retirement from international football.

There were no goals in the second half, though Holland came out vigorously to play, and Maier had to make a splendid stop from Neesken's volley. They were obliged to put on Van de Kerkhof for Rensenbrink, who had passed a very late fitness test after pulling a muscle, and eventually replaced the injured, highly effective, Rijsbergen with De Jong. But the truth of it was that the early goal was a snare and a delusion. Cruyff was never allowed to run riot; and West Germany regained the Cup.

## GROUP 1
Berlin, 14 June 1974
West Germany (1) 1                    Chile (0) 0
*West Germany:* Maier; Vogts, Brietner, Schwarzenbeck, Beckenbauer, Cullmann, Grabowski, Hoeness, Müller, Overath (Holzenbein), Heynckes.
*Chile:* Vallejos; Garcia, Quintano, Arias, Figueroa, Rodriguez (Lara), Caszely, Valdes (Veliz), Ahumada, Reinoso, Paez.
*Scorer:* Breitner for West Germany.

Hamburg, 14 June 1974
East Germany (0) 2                    Australia (0) 0
*East Germany:* Croy; Kische, Bransch, Weise, Waetzlich, Irmscher, Pommerenke, Sparwasser, Loewe (Hoffmann), Streich, Vogel.
*Australia:* Reilly; Utjesenevic, Wilson, Schaefer, Curran, Richards, Rooney, Mackay, Warren, Alston, Buljevic.
*Scorers:* Curran (o.g.), Streich for East Germany.

Hamburg, 18 June 1974
West Germany (2) 3                    Australia (0) 0
160

*West Germany:* Maier; Vogts, Breitner, Schwarzenbeck, Beckenbauer, Cullman (Wimmer), Grabowski, Heynckes (Holzenbein), Overath, Müller, Hoeness.
*Australia:* Reilly; Utjesenovic, Wilson, Schaefer, Curran, Richards, Rooney, Mackay, Campbell (Abonyi), Alston, Buljevic (Ollerton).
*Scorers:* Overath, Cullmann, Müller for West Germany.

West Berlin, 18 June 1974
East Germany (0) 1                    Chile (0) 1
*East Germany:* Croy; Bransch, Kische, Weise, Waetzlich, Irmscher, Seguin (Kreische), Sparwasser, Hoffmann, Streich, Vogel (Ducke).
*Chile:* Vallejos; Garcia, Figueroa, Quintano, Arias, Paez, Valdes (Yavar), Reinoso, Socias (Farias), Ahumada, Veliz.
*Scorers:* Hoffman for East Germany, Ahumada for Chile.

Hamburg, 22 June 1974
East Germany (1) 1                    West Germany (0) 0
*East Germany:* Croy; Kurbjuweit, Bransch, Weise, Kreische, Waetzlich, Lauck, Sparwasser, Irmscher, (Hamann), Kische, Hoffmann.
*West Germany:* Maier; Vogts, Schwarzenbeck (Hottges), Beckenbauer, Breitner, Hoeness, Overath (Netzer), Cullmann, Grabowski, Müller, Flohe.
*Scorer:* Sparwasser for East Germany.

Berlin, 22 June 1974
Chile (0) 0                    Australia (0) 0
*Chile:* Vallejos; Garcia, Quintano, Figueroa, Arias, Paez, Valdes (Farias), Caszely, Ahumada, Reinoso, Veliz (Yavar).
*Australia:* Reilly; Utjesenovic, Wilson, Schaefer, Curran (Williams), Richards, Rooney, Mackay, Abonyi, Alston (Ollerton), Buljevic.

|              | P | W | D | L | F | A | Pts |
|--------------|---|---|---|---|---|---|-----|
| East Germany | 3 | 2 | 1 | 0 | 4 | 1 | 5   |
| West Germany | 3 | 2 | 0 | 1 | 4 | 1 | 4   |
| Chile        | 3 | 0 | 2 | 1 | 1 | 2 | 2   |
| Australia    | 3 | 0 | 1 | 2 | 0 | 5 | 1   |

## GROUP 2
Frankfurt, 13 June 1974
Brazil (0) 0                    Yugoslavia (0) 0
*Brazil:* Leao; Nelhinho, Luis Pereira, M. Marinho, F. Marinho, Wilson Piazza, Rivelino, Paulo César Lima, Valdomiro, Jairzinho, Leivinha.
*Yugoslavia:* Maric; Buljan, Katalinski, Bogicevic, Hadziabdic, Muzinic, Oblak, Acimovic, Petkovic, Surjak, Dzajic.

Dortmund, 14 June 1974
Scotland (2) 2                    Zaire (0) 0
*Scotland:* Harvey; Jardine, McGrain, Bremner, Holton, Blackley, Dalglish (Hutchison), Hay, Lorimer, Jordan, Law.

161

*Zaire:* Kazadi; Mwepu, Mukombo, Buhanga, Lobilo, Kilasu, May-anga (Kembo), Mana, Ndaye, Kidumu (Kiwonge), Kakodo.
*Scorers:* Lorimer, Jordan for Scotland.

Frankfurt, 18 June 1974
Brazil (0) 0                                    Scotland (0) 0
*Brazil:* Leao; Nelinho, Luis Pereira, M. Marinho, F. Marinho, Wilson Piazza, Rivelino, Paulo César Lima, Jairzinho, Mirandinha, Leivinha (Paulo César Carpegiani).
*Scotland:* Harvey; Jardine, McGrain, Holton, Buchan, Bremner, Hay, Dalglish, Morgan, Jordan, Lorimer.

Gelsenkirchen, 18 June 1974
Yugoslavia (6) 9                               Zaire (0) 0
*Yugoslavia:* Maric; Buljan, Katalinski, Hadziabdic, Bogicevic, Pet-kovic, Oblak, Acimovic, Surjak, Bajevic, Dzajic.
*Zaire:* Kazadi (Tubilandu); Mwepu, Mukombo, Bwanga, Lobilo, Kilasu, Ndaye, Mana, Kembo, Kidumu, Kakoko (Mayanga).
*Scorers:* Bajeriz (3), Dzajic, Surkaj, Katalinski, Bogiceviz, Oblak, Petkovic for Yugoslavia.

Frankfurt, 22 June 1974
Scotland (0) 1                                 Yugoslavia (0) 1
*Scotland:* Harvey; Jardine, McGrain, Holton, Buchan, Bremner, Dalglish (Hutchison), Hay, Morgan, Jordan, Lorimer.
*Yugoslavia:* Maric; Buljan, Hadziabdic, Oblak, Katalinski, Bogicevic, Petkovic, Acimovic, Bajevic (Karasi), Surjak, Dzajic.
*Scorers:* Jordan for Scotland; Karasi for Yugoslavia.

Gelsenkirchen, 22 June 1974
Brazil (1) 3                                    Zaire (0) 0
*Brazil:* Leao; Nelinho, Luis Pereira, S. Marinho, F. Marinho, Wilson Piazza (Mirandinha), Rivelino, Leivinha (Valdomiro), Paulo César Lima, Jairzinho, Edu.
*Zaire:* Kazadi; Mwepu, Mukombo, Bwanga, Lobilo, Kibonge, Tshinabu (Kembo), Mana, Ntumba, Kidumu (Kilasu), Mayanga.
*Scorers:* Jairzinho, Rivelino, Valdomiro for Brazil.

|            | P | W | D | L | F | A  | Pts |
|------------|---|---|---|---|---|----|-----|
| Yugoslavia | 3 | 1 | 2 | 0 | 10 | 1  | 4   |
| Brazil     | 3 | 1 | 2 | 0 | 3 | 0  | 4   |
| Scotland   | 3 | 1 | 2 | 0 | 3 | 1  | 4   |
| Zaire      | 3 | 0 | 0 | 3 | 0 | 14 | 0   |

**GROUP 3**
Hanover, 15 June 1974
Netherlands (1) 2                              Uruguay (0) 0
*Netherlands:* Jongbloed; Suurbier, Rijsbergen, Haan, Krol, Jansen, Neeskens, Van Hanegem, Cruyff, Rep, Rensenbrink.

162

*Uruguay:* Mazurkiewicz; Jauregui, Masnik, Forlan, Pavoni, Esparrago, Montero Castillo, Rocha, Cubilla (Milar), Morena, Mantegazza.
*Scorer:* Rep (2) for Netherlands.

Dusseldorf, 15 June 1974
Sweden (0) 0                          Bulgaria (0) 0
*Sweden:* Hellstroem; Olsson, Karlsson, Bo Larsson, Andersson, Kind-vall (Magnusson), Tapper, Grahn, Torstensson, Sandberg, Edstroem.
*Bulgaria:* Goranov; Velitchkov, Kolev, Penev, Voinov (Mikhailov), Bonev, Devev, Panov (M. Vassilev), Nikodimov, Z. Vassilev, Ivkov.

Dortmund, 19 June 1974
Netherlands (0) 0                     Sweden (0) 0
*Netherlands:* Jongbled; Suurbier, Haan, Krol, Rijsbergen, Jansen, Neeskens, Van Hanegem (De Jong), Rep, Cruyff, Keizer.
*Sweden:* Hellstroem; Olsson (Grip), Andersson, Karlsson, Nordqvist, Bo Larsson, Ejderstedt, Tapper (Persson), Edstroem, Grahn, Sandberg.

Hanover, 19 June 1974
Bulgaria (0) 1                        Uruguay (0) 1
*Bulgaria:* Goranov; Velitchkov, Ivkov, Kolev, Z. Vassilev, Penev, Voinov, Bonev, Denev, Panov, Nikodimov (Mikhailov).
*Uruguay:* Mazurkiewicz; Jauregui, Forlan, Pavoni, Esparrago, Morena, Rocha, Garisto (Masnik), Mantegazza (Cardaccio), Milar, Corbo.
*Scorers:* Bonev for Bulgaria; Pavoni for Uruguay.

Dortmund, 23 June 1974
Netherlands (2) 4                     Bulgaria (0) 1
*Netherlands:* Jongbled; Suurbier, Haan, Rijsbergen, Krol, Neeskens (De Jong), Van Hanegem (Israel), Jansen, Rep, Cruyff, Rensenbrink.
*Bulgaria:* Staikov; Velitchkov, Ivkov, Penev, Z. Vassilev, Stoyanov (Mikhailov), Bonev, Kolev, Voinov, Panov (Borisov), Denev.
*Scorers:* Neeskens (2 pens), Rep, De Jong for Netherlands; Krol (o.g.) for Bulgaria.

Dusseldorf, 23 June 1974
Sweden (0) 3                          Uruguay (0) 0
*Sweden:* Hellstroem; Andersson, Grip, Karlsson, Nordqvist, Bo Larsson, Grahn, Kindvall (Torstensson), Edstroem, Magnusson (Ahlstroem), Sandberg.
*Uruguay:* Mazurkiewicz; Jauregui, Forlan, Pavoni, Garisto (Masnik), Esparrago, Rocha, Mantegazza, Milar, Morena, Corbo (Cubilla).
*Scorers:* Edstroem (2), Sandberg.

|             | P | W | D | L | F | A | Pts |
|-------------|---|---|---|---|---|---|-----|
| Netherlands | 3 | 2 | 1 | 0 | 6 | 1 | 5   |
| Sweden      | 3 | 1 | 2 | 0 | 3 | 0 | 4   |
| Bulgaria    | 3 | 0 | 2 | 1 | 2 | 5 | 2   |
| Uruguay     | 3 | 0 | 1 | 2 | 1 | 6 | 1   |

## GROUP 4

Munich, 15 June 1974
Italy (0) 3                              Haiti (0) 1
*Italy:* Zoff; Spinosi, Morini, Burgnich, Facchetti, Mazzola, Capello, Rivera, Benetti, Chinaglia (Anastasi), Riva.
*Haiti:* Francillon; Bayonne, Jean Joseph (Barthelemy), Nazaire, Auguste, Antoine, Desir, Vorbe, Francois, G. Saint-Vil, Sanon.
*Scorers:* Rivera, Benetti, Anastasi for Italy; Sanon for Haiti.


Stuttgart, 15 June 1974
Poland (2) 3                            Argentina (0) 2
*Poland:* Tomaszewski; Gorgon, Szymanowski, Zmuda, Musial, Kasperczak, Deyna, Maszczyk, Lato, Szarmach (Domarski), Gadocha (Cmikiewicz).
*Argentina:* Carnevali; Perfumo, Wolff, Heredia, Sa, Bargas (Telch), Babington, Brindisi (Houseman), Kempes, Ayala, Balbuena.
*Scorers:* Lato (2), Szarmach for Poland; Heredia, Babington for Argentina.


Stuttgart, 19 June 1974
Argentina (1) 1                         Italy (1) 1
*Argentina:* Carnevali; Wolff (Glaria), Perfumo, Heredia, Sa, Telch, Houseman, Babington, Ayala, Kempes, Yazalde (Chazarreta).
*Italy:* Zoff; Spinosi, Facchetti, Benetti, Morini (Wilson), Burgnich, Mazzola, Capello, Anastasi, Rivera (Causio), Riva.
*Scorers:* Houseman for Argentina; Perfumo (o.g.) for Italy.


Munich, 19 June 1974
Poland (5) 7                            Haiti (0) 0
*Poland:* Tomaszewski; Szymanowski, Gorgon, Zmuda, Musial (Gut), Deyna, Kasperczak, Lato, Maszczyk (Cmikiewicz), Szarmach, Gadocha.
*Haiti:* Francillon; Auguste, Bayonne, Vorbe, Nazaire, Antoine, André (Barthelemy), Francois, R. Saint-Vil (Racine), Desir, Sanon.
*Scorers:* Lato (2), Deyna, Szarmach (3), Gorgon for Poland.


Munich, 23 June 1974
Argentina (2) 4                         Haiti (0) 1
*Argentina:* Carnevali; Wolff, Heredia, Perfumo, Sa, Babington, Telch, Houseman (Brindisi), Yazalde, Ayala, Kempes (Balbuena).
*Haiti:* Francillon; Ducoste, Bayonne, Vorbe, Desir, Antoine, G. St Vil (F. Leandre), Racine, Nazaire (M. Leandre), Sanon, Louis.
*Scorers:* Yazalde (2), Houseman, Ayala for Argentina; Sanon for Haiti.


Stuttgart, 23 June 1974
Poland (2) 2                            Italy (0) 1
*Poland:* Tomaszewski; Szymanowski, Gorgon, Musial, Zmuda, Kasperczak, Deyna, Maszczyk, Gadocha, Szarmach (Cmikiewicz), Lato.

164

*Italy:* Zoff; Spinosi, Facchetti, Benetti, Morini, Burgnich (Wilson), Causio, Mazzola, Capello, Anastasi, Chinaglia (Boninsegna).
*Scorers:* Szarmach, Deyna for Poland; Capello for Italy.

|           | P | W | D | L | F  | A  | Pts |
|-----------|---|---|---|---|----|----|-----|
| Poland    | 3 | 3 | 0 | 0 | 12 | 3  | 6   |
| Argentina | 3 | 1 | 1 | 1 | 7  | 5  | 3   |
| Italy     | 3 | 1 | 1 | 1 | 5  | 4  | 3   |
| Haiti     | 3 | 0 | 0 | 3 | 2  | 14 | 0   |

## GROUP A

Hanover, 26 June 1974
Brazil (0) 1          East Germany (0) 0
*Brazil:* Leao; Zé Maria, Luis Pereira, M. Marinho, F. Marinho, Paulo César Carpegiani, Rivelino, Dirceu, Valdomiro, Jairzinho, Paulo César Lima.
*East Germany:* Croy; Kurbjuweit, Bransch, Weise, Streich, Waetzlich, Lauck (Loewe), Sparwasser, Hamann (Irmscher), Kische, Hoffmann.
*Scorer:* Rivelino for Brazil.

Gelsenkirchen, 26 June 1974
Netherlands (2) 4        Argentina (0) 0
*Netherlands:* Jongbloed; Suurbier (Israel), Haan, Rijsbergen, Krol, Jansen, Neeskens, Van Hanegem, Rep, Cruyff, Rensenbrink.
*Argentina:* Carnevali; Perfumo, Sa, Wolff (Glaria), Telch, Heredia, Balbuena, Yazalde, Ayala, Squeo, Houseman (Kempes).
*Scorers:* Cruyff (2), Krol, Rep for Netherlands.

Gelsenkirchen, 30 June 1974
Netherlands (1) 2        East Germany (0) 0
*Netherlands:* Jongbloed; Suurbier, Haan, Rijsbergen, Krol, Jansen, Neeskens, Van Hanegem, Rep, Cruyff, Rensenbrink.
*East Germany:* Croy; Kische, Bransch, Weise, Kurbjuweit, Pommerenke, Schnuphase, Lauck (Kreische), Loewe (Ducke), Sparwasser, Hoffmann.
*Scorers:* Neeskens, Rensenbrink for Netherlands.

Hanover, 30 June 1974
Brazil (1) 2          Argentina (1) 1
*Brazil:* Leao; Zé Maria, Luis Pereira, M. Marinho, F. Marinho, Paulo César Carpegiani, Rivelino, Dirceu, Valdomiro, Jairzinho, Paulo César Lima.
*Argentina:* Carnevali; Glaria, Heredia, Bargas, Sa (Carrascosa), Brindisi, Squeo, Babington, Balbuena, Ayala, Kempes (Houseman).,
*Scorers:* Rivelino, Jairzinho for Brazil; Brindisi for Argentina.

Dortmund, 3 July 1974
Netherlands (0) 2        Brazil (0) 0
*Netherlands:* Jongbloed; Suurbier, Haan, Rijsbergen, Krol, Neeskens (Israel), Van Hanegem, Jansen, Rep, Cruyff, Rensenbrink (De Jong).

165

*Brazil:* Leao; Zé Maria, Luis Pereira, M. Marinho, F. Marinho, Paulo César Carpegiani, Rivelino, Dirceu, Paulo César Lima (Mirandinha), Jairzinho, Valdomiro.
*Scorers:* Neeskens, Cruyff for Netherlands.

Gelsenkirchen, 3 July 1974
   Argentina (1) 1                   East Germany (1) 1
*Argentina:* Fillol; Wolff, Heredia, Bargas, Carrascosa, Brindisi, Telch, Babington, Houseman, Ayala, Kempes.
*East Germany:* Croy; Kurbjuweit, Bransch, Weise, Schnuphase, Pommerenke, Loewe (Vogel), Streich (Ducke), Sparwasser, Kische, Hoffmann.
*Scorers:* Houseman for Argentina; Streich for East Germany.

|              | P | W | D | L | F | A | Pts |
|--------------|---|---|---|---|---|---|-----|
| Netherlands  | 3 | 3 | 0 | 0 | 8 | 0 | 6   |
| Brazil       | 3 | 2 | 0 | 1 | 3 | 3 | 4   |
| East Germany | 3 | 0 | 1 | 2 | 1 | 4 | 1   |
| Argentina    | 3 | 0 | 1 | 2 | 2 | 7 | 1   |

## GROUP B
Stuttgart, 26 June 1974
Poland (1) 1                     Sweden (0) 0
*Poland:* Tomaszewski; Szymanowski, Gorgon, Zmuda, Gut, Deyna, Kasperczak, Maszczyk, Lato, Szarmach (Kmiecik), Gadocha.
*Sweden:* Hellstroem; Karlsson, Grip, Nordqvist, Andersson (Augustsson), Grahn, Tapper (Ahlstroem), Bo Larsson, Torstensson, Sandberg, Edstroem.
*Scorer:* Lato for Poland.

Dusseldorf, 26 June 1974
West Germany (1) 2              Yugoslavia (0) 0
*West Germany:* Maier; Vogts, Schwarzenbeck, Beckenbauer, Breitner Bonhof, Wimmer (Hoeness), Holzenbein (Flohe), Overath, Müller, Herzog.
*Yugoslavia:* Maric; Buljan, Hadziabdic, Muzinic, Katalinski, Oblak, (Jerkovic), Popivoda, Acimovic, Surjak, Karasi, Dzajic (Petkovic).
*Scorers:* Breitner, Müller for West Germany.

Frankfurt, 30 June 1974
Poland (1) 2                    Yugoslavia (1) 1
*Poland:* Tomaszewski; Szymanowski, Gorgon, Zmuda, Musial, Kasperczak, Maszczyk, Deyna (Domarski), Lato, Szarmach (Cmikiewicz), Gadocha.
*Yugoslavia:* Maric; Buljan, Hadziabdic, Bogicevic, Katalinski, Oblak (Jerkovic), Petkovic (V. Petrovic), Karasi, Bajevic, Acimovic, Surjak.
*Scorers:* Deyna (pen), Lato for Poland; Karasi for Yugoslavia.

Dusseldorf, 30 June 1974
West Germany (0) 4             Sweden (1) 2

*West Germany:* Maier; Vogts, Schwarzenbeck, Beckenbauer, Breitner, Hoeness, Overath, Bonhof, Holzenbein (Flohe), Müller, Herzog (Grabowski).
*Sweden:* Hellstroem; Olsson, Augustsson, Karlsson, Nordqvist, Bo Larsson (Ejderstedt), Torstensson, Tapper, Edstroem, Grahn, Sandberg.
*Scorers:* Overath, Bonhof, Grabowski, Hoeness (pen) for West Germany; Edstroem, Sandberg for Sweden.

Dusseldorf, 3 July 1974
Sweden (1) 2                        Yugoslavia (1) 1
*Sweden:* Hellstroem; Olsson, Karlsson, Nordqvist, Augustsson, Tapper, Grahn, Persson, Torstensson, Edstroem, Sandberg.
*Yugoslavia:* Maric; Buljan, Hadziabdic, Katalinski, Bogicevic, Pavlovic (Peruzovic), V. Petrovic (Karasi), Jerkovic, Surjak, Acimovic, Dzajic.
*Scorers:* Edstroem, Torstensson for Sweden; Surjak for Yugoslavia.

Frankfurt, 3 July 1974
West Germany (0) 1                 Poland (0) 0
*West Germany:* Maier; Vogts, Schwarzenbeck, Beckenbauer, Breitner, Bonhof, Overath, Hoeness, Grabowski, Müller, Holzenbein.
*Poland:* Tomaszewski; Szymanowski, Gorgon, Zmuda, Musial, Kasperczak (Cmikiewicz), Deyna, Maszczyk (Kmiecik), Lato, Domarski, Gadocha.
*Scorer:* Müller for West Germany.

|               | P | W | D | L | F | A | Pts |
|---------------|---|---|---|---|---|---|-----|
| West Germany  | 3 | 3 | 0 | 0 | 7 | 2 | 6   |
| Poland        | 3 | 2 | 0 | 1 | 3 | 2 | 4   |
| Sweden        | 3 | 1 | 0 | 2 | 4 | 6 | 2   |
| Yugoslavia    | 3 | 0 | 0 | 3 | 2 | 6 | 0   |

**THIRD PLACE MATCH**
Munich, 6 July 1974
Poland (0) 1                        Brazil (0) 0
*Poland:* Tomaszewski; Szymanowski, Gorgon, Zmuda, Musial, Maszczyk, Deyna, Kasperczak (Cmikiewicz), Lato, Szarmach (Kapka), Gadocha.
*Brazil:* Leao, Zé Maria, Alfredo, M. Marinho, F. Marinho, Paulo César Carpegiani, Rivelino, Ademir da Guia (Mirandinha), Valdomiro, Jairzinho, Dirceu.
*Scorer:* Lato for Poland.

**FINAL**
Munich, 7 July 1974
West Germany (2) 2                 Netherlands (1) 1
*West Germany:* Maier; Vogts, Schwarzenbeck, Beckenbauer, Breitner, Bonhof, Hoeness, Overath, Grabowski, Müller, Holzenbein.
*Netherlands:* Jongbloed; Suurbier, Rijsbergen (De Jong), Haan, Krol, Jansen, Van Hanegem, Neeskens, Rep, Cruyff, Rensenbrink (R. Van der Kerkhof).

167

*Scorers:* Breitner (pen), Müller for West Germany; Neeskens (pen) for Netherlands.

**LEADING SCORERS**
7 – Lato (Poland); 5 – Szarmach (Poland), Neeskens (Netherlands); 4 – Rep (Netherlands), Edstroem (Sweden), Müller (West Germany); 3 – Bajevic (Yugoslavia), Rivelino (Brazil), Deyna (Poland), Cruyff (Netherlands), Houseman (Argentina), Breitner (West Germany).


CHAPTER THIRTEEN

# The European Football Championship

This was initiated in 1958 as a home and away knockout tournament, with the semi-finals and final to be played in one country, along the lines of the World Cup. The title of the tournament was changed from the European Nations Cup to the European Football Championship for the 1966–68 episode.

**EUROPEAN NATIONS CUP 1958–60**

The first tournament dragged on till 1960 and a somewhat anti-climactic finish in Paris. Russia won it, but they had been favoured by the withdrawal of Spain, whom they were due to meet in the quarter-final. No British country competed. The final rounds were notable for the superb form of Russia's goalkeeper, Lev Yachin.

**Preliminary Round**
Eire 2, Czechoslovakia 0
Czechoslovakia 4, Eire 0
Czechoslovakia 5, Denmark 1
Poland 2, Spain 4
Spain 3, Poland 0

**First Round**
France 7, Greece 1
Greece 1, France 1
Russia 3, Hungary 1
Hungary 0, Russia 1
Romania 3, Turkey 0
Turkey 2, Romania 0
Norway 0, Austria 1
Austria 5, Norway 2
Yugoslavia 2, Bulgaria 0
Bulgaria 1, Yugoslavia 1
Portugal 2, East Germany 0
East Germany 2, Portugal 3
Denmark 2, Czechoslovakia 2

**Quarter-finals**
Portugal 2, Yugoslavia 1
Yugoslavia 5, Portugal 1
France 5, Austria 2
Austria 2, France 0
Romania 0, Czechoslovakia 2
Czechoslovakia 3, Romania 0
Russia beat Spain who withdrew

**Semi-finals**
Yugoslavia 5, France 4 (Paris)
Russia 3, Czechoslovakia 0
(Marseilles)

Final Paris, 10 July 1960
Russia 2, Yugoslavia 1 after extra time
*Russia:* Yachin; Tchekeli, Kroutikov; Voinov, Maslenkin, Netto; Metreveli, Ivanov, Ponedelnik, Bubukin, Meshki.
*Yugoslavia:* Vidinic; Durkovic, Jusufi; Zanetic, Miladinovic, Perusic; Sekularac, Jerkovic, Galic, Matus, Kostic.
*Scorers:* Metreveli, Ponedelnik for Russia; Netto (o.g.) for Yugoslavia.

## EUROPEAN NATIONS CUP 1962–64

This time, England, Northern Ireland, and Wales competed, but Scotland inexcusably and inexplicably stayed out. England's performance was far from glorious. After struggling to draw with France at Sheffield, they played the return during the bitter winter of 1963, took a floundering team to Paris, poorly selected (no scheming inside-forward) and with a goalkeeper out of practice and form, to lose 5–2.

Northern Ireland did better, playing gallantly to beat Poland, and exceedingly well to hold Spain to a draw away. For the return, however, Spain recalled their Italian-based stars, Del Sol and Suarez, and just squeezed through in Belfast. The Welsh, meanwhile, had already gone out to Hungary. Spain did not need Del Sol and Suarez to put out Eire, which they did with ease, while Hungary surprised France in Paris; a revitalised team.

The closing rounds, played in Spain, not surprisingly saw the home team prevail, though not without infinite trouble. After narrowly prevailing against Hungary, Spain ran up against a packed Russian defence, scored in five minutes, let in an eighth-minute equaliser, then inspired by Suarez had enough of the play for Marcellino to give them the game with a brilliant opportunist goal. The Russians used Kornaev as an extra defender. Hungary took third place with a laborious win over Denmark.

**Third Place Match**
Hungary 3, Denmark 1 after extra time

Final Madrid, 21 June 1964
Spain (1) 2, Russia (1) 1
*Spain:* Iribar; Rivilla, Calleja; Fuste, Olivella, Zoco; Amancio, Pereda, Marcellino, Suarez, Lapetra.
*Russia:* Yachin; Chustikov, Mudrik; Voronin, Chesternjiev, Anitchkine; Chislenko, Ivanov, Ponedelnik, Kornaev, Khusainov.
*Scorers:* Pereda, Marcellino for Spain; Khusainov for Russia.

## EUROPEAN FOOTBALL CHAMPIONSHIP 1966–68

Italy won a most unsatisfactory final series, on their own soil. In the semi-finals, they drew with Russia after extra time at Naples and won the toss: a competition rule which properly met with bitter criticism. In the final, a late goal from a free kick gave them a lucky draw against the superior Yugoslav side. The replay, two days later, found

Yugoslavia exhausted, Italy reinforced by capable reserves, and the Italians won with some ease. Previously, in a brutally hard match, Yugoslavia had put out England in Florence through a late goal by Dzajic.

England had qualified for the quarter-finals by winning the home international championship. Beaten at Wembley by Scotland, they drew the vital match at Hampden in February 1968. The Scots threw away points against weaker opposition. England went on to eliminate Spain in the quarter-finals, playing specially well in Madrid.

The competition was this time divided into eight qualifying groups, in which the results were as follows:

**Group I**
Eire 0, Spain 0
Eire 2, Turkey 0
Spain 2, Eire 0
Turkey 0, Spain 0
Turkey 2, Eire 1
Eire 0, Czechoslovakia 2
Spain 2, Turkey 0
Czechoslovakia 1, Spain 0
Spain 2, Czechoslovakia 1
Czechoslovakia 4, Turkey 0
Turkey 0, Czechoslovakia 0
Czechoslovakia 1, Eire 2

**Group II**
Norway 0, Bulgaria 2
Portugal 1, Sweden 2
Bulgaria 0, Norway 2
Sweden 1, Portugal 1
Norway 1, Portugal 2
Sweden 0, Bulgaria 2
Norway 3, Sweden 1
Sweden 5, Norway 1
Bulgaria 3, Sweden 0
Portugal 2, Norway 1
Bulgaria 1, Portugal 0
Portugal 0, Bulgaria 0

**Group III**
Finland 0, Austria 0
Greece 2, Finland 1
Finland 1, Greece 1
Russia 4, Austria 3
Russia 2, Finland 0
Finland 2, Russia 5
Austria 2, Finland 1
Greece 4, Austria 0

Austria 1, Russia 0
Greece 0, Russia 1
Austria 1, Greece 1
Russia 4, Greece 1

**Group IV**
Albania 0, Yugoslavia 2
West Germany 6, Albania 0
Yugoslavia 1, West Germany 0
West Germany 3, Yugoslavia 1
Yugoslavia 4, Albania 0
Albania 0, West Germany 0

**Group V**
Netherlands 2, Hungary 2
Hungary 6, Denmark 0
Netherlands 2, Denmark 0
East Germany 4, Netherlands 3
Hungary 2, Netherlands 1
Denmark 0, Hungary 2
Denmark 1, East Germany 1
Netherlands 1, East Germany 0
Hungary 3, East Germany 1
Denmark 3, Netherlands 2
East Germany 3, Denmark 2
East Germany 1, Hungary 0

**Group VI**
Cyprus 1, Romania 5
Romania 4, Switzerland 2
Italy 3, Romania 1
Cyprus 0, Italy 2
Romania 7, Cyprus 0
Switzerland 7, Romania 1
Italy 5, Cyprus 0
Switzerland 5, Cyprus 0
Switzerland 2, Italy 2

Italy 4, Switzerland 0
Cyprus 2, Switzerland 1
Romania 0, Italy 1

**Group VII**
Poland 4, Luxembourg 0
France 2, Poland 1
Luxembourg 0, France 3
Luxembourg 0, Belgium 5
Luxembourg 0, Poland 0
Poland 3, Belgium 1
Belgium 2, France 1
Poland 1, France 4
Belgium 2, Poland 4
France 1, Belgium 1
Belgium 3, Luxembourg 0
France 3, Luxembourg 1

**Group VIII**
Northern Ireland 0, England 2
Wales 1, Scotland 1
England 5, Wales 1
Scotland 2, Northern Ireland 1
Northern Ireland 0, Wales 0
England 2, Scotland 3
Wales 0, England 3

Northern Ireland 1, Scotland 0
England 2, Northern Ireland 0
Scotland 3, Wales 2
Scotland 1, England 1
Wales 2, Northern Ireland 0

**Quarter-finals**
England 1, Spain 0
Spain 1, England 2
Bulgaria 3, Italy 2
Italy 2, Bulgaria 0
France 1, Yugoslavia 1
Yugoslavia 5, France 1
Hungary 2, Russia 0
Russia 3, Hungary 0

**Semi-finals** (Italy)
Yugoslavia 1, England 0
Italy 0, Russia 0, Italy won toss

**Third-place match** (Rome)
England 2, Russia 0

**Final** (Rome)
Italy 1, Yugoslavia 1

**Replayed Final** Rome, 10 June 1968
Italy (2) 2, Yugoslavia (0) 0
*Italy:* Zoff; Burgnich, Facchetti; Rosato, Guarneri, Salvadore; Domenghini, Mazzola, Anastasi, De Sisti, Riva.
*Yugoslavia:* Pantelic; Fazlagic, Damjanovic; Pavlovic, Paunovic, Holcer; Hosic, Acimovic, Musemic, Trivic, Dzajic.
*Scorers:* Riva, Anastasi for Italy.

## EUROPEAN FOOTBALL CHAMPIONSHIP 1970–72

This tournament was won gloriously by West Germany, a team excitingly dedicated to attack in the style of 'total football'. Franz Beckenbauer played in his favourite role as a mobile sweeper, magnificently abetted by Günter Netzer in midfield and the opportunism of the prolific Gerd Müller. It was a total departure from the old German school of physical football.

England, ineptly choosing a team with no midfield half-back to confront Netzer, were thrashed 3–1 at Wembley, though they gained a futile draw with harsh, negative tactics in Berlin; an odd aberration by Sir Alf Ramsey.

The West Germans then beat Belgium in the semi-final in Antwerp in an exciting game, while Russia got the better of Hungary in Brussels, a game watched by only a few thousand because the other was televised. In the final, West Germany outplayed the heavy Russians, and had it not been for the goalkeeping of Rudakov they would have won much more easily than 3–0.

**Group I**

Czechoslovakia 1, Finland 1
Romania 3, Finland 0
Wales 0, Romania 0
Wales 1, Czechoslovakia 3
Finland 0, Wales 1
Czechoslovakia 1, Romania 0
Finland 0, Czechoslovakia 4
Finland 0, Romania 4
Wales 3, Finland 0
Czechoslovakia 1, Wales 0
Romania 2, Czechoslovakia 1
Romania 2, Wales 0

**Group II**

Norway 1, Hungary 3
France 3, Norway 1
Bulgaria 1, Norway 1
Hungary 1, France 1
Bulgaria 3, Hungary 0
Norway 1, Bulgaria 4
Norway 1, France 3
Hungary 2, Bulgaria 0
France 0, Hungary 2
Hungary 4, Norway 0
France 2, Bulgaria 1
Bulgaria 2, France 1

**Group III**

Greece 0, Switzerland 1
Malta 1, Switzerland 2
Malta 0, England 1
England 3, Greece 0
Switzerland 5, Malta 0
England 5, Malta 0
Malta 1, Greece 1
Switzerland 1, Greece 0
Greece 2, Malta 0
Switzerland 2, England 3
England 1, Switzerland 1
Greece 0, England 2

**Group IV**

Spain 3, Northern Ireland 0
Cyprus 0, Northern Ireland 3

Northern Ireland 5, Cyprus 0
Cyprus 1, Russia 3
Cyprus 0, Spain 2
Russia 2, Spain 1
Russia 6, Cyprus 1
Russia 1, Northern Ireland 0
Northern Ireland 1, Russia 1
Spain 0, Russia 0
Spain 7, Cyprus 0
Northern Ireland 1, Spain 1

**Group V**

Denmark 0, Portugal 1
Scotland 1, Denmark 0
Belgium 2, Denmark 0
Belgium 3, Scotland 0
Belgium 3, Portugal 0
Portugal 2, Scotland 0
Denmark 1, Scotland 0
Portugal 5, Denmark 0
Denmark 1, Belgium 2
Scotland 2, Portugal 1
Scotland 1, Belgium 0
Portugal 1, Belgium 1

**Group VI**

Eire 1, Sweden 1
Sweden 1, Eire 0
Austria 1, Italy 2
Italy 3, Eire 0
Eire 1, Italy 2
Eire 1, Austria 4
Sweden 1, Austria 0
Sweden 0, Italy 0
Austria 1, Sweden 0
Austria 6, Eire 0
Italy 2, Austria 2
Italy 3, Sweden 0

**GROUP VII**

Netherlands 1, Yugoslavia 1
East Germany 1, Netherlands 0
Luxembourg 0, East Germany 5
Yugoslavia 2, Netherlands 0

172

as a token of sympathy for the Munich air crash disaster, they were meanly frustrated. The League forbade them to enter, maintaining that this was a competition for national champions, and United had not won the League title (thus claiming to make UEFA's rules for them). United appealed successfully to the Football Association but the League, in turn, were upheld in their decision by a joint F.A.–F.L. body. It was a thoroughly shabby episode.

The feature of the first five European Cups was the extraordinary dominance of Real Madrid. Off the field, the credit belonged to their vigorous President, Santiago Bernabeu; but on it, to the great Argentinian centre-forward, Alfredo Di Stefano. Long before the coming of Puskas, Di Stefano had inspired his team to bestride Europe. Not until 1960–61 did Barcelona at last become the first team to knock Real out of the European Cup.

## EUROPEAN CUP 1955–56

With no entry from England, Hibernian of Edinburgh were the sole representatives of Britain and they reached the semi-finals with an excellent team which included Tommy Younger in goal, and a forward-line of Gordon Smith, Combe, Reilly, Turnbull, and Ormond. A brilliant 4–0 away win against Rot Weiss Essen took them through the first round; Djurgarden of Sweden were twice beaten on Scottish soil in the second, but Reims proved too strong for them in the semi-final. The return match, at Easter Road, was a brilliant one, with Kopa and Bob Jonquet in splendid form for Reims, but Hibernian having most of the play – and failing to score.

The final, in Paris, provided a splendid match between Reims and Real, in which Di Stefano and Kopa reached great heights of technique and organisation. Leblond and Templin gave Reims a 2–0 lead in the first ten minutes, it was 2–2 at half time, Hidalgo restored the lead for Reims, but a remarkable individual goal by the Real centre-half Marquitos equalised, and Rial, the Argentinian-born inside-left scored the winner, 11 minutes from time.

**First Round**

Sporting Lisbon 3, Partizan Belgrade 3

Partizan Belgrade 5, Sporting Lisbon 2

Voros Logobo 6, Anderlecht 3

Anderlecht 1, Voros Logobo 4

Servette Geneva 0, Real Madrid 2

Real Madrid 5, Servette 0

Rot Weiss Essen 0, Hibernian 4

Hibernian 1, Rot Weiss Essen 1

Aarhus 0, Reims 2

Reims 2, Aarhus 2

Rapid Vienna 6, Eindhoven 1

Eindhoven 1, Rapid 0

Djurgarden 0, Gwardia Warsaw 0

Gwardia 1, Djurgarden 4

AC Milan 3, Saarbrücken 4

Saarbrücken 1, AC Milan 4

**Quarter-finals**

Hibernian 3, Djurgarden 1

Djurgarden 0, Hibernian 1
(*in Edinburgh*)

Reims 4, Voros Logobo 2

Voros Logobo 4, Reims 4

Real Madrid 4, Partizan Belgrade 0

Partizan Belgrade 3, Real Madrid 0

East Germany 2, Luxembourg 1
Netherlands 6, Luxembourg 0
Luxembourg 0, Yugoslavia 2
Netherlands 3, East Germany 2
East Germany 1, Yugoslavia 2
Yugoslavia 0, East Germany 0
Luxembourg 0, Netherlands 8
Yugoslavia 2, Luxembourg 0


**Group VIII**
Poland 3, Albania 0
West Germany 1, Turkey 1
Turkey 2, Albania 1
Albania 0, West Germany 1
Turkey 0, West Germany 3
Albania 1, Poland 1
West Germany 2, Albania 0
Poland 5, Turkey 1
Poland 1, West Germany 3
Albania 3, Turkey 0

West Germany 0, Poland 0
Turkey 1, Poland 0

**Quarter-Finals**
England 1, West Germany 3
West Germany 0, England 0
Italy 0, Belgium 0
Belgium 2, Italy 1
Hungary 1, Romania 1
Romania 2, Hungary 2
Hungary 2, Romania 1
Yugoslavia 0, Russia 0
Russia 3, Yugoslavia 0

**Semi-finals** (Belgium)
Belgium 1, West Germany 2
   (Antwerp)
Russia 1, Hungary 0 (Brussels)

**Third Place Match** (Liège)
Belgium 2, Hungary 1

Final Brussels, 18 June 1972
West Germany (1) 3, Russia (0) 0
*West Germany:* Maier; Hottges, Breitner, Beckenbauer, Schwarzen-
beck, Wimmer, Heynckes, Hoeness, Müller, Netzer, Kremer.
*Russia:* Rudakov; Dzodzuashvili, Khurtsilava, Kaplichnyi, Istomine,
Troshkine, Kolotov, Baidnachyi, Konkov (Dolmatov), Banichevski
(Kozinkevich), Onishenko.
*Scorers:* Müller (2), Wimmer for West Germany.


CHAPTER FOURTEEN

# The European Cup History

The European Cup was the brainchild of the veteran French jour
selector and international player, Gabriel Hanot, and his Parisia
paper, *L'Equipe*. Confined to clubs which have won their
League championship (though the holders' country may ente
team), matches preceding the Final are decided on a home
goal aggregate basis.

Though Scotland entered at once when the tournam
1955, England did not. The Football League refused C
English champions, permission to take part, and the
advised Manchester United not to enter. Fortuna
have no truck with such negative counsel, and d
1958, when the organisers generously invited the

Rapid Vienna 1, Milan 1                   Hibernian 0, Reims 1
Milan 7, Rapid Vienna 2                   Real Madrid 4, Milan 2
                                          Milan 2, Real Madrid 1

**Semi-finals**
Reims 2, Hibernian 0

**Final** Paris, 13 June 1956
Real Madrid (2) 4, Reims (2) 3
*Real:* Alonso; Atienza, Lesmes; Munoz, Marquitos, Zarraga; Joseito;
Marchal, Di Stefano, Rial, Gento.
*Reims:* Jacquet; Zimny, Giraudo; Leblond, Jonquet, Siatka; Hidalgo,
Glovacki, Kopa, Bliard, Templin.
*Scorers:* Leblond, Templin, Hidalgo for Reims, Di Stefano, Rial (2),
Marquitos for Real Madrid.


## EUROPEAN CUP 1956–57

Manchester United now entered the lists for England, and put up
an excellent performance, reaching the semi-finals with a dazzling
young team among whose stars were Roger Byrne, Duncan Edwards
and Tommy Taylor – all to die at Munich. Their ten-goal win over
Anderlecht, at Maine Road, was a remarkable one. Denis Viollet, their
inside-left, scored four of the goals. The third round, in Bilbao, saw
United beaten 5–3 on a very heavy pitch, but they recovered for a
splendid 3–0 victory in the return, and went through to the semi-
finals, where the power of Real was just too much for them.

Rangers, Scotland's entry, went out ingloriously to Nice.

In the final, Italy's gifted Fiorentina side, which had splendid South
American forwards in Julinho and Montuori, succumbed to Real, on
Real's own ground.

**First Round (Preliminary)**
Dortmund Borussia 4, Spora
  Luxemburg 3
Spora Luxemburg 2, Dortmund
  Borussia 1
Dortmund Borussia 7, Spora
  Luxemburg 0
Dynamo Bucharest 3,
  Galatasaray 1
Galatasaray 2, Dynamo
  Bucharest 1
Slovan Bratislava 4, CWKS
  Warsaw 0
CWKS Warsaw 2, Slovan
  Bratislava 0
Anderlecht 0, Manchester United
  2
Manchester United 10,
  Anderlecht 0

Aarhus 1, Nice 1
Nice 5, Aarhus 1
Porto 1, Atlético Bilbao 2
Atlético Bilbao 3, Porto 2
Byes: *Real Madrid, CDNA Sofia,*
  *Grasshoppers, Rangers, Rapid*
  *Vienna, Rapid Heerlen, Red*
  *Star Belgrade, Fiorentina, Norr-*
  *köping, Honved.*

**First Round Proper**
Manchester United 3, Dortmund
  Borussia 2
Dortmund Borussia 0, Manchester
  United 0
CDNA Sofia 8, Dynamo
  Bucharest 1
Dynamo Bucharest 3, CDNA
  Sofia 2

Slovan Bratislava 1, Grasshoppers 0
Grasshoppers 2, Slovan Bratislava 0
Rangers 2, Nice 1
Nice 2, Rangers 1
Rangers 1, Nice 3
Real Madrid 4, Rapid Vienna 2
Rapid Vienna 3, Real Madrid 1
Real Madrid 2, Rapid Vienna 0
Rapid Juliana 3, Red Star Belgrade 4
Red Star Belgrade 2, Rapid Juliana 0
Fiorentina 1, Norrköping 1
Norrköping 0, Fiorentina 1
Atlético Bilbao 3, Honved 2
Honved 3, Atlético Bilbao 3

**Quarter-finals**
Atlético Bilbao 5, Manchester United 3
Manchester United 3, Atlético Bilbao 0
Fiorentina 3, Grasshoppers 1
Grasshopers 2, Fiorentina 2
Red Star 3, CDNA Sofia 1
CDNA Sofia 2, Red Star 1
Real Madrid 3, Nice 0
Nice 2, Real Madrid 3
**Semi-finals**
Red Star 0, Fiorentina 1
Fiorentina 0, Red Star 0
Real Madrid 3, Manchester United 1
Manchester United 2, Real Madrid 2

**Final** Madrid, 30 May 1957
*Real Madrid (0) 2, Fiorentina (0) 0*
*Real:* Alonso; Torres, Lesmes; Munoz, Marquitos, Zarraga; Kopa, Mateos, Di Stefano, Rial, Gento.
*Fiorentina:* Sarti; Magnini, Cervato; Scaramucci, Orzan, Segato; Julinho, Gratton, Virgili, Montuori, Bizzarri.
*Scorers:* Di Stefano (pen), Gento for Real Madrid.

## EUROPEAN CUP 1957–58

For British football, this was the European Cup which was cruelly overshadowed by the Munich disaster, when the Elizabethan carrying Manchester United back from their match in Belgrade crashed on take-off, killing seven players. United had already qualified for the semi-finals, and their patched-up team made a brave show against Milan, winning the first leg in Manchester 2–1, Ernie Taylor getting the winner from a penalty, but losing the return 4–0. Rangers, who knocked out St Etienne, had been comfortably despatched by Milan in the eighth-finals.

Real, who now had Santamaria at centre-half, were lucky to get the better of Milan in a really thrilling final. Real survived when a shot by Cucchiaroni hit the bar, and went on to win in extra-time with a 107th-minute goal by Gento. It was a fine day for the Milan inside-forwards, Nils Liedholm and Argentina's Ernesto Grillo.

**Preliminary Round**
Rangers 3, St Etienne 1
St Etienne 2, Rangers 1
CNDA Sofia 2, Vasas Budapest 1
Vasas Budapest 6, CDNA Sofia 1
Red Star Belgrade 5, Stade Dudelange 0
Stade Dudelange 1, Red Star Belgrade 9
Aarhus 0, Glenavon 0

Glevavon 0, Aarhus 3
Gwardia Warsaw 3, Wismut Karl-Marx-Stadt 1
Wismut Karl-Marx-Stadt 2, Gwardia Warsaw 0
Wismut Karl-Marx-Stadt 1, Gwardia Warsaw 1 (*Wismut won the toss*)
Seville 3, Benfica 1
Benfica 0, Seville 0
Shamrock Rovers 0, Manchester United 6
Manchester United 3, Shamrock Rovers 2
Milan 4, Rapid Vienna 1
Rapid Vienna 5, Milan 2
Milan 4, Rapid Vienna 2
Byes: *Antwerp, Real Madrid, Norrköping, Ajax Amsterdam, Dukla Prague, Young Boys Berne, Borussia Dortmund, CCA Bucharest.*

**First Round Proper**
Antwerp 1, Real Madrid 2
Real Madrid 6, Antwerp 0
Norrköping 2, Red Star 2
Red Star 2, Norrköping 1
Wismut Karl-Marx-Stadt 1, Ajax Amsterdam 3
Ajax Amsterdam 1, Wismut Karl-Marx-Stadt 0

Manchester United 3, Dukla Prague 0
Dukla Prague 1, Manchester United 0
Young Boys Berne 1, Vasas 1
Vasas 2, Young Boys Berne 1
Rangers 1, Milan 4
Milan 2, Rangers 0
Seville 4, Aarhus 0
Aarhus 2, Seville 0
Dortmund Borussia 4, CCA Bucharest 2
CCA Bucharest 3, Dortmund Borussia 1
Dortmund Borussia 3, CCA Bucharest 1

**Quarter-finals**
Manchester United 2, Red Star 1
Red Star 3, Manchester United 3
Real Madrid 8, Seville 0
Seville 2, Real Madrid 2
Ajax Amsterdam 2, Vasas 2
Vasas 4, Ajax Amsterdam 0
Dortmund Borussia 1, Milan 1
Milan 4, Dortmund Borussia 1

**Semi-finals**
Real Madrid 4, Vasas Budapest 0
Vasas 2, Real Madrid 0
Manchester United 2, Milan 1
Milan 4, Manchester United 0

**Final** Brussels, 28 May 1958
Real Madrid (0) 3, Milan (0) 2 after extra time
*Real Madrid:* Alonso; Atienza, Lesmes; Santisteban, Santamaria, Zarraga; Kopa, Joseito, Di Stefano, Rial, Gento.
*Milan:* Soldan; Fontana, Beraldo; Bergamaschi, Maldini, Radice; Danova, Liedholm, Schiaffino, Grillo, Cucchiaroni.
*Scorers:* Schiaffino, Grillo for Milan; Di Stefano, Rial, Gento for Real Madrid.

**EUROPEAN CUP 1958–59**
After the champagne of Manchester United, the rather flat beer of the Wolves, who were put out, somewhat obscurely, by Schalke 04 in the first round. As for Hearts, the coloured Liège centre-forward, quaintly named Bonga-Bonga, tore their defence to shreds. Real proved more majestic than ever, especially in the crushing of Wiener Sport-

klub. But the all-Madrid semi-final with Atlético turned out to be a frighteningly close affair, in which Atlético (led by Brazil's Vavá) fought with magnificent spirit, forcing a third match. The final, against Reims, was anti-climax; a dull match which Real won despite an injury to Kopa, playing against his old club.

## Preliminary Round

Boldklub Copenhagen 3, Schalke 04 0

Schalke 04 5, Boldklub Copenhagen 2

Schalke 04 3, Boldklub Copenhagen 1

Standard Liège 5, Hearts 1

Hearts 2, Standard Liège 1

Dynamo Zagreb 2, Dukla Prague 1

Dukla Prague 2, Dynamo Zagreb 1

Jeunesse Esch 1, Gothenburg 2

Gothenburg 0, Jeunesse Esch 1

Gothenburg 5, Jeunesse Esch 1

Wismut Karl-Marx-Stadt 4, Petrolul Ploesti 2

Petrolul Ploesti 2, Wismut Karl-Marx-Stadt 0

Wismut Karl-Marx-Stadt 4, Petrolul Ploesti 0

Polonia Bytom 0, MTK Budapest 3

MTK Budapest 3, Polonia Bytom 0

Atlético Madrid 8, Drumcondra 0

Drumcondra 1, Atlético Madrid 5

DSO Utrecht 3, Sporting Lisbon 4

Sporting Lisbon 2, DSO Utrecht 1

Ards 1, Reims 4

Reims 6, Ards 2

Juventus 3, Wiener SK 1

Wiener SK 7, Juventus 0

Byes: *Real Madrid, CDNA Sofia, Wolverhampton Wanderers, Palloseura Helsinki.* Walk-overs: *Young Boys Berne, Besiktas.*

## First Round Proper

Sporting Lisbon 2, Standard Liège 3

Standard Liège 2, Sporting Lisbon 0

MTK 1, Young Boys Berne 2

Young Boys Berne 4, MTK 1

Wiener SK 3, Dukla Prague 1

Dukla Prague 1, Weiner SK 0

Atletico Madrid 2, CDNA Sofia 1

CDNA Sofia 1, Atlético Madrid 0

Atlético Madrid 3, CDNA Sofia 1 after extra time

Gothenburg 2, Wismut Karl-Marx-Stadt 2

Wismut Karl-Marx-Stadt 4, Gothenburg 0

Wolverhampton Wanderers 2, Schalke 04 2

Shalke 04 2, Wolverhampton Wanderers 1

Real Madrid 2, Besiktas Istanbul 0

Besiktas Istanbul 1, Real Madrid 1

Reims 4, Palloseura Helsinki 0

Reims 3, Palloseura Helsinki 0

## Quarter-finals

Standard Liège 2, Reims 0

Reims 3, Standard Liège 0

Atlético Madrid 3, Schalke 04 0

Schalke 04 1, Atlético Madrid 1

Wiener SK 0, Real Madrid 0

Real Madrid 7, Wiener SK 1

Young Boys 2, Wismut Karl-Marx-Stadt 2

Wismut Karl-Marx-Stadt 0, Young Boys 0

Young Boys 2, Wismut Karl-Marx-Stadt 1

## Semi-finals

Young Boys 1, Reims 0

Reims 3, Young Boys 0

Real Madrid 2, Atlético Madrid 1

Atlético Madrid 1, Real Madrid 0

Real Madrid 2, Atlético Madrid 1

**Final** Stuttgart, 2 June 1959
*Real Madrid* (1) 2, *Reims* (0) 0
*Real Madrid:* Dominguez; Marquitos, Zarraga; Santisteban, Santa-maria, Ruiz; Kopa, Mateos, Di Stefano, Rial, Gento.
*Reims:* Colonna; Rodzik, Giraudo; Penverne, Jonquet, Leblond; Lamartine, Bliard, Fontaine, Piantoni, Vincent.
*Scorers:* Mateos, Di Stefano for Real Madrid.


# EUROPEAN CUP 1959–60

The year 1960 produced one of the finest and most spectacular finals, a match in which Real – who now had the great Puskas in the side, with tireless Del Sol at inside-right – easily rode an early goal by Eintracht, to crush them 7–3. The immense Hampden crowd gave them a memorable ovation after the match. Di Stefano and Puskas were peerlessly brilliant, Puskas getting four of the goals, his left foot as ferocious as ever, with Di Stefano, tirelessly inventive, scoring the other three.

But Eintracht must not be written off; their progress to the final was splendid, not least their contemptuous home and away thrashing of Rangers. Their veteran inside-left, Pfaff, was a major star.

Nor must one forget the virtuosity of Barcelona and their polyglot team, under the flamboyant Herrera – who was abused by fans and sacked, after the elimination by Real in two awe-inspiring matches. Previously, they had killed the legend that Continentals cannot play in thick mud by humiliating Wolves on just such a pitch at Molineux. Of all the European Cups played, this was so far the most exciting and glittering.

**Preliminary Round**
Nice 3, Shamrock Rovers 2
Shamrock Rovers 1, Nice 1
CDNA Sofia 2, Barcelona 2
Barcelona 6, CDNA Sofia 2
Linfield 2, IFK Gothenburg 1
IFK Gothenburg 6, Linfield 1
Jeunesse Esch 5, Lodz 1
Lodz 2, Jeunesse Esch 1
Wiener SK 0, Petrolul Ploesti 0
Petrolul Ploesti 1, Wiener SK 2
Olympiakos 2, Milan 2
Milan 3, Olympiakos 1
Fenerbahce 1, Csepel 1
Fenerbahce 3, Csepel 2
Rangers 5, Anderlecht 2
Anderlecht 0, Rangers 2
Red Star Bratizlava 2, Porto 1
Porto 0, Red Star Bratislava 2
Vorwaerts Berlin 2,
   Wolverhampton Wanderers 1

Wolverhampton Wanderers 2,
   Vorwaerts Berlin 0
Byes: *Real Madrid, Odense BK09, Young Boys Berne, Sparta Rotterdam, Red Star Belgrade*. Walk-over: *Eintracht Frankfurt.*


**First Round**
Real Madrid 7, Esch 0
Esch 2, Real Madrid 5
Odense BK 09 0, Weiner SK 3
Weiner SK 2, Odense BK 09 2
Sparta Rotterdam 3, IFK
   Gothenburg 1
IFK Gothenburg 3, Sparta
   Rotterdam 1
Sparta Rotterdam 3, IFK
   Gothenburg 1
Milan 0, Barcelona 2
Barcelona 5, Milan 1

Young Boys Berne 1, Eintracht
Frankfurt 4
Eintracht Frankfurt 1, Young
Boys Berne 1
Red Star Belgrade 1,
Wolverhampton Wanderers 1
Wolverhampton Wanderers 3,
Red Star Belgrade 0
Rangers 4, Red Star Bratislava 3
Red Star Bratislava 1, Rangers 1
Fenerbahce 2, Nice 1
Nice 2, Fenerbahce 1
Nice 5, Fenerbahce 1

Real Madrid 4, Nice 0
Barcelona 4, Wolverhampton
Wanderers 0
Wolverhampton Wanderers 2,
Barcelona 5
Eintracht 2, Wiener SK 1
Wiener SK 1, Eintracht 1
Rangers 3, Sparta 2
Sparta 1, Rangers 0
Rangers 3, Sparta 2

**Quarter-finals**
Nice 3, Real Madrid 2

**Semi-finals**
Eintracht 6, Rangers 1
Rangers 3, Eintracht 6
Real Madrid 3, Barcelona 1
Barcelona 1, Real Madrid 3

**Final** Glasgow, 18 May 1960
*Real Madrid* (3) 7, *Eintracht Frankfurt* (1) 3
*Real Madrid:* Dominguez; Marquitos, Pachin; Vidal, Santamaria,
Zarraga; Canario, Del Sol, Di Stefano, Puskas, Gento.
*Eintracht:* Loy; Lutz, Hoefer; Wellbaecher, Eigenbrodt, Stinka;
Kress, Lindner, Stein, Pfaff, Meier.
*Scorers:* Di Stefano (3), Puskas (4) for Real; Kress, Stein (2) for
Eintracht.

## EUROPEAN CUP 1960–61

At long last, the reign of Real Madrid was brought to an end. But
the team that eliminated them – Barcelona, taking revenge for the
previous year – did not win the Cup. Instead, it went, against all ex-
pectation, to Benfica, the Portuguese club, managed with immense
shrewdness by the veretan Hungarian, Bela Guttmann. Benfica may
have had a little luck in the final, when the sun dazzled Ramallets, and
he let in a couple of simple goals, but they undoubtedly had a splendid
team. Germano, the centre-half, was the best and most mobile in
Europe, Coluna a superb midfield player, and Aguas a mature centre
forward.

Burnley, England's representatives, played skilful football, but failed
badly against Hamburg in their return quarter-final, when they had
enough of the play to have won. Hearts were unfortunate enough to
meet Benfica in the first round.

**Preliminary Round**
Frederikstadt 4, Ajax
Amsterdam 3
Ajax Amsterdam 0,
Frederikstadt 0
Limerick 0, Young Boys Berne 6
Young Boys Berne 4, Limerick 2

Kamraterna 1, IFK Malmö 3
IFK Malmö 2, Kamraterna 1
Reims 6, Jeunesse Esch 1
Jeunesse Esch 0, Reims 5
Rapid Vienna 4, Besiktas
Istanbul 0
Besiktas Istanbul 1, Rapid
Vienna 0

Juventus 2, CDNA Sofia 0
CDNA Sofia 4, Juventus 1
Aarhus GF 3, Legia Warsaw 0
Legia Warsaw 1, Aarhus GF 0
Red Star Belgrade 1, Ujpest
    Dozsa 2
Ujpest Dozsa 3, Red Star
    Belgrade 0
Barcelona 2, Lierse SK 0
Lierse SK 0, Barcelona 3
Hearts 1, Benfica 2
Benfica 3, Hearts 0
CCA Bucharest 0, Spartak
    Kralove 3
Forfeited *Glenavon and CCA
Bucharest*
Byes: *Real Madrid, Panathinaikos
SV Hamburg, Burnley.* Walk-over:
*Wismut Karl-Marx-Stadt.*

**First Round**
Aarhus GF 3, Frederikstadt 0
Frederikstadt 0, Aarhus GF 1
IFK Malmö 1, CDNA Sofia 0
CDNA Sofia 1, IFK Malmö 0
Young Boys 0, SV Hamburg 5
SV Hamburg 3, Young Boys 3
Spartak Kralove 1,
    Panathinaikos 0
Panathinaikos 0, Spartak
    Kralove 0

**Final** Berne, 31 March 1961

Benfica 6, Ujpest 2
Ujpest 2, Benfica 1
Real Madrid 2, Barcelona 2
Barcelona 2, Real Madrid 1
Rapid Vienna 3, Wismut
    Karl-Marx-Stadt 1
Wismut Karl-Marx-Stadt 2,
    Rapid Vienna 0
Rapid Vienna 1, Wismut
    Karl-Marx-Stadt 0
Burnley 2, Reims 0
Reims 3, Burnley 2

**Quarter-finals**
Burnley 3, Hamburg 1
Hamburg 4, Burnley 1
Barcelona 4, Spartak Kralove 0
Spartak Kralove 1, Barcelona 1
Benfica 3, Aarhus 1
Aarhus 2, Benfica 4
Rapid Vienna 2, IFK Malmö 0
IFK Malmö 0, Rapid Vienna 2

**Semi-finals**
Barcelona 1, Hamburg 0
Hamburg 2, Barcelona 1
Barcelona 1, Hamburg 0
Benfica 3, Rapid Vienna 0
Rapid Vienna 1, Benfica 1

*Benfica* (2) 3, *Barcelona* (1) 2

*Benfica:* Costa Pereira; Joao, Angelo; Netto, Germano, Cruz; Augusto, Santana, Aguas, Coluna, Cavem.

*Barcelona:* Ramallets; Foncho, Gracia; Verges, Garay, Gensana; Kubala, Kocsis, Evaristo, Suarez, Czibor.

*Scorers:* Aguas, Ramallets (own goal), Coluna for Benfica; Kocsis, Czibor for Barcelona.


## EUROPEAN CUP 1961–62

It was now the turn of the brilliant Spurs team to represent England. They played some memorable matches, not least the one in which they crushed Gornik of Poland 8–1 in a frenzied atmosphere of partisan passion, after losing the first leg. But over-emphasis on defence in Lisbon, mistakes by the backs, and a little bad luck in a frenetic return, against Benfica, cost them the semi-finals. Benfica went on to win a marvellous final against Real, in Amsterdam, proving that their success the season before had been no fluke. They survived a fine early goal worked out by Di Stefano and Puskas, and the shooting in this match from Puskas, Coluna, Eusebio, and Cavem really had to be seen to be believed.

Rangers, once again representing Scotland, had a creditable passage, but failed sadly and surprisingly in Liège against Standard.

**Preliminary Round**

Nuremberg 5, Drumcondra 0
Drumcondra 1, Nuremberg 4
Vorwaerts 3, Linfield 0
(*Linfield gave Vorwaerts a walkover in the second leg when the East Germans were refused visas*).
Spora Luxemburg 0, Odense BK 09 6
Odense BK 09 9, Spora Luxemburg 2
Monaco 2, Rangers 3
Rangers 3, Monaco 2
Vasas Budapest 0, Real Madrid 2
Real Madrid 3, Vasas Budapest 1
CDNA Sofia 4, Dulka 4
Dulka 2, CDNA Sofia 1
Standard Liège 2, Frederikstadt 1
Frederikstadt 0, Standard Liège 2
IFK Gothenburg 0, Feyenoord 3
Feyenoord 8, IFK Gothenburg 2
Servette 5, Valetta 0
Valetta 1, Servette 2
Gornik Zabrze 4, Tottenham Hotspur 2
Tottenham Hotspur 8, Gornik Zabrze 1
Sporting Lisbon 1, Partizan Belgrade 1
Partizan Belgrade 2, Sporting Lisbon 0
Panathinaikos 1, Juventus 1
Juventus 2, Panathinaikos 1
Bucharest 0, FK Austria 0
FK Austria 2, Bucharest 0
Byes: *Benfica, Valkeakosken, Fenerbahce*.

**First Round**

Odense BK 09 0, Real Madrid 3
Real Madrid 9, Odense BK 09 0
Fenerbahce 1, Nuremberg 2
Nuremberg 1, Fenerbahce 0
Standard Liège 5, Valkeakosken 1
Valkeakosken 0, Standard Liège 2
FK Austria 1, Benfica 1
Benfica 5, FK Austria 1
Servette 4, Dukla 3
Dukla 2, Servette 0
Feyenoord 1, Tottenham Hotspur 3
Tottenham Hotspur 1, Feyenoord 1
Partizan 1, Juventus 2
Juventus 5, Partizan 1
Vorwaerts Berlin 1, Rangers 2
Rangers 4, Vorwaerts Berlin 1

**Quarter-finals**

Nuremberg 3, Benfica 1
Benfica 6, Nuremberg 0
Standard Liège 4, Rangers 1
Rangers 2, Standard Liège 0
Dukla 1, Tottenham Hotspur 0
Tottenham Hotspur 4, Dukla 1
Juventus 0, Real Madrid 1
Real Madrid 0, Juventus 1
Real Madrid 3, Juventus 1

**Semi-finals**

Benfica 3, Tottenham Hotspur 1
Tottenham Hotspur 2, Benfica 1
Real Madrid 4, Standard Liège 0
Standard Liège 0, Real Madrid 2

Final Amsterdam, 2 May 1962
*Benfica* (2) 5, *Real Madrid* (3) 3
Benfica: Costa Pereira; Joao, Angelo; Cavem, Germano, Cruz; Augusto, Eusebio, Aguas, Coluna, Simoes.

*Real Madrid:* Araquistain; Cassado, Miera; Felo, Santamaria, Pachin; Tejada, Del Sol, Di Stefano, Puskas, Gento.
*Scorers:* Puskas (3) for Real Madrid; Aguas, Cavem, Coluna, Eusebio (2) for Benfica.

## EUROPEAN CUP 1962–63

For the third successive time, Benfica reached the final, but this one was to end in their defeat. Milan beat them at Wembley in a slightly disappointing game. Managed now by the Chilean, Riera, instead of Guttmann, Benfica had gone over to 4–2–4 and a more defensive outlook, partly dictated by the loss of Germano through injury, Aguas through form. Milan, well generalled by the precocious young Rivera, hit back with two goals by Brazil's Altafini (the second of which looked offside) after Eusebio had put Benfica ahead. But an injury to Coluna who had to go off in the second half, badly affected them.

Ipswich, England's representatives, and Dundee both went out to Milan. Ipswich floundered in heavy rain in Milan, played more briskly in the return – and won – but Dundee were a revelation. Clever breakaway tactics and a defence splendidly marshalled by Ian Ure enabled them to become the dark horse of the tournament. For Real, knocked out in Belgium by a goal from Jef Jurion, this was a season of relative twilight.

**Preliminary Round**
Linfield 1, Esbjerg 2
Esbjerg 0, Linfield 0
Real Madrid 3, Anderlecht 3
Anderlecht 1, Real Madrid 0
Floriana Malta 1, Ipswich Town 4
Ipswich Town 10, Floriana
  Malta 0
Dundee 8, Cologne 1
Cologne 4, Dundee 0
Shelbourne 0, Sporting Lisbon 2
Sporting Lisbon 5, Shelbourne 1
Vorwaerts 0, Dukla Prague 3
Dukla Prague 1, Vorwaerts 0
Norrköping 9, Partizan Tirana 2
Partizan Tirana 1, Norrköping 1
Dynamo Bucharest 1,
  Galatasaray 1
Galatasaray 3, Dynamo
  Bucharest 0
Servette Geneva 1, Feyenoord 3
Feyenoord 1, Servette Geneva 3
Servette Geneva 1, Feyenoord 3
Polonia 2, Panathinaikos 1
Panathinaikos 1, Polonia 4
Frederikstadt 1, Vasas Budapest 4

Vasas Budapest 7, Frederikstadt 0
FK Austria 5, Kamraterna
  Helsinki 3
Kamraterna Helsinki 0,
  FK Austria 2
CDNA Sofia 2, Partizan
  Belgrade 1
Partizan Belgrade 1, CDNA
  Sofia 4
Milan 8, US Luxemburg 0
US Luxemburg 0, Milan 6
Byes: *Benfica, Reims*

**First Round**
FK Austria 3, Reims 2
Reims 5, FK Austria 0
Sporting Lisbon 1, Dundee 0
Dundee 4, Sporting Lisbon 1
Norrköping 1, Benfica 1
Benfica 5, Norrköping 1
Galatasaray 4, Polonia Bytom 1
Polonia Bytom 1, Galatasaray 0
Esbjerg 0, Dukla 0
Dukla 5, Esbjerg 0
Feyenoord 1, Vasas 1
Vasas 2, Feyenoord 2

Feyenoord 1, Vasas 0
Milan 3, Ipswich Town 0
Ipswich Town 2, Milan 1

Dukla 0, Benfica 0
Reims 0, Feyenoord 1
Feyenoord 1, Reims 1

**Quarter-finals**
Anderlecht 1, Dundee 4
Dundee 2, Anderlecht 1
Galatasaray 1, Milan 3
Milan 5, Galatasaray 0
Benfica 2, Dukla 1

**Semi-finals**
Milan 5, Dundee 1
Dundee 1, Milan 0
Benfica 3, Feyenoord 1
Feyenoord 0, Benfica 0

**Final** Wembley Stadium, 22 May 1963
Milan (0) 2, Benfica (1) 1
*Milan:* Ghezzi; David, Trebbi; Benitez, Maldini, Trapattoni; Pivatelli, Sani, Altafini, Rivera, Mora.
*Benfica:* Costa Pereira; Cavem, Cruz; Humberto, Raul, Coluna; Augusto, Santana, Torres, Eusebio, Simões.
*Scorers:* Eusebio for Benfica; Altafini (2) for Milan.


# EUROPEAN CUP 1963–64

Britain's challenge disappeared with depressing speed. Rangers, somewhat unlucky to lose to a late goal by Puskas in a breakaway at Ibrox, were torn apart in Madrid, where Puskas showed much of his old form. It must be said in Rangers' defence that they lacked several experienced forwards. Everton were baffled by the reinforced Inter defence at Goodison, though many feel they did breach it, when a goal by Vernon was narrowly judged offside. In Milan, they themselves employed massive defence, and it was only a freak goal from near the by-line, scored by Jair, which beat them.

Benfica, lacking Costa Pereira and Eusebio, were thrashed in their return match with Borussia Dortmund who went on to eliminate Dukla. A superb display in Madrid enabled Real to eliminate Milan, while Inter's massive defence and breakaway attacks accounted for Monaco, Partizan, and Borussia. In the final, Inter left out their extra defender, Szymaniak, gambled on a genuine leader in Milani, blotted out Real's attack, and exploited the mistakes of their defence. Mazzola scored from long range just before half-time. Poor goalkeeping gave Milani a second, Felo headed in from a corner, but an incredible blunder by Santamaria presented Mazzola with the third.

**Preliminary Round**
Galatasary 4, Ferencvaros 0
Ferencvaros 2, Galatasaray 0
Partizan Belgrade 3, Anorthosis 0
Anorthosis 1, Partizan Belgrade 3
Dundalk 0, FC Zürich 3
FC Zürich 1, Dundalk 2
Lyn Oslo 2, Borussia
  Dortmund 4

Borussia Dortmund 3, Lyn Oslo 1
Dukla Prague 6, Valetta 0
Valetta 0, Dukla Prague 2
Everton 0, Internazionale 0
Internazionale 1, Everton 0
Gornik Zabrze 1, FK Austria 0
FK Austria 1, Gornik Zabrze 0
Gornik Zabrze 2, FK Austria 1
Monaco 7, AEK Athens 2

AEK Athens 1, Monaco 1
Dynamo Bucharest 2, Motor
  Jena 0
Motor Jena 0, Dynamo
  Bucharest 1
Valkeakosken 4, Jeunesse Esch 1
Jeunesse Esch 4, Valkaekosken 0
Standard Liège 1, Norrköping 0
Norrköping 2, Standard Liège 0
Tirania 1, Spartak Plovdiv 0
Spartak Plovdiv 3, Tirania 1
Eindhoven 7, Esbjerg 1
Esbjerg 3, Eindhoven 4
Distillery 3, Benfica 3
Benfica 5, Distillery 0
Rangers 0, Real Madrid 1
Real Madrid 6, Rangers 0
Bye: *Milan*

**First Round**
Benfica 2, Borussia Dortmund 1
Borussia Dortmund 5, Benfica 0
Internazionale 1, Monaco 0
Monaco 0, Internazionale 3
Norrköpping 1, Milan 1
Milan 5, Norrköpping 2
FC Zürich 3, Galatasaray 0
Galatasaray 2, FC Zürich 0
Gornik 2, Dukla 0
Dukla 4, Gornik 1

Jeunesse Esch 2, Partizan
  Belgrade 1
Partizan Belgrade 6, Heunesse
  Esch 2
Spartak Plovdiv 0, Eindhoven 1
Eindhoven 0, Spartak Plovdiv 0
Dynamo Bucharest 1, Real
  Madrid 3
Real Madrid 5, Dynamo
  Bucharest 3

**Quarter-finals**
Real Madrid 4, Milan 1
Milan 2, Real Madrid 0
Partizan Belgrade 0,
  Internazionale 3
Internazionale 2, Partizan
  Belgrade 1
Eindhoven 1, FC Zürich 0
FC Zürich 3, Eindhoven 1
Dukla 0, Borussia Dortmund 4
Borussia Dortmund 1, Dukla 3

**Semi-finals**
Borussia Dortmund 2,
  Internazionale 2
Internazionale 2, Borussia
  Dortmund 0
FC Zürich 1, Real Madrid 2
Real Madrid 6, FC Zürich 0

**Final** Vienna, 27 May 1964
Internazionale 3, Real Madrid 1
*Internazionale:* Sarti; Burgnich, Facchetti; Tagnin, Guarneri, Picchi;
Jair, Mazzola, Milani, Suarez, Corso.
*Real Madrid:* Vicente; Isidro, Pachin; Muller, Santamaria, Zoco;
Amancio, Felo, Di Stefano, Puskas, Gento.
*Scorers:* Mazola (2), Milani for Internazionale; Felo for Real Madrid.

## EUROPEAN CUP 1964–65
Once again, Inter won the tournament, though not without considerable difficulty, on the way. Much of this was gallantly provided by
Liverpool who, three days after a bruising Cup final, involving extra
time, and playing without two key men, brilliantly defeated them at
Anfield. Inter, however, recovered to win in Milan, though Peiró's gaol,
after a challenge on goalkeeper Lawrence, which is still a subject of dis-
pute. Previously, Liverpool had had a notable success against an
Anderlecht team till then in splendid form. A clever tactical plan, using

185

Smith as a second centre-half, was their chief weapon, but they were very lucky indeed to win the toss in Rotterdam against a brave 10-man Cologne team, which fought back from 0–2.

Rangers also did well, and might have done better still, had not Jim Baxter broken a leg, while helping materially to get them through, in Vienna.

In the final, Inter won laboriously and unconvincingly against a brave Benfica side, naturally reluctant to play it on Inter's own ground. Benfica lost Costa Pereira, their goalkeeper, half-an-hour from time, but the score remained unchanged. And the goal, by Jair, was really a result of the appalling, rainy conditions, for his shot slipped under Costa Pereira's body.

**Preliminary Round**

Anderlecht 1, Bologna 0
Bologna 2, Anderlecht 1
Anderlecht 0, Bologna 0 (*in Barcelona*)
(Anderlecht *won toss*)
Rangers 3, Red Star Belgrade 1
Red Star Belgrade 4, Rangers 2
Rangers 3, Red Star Belgrade 1 (*at Highbury*)
Chemie Leipzig 0, Vasas Gyor 2
Vasas Gyor 4, Chemie Leipzig 2
Dukla Prague 4, Gornik Zabrze 1
Gornik Zabrze 3, Dukla Prague 0
Gornik Zabrze 0, Dukla Prague 0 (*in Duisberg*)
(Dukla *won toss*)
Reipas Lahti 2, Lyn Oslo 1
Lyn Oslo 3, Reipas Lahti 0
Partizan Tirana 0, Cologne 0
Cologne 2, Partizan Tirana 0
St Eteinne 2, Chaux de Fonds 2
Chaux de Fonds 2, St Etienne 1
Glentoran 2, Panathinaikos 2
Panathinaikos 3, Glentoran 2
Odense BK 09 2, Real Madrid 5
Real Madrid 4, Odense BK 09 0
Aris 1, Benfica 5
Benfica 5, Aris 1
DWS Amsterdam 3, Fenerbahce 0
Fenerbahce 0, DWS Amsterdam 1
Rapid Vienna 3, Shamrock Rovers 0
Shamrock Rovers 0, Rapid Vienna 2

Lokomotiv Sofia 8, Malmö 3
Malmö 2, Lokomotiv Sofia 0
Reykjavic 0, Liverpool 5
Liverpool 6, Reykjavic 1
Dynamo Bucharest 5, Sliema Wanderers 0
Sliema Wanderers 0, Dynamo Bucharest 2
Bye: *Internazionale*

**First Round**

Panathinaikos 1, Cologne 1
Cologne 2, Panathinaikos 1
Internazionale 6, Dynamo Bucharest 0
Dynamo Bucharest 0, Internazionale 1
Vasas Gyor 5, Lokomotiv Sofia 3
Lokomotiv Sofia 4, Vasas Gyor 3
Rangers 1, Rapid Vienna 0
Rapid Vienna 0, Rangers 2
Real Madrid 4, Dukla 0
Dukla 2, Real Madrid 2
Liverpool 3, Anderlecht 0
Anderlecht 0, Liverpool 1
DWS Amsterdam 5, Lyn 0
Lyn 1, DWS Amsterdam 3
Chaux de Fonds 1, Benfica 1
Benfica 5, Chaux de Fonds 0

**Quarter-finals**

Cologne 0, Liverpool 0
Liverpool 0, Cologne 0
Liverpool 2, Cologne 2 (*in Rotterdam*)
Liverpool *won toss*

Internazionale 3, Rangers 1
Rangers 1, Internazionale 0
Benfica 3, Real Madrid 1
Real Madrid 2, Benfica 1
DWS Amsterdam 1, Vasas
  Gyor 1
Vasas Gyor 1, DWS
  Amsterdam 0

**Final** Milan, 27 May 1965
Internazionale (1) 1, Benfica (0) 0
*Internazionale:* Sarti; Burgnich, Facchetti; Bedin, Guarneri, Picchi; Jair, Mazzola, Peiró, Suarez, Corso.
*Benfica:* Costa Pereira; Cavem, Cruz; Netto, Germano, Raul; Augusto, Eusebio, Torres, Coluna, Simões.
*Scorer:* Jair for Inter.

**Semi-finals**
Vasas Gyor 0, Benfica 1
Benfica 4, Vasas Gyor 0
Liverpool 3, Internazionale 1
Internazionale 3, Liverpool 0

## EUROPEAN CUP 1965–66

Once again, Manchester United reached the semi-finals – and folded up. Once again Real Madrid, for the sixth time in their history, took the Cup. The virtual final was composed by their two matches against Inter, the holders and favourites, who made the mistake of fielding a defensive formation against them in the first leg of the semi-finals, in Madrid. Real got through by the only goal and, at San Siro, virtually settled matters when they took the lead through Amancio. Inter equalised, but never seemed likely to win.

In the final, Real, a young, vigorous side with none of the high quality of the Di Stefano days, duly beat Partizan, the Belgrade dark horses, despite falling behind to a goal by Vasovic 10 minutes after half-time.

Previously, Partizan had beaten a sloppy Manchester United side in Belgrade, and held them to a single, rather lucky, goal by Stiles, at Old Trafford, where United were without Best, Partizan without their midfield schemer, Kovacevic – and without Galic, doing his military service but recalled for the final, in Brussels. United had the consolation of putting up perhaps the finest display of the competition, when they brilliantly thrashed Benfica in Lisbon, in the return leg of the quarter-finals. George Best, irresistible, scored the two opening goals in the first 12 minutes.

**Preliminary Round**
Lyn 5, Derry City 3
Derry City 5, Lyn 1
Feyenoord 2, Real Madrid 1
Real Madrid 5, Feyenoord 0
Kevflavik 1, Ferencvaros 4
Ferencvaros 9, Kevflavik 1
Fenerbahce 0, Anderlecht 0
Anderlecht 5, Fenerbahce 1

Tirania 0, Kilmarnock 0
Kilmarnock 1, Tirania 0
Djurgarden 2, Levski 1
Levski 6, Djurgarden 0
Drumcondra 1, Vorwaerts
  Berlin 0
Vorwaerts Berlin 2,
  Drumcondra 0
Linz 1, Gornik Zabrze 3

187

Gornik Zabrze 2, Linz 1
Partizan Belgrade 2, Nantes 0
Nantes 2, Partizan Belgrade 2
HJK Helsinki 2, Manchester
United 3
Manchester United 6,
HJK Helsinki 0
Lausanne 0, Sparta Prague 0
Sparta Prague 4, Lausanne 0
Dundelange 0, Benfica 8
Benfica 10, Dundelange 0
Panathinaikos 4, Sliema 1
Sliema 1, Panathinaikos 0
Hapoel Nicosia 0, Werder
Bremen 5 (Bremen)
Werder Bremen 5, Hapoel
Nicosia 0
Dynamo Bucharest 4, Odense
BK 09 0
Odense BK 09 2, Dynamo
Bucharest 3
Bye: *Internazionale*

### First Round
Partizan 3, Werder Bremen 0
Werder Bremen 1, Partizan 0
Levski 2, Benfica 2
Benfica 3, Levski 2
Ferencvaros 0, Panathinaikos 0
Panathinaikos 1, Ferencvaros 3

Kilmarnock 2, Real Madrid 2
Real Madrid 5, Kilmarnock 1
Vorwaerts 0, Manchester
United 2
Manchester United 3,
Vorwaerts 1
Sparta 3, Gornik 0
Gornik 1, Sparta 2
Dynamo Bucharest 2,
Internazionale 1
Internazionale 2, Dynamo
Bucharest 0
Anderlecht 9, Derry City 0
(*no return match*)

### Second Round
Manchester United 3, Benfica 2
Benfica 1, Manchester United 5
Anderlecht 1, Real Madrid 0
Real Madrid 4, Anderlecht 2
Sparta 4, Partizan 1
Partizan 5, Sparta 0
Internazionale 4, Ferencvaros 0
Ferencvaros 1, Internazionale 1

### Semi-finals
Partizan 2, Manchester United 0
Manchester United 1, Partizan 0
Real Madrid 1, Internazionale 0
Internazionale 1, Real Madrid 1

**Final** Brussels, 11 May 1966
Real Madrid (0) 2, Partizan (0) 1
*Real Madrid:* Araquistain; Pachin, Sanchis; Pirri, De Felipe, Zoco;
Serena, Amancio, Grosso, Velasquez, Gento.
*Partizan:* Soskic; Jusufi, Milhailovic; Becejac, Rasovic, Vasovic;
Bakic, Kovacevic, Hasanagic, Galic, Primajer.
*Scorers:* Amancio and Serena for Real; Vasovic for Partizan.

## EUROPEAN CUP 1966–67
To the general surprise, and delight, the Cup was won by a Celtic
team competing in it for the first time; one, moreover, which overwhelmed a weary and pathetically negative Inter in the final, at Lisbon.
Shrewdly and forcefully managed by their old centre-half, Jock Stein,
Celtic's football was (with the exception of a cautious holding action
away to Dukla) fast, muscular, and attacking. Gemmell overlapped
powerfully at left-back, scoring a magnificent, half-volleyed goal in the
final, Auld was a fine midfield player, little Johnstone a superb outside-
right.

Inter reached their zenith in the quarter-finals, when they took an ample revenge on Real Madrid for the previous year's elimination. Cappellini, then, looked an impressive new centre-forward. Then the bubble burst, and they made pitifully heavy weather disposing, in three matches, of the honest, modest CSKA Sofia, previously much troubled by Linfield.

Liverpool were thrashed by a splendid Ajax forward-line, in Amsterdam; finely led by Cruyff; but Dukla knew too much for Ajax. Torpedo, Russia's first entrants, put up a sturdy fight against Inter, in Milan, but went out by the only goal – Voronin's own goal – of the tie.

In the final, Inter, without their midfield general Suarez, and with Mazzola not fully fit, took the lead from a penalty when, in the eighth minute, Craig tripped Cappellini, then bolted back into defence, to be besieged for the rest of the game. Gemmell equalised after 63 minutes, and Chalmers got the winner five minutes from time.

**Preliminary Round**

Sliema Wanderers 1, CSKA Sofia 2
CSKA Sofia 4, Sliema Wanderers 0
Waterford 1, Vorwaerts Berlin 6
Vorwaerts Berlin 6, Waterford 0

**First Round**

Reykjavik 2, Nantes 3
Nantes 5, Reykjavik 2
Aris Bonnevoie 3, Linfield 3
Linfield 6, Aris Bonnevoie 1
Admira 0, Vojvodina 1
Vojvodina 0, Admira 0
Anderlecht 10, Valkeakovski 1
Valkeakovski 0, Anderlecht 2
  (in Brussels)
Munich 1860 8, Nicosia 0
Nicosia 1, Munich 1860 2
  (in Munich)
Liverpool 2, Petrolul Ploesti 0
Petrolul Ploesti 3, Liverpool 1
Liverpool 2, Petrolul Ploesti 0
  (in Brussels)
Celtic 2, Zürich 0
Zürich 0, Celtic 3
Malmö 0, Atlético Madrid 2
Atletico Madrid 3, Malmö 1
Esbjerg 0, Dukla Prague 2
Dukla Prague 4, Esbjerg 0
Ajax Amsterdam 2, Besiktas 0
Besiktas 1, Ajax Amsterdam 2

Vasas Budapest 5, Sporting Lisbon 0
Sporting Lisbon 0, Vasas Budapest 2
CSKA 3, Olimpiakos Piraeus 1
Olimpiakos Piraeus 1, CSKA 0
Gornik Zabrze 2, Vorwaerts 1
Vorwaerts 2, Gornik Zabrze 1
Gornik Zabrze 2, Vorwaerts 1
  (in Budapest)
Internazionale 1, Torpedo 0
Torpedo 0, Internazionale 0
Bye: *Real Madrid*. Walk-over: *Valerengen*

**Second Round**

Valerengen Oslo 1, Linfield 4
Linfield 1, Valerengen Oslo 1
Inter 2, Vasas 1
Vasas 0, Inter 2
Dukla 4, Anderlecht 1
Anderlecht 1, Dukla 2
Munich 1860 1, Real Madrid 0
Real Madrid 3, Munich 1860 1
CSKA 4, Gornik 1
Gornik 3, CSKA 0
Vojvodina 3, Atlético Madrid 1
Atlético Madrid 2, Vojvodina 3
  (in Madrid)
Nantes 1, Celtic 3
Celtic 3, Nantes 1
Ajax 5, Liverpool 1
Liverpool 2, Ajax 2

189

**Quarter-finals**
Inter 1, Real Madrid 0
Real Madrid 0, Inter 2
Linfield 2, CSKA 2
CSKA 1, Linfield 0
Ajax 1, Dukla 1
Dukla 2, Ajax 1
Vojvodina 1, Celtic 0

Celtic 2, Vojvodina 0

**Semi-finals**
Celtic 3, Dukla 1
Dukla 0, Celtic 0
Inter 1, CSKA 1
CSKA 1, Inter 1
Inter 1, CSKA 0 (*in Bologna*)

**Final** Lisbon, 25 May 1967
Celtic (0) 2, Internazionale (1) 1
*Celtic:* Simpson; Craig, Gemmell; Murdoch, McNeill, Clark; Johnstone, Wallace, Chalmers, Auld, Lennox.
*Inter:* Sarti; Burgnich, Facchetti; Bedin, Guarneri, Picchi; Bicicli, Mazzola, Cappellini, Corso, Domenghini.
*Scorers:* Gemmell, Chalmers for Celtic, Mazzola (pen) for Inter.

## EUROPEAN CUP 1967–68

For the first time, the European Cup was won by an English club; most fittingly, Manchester United, who had been semi-finalists on three previous occasions. The final, at Wembley, was remarkable. United dominated the first half, but couldn't turn their advantage into goals, flagged badly late in the second half, when Benfica equalised Charlton's goal, and were ultimately galvanised by a superb goal, early in extra time, scored by George Best.

Previously, they'd had little trouble with the Maltese – though they surprisingly drew 0–0 in Malta – had overcome a rough, determined Sarajevo, and beaten Real Madrid after an astonishing revival at Bernabeu Stadium, centre-half Foulkes getting the equaliser. There was also a memorable quarter-final versus Gornik, who were defied by brilliant goalkeeping at Old Trafford. United then managed to keep the score down to 1–0 on an impossibly Arctic pitch, in Poland.

Celtic, the holders, surprisingly went out to Dynamo Kiev in the first round. Bychevetz was their destroyer in Glasgow, but they were rather unlucky in the return, when Murdoch was sent off, and fighting broke out late in the game. Glentoran, the Irish champions, gave Benfica a terrible fright in the same round, going out only on the newly and dubiously introduced rule whereby away goals, in case of equality, count double. Benfica did not really find form and recover from manager Riera's resignation till the semi-finals, when Vasas were overcome. At Wembley, they lost many friends with their rough treatment of Best.

This was the first European Cup to be seeded.

**First Round**
Glentoran 1, Benfica 1
Benfica 0, Glentoran 0
Besiktas 0, Rapid Vienna 1

Rapid Vienna 3, Besiktas 0
Celtic 1, Dynamo Kiev 2
Dynamo Kiev 1, Celtic 1

Olimpiakos Piraeus 0,
Juventus 0
Juventus 2, Olimpiakos
Piraeus 0
Dundalk 0, Vasas Budapest 1
Vasas Budapest 8, Dundalk 1
Manchester United 4, Hibernian
(Malta) 0
Hibernian (Malta) 0, Manchester
United 0
St Etienne 2, Kuopio 0
Kuopio 3, St Etienne 0
Karl-Marx-Stadt 1, Anderlecht 3
Anderlecht 2, Karl-Marx-Stadt 1
Basel 1, Hvidovre 2
Hvidovre 3, Basel 3
Skeid Oslo 0, Sparta Prague 1
Sparta Prague 1, Skeid Oslo 1
Olympiakos Nicosia 2,
Sarajevo 2
Sarajevo 3, Olympiakos
Nicosia 1
Ajax 1, Real Madrid 1
Real Madrid 2, Ajax 1
Valur 1, Jeunesse Esch 1
Jeunesse Esch 3, Valur 3
Gornik Zabrze 3, Djurgarden 0
Djurgarden 0, Gornik Zabrze 0
Plovdiv Traka 2, Rapid
Bucharest 0
Rapid Bucharest 3, Plovdiv
Traka 0
Walk-over: *Eintracht Brunswick*

**Second Round**
Sarajevo 0, Manchester United 0

Manchester United 2, Sarajevo 1
Hvidovre 2, Real Madrid 2
Real Madrid 4, Hvidovre 1
Rapid Vienna 1, Eintracht
Brunswick 0
Eintracht Brunswick 2, Rapid
Vienna 0
Benfica 2, St Etienne 0
St Etienne 1, Benfica 0
Vasas 6, Reykjavik 0
Reykjavik 1, Vasas 5
Dynamo Kiev 1, Gornik 2
Gornik 1, Dynamo Kiev 1
Juventus 1, Rapid Bucharest 0
Rapid Bucharest 0, Juventus 0
Sparta Prague 3, Anderlecht 2
Anderlecht 2, Sparta Prague 3

**Quarter-finals**
Eintracht Brunswick 3, Juventus 2
Juventus 1, Eintracht Brunswick 0
(*play-off*)
Manchester United 2, Gornik 0
Gornik 1, Manchester United 0
Real Madrid 3, Sparta Prague 0
Sparta Prague 2, Real Madrid 1
Vasas 0, Benfica 0
Benfica 3, Vasas 0

**Semi-finals**
Manchester United 1, Real
Madrid 0
Real Madrid 3, Manchester
United 3
Benfica 0, Juventus 0
Juventos 0, Benfica 1

**Final** Wembley Stadium, 29 May 1968
Manchester United (0) (1) 4, Benfica (0) (1) 1 (after extra time).
*Manchester United:* Stepney; Brennan, Dunne; Crerand, Foulkes,
Stiles; Best, Kidd, Charlton, Sadler, Aston.
*Benfica:* Henrique; Adolfo, Humberto, Jacinto, Cruz; Graça, Coluna;
Augusto, Eusebio, Torres, Simões.
*Scorers:* Charlton (2), Best, Kidd for Manchester United; Graça for
Benfica.

## EUROPEAN CUP 1968–69

Milan won their second European Cup, gathering strength and momentum as the competition progressed, knocking out both Celtic and Manchester United, and finally overwhelming Ajax in a one-sided final. Pierino Prati established himself as one of the game's most dangerous finishers, ruthlessly exploiting a slip by McNeill at a throw-in to put out Celtic in Glasgow, and scoring three times, with much help from Gianni Rivera, in the final, in Madrid.

Mistaken selection and sloppy defensive play helped to put out Manchester United, after they had comfortably accounted for Rapid – Best showing superb form. Surprisingly in the first leg of the quarter-final in Milan, they chose the veteran Foulkes for centre-half; Sormani was thus allowed his best game for months. The inexperienced Rimmer played in goal. United lost 2–0, and though they won an ill-tempered return in Manchester – during which Cudicini was felled by a missile from the notorious Stretford End – they properly went out; once again gifted but maddening.

Ajax, with Cruyff a dazzling centre-forward, were first astonished by Benfica, before astonishing them in their turn. A poor first game by Spartak Trnava's goalkeeper assisted their passage into the final, but there, they were simply outclassed.

All the Iron Curtain teams but the Czech withdrew in protest against a decision to re-draw the First Round.

**First Round**
St Etienne 2, Celtic 0
Celtic 4, St Etienne 0
Waterford 1, Manchester United 3
Manchester United 7, Waterford 1
Manchester City 0, Fenerbahce 0
Fenerbahce 2, Manchester City 1
Anderlecht 3, Glentoran 0
Glentoran 2, Anderlecht 2
AEK Athens 3, Jeunesse Esch 0
Jeunesse Esch 3, AEK Athens 2
Nuremberg 1, Ajax 1
Ajax 4, Nuremberg 0
Malmö 2, Milan 1
Milan 4, Malmö 1
Steaua Bucharest 3, Spartak Trnava 1
Spartak Trnava 4, Steaua Bucharest 0
Zurich 1, AB Copenhagen 3
AB Copenhagen 2, Zurich 2
Trondheim 1, Rapid Vienna 3
Rapid Vienna 3, Trondheim 3
Valetta 1, Repias Lahti 1

Reipas Lahti 2, Valetta 0
Real Madrid 6, Limassol 0
Real Madrid 6, Limassol 0
   (*in Madrid*)
Valur Reykjavik 0, Benfica 0
Benfica 8, Valur Reykjavik 0
Byes: *Milan, Benfica*

**Second Round**
Manchester United 3, Anderlecht 0
Anderlecht 3, Manchester United 1
Celtic 5, Red Star 1
Red Star 1, Celtic 1
Rapid Vienna 1, Real Madrid 0
Real Madrid 2, Rapid Vienna 1
Reipas Lahti 1, Spartak Trnava 9
Spartak Trnava 7, Reipas Lahti 1
AEK 0, AB Copenhagen 0
AB Copenhagen 0, AEK 2
Ajax 2, Fenerbahce 0
Fenerbahce 0, Ajax 2

**Quarter-finals**
Ajax 1, Benfica 3
Benfica 1, Ajax 3
Ajax 3, Benfica 0
Milan 0, Celtic 0
Celtic 0, Milan 1
Manchester United 3,
  Rapid Vienna 0
Rapid Vienna 0, Manchester
  United 0

Spartak Trnava 2, AEK 1
AEK 1, Sparta Trnava 1

**Semi-finals**
Milan 2, Manchester United 0
Manchester United 1, Milan 0
Ajax 3, Spartak Trnava 0
Spartak Trnava 2, Ajax 0

**Final** Madrid, 28 May 1969
Milan (2) 4, Ajax Amsterdam (0) 1
*Milan:* Cudicini; Anquilletti, Schnellinger; Maldera, Rosato, Trapattoni; Hamrin, Lodetti, Sormani, Rivera, Prati.
*Ajax:* Blas, Suurbier (Nuninga), Vasovic, Van Duivenbode, Hulshoff; Pronk, Groot; Swart, Cruyff, Danielsson, Keizer.
*Scorers:* Prati 3, Sormani for Milan; Vasovic (pen) for Ajax.

## EUROPEAN CUP 1969–70

Feyenoord, the second consecutive Dutch team to reach the final of the European Cup, most unexpectedly won it with a fine victory over Celtic. Their superiority in the second half in Milan was such that the game should never have gone to extra time, let alone the closing minutes of extra time when Kindvall got away to score the winner. Feyenoord's performance was all the more meritorious in that it included a deserved victory over the holders, Milan, admittedly much scarred by their harsh encounters with Estudiantes in the world club championship.

The peak of Celtic's achievement was their splendid double over Leeds United, whom they deservedly beat in the semi-finals at Elland Road with an early, deflected goal by Connelly, then overwhelmed in front of an immense, frenzied crowd at Hampden Park, despite Bremner's early goal against the play. Leeds, however, were tired and depleted by their efforts in three major competitions.

Feyenoord's performance in Milan was a marvel of flexibility, severe *catenaccio* modulating in the second half to lively attack, with Hasil brilliant in midfield. Gemmell gave Celtic a rather fortunate lead with a pulverising free kick. From another free kick, Israel, Feyenoord's sweeper, came up to head the equaliser. Kindvall's belated winner followed a break down the left when McNeill misjudged and handled the ball. It was a curiously flaccid and disappointing performance by Celtic, a dazzling one by Feyenoord, accompanied by a myriad of honking Dutch horns.

**Preliminary Round**
Turku Palloseura 0, KB
  Copenhagen 1

KB Copenhagen 3, Turku
  Palloseura 0

**First Round**
Milan 5, Avenir Beggen 0
Avenir Beggen 0, Milan 3
Leeds United 10, Lyn Oslo 0
Lyn Oslo 0, Leeds United 6
Red Star Belgrade 8, Linfield 0
Linfield 2, Red Star Belgrade 4
Basel 0, Celtic 0
Celtic 2, Basel 0
Hibernian (Malta) 2, Spartak
  Trnava 2
Spartak Trnava 4, Hibernian
  (Malta) 0
Galatasaray 2, Waterford 0
Waterford 2, Galatasaray 3
CSKA Sofia 2, Ferencvaros 1
Ferencvaros 4, CSKA Sofia 1
Arad 1, Legia Warsaw 2
Legia Warsaw 8, Arad 0
Vorwaerts 2, Panathinaikos 0
Panathinaikos 1, Vorwaerts 1
Bayern Munich 2, St Etienne 0
St Etienne 3, Bayern Munich 0
Standard Liège 3, Nendori
  Tirana 0
Nendori Tirana 1, Standard
  Liège 1
Feyenoord 12, Reykjavik 0
Reykjavik 0, Feyenoord 4
FK Austria 1, Dynamo Kiev 2
Dynamo Kiev 3, FK Austria 1
Fiorentina 1, Oester 0
Oester 1, Fiorentina 2
Benfica 2, KB Copenhagen 0
KB Copenhagen 2, Benfica 3
Real Madrid 8, Olympiakos
  Nicosia 0

Olympiakos Nicosia 1, Real
  Madrid 6

**Second Round**
Leeds United 3, Ferencvaros 0
Ferencvaros 0, Leeds United 3
Celtic 3, Benfica 0
Benfica 3, Celtic 0
  (*Celtic won toss*)
Dynamo Kiev 1, Fiorentina 2
Fiorentina 0, Dynamo Kiev 0
Milan 1, Feyenoord 0
Feyenoord 2, Milan 0
Spartak Trnava 1, Galatasaray 0
Galatasaray 1, Spartak Trnava 0
  (*Galatasaray won toss*)
Legia Warsaw 2, St Etienne 1
St Etienne 0, Warsaw 1
Vorwaerts 2, Red Star 1
Red Star 3, Vorwaerts 2
Standard Liège 1, Real Madrid 0
Real Madrid 2, Standard Liège 3

**Quarter-finals**
Standard Liège 0, Leeds United 1
Leeds United 1, Standard Liège 0
Celtic 3, Fiorentina 0
Fiorentina 1, Celtic 0
Galatasaray 1, Legia Warsaw 1
Legia Warsaw 2, Galatasaray 0
Vorwaerts 1, Feyenoord 0
Feyenoord 2, Vorwaerts 0

**Semi-finals**
Leeds United 0, Celtic 1
Celtic 2, Leeds United 1
Legia Warsaw 0, Feyenoord 0
Feyenoord 2, Legia Warsaw 0

**Final** San Siro, Milan, 6 May 1970
Feyenoord (1) 2, Celtic (1) 1 after extra time
*Feyenoord:* Pieters Graafland; Romeyn (Haak), Israel, Laseroms,
Jansen, Van Duivenbode; Hasil, Van Hanegem; Wery, Kindvall,
Moulijn.

*Celtic:* Williams; Hay, Gemmell; Murdoch, McNeill, Brogan;
Johnstone, Wallace, Hughes, Auld (Connelly), Lennox.
**Scorers:** Gemmell for Celtic; Israel, Kinvall for Feyenoord.

# EUROPEAN CUP 1970–71

Ajax of Amsterdam became the second consecutive Dutch club to win the European Cup, thus making up for their defeat in the 1969 Final. Though they disappointingly shut up shop at Wembley in the second half against Panathinaikos, they were an admirable side, with a dazzling centre-forward in Johan Cruyff.

Panathinaikos, under the managership of Ferenc Puskas, were remarkable dark horses. They eliminated Everton, forcing a draw at Goodison – indeed, they only lost their early lead in the closing seconds, after resisting heavy pressure – then held them again in Athens and qualified through their away goal. Their methods were often ruthless, yet their achievement in turning a 4–1 deficit into ultimate qualification against Red Star in the semi-finals was extraordinary, and in the final, their conduct was largely good.

Perhaps Red Star would have gone through, had Dragan Dzajic, their star forward, not been controversially suspended for four games, after being sent off in the quarter-finals in Jena.

Celtic reached the quarter-finals but, clearly in a transitional period, were crushed in Amsterdam. Ajax closed their ranks to lose the return by only 1–0, going down by the same score to Atlético in Madrid, but again winning the home leg 3–0 to reach the final.

At Wembley, Van Dijk headed a simple goal from the clever Piet Keizer's centre after only five minutes, and despite Domazos' undoubted skill, the die was cast. Kamaras missed the Greek's best chance just before half-time, and in the second half, Ajax brought on two substitutes, one of whom, Haan, got their second goal by way of a Greek defender, three minutes from the end of a now dull game.

## Preliminary Round
Levski-Spartak 3, FK Austria 1
FK Austria 3, Levski-Spartak 0

## First Round
Everton 6, Keflavik 2
Keflavik 0, Everton 3
Celtic 9, Kokkola 0
Kokkola 0, Celtic 5
Glentoran 1, Waterford 3
Waterford 1, Glentoran 0
Cagliari 3, St Etienne 0
St Etienne 1, Cagliari 0
Slovan Bratislava 2, BK Copenhagen 1
BK Copenhagen 2, Slovan Bratislava 2
Nenduri Tirana 2, Ajax Amsterdam 2
Ajax Amsterdam 2, Nenduri Tirana 0

IFK Gothenburg 0, Legia Warsaw 4
Legia Warsaw 2, IFK Gothenburg 1
Ujpest 2, Red Star 0
Red Star 4, Ujpest 0
Rosenborg 0, Standard Liège 2
Standard Liège 5, Rosenborg 0
Borussia Mönchengladbach 6 EP Larnax (Cyprus) 0
(at Augsberg)
Borussia Mönchengladbach 10 EP Larnax 0
Spartak Moscow 3, Basel 2
Basel 2, Spartak Moscow 1
Feyenoord 1, UT Arad 1
UT Arad 0, Feyenoord 0
Atlético Madrid 2, FK Austria 0
FK Austria 1, Atlético Madrid 2
Jeunesse Esch 1, Panathinaikos 2
Panathinaikos 5, Jeunesse Esch 0

195

Fenerbahce 0, Carl Zeiss Jena 4
Carl Zeiss Jena 1, Fenerbahce 0
Sporting Lisbon 5, Floriana 0
Floriana 0, Sporting Lisbon 4

**Second Round**
Borussia Mönchengladbach 1,
  Everton 1
Everton 1, Borussia
  Mönchengladbach 1
(Everton qualify on new
  penalty-kicks rule)
Waterford 0, Celtic 7
Celtic 3, Waterford 2
Red Star Belgrade 3, UT Arad 0
UT Arad 1, Red Star Belgrade 3
Carl Zeiss Jena 2, Sporting
  Lisbon 1
Sporting Lisbon 1, Carl Zeiss
  Jena 2
Panathinaikos 3, Slovan
  Bratislava 0
Slovan Bratislava 2,
  Panathinaikos 1
Standard Liège 1, Legia Warsaw 0
Legia Warsaw 2, Standard Liège 0
Cagliari 2, Atlético Madrid 1

Atlético Madrid 3, Cagliari 0
Ajax Amsterdam 3, Basel 0
Basel 1, Ajax Amsterdam 2

**Quarter-finals**
Everton 1, Panathinaikos 1
Panathinaikos 0, Everton 0
Ajax Amsterdam 3, Celtic 0
Celtic 1, Ajax Amsterdam 0
Atlético Madrid 1, Legia
  Warsaw 0
Legia Warsaw 2, Atlético
  Madrid 1
Carl Zeiss Jena 3, Red Star
  Belgrade 2
Red Star Belgrade 4, Carl Zeiss
  Jena 0

**Semi-finals**
Red Star Belgrade 4,
  Panathinaikos 1
Panathinaikos 3, Red Star
  Belgrade 0
Atlética Madrid 1, Ajax
  Amsterdam 0
Ajax Amsterdam 3, Atlético
  Madrid 0

**Final** Wembley Stadium, 2 June 1971
Ajax Amsterdam (1) 2, Panathinaikos (0) 0
*Ajax:* Stuy; Neeskens, Vasovic, Hulshoff, Suurbier; Rijnders (Blankenburg), Muhren; Swart (Haan), Cruyff, Van Dijk, Keizer.
*Panathinaikos:* Oeconomopoulos; Tomaras, Vlahos, Eleftherakis, Kamaras, Sourpis, Grammos, Filakouris, Antoniadis, Domazos, Kapsis.
*Scorers:* Van Dijk, Haan for Ajax.

**EUROPEAN CUP 1971–72**
Gathering stature and flexibility, now under the managership of the Romanian Stefan Kovacs, and playing 'total football' with a mobile sweeper, Ajax won more convincingly than in 1971. The final, against Inter in Rotterdam, was the old, sterile *catenaccio* pitted against the dynamic new, which won hands down. Inter's negativity inevitably produced a dour, one-sided game, and it wasn't until the second half that a defensive muddle gave Cruyff a remarkably easy first goal. Later, he headed a second.
  Arsenal were put out by Ajax in the quarter-finals; overplayed in

Amsterdam and losing by an unlucky own goal at Highbury. Celtic, improving by the round, did very well to reach the semi-finals, which ended with stalemate against Inter. The Italians prevailed on penalties, after extra time, 'Dixie' Deans missing the first of Celtic's. Inter were rather lucky to be there at all, their 7–1 defeat by Borussia Mönchengladbach having been annulled because Boninsegna was hit by a beer can.

**Preliminary Round**
Valencia 3, US Luxembourg 1
US Luxembourg 0, Valencia 1
**First Round**
Olympique Marseilles 2, Gornik Zabrze 1
Gornik Zabrze 1, Olympique Marseilles 1
Galatasaray 1, CSKA Moscow 1
CSKA Moscow 3, Galatasaray 0
Akranes 0, Sliema Wanderers 4
Sliema Wanderers 0, Akranes 0
Ujpest Dozsa 4, Malmö 0
Malmö 1, Ujpest Dozsa 0
CSKA Sofia 3, Partizan Tirana 0
Partizan Tirana 0, CSKA Sofia 1
Stromsgodset 1, Arsenal 3
Arsenal 4, Stromsgodset 0
BK 1903 Copenhagen 2, Celtic 1
Celtic 3, BK 1903 0
Standard Liège 2, Linfield 0
Linfield 2, Standard Liège 3
Valencia 0, Hajduk Split 0
Hajduk 1, Valencia 1
Internazionale 4, AEK Athens 1
AEK Athens 3, Internazionale 2
Reipas Lahti 1, Grasshoppers 1
Grasshoppers 8, Reipas Lahti 0
Ajax 2, Dynamo Dresden 0
Dynamo Dresden 0, Ajax 0
Wacker Innsbruk 0, Benfica 4
Benfica 3, Wacker Innsbruck 1
Feyenoord 8, Olympiakos Nicosia 0
Feyenoord 9, Olympiakos Nicosia 0
Dynamo Bucharest 0, Spartak Trnava 0
Spartak Trnava 2, Dynamo Bucharest 2

Cork Hibernians 0, Borussia Mönchengladbach 5
Borussia Mönchengladbach 2, Cork Hibernians 1

**Second Round**
Grasshoppers 0, Arsenal 2
Arsenal 3, Grasshoppers 0
Celtic 5, Sliema Wanderers 0
Sliema Wanderers 1, Celtic 2
Internazionale 4, Borussia Mönchengladbach 2
Borussia Mönchengladbach 0, Internazionale 0
Dynamo Bucharest 0, Feyenoord 3
Feyenoord 2, Dynamo Bucharest 0
Valencia 0, Ujpest 1
Ujpest 2, Valencia 1
CSKA Moscow 1, Standard Liège 0
Standard Liège 2, CSKA Moscow 0
Olympique Marseilles 1, Ajax 2
Ajax 4, Olympique Marseilles 1
Benfica 2, CSKA Sofia 1
CSKA 0, Benfica 0

**Quarter-finals**
Ajax 2, Arsenal 1
Arsenal 0, Ajax 1
Ujpest 1, Celtic 2
Celtic 1, Ujpest 0
Internazionale 1, Standard Liège 0
Standard Liège 2, Internazionale 1
Feyenoord 1, Benfica 0
Benfica 5, Feyenoord 1

**Semi-finals**
Internazionale 0, Celtic 0
Celtic 0, Internazionale 0

*(Inter won on penalties 5–4)*
Ajax 1, Benfica 0
Benfica 0, Ajax 0

**Final** Rotterdam, 31 May 1972
Ajax (0) 2, Internazionale (0) 0
*Ajax:* Stuy; Suurbier, Hulshoff, Blankenburg, Krol; Haan, Neeskens, G. Muhren; Swart, Cruyff, Keizer.
*Internazionale:* Bordon; Bellugi, Burgnich, Giubertoni (Bertini), Facchetti; Oriali, Mazzola, Bedin, Jair (Pellizzaro), Boninsegna, Frustalupi.
*Scorer:* Cruyff (2) for Ajax.

## EUROPEAN CUP 1972–73

Ajax won their third successive title, again beating an Italian club, Juventus, in the final; a very dull match after Ajax's fine beginning, which brought a quick, determining goal headed by Rep from Blankenburg's left wing centre.

Derby County, competing for the first time, did well to reach the semi-finals, where Juventus' expertise proved too much for them. Lacking key players in both matches, they were beaten 3–1 in Turin, largely through Altafini's opportunism, and held 0–0 at Derby. But they had fine home victories over Spartak Trnava and Benfica. Celtic went out to clever Ujpest, who very nearly eliminated Juventus, too. Ajax, however, were once again head and shoulders above the field, their tactics exciting, Cruyff remarkable.

**First Round**
Derby County 2, Zeljeznicar Sarajevo 0
Zeljezinicar 1, Derby County 2
Celtic 2, Rosenborg 1
Rosenborg 1, Celtic 3
Real Madrid 3, Keflavik 0
Keflavik 0, Real Madrid 1
Anderlecht 4, Vejle 2
Vejle 0, Anderlecht 3
Ujpest 2, Basle 0
Basle 2, Ujpest 3
Galatasaray 1, Bayern Munich 1
Bayern Munich 6, Galatasaray 0
Olympique Marseilles 1, Juventus 0
Juventus 3, Olympique Marseilles 0
Malmö 1, Benfica 0
Benfica 4, Malmö 1
T-S Innsbruck 0, Dynamo Kiev 1
Dynamo Kiev 2, T-S Innsbruck 0

CSKA Sofia 2, Panathinaikos 1
Panathinaikos 0, CSKA Sofia 2
Sliema Wanderers 0, Gornik 5
Gornik 5, Sliema Wanderers 0
Magdeburg 6, Turun Palloseura 0
Turun Palloseura 1, Magdeburg 3
Aris 0, Arges Pitesti 2
Arges Pitesti 4, Aris 0
Waterford 2, Omonia Nicosia 1
Omonia Nicosia 2, Waterford 0
Byes: *Ajax Amsterdam, Spartak Trnava*

**Second Round**
Derby County 3, Benfica 0
Benfica 0, Derby County 0
Omonia Nicosia 0, Bayern Munich 9
Bayern Munich 4, Omonia Nicosia 0
Celtic 2, Ujpest 1
Ujpest 3, Celtic 0

Dynamo Kiev 2, Gornik 0
Gornik 2, Dynamo Kiev 1
Juventus 1, Magdeburg 0
Magdeburg 0, Juventus 1
Arges Pitesti 2, Real Madrid 1
Real Madrid 3, Arges Pitesti 1
CSKA Sofia 1, Ajax 3
Ajax 3, CSKA 0
Spartak Trnava 1, Anderlecht 0
Anderlecht 0, Spartak Trnava 1

Derby County 2, Spartak
  Trnava 0
Dynamo Kiev 0, Real Madrid 0
Real Madrid 3, Dynamo Kiev 0
Ajax 4, Bayern Munich 0
Bayern Munich 2, Ajax 1
Juventus 0, Ujpest 0
Ujpest 2, Juventus 2

**Quarter-finals**
Spartak Trnava 1, Derby
  County 0

**Semi-finals**
Juventus 3, Derby County 1
Derby County 0, Juventus 0
Ajax 2, Real Madrid 1
Real Madrid 0, Ajax 1

**Final** Belgrade, 30 May 1973
Ajax (1) 1 Juventus (0) 0
*Ajax:* Stuy; Suurbier, Hulshoff, Blankenburg, Kroll; Neeskens,
Haan, G. Muhren; Rep, Cruyff, Keizer.
*Juventus:* Zoff; Longobucco, Marchetti, Furino, Morini, Salvadore,
Causio (Cuccureddu), Altafini, Anastasi, Capello, Bettega (Haller).
*Scorer:* Rep for Ajax.

### EUROPEAN CUP 1973-74

The departure of Johan Cruyff to Barcelona sabotaged Ajax's attempt
to win the Cup a fourth time, and showed that Total Football or no,
one man can still make a team. CSKA Sofia, whom they easily beat the
previous season, now took advantage of a missed penalty by Mulder in
Amsterdam to beat them.

So the Cup went to West Germany for the first time, though it
was only the dramatic last minute equaliser by their centre-half,
Georg Schwarzenbeck, which saved Bayern in the first final against
Atlético Madrid.

Had Atlético won, it would have been monstrous, for they'd viciously
kicked and maltreated Celtic in the first leg of the semi-final at Park-
head; one more chapter in their manager, Juan Carlos Lorenzo's,
vendetta with British football. UEFA behaved with their usual
flabbiness, suspending six Atlético players but allowing the game to go
on in a boiling Madrid, where Celtic predictably lost.

Liverpool had gone in the second round, victim of a Red Star
Belgrade team which scored two superbly hit goals and played much
glorious football at Anfield.

Bayern had no easy passage. They lost at Atvidaberg, where Paul
Breitner's shin was broken by a stone, then had a hard task beating
the excellent East Germans, Dynamo Dresden, conquerors of Juventus.
But Ujpest were well beaten in the semi-finals, as were Atlético in the
replayed final in Brussels. Bayern nearly lost the first game to a remarkable, late free kick swerved in by Luis, but the replayed final – first
in the history of the tournament – was a procession. Bayern wisely
decided on a much more adventurous policy, Müller and Hoeness ran
riot, Beckenbauer received the Cup.

**First Round**

Jeunesse Esch 1 Liverpool 1
Liverpool 2 Jeunesse Esch 0
TPS Turku 1, Celtic 6
Celtic 3, TPS Turku 0
Crusaders 0, Dynamo Bucharest 1
Dynamo Bucharest 11, Crusaders 0
Benfica 1, Olympiakos 0
Olympiakos 0, Benfica 1
Waterford 2, Ujpest 3
Ujpest 3, Waterford 0
Dynamo Dresden 2, Juventus 0
Juventus 3, Dynamo Dresden 2
Vejle 2, Nantes 2
Nantes 0, Vejle 1
Bayern Munich 3, Atvidaberg 1
Atvidaberg 3, Bayern Munich 1
(*Bayern won on penalties*)
Zaria 2, Apoel 0
Apoel 0, Zaria 1
Red Star Belgrade 2, Stal Mielec 1
Stal Mielec 0, Red Star 1
Bruges 8, Floriana 0
Floriana 0, Bruges 2
Atletico Madrid 0, Galatasaray 1
Galatasary 1, Atletico Madrid 1
Viking Stavanger 1, Spartak
                       Trnava 2
Spartak Trnava 1, Viking Stav. 0
Frem Reykjavik 0, Basle 5
Basle 6, Frem Reykjavik 2
CSKA Sofia 3,
  Wacker Innsbruck 0
Wacker Innsbruck 0, CSKA
  Sofia 1
Bye: *Ajax*

**Second Round**

Red Star Belgrade 2, Liverpool 1
Liverpool 1, Red Star Belgrade 2
Celtic 0, Vejle 0
Vejle 0, Celtic 1
Benfica 1, Ujpest 1
Ujpest 2, Benfica 0
Bayern Munich 4, Dynamo
  Dresden 3
Dynamo Dresden 3, Bayern
  Munich 3
Ajax 1, CSKA Sofia 0
CSKA Sofia 2, Ajax 0
Dynamo Bucharest 0,
  Atletico Madrid 2
Atletico Madrid 2,
Dynamo Bucharest 2
Spartak Trnava 0, Zaria 0
Zaria 0, Spartak Trnava 1
Bruges 2, Basle 1
Basle 6, Bruges 4

**Quarter-finals**

Basle 3, Celtic 2
Celtic 4, Basle 2
Bayern Munich 4, CSKA Sofia 1
CSKA Sofia 2, Bayern Munich 1
Red Star Belgrade 0,
  Atlético Madrid 2
Atlético Madrid 0, Red Star 0
Spartak Trnava 1, Ujpest 1
Ujpest 1, Spartak Trnava 1
(*Ujpest won on penalties*)

**Semi-finals**

Celtic 0, Alético Madrid 0
Atlético Madrid 2, Celtic 0
Ujpest 1, Bayern Munich 1
Bayern Munich 3, Ujpest 0

200

**Final**
Brussels, 15 May 1974
   Atlético Madrid (0) 1            Bayern Munich (0) 1
   (*After extra time, full time*: 0–0)
*Atletico Madrid:* Reina; Melo, Capon, Adelardo, Heredia, Eusebio, Ufarte (Becerra), Luis, Garate, Irureta, Salcedo (Alberto).
*Bayern Munich:* Maier; Hansen, Breitner, Schwarzenbeck, Beckenbauer, Roth, Torstensson (Durnberger), Zobel, Müller, Hoeness, Kappelmann.
*Scorers:* Luis for Atlético; Schwarzenbeck for Bayern.

**Replay**
Brussels, 17 May 1974
   Bayern Munich (1) 4           Atlético Madrid (0) 0
*Bayern Munich:* Maier; Hansen, Breitner, Schwarzenbeck, Beckenbauer, Roth, Torstensson, Zobel, Müller, Hoeness, Kappelmann.
*Atletico Madrid:* Reina; Melo, Capon, Adelardo (Benegas), Heredia, Eusebio, Salcedo, Luis, Garate, Alberto (Ufarte), Becerra.
*Scorers:* Hoeness 2, Müller 2 for Bayern.


CHAPTER FIFTEEN

# The European Cup-Winners' Cup History

This Cup is something of a poor relation to the European Cup, if only because relatively few countries have a *bona fide* Cup competition. Italy, who play theirs off obscurely in midweek, are a notable instance. On the other hand, the decisive matches have often drawn mammoth crowds and evinced huge enthusiasm, while Tottenham's performance in winning the 1963 tournament was of high quality.

## EUROPEAN CUP-WINNERS' CUP 1960–61
This was really Glasgow Ranger's finest hour to date in a European competition. Their appetite whetted by the European Cup, their fans took wholeheartedly to the new tournament, and virtually invaded Wolverhampton on the occasion of the floodlit tie there.

   In the final, however, Fiorentina were a little too well balanced and experienced. Above all, they had in Kurt Hamrin, their Swedish international outside-right, one of the greatest match winners in Europe.

**Qualifying Round**

Vorwaerts Berlin 2, Red Star
  Brno 1
Red Star Brno 2, Vorwaerts
  Berlin 0
Rangers 4, Ferencvaros 2
Ferencvaros 2, Rangers 1

Wolverhampton Wanderers 5,
  FK Austria 0
Borussia Dusseldorf 0, Rangers 3
Rangers 8, Borussia Dusseldorf 0
Lucerne 0, Fiorentina 3
Fiorentina 6, Lucerne 2

**Quarter-finals**

Red Star Brno 0, Dynamo
  Zagreb 0
Dynamo Zagreb 2, Red Star
  Brno 0
FK Austria 2, Wolverhampton
  Wanderers 0

**Semi-finals**

Fiorentina 3, Dynamo Zagreb 0
Dynamo Zagreb 2, Fiorentina 1
Rangers 2, Wolverhampton
  Wanderers 0
Wolverhampton Wanderers 1,
  Rangers 1

**Final**

1st Leg. Glasgow, 17 May 1961
Rangers (0) 0, Fiorentina (1) 2
*Rangers:* Ritchie; Shearer, Caldow; Davis, Paterson, Baxter; Wilson,
McMillan, Scott, Brand, Hume.
*Fiorentina:* Albertosi; Robotti, Castelletti; Gonfiantini, Orzan, Rim-
baldo; Hamrin, Micheli, Da Costa, Milan, Petris.
*Scorer:* Milan (2) for Fiorentina.

2nd Leg. Florence, 27 May, 1961
Fiorentina (1) 2, Rangers (1) 1
*Fiorentina:* Albertosi; Robotti, Castelletti; Gonfiantini, Orzan,
Rimbaldo; Hamrin, Micheli, Da Costa, Milan, Petris.
*Rangers:* Ritchie; Shearer, Caldow; Davis, Paterson, Baxter; Scott,
McMillan, Millar, Brand, Wilson.
*Scorers:* Milan, Hamrin for Fiorentina, Scott for Rangers.

## EUROPEAN CUP-WINNERS' CUP 1961–62

Leicester City took the place of Spurs, who had beaten them in the
final but, having also won the League, were committed to the European
Cup. Spain, entering for the first time in the imposing shape of Atlético
Madrid, won the tournament, beating Leicester on the way and
ultimately defeating Fiorentina in a replayed final – no longer a two-
legged affair.

**Preliminary Round**

Glenavon 1, Leicester City 4
Leicester City 3, Glenavon 1
Dunfermline Ath. 4,
  St Patrick's 1
St Patrick's 0, Dunfermline
  Ath. 4
Swansea Town 2, Motor Jena 2
Motor Jena 5, Swansea Town 1

Chaux de Fonds 6, Leixoes 2
Leixoes 5, Chaux de Fonds 0
Sedan 2, Atlético Madrid 3
Atlético Madrid 4, Sedan 1
Rapid Vienna 0, Spartak Varna 0
Spartak Varna 2, Rapid Vienna 5
Floriana 2, Ujpest Dozsa 5
Ujpest Dozsa 10, Floriana 2

Byes: *Fiorentina, Vardar, Werder, Bremen, Aarhus, Ajax, Olympiakos Piraeus, Dynamo Zilina, Progresul, Allianet Dudelange*

Progresul 0, Leixoes 1
Motor Jena 7, Alliance
  Dudelange 0
Alliance Dudelange 2, Motor
  Jena 2

## First Round
Fiorentina 3, Rapid Vienna 1
Rapid Vienna 2, Fiorentina 6
Leicester City 1, Atlético
  Madrid 1
Atlético Madrid 2, Leicester
  City 0
Dunfermline Ath. 5, Vardar 2
Vardar 2, Dunfermline Ath. 0
Werder Bremen 2, Aarhus 0
Aarhus 2, Werder Bremen 3
Ajax 2, Ujpest 1
Ujpest 3, Ajax 1
Olympiakos Piraeus 2, Dynamo
  Zilina (Czech.) 3
Dynamo Zilina 1, Olympiakos
  Piraeus 0
Leixoes (Portugal) 1, Progresul 1

## Quarter-finals
Atlético Madrid 3, Werder
  Bremen 1
Werder Bremen 1, Atlético
  Madrid 1
Ujpest 4, Dunfermline 3
Dunfermline 0, Ujpest 1
Fiorentina 2, Dynamo Zilina 3
Dynamo Zilina 0, Fiorentina 2
Motor Jena 1, Leixoes 1
Leixoes 1, Motor Jena 3

## Semi-finals
Fiorentina 2, Ujpest 0
Ujpest 0, Fiorentina 1
Atlético Madrid 1, Motor Jena 0
Motor Jena 0, Atlético Madrid 4

**Final** Glasgow, 10 May 1962
Fiorentina (1) 1, Atlético Madrid (1) 1
*Scorers:* Peiro for Atlético Madrid, Hamrin for Fiorentina.
**Replay** Stuttgart, 5 September 1962
Atlético Madrid (2) 3, Fiorentina (0) 0

*Atlético Madrid:* Madinabeytia; Rivilla, Calleja; Ramirez, Griffa, Glaria; Jones, Adelardo, Mendonça, Peirò, Collar.
*Fiorentina:* Albertosi; Robotti, Castelletti; Malatrasi, Orzan, Marchesi; Hamrin, Ferretti, Milani, Dell'Angelo, Petris.
*Scorers:* Jones, Mendonça, Peirò for Atlético Madrid.
Same teams for both matches.

## EUROPEAN CUP-WINNERS' CUP 1962–63
This was most impressively won by Spurs. Invincible at home, they played brilliant football to humiliate Rangers, and recovered impressively after a poor performance in Bratislava. OFK, after losing in Belgrade, never had much of a chance of survival. In the final, though robbed at the last moment of the dynamic Mackay with a stomach injury, Spurs played some magnificent football to defeat Atlético Madrid, dominating the first half, surviving a sticky patch at the beginning of the second, and at last turning the game with a surprising long-range goal by outside-left Terry Dyson.

One must not leave this Cup without recording the brave achievement of the little Welsh non-League club, Bangor City, who actually beat the expensive Naples team and forced them to a third, decisive, game.

**Preliminary Round**

Lausanne 3, Sparta 0
Sparta 4, Lausanne 2
St Etienne 1, Vitoria 1
Vitoria 0, St Etienne 3
Alliance Dudelange 1, Odense 1
Odense 8, Alliance Dudelange 1
Rangers 4, Seville 0
Seville 2, Rangers 0
OFK Belgrade 2, Chemie 0
Chemie 3, OFK Belgrade 3
Steaua 3, Botev 2
Botev 5, Steaua 1
Ujpest Dozsa 5, Zaglebie 0
Zaglebie 0, Ujpest Dozsa 0
Bangor City 2, Naples 0
Naples 3, Bangor City 1
Naples 2, Bangor City 1
  (*at Highbury*)
Byes: *Nuremburg, Atlético Madrid, Hibernian Malta, Shamrock Rovers, Graz, Tottenham Hotspur, Portadown, Slovan Bratislava*

**First Round**

St Etienne 0, Nuremburg 0
Nuremburg 3, St Etienne 0
Atlético Madrid 4, Hibernian
  Malta 0
Hibernian Malta 0, Atlético
  Madrid 1
Botev 4, Shamrock Rovers 0

Shamrock Rovers 0, Botev 1
Graz 1, Odense BK 09 1
Odense BK 09 5, Graz 3
Tottenham Hotspur 5, Rangers 2
Rangers 2, Tottenham Hotspur 3
OFK Belgrade 5, Portadown 1
Portadown 3, OFK Belgrade 2
Lausanne 1, Slovan Bratislava 1
Slovan Bratislava 1, Lausanne 0
Ujpest 1, Naples 1
Naples 1, Ujpest 1
Naples 3, Ujpest 1

**Quarter-finals**

Slovan 2, Tottenham Hotspur 0
Tottenham Hotspur 6, Slovan 0
Odense 0, Nuremburg 1
Nuremburg 6, Odense 0
Botev 1, Atlético Madrd 1
Atlético Madrid 6, Botev 0
OFK Belgrade 2, Naples 0
Naples 3, OFK Belgrade 1
Play off OFK Belgrade 3,
  Naples 1

**Semi-finals**

OFK Belgrade 1, Tottenham
  Hotspur 2
Tottenham Hotspur 3, OFK
  Belgrade 1
Nuremburg 2, Atlético Madrid 1
Atlético Madrid 2, Nuremburg 0

**Final** Rotterdam, 15 May 1963
Tottenham Hotspur (2) 5, Atlético Madrid (0) 1
*Spurs:* Brown; Baker, Henry; Blanchflower, Norman, Marchi; Jones, White, Smith, Greaves, Dyson.
*Atlético Madrid:* Madinabeytia; Rivilla, Rodrigues; Ramiro, Griffa, Glaria; Jones, Adelardo, Chuzo, Mendonça, Collar.
*Scorers:* Greaves (2), White, Dyson (2) for Spurs, Collar (pen) for Atlético Madrid.

**EUROPEAN CUP-WINNERS' CUP 1963–64**
Tottenham's success in 1963 meant that England were able to enter two teams, and as luck would have it, Spurs and Manchester United

were quickly drawn together. A dour first leg at Tottenham saw Spurs get through with great difficulty, 2–0. But in the return the unhappy Mackay fractured a leg, and Manchester United took the game 4–1 and qualified. It was the first time the holders had been eliminated before the final. United, who should have had a bigger lead in their first leg against Sporting, lost the return in Lisbon a few days after an exhausting FA Cup semi-final. Glasgow Celtic were the splendid surprise of the tournament. Qualified only because Rangers, the Scottish Cupholders, were in the European Cup, they sailed through Europe, before falling to MTK in the semi-final. Celtic put up a brave fight, but were overwhelmed in the replay when MTK got their international stars, Sandor and Nagy, back. Sporting won a tremendously tight semi-final series in a third, deciding match; Lyon had a man sent off in the second half. In the final, the opportunism of Sandor enabled MTK to hold their own in Vienna, but the better-balanced Sporting team defeated them in Antwerp. The winning goal was scored by Morais, direct from a corner, in the twentieth minute.

**Preliminary Round**

Fenerbahce 4, Petrolul 1
Petrolul 1, Fenerbahce 0
Basel 1, Celtic 5
Celtic 5, Basel 0
Tilburg Holland 1, Manchester
    United 1
Manchester United 6, Tilburg 1
SV Hamburg 4, US Luxemburg 0
US Luxemburg 2, SV Hamburg 3
Olympiakos Piraeus 2, Zaglebie 1
Zaglebie 1, Olympiakos
    Piraeus 0
Olympiakos Piraeus 2,
    Zaglebie 0
Shelbourne 0, Barcelona 2
Barcelona 3, Shelbourne 1
Lyon 3, Odense 1
Odense 1, Lyon 3
MTK Budapest 1, Slavia 0
Slavia 1, MTK Budapest 1
Linz 1, Dynamo Zagreb 0
Dynamo Zagreb 1, Linz 0
Dynamo Zagreb 1, Linz 1
(*Dynamo Zagreb won the toss*)
Sliema Wanderers 0, Borough
    United 0
Borough United 2, Sliema
    Wanderers 0
Atlanta 2, Sporting Lisbon 0
Sporting Lisbon 3, Atlanta 1

Apoel (Cyprus) 6, Gjoevik
    (Norway) 0
Gjoevik 1, Apoel 0
Palloseura Helsinki 1, Slovan
    Bratislava 4
Slovan Bratislava 8, Palloseura
    Helsinki 1
Byes: *Tottenham Hotspur,
Linfield, Motor Zwickau*


**First Round**

Tottenham Hotspur 2,
    Manchester United 0
Manchester United 4,
    Tottenham Hotspur 1
Fenerbahce 4, Linfield 1
Linfield 2, Fenerbahce 0
Barcelona 4, SV Hamburg 4
SV Hamburg 0, Barcelona 0
SV Hamburg 3, Barcelona 2
Sporting Lisbon 16, Apoel 1
Apoel 0, Sporting Lisbon 2
Lyon 4, Olympiakos 1
Olympiakos 2, Lyon 1
Motor Zwickau 1, MTK
    Budapest 0
MTK Budapest 2, Motor
    Zwickau 0
Celtic 3, Dynamo Zagreb 0
Dynamo Zagreb 2, Celtic 1

Borough United 0, Slovan Bratislava 1
Slovan Bratislava 3, Borough United 0

Celtic 1, Slovan Bratislava 0
Slovan Bratislava 0, Celtic 1
Fenerbahce 1, MTK Budapest 1
MTK Budapest 1, Fenerbahce 0

## Quarter-finals
Manchester United 4, Sporting Lisbon 1
Sporting Lisbon 5, Manchester United 0
SV Hamburg 1, Lyon 1
Lyon 2, SV Hamburg 0

## Semi-finals
Celtic 3, MTK Budapest 0
MTK Budapest 4, Celtic 0
Lyon 0, Sporting Lisbon 0
Sporting Lisbon 1, Lyon 1
Lyon 0, Sporting Lisbon 1

**Final** Brussels, 13 May 1964
MTK Budapest 3, Sporting Lisbon 3 after extra time (full-time 3–3)
*MTK Budapest:* Kovalik; Keszei, Dansky; Jenei, Nagy, Kovaks; Sandor, Vasas, Kuti, Bodor, Halapi.
*Sporting Lisbon:* Carvalho; Gomez, Peridis; Baptista, Carlos, Geo; Mendes, Oswaldo, Mascarenhas, Figueiredo, Morais.
*Scorers:* Sandor (2), Kuti for MTK Budapest; Figueiredo (2), Dansky (o.g.) for Sporting Lisbon.

**Replay** Antwerp, 15 May 1964
MTK Budapest 0, Sporting Lisbon 1
*Scorer:* Morais for Sporting Lisbon.

## EUROPEAN CUP-WINNERS' CUP 1964–65
For the second time in three years, a London team was the winner, and West Ham's splendid performance at Wembley, in an exciting final, was a memorable one. The Hammers' achievement was the more impressive as they had lost Johnny Byrne, their outstanding forward, injured while playing for England against Scotland. This caused him to miss the second leg of the semi-final, in Saragossa, and the final itself. Saragossa were probably the second best team in the competition, with outstanding forwards in Lapetra, on the left wing, and the centre-forward, Marcelino. Mention must also be made of the astonishing achievement of Cardiff City, a Second Division club, in knocking out the holders, Sporting Lisbon. They did almost as well by pulling back two goals to draw in Saragossa, but a defensive slip cost them the return match.

Munich 1860 were a physically strong, direct, intelligent side, thwarted in the final by Standen's splendid goalkeeping. Late in the game, after a rash of missed chances, Alan Sealey scored twice for West Ham, to settle the match.

## Preliminary Round
Admira Vienna 1, Legia Warsaw 3
Legia Warsaw 1, Admira Vienna 0
Lausanne 2, Honved 0

Honved 1, Lausanne 0
US Luxemburg 0, Munich 1960 4
Munich 1860 6, US Luxemburg 0

Valetta 0, Saragossa 3
Saragossa 5, Valetta 1
AEK Athens 2, Dynamo Zagreb 0
Dynamo Zagreb 3, AEK Athens 0
Dynamo Bucharest 3, Derry City 0
Derry City 0, Dynamo Bucharest 2
Magdeburg 1, Galatasaray 1
Galatasaray 1, Magdeburg 1
Magdeburg 1, Galatasaray 1
 (in Vienna)
(Galatasarya won toss)
Esbjerg 0, Cardiff City 0
Cardiff City 1, Esbjerg 0
Skeid Oslo 1, Haka Finland 0
Haka Finland 2, Skeid Oslo 0
Porto 3, Lyon 0
Lyon 0, Porto 1
Sparta Prague 10, St Anorthosis
 (Cyprus) 0
St Anorthosis 0, Sparta 6
La Gantoise 0, West Ham
 United 1
West Ham United 1, La
 Gantoise 1
Torino 3, Fortuna Geelen 1
Fortuna Geelen 2, Torino 2
Slavia Sofia 1, Cork Celtic 1
Cork Celtic 0, Slavia Sofia 2
Byes: *Sporting Lisbon, Dundee*

**First Round**
Dundee 2, Saragossa 2
Saragossa 2, Dundee 1
Slavia 1, Lausanne 0
Lausanne 2, Slavia 1
Lausanne 3, Slavia 2
 (in Rome)

Legia 2, Galatasaray 1
Galatasaray 2, Legia 1
Legia 2, Galatasaray 1
West Ham United 2, Sparta 0
Sparta 2, West Ham United 1
Porto 0, Munich 1860 1
Munich 1860 1, Porto 1
Dynamo Bucharest 1, Dynamo
 Zagreb 1
Dynamo Zagreb 2, Dynamo
 Bucharest 0
Sporting Lisbon 1, Cardiff
 City 2
Cardiff City 0, Sporting Lisbon 0
Torino 5, Haka 0
Haka 0, Torino 1


**Quarter-finals**
Saragossa 2, Cardiff City 2
Cardiff City 0, Saragossa 1
Legia 0, Munich 1860 4
Munich 1860 0, Legia 0
Torino 1, Dynamo Zagreb 1
Dynamo Zagreb 1, Torino 2
Lausanne 1, West Ham United 2
West Ham United 4, Lausanne 3


**Semi-finals**
West Ham United 2, Saragossa 1
Saragossa 1, West Ham United 1
Torino 2, Munich 1860 0
Munich 1860 3, Torino 1
Munich 1860 2, Torino 0
 (in Zurich)

Final Wembley Stadium, 19 May 1965
West Ham United (0) 2, Munich 1860 (0) 0
*West Ham United:* Standen; Kirkup, Burkett; Peters, Brown, Moore;
Sealey, Boyce, Hurst, Dear, Sissons.
*Munich* 1860: Radenkovic; Wagner, Kohlars; Bena, Reich, Luttrop;
Heiss, Kuppers, Brunnenmeier, Grosser, Rebele.
*Scorer:* Sealey (2) for West Ham United.
**EUROPEAN CUP-WINNERS' CUP 1965–66**
Despite getting three of their four entrants into the semi-finals, Britain
failed to retain the Cup, which went to Borussia and Germany —
on merit. The Dortmund team, astoundingly fit and very incisive, broke

wonderfully well from defence, despite the fact that they used Paul as sweeper-up behind four backs. Sigi Held, later to play so well in the World Cup, was a splendid striker, powerfully abetted by the Bundesliga's top scorer, Lothar Emmerich, the nominal left-winger.

Defending powerfully and breaking rapidly, Borussia surprisingly took all West Ham, the holders, could hurl at them at Upton Park and won on a couple of counter-attacks. In the final, they deserved to beat a disappointing Liverpool team, terribly vulnerable through the middle and lucky to equalise when the ball had so clearly crossed the goal line. Celtic, beaten by Liverpool in the semi-final, had an excellent run, and showed how their manager and former centre-half, Jock Stein, had tempered them for major competition.

**First Round**
Reykjavik 1, Rosenberg Trondheim 3
Rosenberg Trondheim 3, Reykjavik 1
Wiener Neustadt 0, Stintza Cluj 1
Stintza Cluj 2, Wiener Neustadt 0
Reipas Lahti 2, Honved 10
Honved 6, Reipas Lahti 2
Coleraine 1, Dynamo Kiev 6
Dynamo Kiev 4, Coleraine 0
Sion 5, Galatasaray 1
Galatasaray 2, Sion 1
Alético Madrid 4, Dynamo Zagreb 0
Dynamo Zagreb 0, Atlético Madrid 1
Dukla Prague 2, Rennes 0
Rennes 0, Dukla Prague 0
SC Magdeburg 1, Spora 0
Spora 0, SC Magdeburg 2
Go Ahead Deventer 0, Celtic 6
Celtic 1, Go Ahead Deventer 0
Juventus 1, Liverpool 0
Liverpool 2, Juventus 0
Limerick 1, CSKA Sofia 2
CSKA Sofia 2, Limerick 0
Floriana 1, Borussia Dortmund 5
Borussia Dortmund 8, Floriana 0
Omonia Nicosia 0, Olympiakos 1
Olympiakos 1, Omonia Nicosia 1
Aarhus 2, Vitoria Setubal 1
Vitoria Setubal 1, Aarhus 2
Bye: *West Ham United*

**Second Round**
Dukla 2, Honved 3
Honved 1, Dukla 2
*Honved won on away goals rule*
Borussia Dortmund 3, CSKA 0
CSKA 4, Borussia Dortmund 2
SC Magdeburg 8, Sion 1
Sion 2, SC Magdeburg 2
Stintza Cluj 0, Atlético Madrid 2
Atlético Madrid 4, Stantza Cluj 0
Aarhus 0, Celtic 1
Celtic 2, Aarhus 0
West Ham United 4, Olympiakos Piraeus 0
Olympiakos Piraeus 2, West Ham United 2
Liverpool 3, Standard Liège 1
Standard Liège 1, Liverpool 2
Rosenberg 1, Dynamo Kiev 4
Dynamo Kiev 2, Rosenberg 0

**Quarter-finals**
Celtic 3, Dynamo Kiev 0
Dynamo Kiev 1, Celtic 1
Atlético Madrid 1, Borussia Dortmund 1
Borussia Dortmund 1, Atlético Madrid 0
Honved 0, Liverpool 0
Liverpool 2, Honved 0
West Ham United 1, SC Magdeburg 0
SC Magdeburg 1, West Ham United 1

**Semi-finals**

| | |
|---|---|
| West Ham United 1, Borussia Dortmund 2 | Celtic 1, Liverpool 0 |
| Borussia Dortmund 3, West Ham United 1 | Liverpool 2, Celtic 0 |

**Final** Glasgow, 5 May 1966

Borussia Dortmund (0) 2, Liverpool (0) 1

*Borussia:* Tilkowski; Cyliax, Redder; Kurrat, Paul, Assauer; Libuda, Schmidt, Held, Sturo, Emmerich.

*Liverpool:* Lawrence; Lawler, Byrne; Milne, Yeats, Stevenson; Callaghan, Hunt, St John, Smith, Thompson.

*Scorers:* Held, Yeats (o.g.) for Borussia; Hunt for Liverpool.

## EUROPEAN CUP-WINNERS' CUP 1966–67

After a fine passage to their second Cup-Winners' Cup Final, Rangers found the luck of the (German) venue and Bayern's all-round accomplishment just too much for them.

The competition was played under the highly suspect dispensation of away goals counting double, in the event of two teams finishing level on aggregate. Rangers put out the holders, Borussia Dortmund, beating them in Glasgow more easily than the score suggests, and holding them in Munich, despite an injury to Watson. But they were lucky to get through against Saragossa, on the toss of a coin. Bayern scraped through against a brave Shamrock Rovers, and recovered from defeat in Vienna to beat Rapid in a rough second leg, to take the other semi-final. Müller, their young centre-forward, scored the winner in extra time.

In the final, played at Nuremberg, Rangers dominated the first half, Bayern the second and extra time was again needed. It produced the decisive goal, by Roth.

**Preliminary Round**

Valur Reykjavik 1, Standard Liège 1

Standard Liège 8, Valur Reykjavik 1

**First Round**

Skeid Oslo 3, Saragossa 2

Saragossa 3, Skeid Oslo 1

Rapid Vienna 4, Galatasaray 0

Galatasaray 3, Rapid Vienna 5

Servette Geneva 1, Kamraterna Turku 1

Kamraterna Turku 1, Servette Geneva 2

Glentoran 1, Rangers 1

Rangers 4, Glentoran 0

Swansea Town 1, Slavia Sofia 1

Slavia Sofia 4, Swansea Town 0

Tatan Presov 1, Bayern Munich 1

Bayern Munich 3, Tatan Presov 2

AEK Athens 0, Braga (Portugal)1

Braga 3, AEK Athens 2

Shamrock Rovers 4, Spora Luxemburg 0

Spora 1, Shamrock Rovers 4

Aalborg 0, Everton 0

Everton 2, Aalborg 1

OFK Belgrade 1, Spartak Moscow 3

Spartak Moscow 3, OFK Belgrade 0

Fiorentina 1, Vasas Gyor 0

Vasas Gyor 4, Fiorentina 2

Chemie Leipzig 3, Legia Warsaw 0

Legia Warsaw 2, Chemie Leipzig 2

Strasbourg 1, Steaua Bucharest 0
Steaua Bucharest 1, Strasbourg 1
Floriana Valetta 1, Sparta
  Rotterdam 1
Sparta Rotterdam 6, Floriana
  Valetta 0
Standard Liège 5, Limassol 1
Limassol 0, Standard Liège 1
Bye: *Borussia Dortmund*

**Second Round**
Saragossa 2, Everton 0
Everton 1, Saragossa 0
Shamrock Rovers 1, Bayern
  Munich 1
Bayern Munich 3, Shamrock
  Rovers 2
Vasas Gyor 3, Sporting Braga 0
Sporting Braga 2, Vasas Gyor 0
Spartak Moscow 1, Rapid
  Vienna 1
Rapid Vienna 1, Spartak
  Moscow 0
Servette 2, Sparta Rotterdam 0
Sparta Rotterdam 1, Servette 0
Rangers 2, Borussia Dortmund 1
Borussia Dortmund 0, Rangers 0

Strasbourg 1, Slavia Sofia 0
Slavia Sofia 2, Strasbourg 0
Chemie Liepzig 2, Standard
  Liège 1
Standard Liège 1, Chemie
  Leipzig 0

**Quarter-finals**
Rapid Vienna 1, Bayern
  Munich 0
Bayern Munich 2, Rapid
  Vienna 0
Rangers 2, Saragossa 0
Saragossa 2, Rangers 0
Vasas Gyor 2, Standard Liège 1
Standard Liège 2, Vasas Gyor 0
Servette 1, Slavia Sofia 0
Slavia Sofia 3, Servette 0

**Semi-finals**
Bayern Munich 2, Standard
  Liège 0
Standard Liège 1, Bayern
  Munich 3
Slavia Sofia 0, Rangers 1
Rangers 1, Slavia Sofia 0

**Final** Nuremberg, 31 May 1967
Bayern Munich (0) 1, Rangers (0) 0
*Bayern:* Maier; Nowak, Kupferschmidt; Roth, Beckenbauer, Olk; Nafziger, Ohlhauser, Muller, Koulmann, Brenninger.
*Rangers:* Martin; Johansen, Provan; Jardine, McKinnon, Greig; Henderson, A. Smith, Hynd, D. Smith, Johnstone.
*Scorer:* Roth after extra time.

## EUROPEAN CUP-WINNERS' CUP 1967–68

AC Milan, who in the meantime were comfortably carrying off the Italian Championship, added to it the European Cup-Winners' Cup on their first appearance in the tournament. Their victory over Hamburg in the final, at Rotterdam, was a mere canter. Both goals were scored by the veteran Swedish right-winger, Kurt Hamrin, the second a brilliant individual affair. It was far easier for Milan than their painfully hard qualifications against Vasas Gyor and Standard Liège.

Cardiff City were Britain's most impressive competitors, doing wonderfully well. Shamrock Rovers and Breda were no great problem, and in the quarter-finals they belied recent poor League form by knocking out Torpedo Moscow. They won at home with a fine, late headed goal by Barrie Jones, went down 1–0 in Tashkent then, with five reserves, won the play-off, in Augsburg, 1–0, Toshack heading down for Dean to score. In the semi-finals, still fighting relegation in the League, they held Hamburg (without Seeler and Schulz) to an away draw, then lost unluckily at home.

Spurs went out feebly to Lyon, after a brawl in the away match, and some dismal defence at home. Aberdeen went down to Standard Liège, though they played well at home in the return leg. Standard went on to draw twice with Milan, but lost the play-off. Milan then knocked out the holders, Bayern, in the semi-finals.

**First Round**

FK Austria 0, Steaua Bucharest 2
Steaua Bucharest 2, FK Austria 1
Hamburg 5, Randers Freja 3
Randers Freja 0, Hamburg 2
AC Milan 5, Levski 1
Levski 1, AC Milan 1
Hajduk Split 0, Tottenham Hotspur 2
Tottenham Hotspur 4, Hajduk Split 3
Shamrock Rovers 1, Cardiff City 1
Cardiff City 2, Shamrock Rovers 0
Lausanne Sports 3, Spartak Trnava 2
Spartak Trnava 2, Lausanne Sports 0
Aberdeen 10, Reykjavik 0
Reykjavik 1, Aberdeen 4
Valencia 4, Crusaders 0
Crusaders 2, Valencia 4
Torpedo Moscow 0, Motor Zwickau 0
Motor Zwickau 0, Torpedo Moscow 1
Izmir 2, Standard Liège 3
Standard Liège 0, Izmir 0
Aris Bonnevoie 0, Lyon 3
Lyon 2, Aris Bonnevoie 1
Fredrikstadt 1, Vitoria Setubal 5
Vitoria Setubal 2, Fredrikstadt 1
Vasas Gyor 5, Apollon Limassol 0
Apollon Limassol 0, Vasas Gyor 4
Bayern Munich 5, Panathinaikos 0
Panathinaikos 1, Bayern Munich 2

JHK Helsinki 1, Wislaw Cracow 4
Wislaw Cracow 4, JHK Helsinki 0
Floriana Malta 1, NAC Breda 2
NAC Breda 1, Floriana Malta 0

**Second Round**

Bayern Munich 6, Vitoria Setubal 2
Vitoria Setubal 1, Bayern Munich 1
Wislaw 0, Hamburg 1
Hamburg 4, Wislaw 0
NAC Breda 1, Cardiff City 1
Cardiff City 4, NAC Breda 1
Vasas Gyor 2, AC Milan 2
AC Milan 1, Vasas Gyor 1
Lyon 1, Tottenham Hotspur 0
Tottenham Hotspur 4, Lyon 3
Standard Liège 3, Aberdeen 0
Aberdeen 2, Standard Liège 0
Torpedo Moscow 3, Spartak Trnava 1
Spartak Trnava 1, Torpedo Moscow 3
Steaua Bucharest 1, Valencia 0
Valencia 3, Steaua Bucharest 0

**Quarter-finals**

SV Hamburg 2, Lyon 0
Lyon 2, SV Hamburg 0
SV Hamburg 2, Lyon 0
Standard Liège 1, AC Milan 1
AC Milan 1, Standard Liège 1
AC Milan 2, Standard Liège 0
Torpedo Moscow 1, Cardiff City 0
Cardiff City 1, Torpedo Moscow 0
Valencia 1, Bayern Munich 1
Bayern Munich 1, Valencia 0

**211**

**Semi-finals**

SV Hamburg 1, Cardiff City 1    AC Milan 2, Bayern Munich 0
Cardiff City 2, SV Hamburg 3    Bayern Munich 0, AC Milan 0

**Final** Rotterdam, 23 May 1968
AC Milan (2) 2, SV Hamburg (0) 0
*AC Milan:* Cudicini; Anquilletti, Schnellinger; Trappatoni, Rosato, Scala; Hamrin, Lodetti, Sormani, Rivera, Prati.
*SV Hamburg:* Ozcan; Sondemann, Kurbjohn; Dieckemann, Horst, H. Schulz; Dorfel II, Kramer, Seeler, Hornig, Dorfel I.
*Scorer:* Hamrin (2) for Milan.

## EUROPEAN CUP-WINNERS' CUP 1968–69

For the first time, one of the two major European club competitions was won by an Eastern European country; more precisely by the Czech team, Slovan Bratislava. The Soviet invasion of Czechoslovakia the previous summer had led to a refusal by many Western European clubs to play against Eastern clubs. This in turn had led to the 'zoning' of the first round, and all Eastern clubs except Slovan had withdrawn in protest. Slovan's victory was peculiarly appropriate under the circumstances.

Dunfermline, cleverly managed by the old Blackpool goalkeeper, George Farm, did best of the British entry, surviving until the semifinal. After a rough second leg, in which they had a player sent off, they protested at the way they were treated in Bratislava.

West Bromwich Albion, the FA Cup holders, were surprisingly among Dunfermline's victims. After conceding a draw at home, Dunfermline adjusted better to the icy circumstances at The Hawthorns, and won by Gardner's headed goal, scored after only 90 seconds.

Barcelona, if anybody, looked favourites for the final, especially after their fine 4–1 victory over Cologne in the second leg of the semifinals. But for the second time they lost a European final on Swiss soil. Cvetler, Slovan's clever winger, put them ahead in the second minute, and by half-time discomfited Barcelona were 3–1 behind. Though Rexach proceeded to score straight from a corner kick, the Czechs held on to win.

Cardiff, veterans of so many brave battles in this tournament, alas went out at the first hurdle.

**First Round**

Bruges 3, West Bromwich Albion 1
West Bromwich Albion 2, Bruges 0
Dunfermline Ath. 10, Apoel Nicosia 1
Apoel Nicosia 0, Dunfermline Ath. 2

Crusaders 2, Norrköping 2
Norrköping 4, Crusaders 1
Cardiff City 2, Porto 2
Porto 2, Cardiff City 1
Bordeaux 2, Cologne 1
Cologne 3, Bordeaux 0
Slovan Bratislava 3, Bor 0
Bor 2, Slovan Bratislava 0
Partizan Tirana 1, Torino 0

Torino 3, Partizan Tirana 1
Rumelange 2, Sliema Malta 1
Sliema Malta 1, Rumelange 0
Izmir 3, Lyn Oslo 1
Lyn Oslo 4, Izmir 1
Freja 1, Shamrock Rovers 0
Shamrock Rovers 1, Freja 2
Lugano 0, Barcelona 1
Barcelona 3, Lugano 0
Olympiakos Piraeus 2, Frem
  Reykjavik 0
Frem Reykjavik 0, Olympiakos
  Piraeus 2
ADO The Hague 4, Graz 1
Graz 0, ADO The Hague 2
Walk-over: *Dynamo Bucharest*

**Second Round**
Dynamo Bucharest 1, West
  Bromwich Albion 1
West Bromwich Albion 4,
  Dynamo Bucharest 0
Dunfermline 4, Olympiakos 0
Olympiakos 3, Dunfermline 0
Porto 1, Slovan Bratislava 0
Slovan Bratislava 4, Porto 0

Randers Freja 6, Sliema Malta 0
Sliema Malta 0, Randers Freja 2
ADO 0, Cologne 1
Cologne 3, ADO 0
Byes: *Torino, Barcelona*

**Quarter-finals**
Barcelona 3, Lyn Oslo 2
Barcelona 2, Lyn Oslo 2
  (*in Barcelona*)
Cologne 2, Randers Freja 1
Randers Freja 0, Cologne 3
Torino 0, Slovan Bratislava 1
Slovan Bratislava 2, Torino 1
Dunfermline 0, West Bromwich
  Albion 0
West Bromwich Albion 0,
  Dumfermline 1

**Semi-finals**
Dunfermline 1, Slovan
  Bratislava 1
Slovan Bratislava 1,
  Dunfermline 0
Cologne 2, Barcelona 2
Barcelona 4, Cologne 1

**Final** Basel, 21 May 1969
Slovan Bratislava (3) 3, Barcelona (1) 2
*Slovan:* Vencel; Filo, Hrivnak; Jan Zlocha, Horvarth, Hrdlicka;
Cvetler, Moder, Josef Capkovic, Jokl, Jan Capkovic.
*Barcelona:* Sadurni; Franch, Eladio; Rife, Olivella, Zabalza; Pelicer,
Castro, Zaldua, Fuste, Rexach, subs: Pereda, Mendonça.
*Scorers:* Cvetler, Hrivnak, Jan Capkovic for Slovan; Zaldua, Rexach
for Barcelona.

**EUROPEAN CUP-WINNERS' CUP 1969–70**
Manchester City added the Cup-Winners' Cup to the various honours
they had won since 1968, decisively beating Gornik in the final despite
some rough treatment by the Polish defenders. On their way to Vienna,
they beat Atlético Bilbao in the first round, after being at one stage
3–1 down in the first leg, in Spain, but rallying to draw 3–3. Their
League form in mid-season was poor, but they were always able to
produce something extra for their Cup-Winners' Cup matches.
Slovan, the holders, went out in the very first round, to Dynamo
Zagreb. Lierse were thoroughly thrashed in the second round by
Manchester City, Academica Coimbra narrowly beaten in the third.
Schalke won the first leg of the semi-final thanks to a characteristic

individualist goal by Libuda, but City annihilated them at Manchester. Francis Lee, Colin Bell, and Mike Summerbee, till he was hurt, were ebullient.

Gornik beat Roma to reach the final on the toss of a coin. In heavy rain, Lee had another fine match, and City comfortably overcame the loss of Doyle, through injury. Gornik's goal, made by Lubanski for Oslizlo, came too late to matter. Young and Lee – a penalty when Young was fouled – got City's goals.

**Preliminary Round**

Rapid Vienna 0, Torpedo Moscow 0

Torpedo Moscow 1, Rapid Vienna 1

**First Round**

Atlético Bilbao 3, Manchester City 3

Manchester City 3, Atlético Bilbao 0

Ards 0, Roma 0

Roma 3, Ards 1

Rangers 2, Steaua Bucharest 0

Steaua Bucharest 0, Rangers 0

Mjoendalen 1, Cardiff City 7

Cardiff City 5, Mjoendalen 1

Shamrock Rovers 2, Schalke 04 1

Schalke 04 3, Shamrock Rovers 0

Magdeburg 1, MTK Budapest 0

MTK Budapest 1, Magdeburg 1

Dukla Prague 1, Marseilles 0

Marseilles 2, Dukla Prague 0

Rapid Vienna 1, PSV Eindhoven 2

PSV Eindhoven 4, Rapid Vienna 2

Frem Copenhagen 2, St Gallen 1

St Gallen 1, Frem Copenhagen 0

Norrköping 5, Sliema 1

Sliema 1, Norrköping 0

Dynamo Zagreb 3, Slovan Bratislava 0

Slovan Bratislava 0, Dynamo Zagreb 0

Lierse 10, Apoel Cyprus 0

Apoel Cyprus 0, Lierse 1

Olympiakos Piraeus 2, Gornik Zabrze 2

Gornik Zabrze 5, Olympiakos Piraeus 0

Goeztepe Izmir 3, Union Luxemburg 0

Union Luxemburg 2, Goeztepe Izmir 3

IBV Reykjavik 0, Levski Sofia 4

Levski Sofia 4, IBV Reykjavik 0

Academica 0, Palloseura 0

Palloseura 0, Academica 1

**Second Round**

Lierse 0, Manchester City 3

Manchester City 5, Lierse 0

Gornik 3, Rangers 1

Rangers 1, Gornik 3

Goeztepe Izmir 3, Cardiff City 0

Cardiff City 1, Goeztepe Izmir 0

Roma 1, PSV 0

PSV 1, Roma 0

(*Roma won toss*)

Norrköping 0, Schalke 04 0

Schalke 04 1, Norrköping 0

Levski 4, St Gallen 0

St Gallen 0, Levski 0

Magdeburg 1, Academica 0

Academica 2, Magdeburg 0

Marseilles 1, Dynamo Zagreb 1

Dynamo Zagreb 0, Marseilles 0

**Quarter-finals**

Academica 0, Manchester City 0

Manchester City 1, Academica 0

Roma 2, Goeztepe Izmir 0

Goeztepe Izmir 0, Roma 0

Levski 3, Gornik 0

Gornik 2, Levski 1

Dyanamo Zagreb 1, Schalke 04 3

Schalke 04 1, Dynamo Zagreb 0

**Semi-finals**
Schalke 04 1, Manchester City 0
Manchester City 5, Schalke 04 1
Roma 1, Gornik 1

Gornik 2, Roma 2
Gornik 1, Roma 1
   (*at Strasbourg Gornik won
   toss*)

**Final** Vienna, 29 April 1970
Manchester City (2) 2, Gornik (0) 1
*Manchester City:* Corrigan; Book, Booth, Heslop, Pardoe; Doyle (Bowyer), Oakes, Towers; Bell, Lee, Young.
*Gornik:* Kostka; Gorgon, Oslizlo, Latocha, Florenski (Deja), Olek, Szoltysik, Wilczek (Skowronck), Banas, Lubanski, Szarynski.
*Scorers:* Young, Lee for Manchester City; Oslizlo for Gornik.

## EUROPEAN CUP-WINNERS' CUP 1970–71

Chelsea kept the trophy in England, defeating Real Madrid in a re-played final in Athens, having knocked out the holders, Manchester City, in the semi-finals. Injuries seriously afflicted City's hopes of retaining the Cup. Chelsea's victory in Athens owed much to the splendid form in midfield of the unpredictable Charlie Cooke, on this occasion displaying the full range of his exceptional talent.

Cardiff City yet again gave an excellent account of themselves in this competition, thrashing Nantes and giving Real Madrid a good run for their money.

After a shaky beginning against Linfield, Manchester City got into their stride, defeating Honved and Gornik (in a play-off) and revealing such fine new, locally developed players as the slim Mellor and the powerfully versatile Jeffries. The absence of both wing-halves, Doyle and Oakes, and above all the splendid Colin Bell, however, ruined their chances against Chelsea. These semi-final games had, absurdly, to be fitted in with the Easter programme, and were something of a fiasco. Chelsea, themselves without Peter Osgood, made heavy weather of beating City at Stamford Bridge, the South African Derek Smethurst at last getting the only goal from Webb's pass. Lee was the best player on the field. Chelsea also won the return against what amounted to a reserve City side, their young goalkeeper, Healey, carrying Weller's indirect free kick over his own line for the only goal.

But Chelsea, who had previously and convincingly beaten Aris, CSKA Sofia and Bruges, were not be undervalued. In the final, in Athens, still without the thrustful Hutchinson, and with Hollins and Osgood patched up for the fray, they took the lead ten minutes after half-time through Osgood; later obliged to hobble off. Real, largely the better side, equalised when Dempsey miskicked and Zoco seized the chance. Webb and Bonetti kept Real out in extra time.

Switching boldly to 4–2–4 in the replay, Chelsea owed much to Bonetti's goalkeeping, Cooke's skill, and Baldwin's thrust. He made the second goal for Osgood, Dempsey having got the first after a corner. Fleitas scored a fine goal for Real 15 minutes from time, but Real, with Pirri nursing his injured arm, had nobody to match Cooke.

**Preliminary Round**
Bohemians 1, Gottwaldov 2
Gottwaldov 2, Bohemians 1

**First Round**
Aberdeen 3, Honved 1
Honved 3, Aberdeen 1
(*Honved won on penalties*)
Cardiff City 8, Larnaca Cyprus 0
Larnaca 0, Cardiff City 0
Aris Salonika 1, Chelsea 1
Chelsea 5, Aris Salonika 1
Manchester City 1, Linfield 0
Linfield 2, Manchester City 1
Hibernians Malta 0, Real Madrid 0
Real Madrid 5, Hibernians Malta 0
Gottwaldov 2, PSV Eindhoven 1
PSV Eindhoven 1, Gottwaldov 0
Olympic Ljubljana 1, Benfica 1
Benfica 8, Olympic Ljubljana 1
Stromsgodset 0, Nantes 5
Nantes 2, Stromsgodset 3
Wacker Innsbruck 3, Partizan
  Tirana 2
Partizan Tirana 1, Wacker Inns-
  bruck 2
CSKA Sofia 9, Valkeakosken 0
Valkeakosken 1, CSKA Sofia 2
Vorwearts 0, Bologna 0
Bologna 1, Vorwaerts 1
Offenbach Kickers 2, Bruges 1
Bruges 2, Offenbach Kickers 0
Goeztepe Izmir 5, US Luxem-
  burg 0
US Luxemburg 1, Goeztepe
  Izmir 0
Aalborg 0, Gornik 1
Gornik 8, Aalborg 0
Akureyri Iceland 1, Zurich 7
Zurich 7, Akureyri 0
Steaua Bucharest 1, Karpaty
  Lvov 0

Karpaty Lvov 0, Steaua
  Bucharest 1

**Second Round**
CSKA Sofia 0, Chelsea 1
Chelsea 1, CSKA Sofia 0
Honved 1, Manchester City 0
Manchester City 2, Honved 0
Goztepe Izmir 0, Gornik 1
Gornik 3, Goztepe Izmir 0
PSV Eindhoven 4, Steaua Bucha-
  rest 0
Steaua Bucharest 0, PSV Eind-
  hoven 3
Benfica 2, Vorwaerts 0
Vorwaerts 2, Benfica 0
Vorwaerts won on penalties
Bruges 2, Zurich 0
Zurich 3, Bruges 2
Cardiff City 5, Nantes 1
Nantes 1, Cardiff City 2
Real Madrid 0, Wacker Inns-
  bruck 1
Wacker Innsbruck 0, Real
  Madrid 2

**Quarter-finals**
Cardiff City 1, Real Madrid 0
Real Madrid 2, Cardiff City 0
Bruges 2, Chelsea 0
Chelsea 4, Bruges 0
Gornik 2, Manchester City 0
Manchester City 2, Gornik 0
Manchester City 3, Gornik 1
PSV Eindhoven 2, Vorwaerts 0
Vorwearts 1, PSV Eindhoven 0

**Semi-finals**
Chelsea 1, Manchester City 0
Manchester City 0, Chelsea 1
PSV Eindhoven 0, Real Madrid 0
Real Madrid 2, PSV Eindhoven 1

**Final** (Replay)
Athens, 21 May 1971
Chelsea (2) 2, Real Madrid (0) 1
*Chelsea:* Bonetti; Boyle, Harris; Cooke, Dempsey, Webb; Weller,
Baldwin, Osgood (Smethurst), Hudson, Houseman.

*Real Madrid:* Borja; José Luis, Zunzunegui; Pirri, Benito, Zoco; Fleitas, Amancio, Grosso, Velazquez, (Gento), Bueno (Grande).
*Scorers:* Dempsey, Osgood for Chelsea; Fleitas for Real.

## EUROPEAN CUP-WINNERS' CUP 1971–72

A notable if somewhat Pyrrhic victory for Rangers, playing their third and first successful final in the competition. They duly defeated Moscow Dynamo, first Iron Curtain team to reach a major European final, in Barcelona, but such were the drunken excesses of their supporters in the stadium afterwards that they were banned by UEFA from defending it. A severe penalty indeed.

Rangers had a strange shock at Lisbon in the second round when, having clearly qualified on away goals, the referee obliged both teams to take penalties after extra time; and Sporting 'won'. Rangers appealed; and prevailed. In Turin, they played an exaggeratedly defensive game and drew, then beat Torino in the return more comfortably than the `1–0 score suggests. Their victory over Bayern Munich, their conquerors in the 1967 final, was splendid. Drawing a little fortunately in Munich, they overwhelmed the Germans at Ibrox, where Parlane made a spectacular debut at centre-forward, scoring the second goal. In the final, Rangers' rhythm was too much for Dynamo, who went 3–0 down before a late rally brought them two goals.

**Preliminary Round**
BK 69 Odense 4, FK Austria 2
FK Austria 2, BK 69 Odense 0
Fram Reykjavik 0, Hibernians Malta 3
Hibernians 2, Fram 0

**First Round**
Dynamo Berlin 1, Cardiff City 1
Cardiff City 1, Dynamo Berlin 1
*Dynamo won on penalties*
Jeunesse Hautcharage 0 Chelsea 8
Chelsea 13 Jeunesse Hautcharage 0
Rennes 1 Rangers 1
Rangers 1, Rennes 0
Servette 2, Liverpool 1
Liverpool 2, Servette 0
Distillery 1, Barcelona 3
Barcelona 4, Distillery 0
Sporting Lisbon, 4, Lyn Oslo 0
Lyn Oslo 0, Sporting Lisbon 3
Olympiakos Piraeus 0, Moscow Dynamo 2
Moscow Dynamo 1, Olympiakos Piraeus 2

Banyasz 2, Red Star Belgrade 7
Red Star 1, Banyasz 2
Dynamo Tirana 1, FK Austria 1
FK Austria 1, Dynamo Tirana 0
Zaglebie Sosnowicz 3, Atvidaberg 4
Atvidaberg 1, Zaglebie 1
Mikkeli 0, Eskisehirspor 0
Eskisehirspor 4, Mikkeli 0
Limerick 0, Torino 1
Torino 4, Limerick 0
Skoda Pilsen 0, Bayern Munich 1
Bayern Munich 6, Skoda Pilsen 1
Levski Sofia 1, Sparta Rotterdam 1
Sparta Rotterdam 2, Levski Sofia 0
Beerschot 7 Famagusta 0
Famagusta 0 Beerschot 1
Hibernians Malta 0 Steaua Bucharest 0
Steaua 1, Hibernians Malta 0

**Second Round**
Rangers 3, Sporting Lisbon 2
Sporting Lisbon 4, Rangers 3

Sparta Rotterdam 1, Red Star Belgrade 1
Red Star 2, Sparta 1
Atvidaberg 0, Chelsea 0
Chelsea 1, Atvidaberg 1
Torino 1, FK Austria 0
FK Austria 0, Torino 0
Liverpool 0, Bayern Munich 0
Bayern Munich 3, Liverpool 1
Beerschot 1, Dynamo Berlin 3
Dynamo Berlin 3, Beerschot 1
Eskisehirspor 0, Moscow Dynamo 1
Moscow Dynamo 1, Eskisehirspor 0
Barcelona 0, Steaua Bucharest 1
Steaua Bucharest 2, Barcelona 1

**Quarter Finals**
Torino 1, Rangers 1
Rangers 1, Torino 0

Steaua Bucharest 1, Bayern Munich 1
Bayern Munich 0, Steaua Bucharest 0
Atvidaberg 0, Dynamo Berlin 2
Dynamo Berlin 2, Atvidaberg 2
Red Star Belgrade 1, Moscow Dynamo 2
Moscow Dynamo 1, Red Star Belgrade 1

**Semi Finals**
Bayern Munich 1, Rangers 1
Rangers 2, Bayern Munich 0
Dynamo Berlin 1, Moscow Dynamo 1
Moscow Dynamo 1, Dynamo Berlin 1
*Moscow Dynamo won on penalties*

**Final** Barcelona, 24 May 1972
Rangers (2) 3, Moscow Dynamo (0) 2
*Rangers:* McCloy; Jardine, Mathieson; Greig, Johnstone, Smith, McLean, Conn, Stein, MacDonald, Johnston.
*Moscow Dynamo:* Pilgui; Basalacev, Dolmatov, Zikov, Dolbonosov, Zukov, Baidazhnyi, Jakobik (Eschtrekov), Sabo, Mahovikov, Evriuschkin.
*Scorers:* Stein, Johnston (2) for Rangers; Eschtrekov, Mahovikov for Moscow Dynamo.

## EUROPEAN CUP-WINNERS' CUP 1972–73

If ever a team was entitled to raise the old boxing manager's cry of 'We was robbed!' it was surely Leeds United. So deplorably biased was the refereeing of the ill-tempered final in Salonica by the Greek Michas that he was suspended by UEFA and his own Federation. Yet no enquiry followed to determine *why* he had been so inept. The darkest suspicions were thus given apparent justification.

Leeds lost the final to an early goal from a free-kick by Chiarugi, but might themselves have had at least a couple of penalties. Leeds had reached the final with increasing power and efficiency. The Turks of Ankaragucu put up a bruising resistance at Elland Road, and Hajduk of Split proved hard opponents in the semi-final, but Leeds' defence gave away only a couple of goals until the final; of which, despite the vital lack of their midfield generals Bremner and Giles and their striker Clarke, they were unquestionably the moral victors. A tournament that left a bad taste; though Third Division Wrexham proved notable giantkillers.

**First Round**

Bastia 0, Atlético Madrid 0
Atlético Madrid 2, Bastia 1
Floriana 1, Ferencvaros 0
Ferencvaros 6, Floriana 0
Schalke 04 2, Slavia Sofia 1
Slavia Sofia 3, Schalke 04 1
Standard Liège 1, Sparta Prague 0
Sparta Prague 4, Standard Liège 2
Spartak Moscow 1, Den Haag 0
Den Haag 0, Spartak Moscow 0
Vikingur Reykjavik 0, Legia
   Warsaw 2
Legia Warsaw 9, Vikingur
   Reykjavik 0
Ankaragucu 1, Leeds United 1
Leeds United 1, Ankaragucu 0
Hajduk Split 1, Frederikstad 0
Frederikstad 0, Hajduk 1
Rapid Vienna 0, POAK
   Salonica 0
POAK Salonica 2, Rapid
   Vienna 2
Zurich 1, Wrexham 1
Wrexham 2, Zurich 1
Sporting Lisbon 2, Hibernian 1
Hibernian 6, Sporting Lisbon 1
Rapid Bucharest 3, Landskrona 0
Landskrona 1, Rapid Bucharest 0
Pesoporikos Larna 1, Cork
   Hibernian 2
Cork Hibernian 4, Pesoporikos
   Larna 1
Fremad 1, Besa 1
Besa 0, Fremad 0
Carl Zeiss Jena 6, Mikkelin 1
Mikkelin 3, Carl Zeiss Jena 2
Red Boys Differdange 1,
   Milan 4
Milan 3, Red Boys 0

**Second Round**

Rapid Vienna 1, Rapid
   Bucharest 1
Rapid Bucharest 3, Rapid
   Vienna 1
Carl Zeiss Jena 0, Leeds United 0
Leeds United 2, Carl Zeiss Jena 0
Wrexham 3, Hajduk Split 1
Hajduk 2, Wrexham 0
Cork Hibernian 0, Schalke 04 0
Schalke 04 3, Cork Hibernian 0
Atlético Madrid 3, Spartak
   Moscow 4
Spartak Moscow 1, Atlético
   Madrid 2
Hibernian 7, Besa 1
Besa 1, Hibernian 1
Ferencvaros 2, Sparta Prague 0
Sparta Prague 4, Ferencvaros 1
Legia Warsaw 1, Milan 1
Milan 2, Legia Warsaw 1

**Quarter-Finals**

Leeds United 5, Rapid
   Bucharest 1
Rapid Bucharest 1,
   Leeds United 3
Hibernian 4, Hadjuk Split 2
Hajduk Split 3, Hibernian 0
Schalke 04 2, Sparta Prague 1
Sparta Prague 3, Schalke 04 0
Spartak Moscow 0, Milan 1
Milan 1, Spartak Moscow 1

**Semi-Finals**

Leeds United 1, Hajduk Split 1
Hajduk Split 0, Leeds United 0
Milan 1, Sparta Prague 0
Sparta Prague 0, Milan 1

**Final** Salonika, 16 May 1973
Milan (1) 1, Leeds United (0) 0
*Milan:* Vecchi; Sabadini, Zignoli, Anquilletti, Turone, Rosato (Dolci),
Sogliano, Benetti, Bigon, Rivera, Chiarugi.
*Leeds United:* Harvey; Reaney, Cherry; Bates, Madeley, Hunter;
Lorimer, Jordan, Jones, F. Gray, Yorath (McQueen).
*Scorer:* Chiarugi for Milan.

# EUROPEAN CUPWINNERS' CUP 1973–74

For the first time, an East European team won this Cup, when Magdeburg thoroughly beat an ailing Milan in the sparsely attended final. This time, Milan had no Greek referee to get them off the hook though they certainly benefited from some weird decisions by the Spaniard, Martinez, in their return semi-final away to Borussia Münchengladbach.

Borussia accounted for both Rangers and Glentoran, who went farthest of the British teams, while Sporting Lisbon knocked out Cardiff and Sunderland, but fell in the semi-finals to Magdeburg.

In the final, at Rotterdam, the East Germans were much faster and stronger than the Italians, had outstanding players in Sparwasser and Pommerenke, and scored once in each half.

**First Round**

Vasas 0, Sunderland 2
Sunderland 1, Vasas 0
Ankaragucu 0, Rangers 2
Rangers 4, Ankaragucu 0
Cardiff City 0, Sporting Lisbon 0
Sporting Lisbon 2, Cardiff City 1
Chimia 2, Glentoran 2
Glentoran 2, Chimia 0
Banik Ostrava 1, Cork Hibs. 0
Cork Hibs 1, Banik Ostrava 2
Reipas 0, Lyon 0
Lyon 2, Reipas 0
Gzira United 0, Brann Bergen 2
Brann Bergen 7, Gzira United 0
Milan 3, Dynamo Zagreb 1
Dynamo Zagreb 0, Milan 1
Pezoporikos 0, Malmö 0
Malmö 11, Pezoporikos 0
Anderlecht 3, Zurich 2
Zurich 1, Anderlecht 0
Vestmannaeyia 0, Borussia
  Münchengladbach 7
Borussia Munchengladbach 9,
  Vestmannaeyia 1
Torpedo Moscow 0,
  Atlético Bilbao 0
Atlético Bilbao 2,
  Torpedo Moscow 0

NAC Breda 0, Magdeburg 0
Magdeburg 2, NAC Breda 0
Randers Freja 0, Rapid Vienna 0
Rapid Vienna 2, Randers Freja 1
Legia Warsaw 1,
  PAOK Salonica 1
PAOK Salonica 1,
  Legia Warsaw 0
Fola Esch 0, Beroe 7
Beroe 4, Fola Esch 1

**Second Round**

Sunderland 2, Sporting Lisbon 0
Sporting Lisbon 2, Sunderland 0
Borussia Münchengladbach 3,
  Rangers 0
Rangers 3,
  Borrussia Münchengladbach 2
Brann Bergen 1, Glentoran 1
Glentoran 3, Brann Bergen 1
Milan 0, Rapid Vienna 0
Rapid Vienna 0, Milan 2
Zurich 0, Malmö 0
Malmö 1, Zurich 1
Beroe 3, Atlético Bilbao 0
Atlético Bilbao 1, Beroe 0
Lyon 3, PAOK Salonica 3
PAOK Salonica 4, Lyon 0
Banik Ostrava 2, Magdeburg 0
Magdeburg 3, Banik Ostrava 0

**Quarter-finals**
Magdeburg 2, Beroe 0
Beroe 1, Magdeburg 1
Milan 3, PAOK Salonika 0
PAOK Salonika 2, Milan 2
Borussia Münchengladbach 5,
  Glentoran 0
Glentoran 0, Borussia München-
gladbach 2
Sporting Lisbon 3, Zurich 0
Zurich 1, Sporting Lisbon 1

**Semi-finals**
Milan 2,
  Borussia Münchengladbach 0
Borussia Münchengladbach 1,
  Milan 0
Sporting Lisbon 1, Magdeburg 1
Magdeburg 2, Sporting Lisbon 1

**Final** Rotterdam, 8 May, 1974
  Magdeburg (1) 2,                    Milan (0) 0
*Magdeburg:* Schulze; Enge, Zapf, Gaube, Abraham, Tyll, Pommer-
enke, Seguin, Raugust, Sparwasser, Hoffmann.
*Milan:* Pizzaballa; Anquilletti, Sabadini, Lanzi, Schnellinger, Maldera,
Tresoldi, Benetti, Bigon, Rivera, Bergamaschi (Tresoldi).
*Scorers:* Lanzi (o.g.), Seguin for Magdeburg.

# CHAPTER SIXTEEN

# The European Inter-Cities Fairs and UEFA Cup History

This competition, which made a creaking start, taking an unconscionable time a-playing, has since gathered prestige and popularity. It was nominally open to cities which put on trade fairs, and initially, London entered a representative team, later falling into line and putting out club sides. Home and away aggregate decides. In 1971 it became the European Union (UEFA) Cup.

**1955–58**
London eliminated Basel, Frankfurt, and Lausanne, but lost in the final to Barcelona. Birmingham City knocked out Inter and Zagreb, but lost (4–3, 0–1, 1–2 at Basel) to Barcelona.
London 2, Barcelona 2 (Chelsea)
*Scorers:* Greaves, Langley (pen) for London; Tejada, Martínez for Barcelona.
Barcelona 6, London 0
*Scorers:* Suarez (2), Martínez, Evaristo (2), Verges for Barcelona.

**1958–60**
Chelsea, representing London, went out in the second round (1–0, 1–4) to Belgrade. Birmingham eliminated Cologne (2–2, 2–0), Zagreb (2–0 3–3) and Union St Gilloise (4–2, 4–2) but lost to Barcelona in the final.
Birmingham 0, Barcelona 0
Barcelona 4, Birmingham 1
*Scorers:* Martínez, Czibor (2), Coll for Barcelona, Hooper for Birmingham.

**1960–61**
By now the competition had been properly stabilised, and played off within one season. Hibernian, representing Scotland, put out Barcelona in the second round. The decisive match at Edinburgh produced violent scenes, as the Barcelona players ran riot. Hibernian, having drawn 4–4 in Barcelona, won this second leg 3–2.

Birmingham City eliminated BK Copenhagen (4–4, 5–0), having previously put out Ujpest of Hungary, while Hibernian had a walkover against Lausanne.

In the semi-finals, Birmingham maintained their fine record in this contest by defeating Inter 2–1 both at home and away. But Hibernian, having drawn 2–2 and 3–3 with Roma, crashed 6–0 in the play-off.

In the final, Roma beat Birmingham.
Birmingham City 2, Roma 2
*Scorers:* Hellawell, Orritt for Birmingham; Manfredini (2) for Roma.
Roma 2, Birmingham City 0
*Scorers:* Farmer (o.g.), Pestrin for Roma.

**1961–62**

The Spaniards now succeeded in getting the entry temporarily increased to three clubs per country; and one of their own clubs, Valencia, was successful.

Of the British clubs, Sheffield Wednesday knocked out Lyon and Roma, but were eliminated by Barcelona 4–3 on aggregate, in the quarter-finals. Valencia crushed Nottingham Forest 7–1 on aggregate in the first round, but Hearts eliminated Union St Gilloise (5–1 on aggregate). In the next round, however, Inter put them out 5–0 on aggregate.

In the final, Valencia, having accounted for Inter in the quarter-finals, convincingly won an all-Spanish clash with Barcelona.

Valencia 6, Barcelona 2
*Scorers:* Not known for Valencia, Kocsis (2) for Barcelona.
Barcelona 1, Valencia 1
*Scorers:* Kocsis for Barcelona, Guillot for Valencia.


**1962–63**

Valencia, their teeth now well into this trophy, won it again. Everton, coming in for the first time, were surprisingly knocked out (1–0 and 0–2) by the compact Dunfermline side. Hibernian had another excellent run, beating Staevnet of Copenhagen 4–0 and 3–2, Utrecht of Holland 1–0 and 2–1, and finally going out, 0–5, 2–1, to Valencia, who had beaten Dunfermline in a third match decider in the second round. Dunfermline lost away, 4–0, but won gallantly at home, 6–2.

Dynamo Zagreb 1, Valencia 2
*Scorers:* Zambata for Dynamo; Waldo, Urtiaga for Valencia.
Valencia 2, Dynamo Zagreb 0
*Scorers:* Mañó, Núñez for Valencia.


**1963–64**

In an all-Spanish final at Barcelona, Saragossa narrowly got home against Valencia.


**First Round**

| (Results of British teams only) | Sheffield Wednesday 1, Cologne 2 |
|---|---|
| Staevnet Copenhagen 1, Arsenal 7 | Arsenal 1, Liège 1 |
| Arsenal 2, Staevnet Copenhagen 3 | Liège 3, Arsenal 1 |
| Utrecht 1, Sheffield Wednesday 4 | Partick Thistle 3, Spartak Brno 2 |
| Sheffield Wednesday 4, Utrecht 1 | Spartak Brno 4, Partick Thistle 0 |
| Glentoran 1, Partick Thistle 4 | Lausanne 1, Saragossa 2 |
| Partick Thistle 3, Glentoran 0 | Saragossa 3, Lausanne 0 |
| Lausanne 2, Hearts 2 | Juventus 1, Atlético Madrid 0 |
| Hearts 2, Lausanne 2 | Atlético Madrid 1, Juventus 2 |
| Lausanne 3, Hearts 2 | Juventus 1, Atlético Madrid 0 |
|  | Atlético Madrid 1, Juventus 2 |

**Second Round**

| | Valencia 0, Rapid Vienna 0 |
|---|---|
| Cologne 3, Sheffield Wednesday 2 | Rapid Vienna 2, Valencia 3 |

Ujpest Dozsa 0, Lokomotiv
    Plovdiv 0
Lokomotive Plovdiv 1, Ujpest
    Dozsa 3

Spartak Brno 2, Liège 0
Liège 1, Spartak Brno 0
Valencia 5, Ujpest 2
Ujpest 3, Valencia 1

**Quarter-finals**
Roma 3, Cologne 1
Cologne 4, Roma 0
Saragossa 3, Juventus 2
Juventus 0, Saragossa 0
Liège 2, Spartak Brno 0

**Semi-finals**
Valencia 4, Cologne 1
Cologne 2, Valencia 0
Liège 1, Saragossa 0
Saragossa 2, Liège 0

**Final**
Saragossa 2, Valencia 1
*Scorers:* Villa, Marcelino for Saragossa; Urtiaga for Valencia.

# EUROPEAN INTER-CITIES FAIRS CUP 1964–65

A tournament surprisingly and meritoriously won by Ferencvaros of Budapest – very much the outsiders from the semi-finals onward, despite a forward-line which included the internationals Albert, Rakosi, and Fenyvesi, whose goal beat Juventus in the final. Manchester United, England's hopes, who had won an all-English clash with Everton on the way, slipped badly in the semi-finals, confirming the fears of those who believed their organisation hardly matched their talent. The first of their two matches in Budapest, won by Ferencvaros with a disputed penalty, was bad tempered and unpleasant; a man from each side was sent off. Juventus, after making a very laborious way to the semi-final, suddenly found some form and recovered against Atlético Madrid, but in the end went down at home to Ferencvaros – and Dr Fenyvesi.

**Preliminary Round**
Eintracht Frankfurt 3,
    Kilmarnock 0
Kilmarnock 5, Eintracht
    Frankfurt 1
Wiener Sportklub 2, Lokomotiv
    Leipzig 1
Lokomotiv Leipzig 0, Wiener
    Sportklub 1
Strasbourg 2, Milan 0
Milan 1, Strasbourg 0
Basel 2, Spora Luxemburg 0
Spora Luxemburg 0, Basel 1
Atlético Bilbao 2, OFK Belgrade 2
OFK Belgrade 0, Atlético Bilbao 2
Ferencvaros 2, Spartak Brno 0
Spartak Brno 1, Ferencvaros 0

Goztep Smyrna 0, Petrolol
    Ploesti 1
Petrolul Ploesti 2, Goztep
    Smyrna 1
Odense BK 1913 1, VfB
    Stuttgart 3
VfB Stuttgart 1, Odense BK
    1913 0
Betis Seville 1, Stade Français 1
Stade Français 2, Betis Seville 0
Dynamo Zagreb 3, Grazer AK 2
Grazer AK 0, Dynamo Zagreb 6
Borussia Dortmund 4, Bordeaux 1
Bordeaux 2, Borussia Dortmund 0
Union St Gilloise 0, Juventus 1
Juventus 1, Union St Gilloise 0
Valencia 1, Liège 1

Liège 3, Valencia 1
Vojvodina 1, Lokomotiv
  Plovdiv 1
Lokomotiv Plovdiv 1,
  Vojvodina 1
Lokomotiv Plovdiv 2,
  Vojvodina1 (Sofia)
Djugaarden 1, Manchester
  United 1
Manchester United 6,
  Djugaarden 1
Valerenger 2, Everton 5
Everton 4, Valerenger 2
Leixoes 1, Celtic 1
Celtic 3, Leixoes 0
Barcelona 0, Fiorentina 1
Fiorentina 0, Barcelona 2
Aris 0, Roma 0
Roma 3, Aris 0
Belenenses 1, Shelbourne 1
Shelbourne 0, Belenenses 0
Shelbourne 2, Belenenses 1
  (Dublin)
Dunfermline Ath. 4, Oergryte 2
Oergryte 0, Dunfermline Ath. 0
Hertha Berlin 2, Antwerp 1
Antwerp 2, Hertha Berlin 0
BK Copenhagen 3, DOS
  Utrecht 4
DOS 2, BK Copenhagen 1
Servette 2, Atlético Madrid 2
Atlético Madrid 6, Servette 1

**First Round**
Dynamo Zagreb 1, Roma 1
Roma 1, Dynamo Zagreb 0
Stade Français 0, Juventus 0
Juventus 1, Stade Français 0
Basel 0, Strasbourg 1
Strasbourg 5, Basel 2
Kilmarnock 0, Everton 2
Everton 4, Kilmarnock 1
Petrolul 1, Lokomotiv Plovdiv 0
Lokomotiv Plovdiv 2, Petrolul 0
Borussia Dortmund 1,
  Manchester United 6
Manchester United 4,
  Borussia Dortmund 0
Dunfermline 1, VfB Stuttgart 0

VfB Stuttgart 0, Dunfermline 0
Atlético Bilbao 2, Antwerp 0
Antwerp 0, Atlético Bilbao 1
Barcelona 3, Celtic 1
Celtic 0, Barcelona 0
Utrecht 0, Liège 2
Liège 2, Utrecht 0
Ferencvaros 1, Weiner SK 0
Wiener SK 0, Ferencvaros 0
Shelbourne 0, Atlético Madrid 1
Atlético Madrid 1, Shelbourne 0

**Second Round**
Strasbourg 0, Barcelona 0
Barcelona 2, Strasbourg 2
Barcelona 0, Strasbourg 0
  (Barcelona)
  Strasbourg won toss
Manchester United 1, Everton 1
Everton 1, Manchester United 2
Juventus 1, Lokomotiv Plovdiv 1
Lokomotiv Plovdiv 1, Juventus 1
Juventus 2, Lokomotiv 1 (Turin)
Atlético Bilbao 1, Dunfermline 0
Dunfermline 1, Atlético Bilbao 0
Atlético Bilbao 2, Dunfermline 1
  (Bilbao)
Roma 1, Ferencvaros 2
Ferencvaros 1, Roma 0
Liège 1, Atlético Madrid 0
Atlético Madrid 2, Liège 0

**Quarter-finals**
Ferencvaros 1, Atlético Bilbao 0
Atlético Bilbao 1, Ferencvaros 0
Ferencvaros 3, Atlético Bilbao 0
  (Budapest)
Strasbourg 0, Manchester
  United 5
Manchester United 0,
  Strasbourg 0
Byes: *Juventus: Atletico Madrid*

**Semi-finals**
Manchester United 3,
  Ferencvaros 2
Ferencvaros 1, Manchester
  United 0

Ferencvaros 2, Manchester
United 1 (Budapest)
Atlético Madrid 3, Juventus 1

Juventus 3, Atlético Madrid 1
Juventus 3, Atlético Madrid 1
(Turin)

**Final** Turin
Juventus (0) 0, Ferencvaros (0) 1
*M. Fenyvesi*

## EUROPEAN INTER-CITIES FAIRS CUP 1965–66

A tournament which produced a rash of violent matches ended in anticlimax, the two Spanish finalists being ordered by their Federation to postpone the two-legged final till the following season. When it was at last played, it turned out to be thoroughly dramatic. Winning on Barcelona's ground, Saragossa proceeded to lose on their own, three of Barcelona's goals being scored by a young newcomer to the attack, Pujol.

Chelsea's young team did well, none better than the brilliant young forward, Peter Osgood. Their three ties with Milan were memorable, above all the game at Stamford Bridge, when Schnellinger gave a performance for Milan which was matchlessly combative. Memorable for more sisnister reasons was the previous round's game in Rome, where the players were bombarded with missiles. Leeds' home game against Valencia gave rise to a disgraceful brawl. But it was Saragossa who eventually eliminated them, with surprising ease, in a decider played at Leeds.

**First Round**
Union Luxembourg 0, Cologne 4
Cologne 13, Union Luxembourg 0
Hibernian 2, Valencia 0
Valencia 2, Hibernian 0
Valencia 3, Hibernian 0
Liège 1, Dynamo Zagreb 0
Dynamo Zagreb 2, Liège 0
Red Star Belgrade 0,
   Fiorentina 4
Fiorentina 3, Red Star
   Belgrade 1
Stade Français 0, Porto 0
Porto 1, Stade Français 0
Malmö 0, Munich 1860 3
Munich 1860 4, Malmö 0
Bordeaux 0, Sporting Lisbon 4
Sporting Lisbon 6, Bordeaux 1
Milan 1, Strasbourg 0
Strasbourg 2, Milan 1
Milan 1, Strasbourg 1
(Milan won toss)

Chelsea 4, Roma 1
Roma 0, Chelsea 0
Spartak Brno 2, Lokomotiv
   Plovdiv 0
Lokomotiv Plovdiv 1, Spartak
   Brno 0
Nuremberg 1, Everton 1
Everton 1, Nuremberg 0
Antwerp 1, Glentoran 0
Glentoran 3, Antwerp 3
Wiener SK 6, PAOK Salonika 0
PAOK Salonika 2, Wiener SK 1
Leeds United 2, Torino 1
Torino 0, Leeds United 0
DSO Utrecht 0, Barcelona 0
Barcelona 7, DSO Utrecht 1
Alk Stockholm 3, Daring
   Brussels 1
Daring Brussels 0, Alk
   Stockholm 0
Byes: *Hanover 96, Español Barce-
lona, Red Flag Brasov, Goeztepe*

226

*Izmir, Servette Geneva, CUF Setubal, Lokomotiv Leipzig, Basle, Aris Salonika, Ujpest Dozsa, BK Copenhagen, Dunfermline Ath., Hearts, Valerengen, Shamrock Rovers, Saragossa.*

## Second Round
Aris Salonika 2, Cologne 1
Cologne 2, Aris Salonika 0
Goeztepe Izmir 2, Munich 1860 1
Munich 1860 9, Goeztepe Izmir 1
Ujpest 3, Everton 0
Everton 2, Ujpest 1
Dunfermline 5, BK Copenhagen 0
BK Copenhagen 2, Dunfermline 4
Hanover 96 5, Porto 0
Porto 2, Hanover 96 1
Sporting Lisbon 2, Español Barcelona 1
Español Barcelona 4, Sporting Lisbon 3
Español Barcelona 2, Sporting Lisbon 1
Dynamo Zagreb 2, Red Flag Brasov 2
Red Flag Brasov 1, Dynamo Zagreb 0
Antwerp 2, Barcelona 1
Barcelona 2, Antwerp 0
Shamrock Rovers 1, Saragossa 1
Saragossa 2, Shamrock Rovers 1
Wiener SK 1, Chelsea 0
Chelsea 2, Wiener SK 0
Lokomotiv Leipzig 1, Leeds United 2
Leeds United 0, Lokomotiv Leipzig 0
CUF Setubal 2, Milan 0
Milan 2, CUF Setubal 0
Milan 1, CUF Setubal 0
Basel 1, Valencia 3
Valencia 5, Basel 1
Fiorentina 2, Spartak Brno 0
Spartak Brno 4, Fiorentina 0
Alk Stockholm 2, Servette Geneva 1

Servette Geneva 4, Alk Stockholm 1
Hearts 1, Valerengen 0
Valerengen 1, Hearts 3

## Third Round
Hearts 3, Saragossa 3
Saragossa 2, Hearts 2
Saragossa 1, Hearts 0
Leeds United 1, Valencia 1
Valencia 0, Leeds United 1
Hanover 96 2, Barcelona 1
Barcelona 1, Hanover 96 0
Hanover 96 1, Barcelona 1
(Barcelona won toss)
Cologne 3, Ujpest 2
Ujpest 4, Cologne 0
Dunfermline 2, Spartak Brno 0
Spartak Brno 0, Dunfermline 0
Español 3, Red Flag Brasov 1
Red Flag Brasov 4, Español 2
Español 1, Red Star Brasov 0
Milan 2, Chelsea 1
Chelsea 2, Milan 1
Milan 1, Chelsea 1
(Chelsea won toss)
Servette Geneva 1, Munich 1860 1
Munich 1860 4, Servette Geneva 1

## Fourth Round
Leeds United 4, Ujpest 1
Ujpest 1, Leeds United 1
Munich 1860 2, Chelsea 2
Chelsea 1, Munich 1860 0
Dunfermline 1, Saragossa 0
Saragossa 4, Dunfermline 2
Barcelona 1, Español 0
Español 0, Barcelona 1

## Semi-finals
Saragossa 1, Leeds United 0
Leeds United 2, Saragossa 1
Leeds United 1, Saragossa 3
Barcelona 2, Chelsea 0
Chelsea 2, Barcelona 0
Barcelona 5, Chelsea 0

**Final**
Barcelona 0, Saragossa 1
*Scorer:* Canario for Saragossa.
Saragossa 2, Barcelona 4
*Scorers:* Marcelino (2) for Saragossa; Pujol (3), Zaballa for Barcelona.


## EUROPEAN INTER-CITIES FAIRS CUP 1966–67

Postponed for the second time until the following season, the final of the 1966–67 competition was ultimately won by Dynamo Zagreb, at the expense of Leeds United. In Zagreb, they deservedly won, both goals being scored by their 18-year-old outside-right, Cercek. At Elland Road, their defence, with Skoric excellent in goal, massed to keep out the Leeds attack. Two other well-known internationals, Belin, the right-half, and Zambata, the striker, also increased their reputations.

Barcelona, the holders, had gone out to Dundee United only a matter of weeks after winning the postponed 1966 final. United shocked them by beating them on their own ground, Seemann and Persson, their Scandinavian wingers, playing splendidly. Juventus, however, were too strong for them in the Third Round, even though United won the return in Dundee.

Burnley had a very good run, beating VfB Stuttgart, Lausanne, and Naples – where, in the return match, they had to survive a short and vicious riot, involving Naples players and spectators.

Burnley's own robust tactics provoked a brawl late in the home game against Eintracht, which they surprisingly lost – thus going out of the competition.

Leeds United did very well to beat Valencia away from home, got through against Bologna on the toss of a coin, and competently disposed of Kilmarnock on their way to the final. But Benfica, on their first appearance in the tournament, surprisingly went out to Leipzig in the Third Round. Dynamo Zagreb had a splendid 3–0 home win to put out Juventus in the quarter finals, then turned a 3–0 deficit into a 4–3 aggregate win over Eintracht in the semis.

**First Round**

Juventus 5, Aras Salonika 0
Aris Salonika 0, Juventus 2
Olympija Ljubljana 3, Ferencvaros 3
Ferencvaros 3, Olympija Ljubljana 0
DOS Utrecht 2, Basel 1
Basel 2, DOS Utrecht 2
Vfb Stuttgart 1, Burnley 1
Burnley 2, VfB Stuttgart 0
Frigg Oslo 1, Dunfermline Ath. 3
Dunfermline Ath. 3, Frigg Oslo 1

Red Star Belgrade 4, Atlético Bilbao 0
Atlético Bilbao 2, Red Star Belgrade 0
Valencia 2, Nuremberg 1
Nuremberg 0, Valencia 2
Drumcondra 0, Eintracht Frankfurt 2
Eintracht Frankfurt 5, Drumcondra 1
Naples 3, Wiener SK 1
Wiener SK 1, Naples 2
Porto 2, Bordeaux 1

Bordeaux 2, Porto 1
(Bordeaux won toss)
Nice 2, Oergryte Gothenburg 2
Oergryte Gothenberg 2, Nice 1
Djurgaarden 1, Lokomotiv
   Leipzig 3
Lokomotiv Leipzig 2, Djurgaar-
   den 1
Dynamo Pitesti 2, Seville 0
Seville 2, Dynamo Pitesti 2
Spartak Brno 2, Dynamo
   Zagreb 0
Dynamo Zagreb 2, Spartak
   Brno 0
(Dynamo won toss)
US Luxemberg 0, Antwerp 1
Antwerp 4, US Luxemberg 0
Bologna 3, Goeztepe 1
Goeztepe 1, Bologna 2
Byes: *Toulouse, Barcelona, Dun-
   dee United, Vitoria Setubal,
   Odense BK 09, Lausanne, BK
   Copenhagen, La Gantoise, Kil-
   marnock, Spartak Plovdiv, Ben-
   fica, Liege, Sparta Prague, West
   Bromwich Albion, DWS Am-
   sterdam, Leeds United.*

**Second Round**
DWS 1, Leeds United 3
Leeds United 5, DWS 1
Lokomotiv Leipzig 0, Liège 0
Liège 1, Lokomotiv Leipzig 2
Lausanne 1, Burnley 3
Burnley 5, Lausanne 0
La Gantoise 1, Bordeaux 0
Bordeaux 0, La Gantoise 0
Oergryte 0, Ferencvaros 0
Ferencvaros 7, Oergryte 1
Toulouse 3, Dynamo Pitesti 0
Dynamo Pitesti 5, Toulouse 1
Dunfermline 4, Dynamo Zagreb 2
Dynamo Zagreb 2, Dunfermline 0
Barcelona 1, Dundee United 2
Dundee United 2, Barcelona 0
Odense BK 09 1, Naples 4
Naples 2, Odense BK 09 1
Antwerp 1, Kilmarnock 1

Kilmarnock 7, Antwerp 2
Valencia 1, Red Star Belgrade 0
Red Star Belgrade 1, Valencia 2
Sparta Prague 2, Bolgona 2
Bologna 2, Sparta Prague 1
Spartak Plovdiv 1, Benfica 1
Benfica 2, Spartak Plovdiv 0
DOS Utrecht 1, West Bromwich
   Albion 1
West Bromwich Albion 5, DOS
   Utrecht 2
Juventus 3, Setubal 1
Setubal 0, Juventus 2
Eintracht 5, BK Copenhagen 1
BK Copenhagen 2, Eintracht 2
**Third Round**
Lokomotiv Leipzig 3, Benfica 1
Benfica 2, Lokomotiv Leipzig 1
Kilmarnock 1, La Gantoise 0
La Gantoise 1, Kilmarnock 2
Burnley 3, Naples 0
Naples 0, Burnley 0
Leeds United 1, Valencia 1
Valencia 0, Leeds United 2
Bologna 3, West Bromwich
   Albion 0
West Bromwich Albion 1,
   Bologna 3
Juventus 3, Dundee United 0
Dundee United 1, Juventus 0
Dynamo Zagreb 1, Dynamo
   Pitesti 0
Dynamo Pitesti 0, Dynamo Zag-
   reb 0
Eintracht 4, Ferencvaros 1
Ferencvaros 2, Eintracht 1
**Quarter-finals**
Bologna 1, Leeds United 0
Leeds United 1, Bologna 0
(Leeds won toss)
Juventus 2, Dynamo Zagreb 2
Dynamo Zagreb 3, Juventus 0
Eintracht 1, Burnley 1
Burnley 1, Eintracht 2,
Lokomotiv Leipzig 1,
   Kilmarnock 0
Kilmarnock 2, Lokomotiv Leip-
   zig 0

**Semi-finals**

Leeds United 4, Kilmarnock 2            Eintracht 3, Dynamo Zagreb 0
Kilmarnock 0, Leeds United 0           Dynamo Zagreb 4, Eintracht 0

**Final** 30 August 1967
Dynamo Zagreb (1) 2, Leeds United (0) 0
*Scorer:* Cercek (2) for Dynamo Zagreb.
6 September 1967
Leeds United (0) 0, Dynamo Zagreb (0) 0

## EUROPEAN INTER-CITIES FAIRS CUP 1967–68

This time, Leeds United, in another postponed final – or finals – consoled themselves for the previous year's disappointment by defeating Ferencvaros to win. They were two hard games, each on the same pattern; an away team clamming up in defence and allowing the home team to come at them. Leeds won the first game and scored the only goal of the finals in controversial circumstances; Jackie Charlton stood on the goal line at a corner and blocked the goalkeeper's path while Jones thumped the ball home.

On their way to the final, Leeds had tough opposition from Partizan Belgrade and Hibernian – who had rallied superbly in their return match with Naples, winning 5–0 after losing 4–1 away – but didn't concede a goal against Rangers.

Ferencvaros, winners of the trophy in 1965, played beautiful football at Liverpool, where Munich had crashed – and were cheered off the field by the Kop. Bologna pushed them very hard in the semi-finals.

Dundee had a splendid run into the semi-finals, but Leeds were again too good for them, defeating a Scottish side for the third time in the competition. The return match at Elland Road was played during an accumulation of postponed matches and won by an Eddie Gray goal nine minutes from time.

**First Round**

Spora Luxemburg 0, Leeds
  United 9
Leeds United 7, Spora
  Luxemburg 0
PAOK Salonika 0, Liège 2
Liège 3, PAOK Salonika 2
Wiener SK 0, Atletico Madrid 5
Atletico Madrid 2, Wiener SK 1
St Patrick's Athletic 1,
  Bordeaux 3
Bordeaux 6, St. Patrick's
  Athletic 3
DOS Utrecht 3, Saragossa 2
Saragossa 3, DOS Utrecht 1
Naples 4, Hanover 96 0
Hanover 96 1, Naples 1

Bologna 2, Lyn Oslo 0
Lyn Oslo 0, Bologna 0
Nice 0, Fiorentina 1
Fiorentina 4, Nice 0
Dresden Dynamo 1, Rangers 1
Rangers 2, Dresden Dynamo 1
Argesul Pitesti 3, Ferencvaros 1
Ferencvaros 4, Argesul Pitesti 0
Malmö 0, Liverpool 2
Liverpool 2, Malmö 1
Hibernian 3, Porto 0
Porto 3, Hibernian 1
Eintracht Frankfurt 0, Notting-
  ham Forest 1
Nottingham Forest 4, Eintracht
  Frankfurt 0

Dynamo Zagreb 5, Petrolul Ploesti 0
Petrolul Ploesti 2, Dynamo Zagreb 0
Servette Geneva 2, Munich 1860 2
Munich 1860 4, Servette Geneva 2
Bruges 0, Sporting Lisbon 0
Sporting Lisbon 2, Bruges 1
Frem Copenhagen 0, Atlético Bilbao 1
Atlético Bilbao 3, Frem Copenhagen 2
Zurich 3, Barcelona 1
Barcelona 1, Zurich 0
Lokomotiv Leipzig 5, Linfield 1
Linfield 1, Lokomotiv Leipzig 0
DWS Amsterdam 2, Dundee 1
Dundee 3, DWS Amsterdam 0
Partizan 5, Lokomotiv Plovdiv 1
Lokomotiv Plovdiv 1, Partizan 1
Vojvodina 1, CUF 0
CUF 1, Vojvodina 3
Cologne 2, Slavia Prague 0
Slavia Prague 2, Cologne 2
Royal Antwerp 1, Goeztepe Izmir 2
Goetzepe Izmir 0, Royal Antwerp 0

**Second Round**
Nottingham Forest 2, Zurich 1
Zurich 1, Nottingham Forest 0
Bordeaux 1, Atlético Bilbao 3
Atlético Bilbao 1, Bordeaux 0
Dundee 3, Liège 1
Liège 1, Dundee 4
Vojvodina 0, Lokomotiv Leipzig 0
Lokomotiv Leipzig 0, Vojvodina 2
Saragossa 2, Ferencvaros 1
Ferencvaros 3, Saragossa 0

**Final**
Leeds United 1, Ferencvaros 0
*Scorer:* Jones for Leeds United.
Ferencvaros 0, Leeds United 0

Liverpool 8, Munich 1860 0
Munich 1860 2, Liverpool 1
Rangers 3, Cologne 0
Cologne 3, Rangers 1
Bologna 0, Dynamo Zagreb 0
Dynamo Zagreb 1, Bologna 2
Naples 4, Hibernian 1
Hibernian 5, Naples 0
Partizan 1, Leeds United 2
Leeds United 1, Partizan 1
Fiorentina 1, Sporting Lisbon 1
Sporting Lisbon 2, Fiorentina 1

**Third Round**
Ferencvaros 1, Liverpool 0
Liverpool 0, Ferencvaros 1
Leeds United 1, Hibernian 0
Hibernian 1, Leeds United 1
Vojvodina 1, Goeztepe Izmir 0
Goeztepe Izmir 0, Vojvodina 1
Zurich 3, Sporting Lisbon 0
Sporting Lisbon 1, Zurich 0
Byes: *Atlético Bilbao, Dundee, Rangers, Bologna*

**Quarter-finals**
Ferencvaros 2, Bilbao 1
Bilbao 2, Ferencvaros 2
Rangers 0, Leeds United 0
Leeds United 2, Rangers 0
Dundee 1, F.C. Zurich 0
F.C. Zurich 0, Dundee 1
Bologna 0, Vojvodina 0
Vojvodina 0, Bologna 2

**Semi-finals**
Dundee 1, Leeds United 1
Leeds United 1, Dundee 0
Ferencvaros 3, Bologna 2
Bologna 2, Ferencvaros 2

# EUROPEAN INTER-CITIES FAIRS CUP 1968–69

For the second successive year, an English club won the Fairs Cup; surprisingly and laudably it was Newcastle United, on their first entry into European competition. After a somewhat erratic beginning, in which they played irresistibly at home and indifferently away, they reached a brilliant crescendo in the two-legged final against Ujpest – conquerors of the holders, Leeds United.

Having soundly beaten them at Gallowgate, thanks to two goals by their normally defensive half-back, Bobby Moncur, they rode a two-goal deficit in Budapest to win dramatically, 3–2.

Leeds might have done rather better had they not become so intensely engaged with the League Championship. They put out Standard Liège, were lucky to eliminate Naples on the iniquitous toss of a coin (Naples must be getting used to it; a similar expedient decided the 1960 Olympic semi-final and the 1968 European Nations semi-final, at Fuorigrotta), annihilated Hanover, but were well beaten, home and away, by Ujpest.

Newcastle overcame Feyenoord, Sporting Lisbon, Saragossa, Vitoria Setubal, then Rangers. 'Away goals' allowed them to scrape through against the Spanish team, but Rangers couldn't score a goal against them. Their failure provoked a barbaric invasion of the Newcastle pitch by Rangers' fans, and a prolonged stoppage of the game.

Thus to the final, in which Moncur got yet another fine goal in Budapest, and young Foggon, coming on as substitute, raced splendidly through alone to score the winner.

## First Round

Chelsea 5, Morton 0
Morton 3, Chelsea 4
Newcastle United 4, Feyenoord 0
Feyenoord 2, Newcastle United 0
Slavia Sofia 0, Aberdeen 0
Aberdeen 2, Slavia Sofia 0
Atlético Bilbao 2, Liverpool 1
Liverpool 2, Atlético Bilbao 1
Atlético won the toss
Rangers 2, Vojvodina 0
Vojvodina 1, Rangers 0
Ljubjana 0, Hibernian 3
Hibernian 2, Ljubjana 1
OFK Belgrade 6, Rapid Bucharest 1
Rapid Bucharest 3, OFK Belgrade 1
Wiener Sportklub 1, Slavia Prague 0
Slavia Prague 5, Weiner Sportklub 0
Skeid Oslo 1, AIK Stockholm 1

AIK Stockholm 2, Skeid Oslo 1
Trakia Plovdiv 3, Real Saragossa 1
Real Saragossa 2, Trakia Plovdiv 0
Dynamo Zagreb 1, Fiorentina 1
Fiorentina 2, Dynamo Zagreb 1
Legia Warsaw 6, Munich 1860 0
Munich 1860 2, Legia Warsaw 3
Daring Brussels 2, Panathinaikos 1
Panathinaikos 2, Daring Brussels 0
Wacker Innsbruck, 2 Eintracht Frankfurt 2
Eintracht Frankfurt 3, Wacker Innsbruck 0
Sporting Lisbon 4, Valencia 0
Valencia 4, Sporting Lisbon 1
Bologna 4, Basel 1
Basel 1, Bologna 2
Aris Salonika 1, Hibernian Malta 0

Hibernian Malta 0, Aris
  Salonika 6
DOS Utrecht 1, Dundalk 1
Dundalk 2, DOS Utrecht 1
Hansa Rostock 3, OGC Nice 0
OGC Nice 2, Hansa Rostock 1
Atlético Madrid 2, Waregem 1
Waregem 1, Atlético Madrid 0
Goeztepe Izmir 2, Marseilles 0
Marseilles 2, Goeztepe Izmir 0
Goeztepe won the toss
Metz 1, Hamburg SV 4
Hamburg SV 3, Metz 2
Lyon 1, Coimbra Academica 0
Coimbra Academica 1, Lyon 0
Lyon won the toss
Lausanne 0, Juventus 2
Juventus 2, Lausanne 0
Beerschot 1, DWS Amsterdam 1
DWS Amsterdam 2, Beerschot 1
Odense BK 09 1, Hanover 96 3
Hanover 96 1, Odense BK 09 0
Vitoria Setubal 3, Linfield 0
Linfield 1, Vitoria Setubal 3
Standard Liège 0, Leeds United 0
Leeds United 3, Standard Liège 2
Naples 3, Grasshoppers 1
Grasshoppers 1, Naples 0
Byes: *Argesul Pitesti, Lokomotiv
  Leipzig, Ujpest Dozsa*

**Second Round**
Hibernian 3, Lokomotiv Leipzig 1
Lokomotiv 0, Hibernian 1
Leeds United 2, Naples 0
Naples 2, Leeds United 0
Leeds won the toss
Rangers 6, Dundalk 1
Dundalk 0, Rangers 3
Aberdeen 2, Real Saragossa 1
Real Saragossa 3, Aberdeen 0
Chelsea 0, DWS Amsterdam 0
DWS Amsterdam 0, Chelsea 0
DWS won the toss
Sporting Lisbon 1, Newcastle
  United 1
Newcastle United 1, Sporting
  Lisbon 0
Vitoria Setubal 5, Lyon 0

Lyon 1, Vitoria Setubal 2
Goeztepe Izmir 3, Argesul Pitesti 0
Argesul Pitesti 3, Goeztepe Izmir 2
Hansa Rostock 3, Fiorentina 2
Fiorentina 2, Hansa Rostock 1
Hamburg SV 4, Slavia Prague 1
Slavia Prague 3, Hamburg SV 1
Panathinaikos 0, Atlético
  Bilbao 0
Bilbao Atlético 1,
  Panathinaikos 0
OFK Belgrade 1, Bologna 0
Bologna 1, OFK Belgrade 1
Aris Salonika 1, Ujpest 2
Ujpest 9, Aris Salonika 1
AIK Stockholm 4, Hanover 96 2
Hanover 96 5, AIK Stockholm 2
Juventus 0, Eintracht Frankfurt 0
Eintracht Frankfurt 1, Juventus 0
Waragem 1, Legia Warsaw 0
Legia Warsaw 2, Waragem 0

**Third Round**
Leeds United 5, Hanover 96 1
Hanover 96 1, Leeds United 2
Hamburg SV 1, Hibernian 0
Hibernian 2, Hamburg SV 1
Legia Warsaw 0, Ujpest 1
Ujpest 2, Legia Warsaw 2
Real Saragossa 3, Newcastle
  United 2
Newcastle United 2, Real
  Saragossa 1
OFK Belgrade 3, Goeztepe Izmir 1
Goeztepe Izmir 2, OFK Belgrade 0
Eintracht Frankfurt 1, Atlético
  Bilbao 1
Atlético Bilbao 1, Eintracht
  Frankfurt 0
DWS Amsterdam 0, Rangers 2
Rangers 2, DWS Amsterdam 1
DWS won the toss
Vitoria Setubal 3, Fiorentina 0
Fiorentina 2, Vitoria Setubal 1

**Quarter-finals**
Newcastle United 5, Vitoria
  Setubal 1
Vitoria Setubal 3, Newcastle
  United 1

Rangers 4, Atlético Bilbao 1
Atlético Bilbao 2, Rangers 0
Leeds United 0, Ujpest 1
Ujpest 2, Leeds United 0
Goztepe Izmir *v.* Hamburg SV
  Hamburg withdrew

**Semi-finals**
Goeztepe Izmir 1, Ujpest 4
Ujpest 4, Goeztepe Izmir 0
Rangers 0, Newcastle United 0
Newcastle United 2, Rangers 0

**Final**
Newcastle United (0) 3, Ujpest (0) 0
*Scorers:* Moncur (2), Scott for Newcastle United.
Ujpest (2) 2, Newcastle United (0) 3
*Scorers:* Bene, Gorocs for Ujpest; Moncur, Arentoft, Foggon for Newcastle.
*Newcastle United's* team in both matches: McFaul; Craig, Clark, Gibb, Burton, Moncur, Scott, Robson, Davies, Arentoft, Sinclair.
Substitute in each match: Foggon.


## EUROPEAN FAIRS CUP 1969–70

Yet again, this now bloated, slightly amorphous competition had an English winner. Though there were moments in the course of the tournament when an Arsenal victory seemed the unlikeliest of outcomes, the North London club finally and impressively prevailed, to win their first major honour since 1953.

They began modestly, actually losing to Glentoran in the first round's return leg. A flaccid Sporting Lisbon team were easily crushed at Highbury, while a hardly more impressive Rouen side gave a startling amount of trouble.

In the quarter-finals, Newcastle United, the holders, were bitterly unlucky to be squeezed out by Anderlecht on a late away goal, while Arsenal thrashed Dynamo Bacau. In the semi-finals, they played vigorously to trounce Ajax 3–0 at home, Cruyff and all, lost the return only 1–0, and so met the powerful Anderlecht in the final.

The Belgians, who had rallied surprisingly to beat Inter at San Siro, after losing at home, were much too good for Arsenal in Brussels. But again Arsenal proved formidable at home, breaking down Anderlecht's defence with a marvellous first half goal by young Kelly, and scoring two more in the second half.

**First Round**
Arsenal 3, Glentoran 0
Glentoran 1, Arsenal 0
Dundee United 1, Newcastle
  United 2
Newcastle United 1, Dundee
  United 0
Liverpool 10, Dundalk 0
Dundalk 0, Liverpool 4
Partizan 2, Ujpest Dozsa 1
Ujpest Dozsa 2, Partizan 0

Sabadel 2, Bruges 0
Bruges 5, Sabadel 1
Las Palmas 0, Hertha Berlin 0
Hertha Berlin 1, Las Palmas 0
Wiener Sportklub 4, Ruch
  Chorzow 2
Ruch Chorzow 4, Wiener
  Sportklub 1
Rouen 2, Twente Enschede 0
Twente Enschede 1, Rouen 0

Vitoria Guimaraes 1, Banik
Ostrava 0
Banik Ostrava 1, Vitoria
Guimaraes 1
Sporting Lisbon 4, Linz ASK 0
Linz ASK 2, Sporting Lisbon 2
Carl Zeiss Jena 1, Altay Izmir 0
Altay Izmir 0, Carl Zeis Jena 0
Lausanne 1, Vasas Györ 2
Vasas Györ 2, Lausanne 1
Rosenborg Trondheim 1,
Southampton 0
Southampton 2, Rosenborg
Trondheim 0
Hansa Rostok 3, Panionios
Athens 0
Panionios Athens 2, Hansa
Rostock 0
Dynamo Bacau 6, Floriana 0
Floriana 0, Dynamo Bacau 1
Slavia Sofia 2, Valencia 0
Valencia 1, Slavia Sofia 1
Internazionale 2, Sparta Prague 0
Sparta Prague 0, Internazionale 1
Juventus 3, Lokomotiv Plovdiv 1
Lokomotiv Plovdiv 1, Juventus 2
VfB Stuttgart 3, Plazs Malmo 0
Plazs Malmo 0, VfB Stuttgart 1
Hanover 96 1, Ajax 0
Ajax 3, Hanover 96 0
Aris Salonika 1, Cagliari 0
Cagliari 3, Aris Salonika 0
Metz 1, Naples 1
Naples 2, Metz 1
Barcelona 4, Odense BK 09 0
Odense BK 09 0, Barcelona 2
Gwardia Warsaw 1, Vojvodina 0
Vojvodina 1, Gwardia Warsaw 1
Dunfermline 4, Bordeaux 1
Bordeaux 2, Dunfermline 0
Zurich 3, Kilmarnock 2
Kilmarnock 3, Zurich 1
Munich 1860 2, Skied Oslo 2
Skeid Oslo 2, Munich 1860 1
Valur Reykjavik 0, Anderlecht 6
Anderlecht 2, Valur Reykjavik 0
Charleroi 2, FNK Zagreb 1
FNK Zagreb 1, Charleroi 3

Hvidovre Copenhagen 1, Porto 2
Porto 2, Hvidovre Copenhagen 0
Jeunesse d'Esch 3, Coleraine 2
Coleraine 4, Jeunesse d'Esch 0
Vitoria Setubal 3, Rapid
Bucharest 1
Rapid Bucharest 1, Vitoria
Setubal 4

**Second Round**
Sporting Lisbon 0, Arsenal 0
Arsenal 3, Sporting Lisbon 0
Anderlecht 6, Coleraine 1
Coleraine 3, Anderlecht 7
Vitoria Setubal 1, Liverpool 0
Liverpool 3, Vitoria Setubal 2
Porto 0, Newcastle United 0
Newcastle United 1, Porto 0
Ajax 7, Ruch Chorzow 0
Ruch Chorzow 1, Ajax 2
Hansa Rostock 2,
Internazionale 1
Internazionale 3, Hansa
Rostock 0
Carl Zeiss Jena 2, Cagliari 0
Cagliari 0, Carl Zeiss Jena 1
Hertha Berlin 3, Juventus 1
Juventus 0, Hertha Berlin 0
Vasas Györ 2, Barcelona 3
Barcelona 2, Vasas Györ 0
VfB Stuttgart 0, Naples 0
Naples 1, VfB Stuttgart 0
Kilmarnock 4, Slavia Sofia 1
Slavia Sofia 2, Kilmarnock 0
Bruges 5, Ujpest 2
Ujpest 3, Bruges 0
Skeid Oslo 0, Dynamo Bacau 0
Dynamo Bacau 2, Skeid Oslo 0
Charleroi 3, Rouen 1
Rouen 2, Charleroi 0
Vitoria Guimaraes 3,
Southampton 3
Southampton 5,
Vitoria Guimaraes 1
Dunfermline 2, Gwardia
Warsaw 1
Gwardia Warsaw 0,
Dunfermline 1

**Third Round**

Newcastle United 0, Southampton 0

Southampton 1, Newcastle United 1

Anderlecht 1, Dunfermline 0

Dunfermline 3, Anderlecht 2

Rouen 0, Arsenal 0

Arsenal 1, Rouen 0

Kilmarnock 1, Dynamo Bacau 1

Dynamo Bacau 2, Kilmarnock 0

Carl Zeiss Jena 1, Ujpest 0

Ujpest 0, Carl Zeiss Jena 3

Barcelona 1, Internazionale 2

Internazionale 1, Barcelona 1

Vitoria Setubal 1, Hertha Berlin 1

Hertha Berlin 1, Vitoria Setubal 0

Naples 1, Ajax 0

Ajax 4, Naples 0

**Quarter-finals**

Carl Zeiss Jena 3, Ajax 1

Ajax 5, Carl Zeiss Jena 1

Hertha Berlin 1, Internazionale 0

Internazionale 2, Hertha Berlin 0

Anderlecht 2, Newcastle United 0

Newcastle United 3, Anderlecht 1

Dynamo Bacau 0, Arsenal 2

Arsenal 7, Dynamo Bacau 1

**Semi-finals**

Anderlecht 0, Internazionale 1

Internazionale 0, Anderlecht 2

Arsenal 3, Ajax 0

Ajax 1, Arsenal 0

**Final** Brussels, 22 April 1970

Anderlecht (2) 3, Arsenal (0) 1

*Anderlecht:* Trappeniers; Heylens, Velkeneers, Kialunda, Cornelis (Peeters), Desengher, Nordahl; Devrindt, Mulder, Van Himst, Puis.

*Arsenal:* Wilson; Storey, McNab; Kelly, McLintock, Simpson; Armstrong, Sammels, Radford, George, Graham.

*Scorers:* Devrindt, Mulder (2) for Anderlecht; Kennedy (sub) for Arsenal.

Highbury, 28 April 1970

Arsenal (1) 3, Anderlecht (0) 0

*Arsenal:* Wilson; Storey, McNab; Kelly, McLintock, Simpson; Armstrong, Sammels, Radford, George, Graham.

*Anderlecht:* Trappeniers; Heylens, Velkeneers, Kialunda, Martens; Nordahl, Desanghere; Devrindt, Mulder, Van Himst, Puis.

*Scorers:* Kelly, Radford, Sammels for Arsenal.

**EUROPEAN FAIRS CUP 1970–71**

This, the last of the Fairs Cups – it would now change its name to the UEFA Cup – was won for the fourth consecutive time by an English club: Leeds United, who themselves had won it three years earlier and were appearing in their third final. Their success was well deserved, crowning a season beset by injury to key players, but it was ironic that they should overcome the fine young Juventus side in the final without beating them in either leg. The absurdity of away goals counting double

236

gave them the trophy. The games were drawn 2–2 in Turin, 1–1 at Elland Road, and excellent games they both were.

On their way to the final, Leeds eliminated Sarpsborg, Dynamo Dresden – on away goals – Sparta Prague, Vitoria Setubal, and Liverpool – with a goal at Anfield by the returning Billy Bremner. Liverpool, who'd thrashed Beckenbauer's Bayern Munich at home in the previous round, had been favoured to win.

Juventus, clearly taking the competition much more seriously than Italian teams are wont to, defeated Barcelona twice, came back powerfully at Enschede to eliminate Twente in the quarter final, then accounted for Cologne. Arsenal, the holders, paid the penalty for a moment's carelessness by their goalkeeper – Bob Wilson let a corner by Cologne at Highbury straight into goal – and some wretched finishing by their own attack.

After their first attempt to play the first leg of the final in Turin was frustrated by rain, Leeds were twice behind to Juventus. But, with Giles in fine form, they twice equalised, thanks to Madeley and Bates. The second goal came after Piloni bungled Giles' cross.

At Elland Road, in the return, Clarke scored after twelve minutes, putting Leeds in an impregnable position on aggregate. 'Juve' scored a fluent equaliser through Anastasi before half -time, but by the interval seemed to have resigned themselves. Cooper had one of his best attacking games for Leeds.

**First Round**

AEK Athens 0, Twente Enschede 1

Twente Enschede 3, AEK Athens 0

Zeleznicar 3, Anderlecht 4

Anderlecht 5, Zeleznicar 4

La Gantoise 0, Hamburg 1

Hamburg 7, La Gantoise 1

Liverpool 1, Ferencvaros 0

Ferencvaros 1, Liverpool 1

Sarpsborg 0, Leeds United 0

Leeds United 5, Sarpsborg 0

Coleraine 1, Kilmarnock 1

Kilmarnock 2, Coleraine 3

Dundee United 3, Grasshoppers 2

Grasshoppers 0, Dundee United 0

Lazio 2, Arsenal 2

Arsenal 2, Lazio 0

GKS Katowice 0, Barcelona 1

Barcelona 3, GKS Katowice 2

Wiener Sportklub 0, Beveren 2

Beveren 3, Wiener Sportklub 0

Ilves 4, Sturm Graz 2

Sturm Graz 3, Ilves 0

Juventus 7, Rumelange 0

Rumelange 0, Juventus 4

Seveille 1, Eskisehirsport 0

Eskisehirsport 3, Seville 1

Vitoria Guimaraes 3, Angouleme 0

Angouleme 3, Vitoria Guimaraes 1

Hajduk Split 3, Slavia Sofia 0

Slavia Sofia 1, Hajduk Split 0

Nykoeping 2, Hertha Berlin 4

Hertha Berlin 4, Nykoeping 1

Partizan Belgrade 0, Dynamo Dresden 0

Dynamo Dresden 6, Partizan Belgrade 0

Barreirense 2, Dynamo Zagreb 0

Dynamo Zagreb 6, Barreirense 1

Ruch Chorzow 1, Fiorentina 1

Fiorentina 2, Ruch Chorzow 0

Sparta Prague 2, Atlético Bilbao 0

Atlético Bilbao 1, Sparta Prague 1

AB Copenhagen 7, Sliema Wanderers 0

Sliema Wanderers 2, AB
Copenhagen 3
Dynamo Bucharest 5, PAOK
Salonika 0
PAOK Salonika 1, Dynamo
Bucharest 0
Lausanne 0, Vitoria Setubal 2
Vitoria Setubal 2, Lausanne 1
Cologne 5, Sedan 1
Sedan 1, Cologne 0
Internazionale 1, Newcastle
United 1
Newcastle United 2,
Internazionale 0
Spartak Trnava 2, Olympique
Marseilles 0
Olympique Marseilles 2, Spartak
Trnava 0
Trnava qualified on penalties
Bayern Munich 1, Rangers 0
Rangers 1, Bayern Munich 1
Cork Hibernian 0, Valencia 3
Valencia 3, Cork Hibernian 1
Hibernian 6, Malmo 0
Malmo 2, Hibernian 3
Universitatea Craiova 2,
Pecsi Dosza 1
Pecsi Dosza 3, Universitatea
Craiova 0
Trakia Plovdiv 1, Coventry
City 4
Coventry City 2, Trakia
Plovdiv 0
Sparta Rotterdam 6, IA
Akranes 0
IA Akranes 0, Sparta
Rotterdam 9

**Second Round**
Sturm Graz 1, Arsenal 0
Arsenal 2, Sturm Graz 0
Sparta Rotterdam 2,
Coleraine 0
Coleraine 1, Sparta
Rotterdam 2
Leeds United 1, Dynamo
Dresden 0
Dynamo Dresden 2, Leeds
United 1

Liverpool 3, Dynamo Bucharest 0
Dynamo Bucharest 1, Liverpool 1
Newcastle United 2, Pecsi
Dosza 0
Pecsi Dosza 2, Newcastle
United 0
Pesci qualified on penalties
Bayern Munich 6, Coventry
City 1
Coventry City 2, Bayern
Munich 1
Sparta Prague 3, Dundee
United 1
Dundee United 1, Sparta
Prague 0
Hibernian 2, Vitoria
Guimaraes 0
Vitoria Guimaraes 2,
Hibernian 1
Eskisehirsport 3, Twente 2
Twente 6, Eskisehirsport 1
AB Copenhagen 1, Anderlecht 3
Anderlecht 4, AB Copenhagen 0
Valencia 0, Baveren 1
Beveren 1, Valencia 1
Hertha Berlin 1, Spartak
Trnava 0
Spartak Trnava 3, Hertha
Berlin 1
Barcelona 1, Juventus 2
Juventus 2, Barcelona 1
Dynamo Zagreb 4, Hamburg 0
Hamburg 1, Dynamo Zagreb 0
Vitoria Setubal 2, Hajduk 0
Hajduk 2, Vitoria Setubal 1
Fiorentina 1, Cologne 2
Cologne 1, Fiorentina 0

**Third Round**
Arsenal 4, Beveren 0
Beveren 0, Arsenal 0
Leeds United 6, Sparta Prague 0
Sparta Prague 2, Leeds United 3
Spartak Trnava 0, Cologne 1
Cologne 3, Spartak Trnava 0
Bayern Munich 2, Sparta
Rotterdam 1
Sparta Rotterdam 1, Bayern
Munich 3

Dynamo Zagreb 2, Twente 2
Twente 1, Dynamo Zagreb 0
Hibernian 0, Liverpool 1
Liverpool 2, Hibernian 0
Pecsi Dosza 0, Juventus 1
Juventus 2, Pecsi Dosza 0
Anderlecht 2, Vitoria Setubal 1
Vitoria Setubal 3, Anderlecht 1

Arsenal 2, Cologne 1
Cologne 1, Arsenal 0
Liverpool 3, Bayern Munich 0
Bayern Munich 1, Liverpool 1
Vitoria Setubal 1, Leeds United 1
Leeds United 2, Vitoria Setubal 1

**Quarter-finals**
Juventus 2, Twente 0
Twente 2, Juventus 2

**Semi-finals**
Liverpool 0, Leeds United 1
Leeds United 0, Liverpool 0
Cologne 1, Juventus 1
Juventus 2, Cologne 0

**Final** Turin, 29 May 1971
Juventus (1) 2    Leeds United (0) 2
*Juventus:* Piloni, Spinosi, Salvadore, Marchetti, Morini, Furino, Haller, Capello, Causio, Anastasi (Novellini), Bettega.
*Leeds United:* Sprake; Reaney, Cooper; Bremner, Charlton, Hunter; Lorimer, Clarke, Jones (Bates), Giles, Madeley.
*Scorers:* Bettega, Capello for Juventus; Madeley, Bates for Leeds.

Leeds, 3 June 1971
Leeds United (1) 1    Juventus (1) 1
*Leeds United:* Sprake; Reaney, Cooper; Bremner, Charlton, Hunter; Lorimer, Clarke, Jones, Giles, Madeley (Bates).
*Juventus:* Tancredi; Spinosi, Salvadore, Marchetti; Morini, Furino, Haller, Capello, Causio, Anastasi, Bettega.
*Scorers:* Clarke for Leeds; Anastasi for Juventus.
*Leeds won on 'away' goals.*

## UEFA CUP 1971-72
This time, Football League clubs went one better than before, providing not only the winners but the runners-up, Spurs beating Wolves in the final. It was the first edition of the European Union Cup, previously and misleadingly named the Fairs Cup, since it had long strayed far from its initial basis. Tottenham's finest achievement was probably their win over a ruthless Milan team in the semi-final, though Milan would not have lost at Tottenham had they not been so defensive after taking the lead. Two shots by Steve Perryman when the ball came out of the box duly sank them, while Alan Mullery, recalled from loan to Fulham to play splendidly, scored in a 1-1 draw at San Siro.

Big Martin Chivers' opportunism won the first leg of the final at Molineux against a Wolves team that had previously played very well to draw away to Juventus and to knock out Ferencvaros, the experienced Hungarians. The second leg, at White Hart Lane, was a hard, fast bruising draw – in which Mullery once again scored the Spurs goal.

## First Round

Glentoran 0, Eintracht Brunswick 1

Eintracht Brunswick 6, Glentoran 1

Keflavik 1, Tottenham Hotspur 6

Tottenham Hotspur 9, Keflavik 0

Lierse 0, Leeds United 2

Leeds United 0, Lierse 4

Dundee 4, AB Copenhagen 2

AB Copenhagen 0, Dundee 1

SV Hamburg 2, St Johnstone 1

St Johnstone 2, SV Hamburg 0

Southampton 2, Atlético Bilbao 1

Atlético Bilbao 2, Southampton 0

Milan 4, Morphou 0

Morphou 0, Milan 3

Fenerbahce 1, Ferencvaros 1

Ferencvaros 3, Fenerbahce 1

Rosenborg 3, IFK Helsinki 0

IFK Helsinki 0, Rosenborg 0

Lugano 1, Legia Warsaw 3

Legia Warsaw 0, Lugano 1

Bologna 1, Anderlecht 1

Anderlecht 0, Bologna 2

Naples 1, Rapid Bucharest 0

Rapid Bucharest 2, Naples 0

Basle 1, Real Madrid 2

Real Madrid 2, Basle 1

Vasas 1, Shelbourne 0

Shelbourne 1, Vasas 1

Celta Vigo 0, Aberdeen 2

Aberdeen 1, Celta Vigo 0

Vitoria Setubal 1, Nimes 0

Nimes 2, Vitoria Setubal 1

Porto 0, Nantes 2

Nantes 1, Porto 0

ADO (Netherlands) 5, Aris 2

Aris 2, ADO (Netherlands) 2

Hertha 3, Elfsborg 1

Elfsborg 1, Hertha 4

Carl Zeiss Jena 3, Lokomotiv Plovdiv 0

Lokomotive Plovdiv 3, Carl Zeiss Jena 1

Chemie Halle 0, PSV Eindhoven 0

*(No return played)*

Zaglebie 1, Union Teplice 0

Union Teplice 1, Zaglebie 3

Marsa Malta 0, Juventus 6

Juventus 5, Marsa Malta 0

UT Arad 4, Austria Salzburg 1

Austria Salzburg 3, UT Arad 1

Atlético Madrid 2, Panionios 1

Panionios 1, Atlético Madrid 0

*Rapid Vienna walkover Vlaznija Alb scr.*

Dynamo Zagreb 6, Botev 1

Botev 1, Dynamo Zagreb 2

Zeljeznicar Sarajevo 3, Brugeois 0

Brugeois 3, Zeljeznicar 1

Saint Etienne 1, Cologne 1

Cologne 2, St Etienne 1

Wolverhampton Wanderers 3, Academica Coimbra 0

Academica Coimbra 1, Wolverhampton Wanderers 4

Spartak Moscow 2, Kosice 0

Kosice 2, Spartak Moscow 1

OFK Belgrade 4, Djurgarden 1

Djurgarden 2, OFK Belgrade 2

## Second Round

ADO 1, Wolverhampton Wanderers 3

Wolverhampton Wanderers 4, ADO 0

Nantes 0, Tottenham Hotspur 0

Tottenham Hotspur 1, Nantes 0

St Johnstone 2, Vasas 0

Vasas 1, St Johnstone 0

Juventus 2, Aberdeen 0

Aberdeen 1, Juventus 1

Cologne 2, Dundee 1

Dundee 4, Cologne 2

Zeljeznicar 1, Bologna 1

Bologna 2, Zeljeznicar 2

Milan 4, Hertha 2

Hertha 2, Milan 1

Ferencvaros 6, Panionios 0

*Panionios expelled for unruly conduct*

Rosenborg 4, Lierse 1

Lierse 3, Rosenborg 0

Rapid Bucharest 4, Legia Warsaw 0

Legia Warsaw 2, Rapid
Bucharest 0
Spartak Moscow 0, Vitoria
Setubal 0
Vitoria Setubal 4, Spartak
Moscow 0
OFK Belgrade 1, Carl Zeiss
Jena 1
Carl Zeiss Jena 4, OFK
Belgrade 0
Real Madrid 3, PSV Eindhoven 1
PSV Eindhoven 2, Real Madrid 0
Zaglebie 1, UT Arad 1
UT Arad 2, Zaglebie 1
Eintracht Brunswick 2,
Atlético Bilbao 1
Atlético Bilbao 2, Eintracht
Brunswick 2
Dynamo Zagreb 2, Rapid
Vienna 2
Rapid Vienna 0, Dynamo
Zagreb 0

**Third Round**
Carl Zeiss Jena 0,
Wolverhampton Wanderers 1
Wolverhampton Wanderers 3,
Carl Zeiss Jena 0
St Johnstone 1, Zeljeznicar 0
Zeljeznicar 5, St Johnstone 0
Milan 3, Dundee 0
Dundee 2, Milan 0
Tottenham Hotspur 3, Rapid
Bucharest 0

Rapid Bucharest 0, Tottenham
Hotspur 2
UT Arad 3, Vitoria Setubal 0
Vitoria Setubal 1, UT Arad 0
Rapid Vienna 0, Juventus 1
Juventus 4, Rapid Vienna 1
PSV Eindhoven 1, Lierse 0
Lierse 4, PSV Eindhoven 0
Eintracht Brunswick 1,
Ferencvaros 1
Ferencvaros 5, Eintracht
Brunswick 2

**Quarter-finals**
UT Arad 0, Tottenham
Hotspur 2
Tottenham Hotspur 1,
UT Arad 1
Milan 2, Lierse 0
Lierse 1, Milan 1
Juventus 1, Wolverhampton
Wanderers 1
Wolverhampton Wanderers 1,
Juventus 0
Ferencvaros 1, Zeljeznicar 2
Zeljeznicar 1, Ferencvaros 2
*Ferencvaros won on penalties*

**Semi-finals**
Tottenham Hotspur 2, Milan 1
Milan 1, Tottenham Hotspur 1
Ferencvaros 2, Wolverhampton
Wanderers 2
Wolverhampton Wanderers 2,
Ferencvaros 1

**Final**

Molineux (Wolverhampton), 3 May 1972
Wolverhampton Wanderers (0) 1    Tottenham Hotspur (0) 2
*Wolverhampton:* Parkes; Shaw, Taylor; Hegan, Munro, McAlle;
McCalliog, Hibbitt, Richards, Dougan, Wagstaffe.
*Tottenham:* Jennings; Kinnear, Knowles; Mullery, England, Beal,
Gilzean, Perryman, Chivers, Peters, Coates (Pratt).
*Scorers:* McCalliog for Wolverhampton; Chivers 2 for Tottenham.


White Hart Lane (London), 17 May 1972
Tottenham Hotspur (1) 1, Wolverhampton Wanderers (1) 1
*Tottenham:* Unchanged; no subs.
*Wolverhampton:* Unchanged. Subs: Bailey for Hibbitt, Curran for
Dougan.
*Scorers:* Mullery for Tottenham; Wagstaffe for Wolverhampton.

## UEFA CUP 1972–73

Liverpool won their first European trophy, after a decade of effort, beating Borussia Mönchengladbach in the final. They had already knocked out Spurs, the holders, in the semi-final thanks to a slice of luck in the tie at White Hart Lane where they lost 2–1 and survived on the 'Away' goal.

The final was a strange affair. The first attempt to play the Liverpool leg was defeated by rain; but not before Liverpool had seen the vulnerability of Borussia in the air. This enabled them to bring in the tall John Toshack in the replayed match next day and his heading powers were decisive. Günter Netzer played a curiously passive game at Anfield as a kind of sweeper, but in Mönchengladbach he was back to his true form and place in midfield; quite irresistible. Liverpool lost, but narrowly hung on to a winning margin on aggregate.

### First Round

Aberdeen 2, Borussia Mönchengladbach 3

Borussia Mönchengladbach 6, Aberdeen 3

Atvidaberg 3, Bruges 5

Bruges 1, Atvidaberg 2

Manchester City 2, Valencia 2

Valencia 2, Manchester City 1

Lyn Oslo 3, Tottenham Hotspur 6

Tottenham Hotspur 6, Lyn Oslo 0

Cologne 2, Bohemians 1

Bohemians 0, Cologne 3

Honved 1, Partick Thistle 0

Partick Thistle 0, Hovend 3

Viking Stavanger 1, Vastmannejar 0

Vastmannejar 0, Viking Stavanger 0

Feyenoord 9, Rumelange 0

Rumelange 0, Feyenoord 12

Liverpool 2, Eintracht 0

Eintracht 0, Liverpool 0

Grasshoppers 2, Nimes 1

Nimes 1, Grasshoppers 2

Vitoria Setubal 6, Zaglebie Sosnowiec 1

Zaglebie Sosnowiec 1, Vitoria Setubal 0

Stoke City 3, Kaiserslautern 1

Kaiserslautern 4, Stoke City 0

Racing White 0, CUF Barreirense 1

CUF Barreirense 2, Racing White 0

Torino 2, Las Palmas 0

Las Palmas 4, Torino 0

Sochaux 1, Frem 3

Frem 2, Sochaux 1

Olympiakos Piraeus 2, Cagliari 1

Cagliari 0, Olympiakos 1

Angers 1, Dynamo Berlin 1

Dynamo Berlin 2, Angers 1

Porto 3, Barcelona 1

Barcelona 0, Porto 1

Universitatea Cluj 4, Levski Sofia 1

Levski Sofia 5, Universitatea Cluj 1

Red Star Belgrade 5, Lausanne 1

Lausanne 3, Red Star Belgrade 2

Internazionale 6, Valetta 1

Valetta 0, Internazionale 1

Beroe Stara 7, FK Austria 0

FK Austria 1, Beroe Stara 3

UT Arad 1, Norrköping 2

Norrköping 2, UT Arad 0

Larna 0, Ararat Erevan 1

Ararat Erevan 1, Larna 0

AEK Athens 3, Salgotarjan 1

Salgotarjan 1, AEK Athens 1

Eskisehirspor 1, Fiorentina 2

Fiorentina 3, Eskisehirspor 0

Dukla 2, OFK Belgrade 2
OFK Belgrade 3, Dukla 1
Slovan Bratislava 6, Vojvodina 0
Vojvodina 1, Slovan Bratislava 2
Dynamo Tbilisi 3, Twente 2
Twente 2, Dynamo Tbilisi 0
Ruch Chorzow 3, Fenerbahce 0
Fenerbahce 1, Ruch Chorzow 0
Dynamo Dresden 2, Vöest Linz 0
Vöest Linz 2, Dynamo Dresden 2
Bye: *Hvidovre Copenhagen*

**Second Round**
Dynamo Berlin 3, Levski Sofia 0
Levski Sofia 2, Dynamo Berlin 0
Borussia Mönchengladbach 3,
  Hvidovre 0
Hvidovre 1, Borussia
  Mönchengladbach 3
Porto 3, Bruges 0
Bruges 3, Porto 2
Tottenham Hotspur 4,
  Olympiakos 0
Olympiakos 1, Tottenham
  Hotspur 0
Red Star Belgrade 3, Valencia 0
Valencia 0, Red Star Belgrade 1
Internazionale 2, Norrköping 2
Norrköping 0, Internazionale 2
Viking Stavanger 1, Cologne 0
Cologne 9, Viking Stavanger 0
Beroe Stara 3, Honved 0
Honved 1, Boroe Stara 0
Feyenoord 4, OFK Belgrade 3
OFK Belgrade 2, Feyenoord 1
Liverpool 3, AEK Athens 0
AEK 1, Liverpool 3
Vitoria Setubal 1, Fiorentina 0
Fiorentina 2, Vitoria Setubal 1
Grasshoppers 1, Ararat Erevan 3
Ararat Erevan 4, Grasshoppers 2
CUF Barreirense 1,
  Kaiserslautern 3
Kaiserslautern 0, CUF
  Barreirense 1
Las Palmas 2, Slovan
  Bratislava 2
Slovan Bratislava 0, Las
  Palmas 1

Ruch Chorzow 0, Dynamo
  Dresden 1
Dynamo Dresden 3, Ruch
  Chorzow 0
Frem 0, Twente 5
Twente 4, Frem 0

**Third Round**
Ararat Erevan 2,
  Kaiserslautern 0
Kaiserslautern 2, Ararat
  Erevan 0
*Kaiserslautern won on penalties*
Cologne 0, Borussia
  Mönchengladbach 0
Borussia Mönchengladbach 5,
  Cologne 0
Dynamo Berlin 0, Liverpool 0
Liverpool 3, Dynamo Berlin 1
Tottenham Hotspur 2, Red Star
  Belgrade 0
Red Star Belgrade 1,
  Tottenham Hotspur 0
Twente 3, Las Palmas 0
Las Palmas 2, Twente 1
Vitoria Setubal 2,
  Internazionale 1
Internazionale 1, Vitoria
  Setubal 0
OFK Belgrade 0, Beroe Stara 0
Beroe Stara 1, OFK Belgrade 3
Porto 1, Dynamo Dresden 2
Dynamo Dresden 1, Porto 0

**Quarter-finals**
Tottenham Hotspur 1, Vitoria
  Setubal 0
Vitoria Setubal 2, Tottenham
  Hotspur 1
Liverpool 2, Dynamo Dresden 0
Dynamo Dresden 0, Liverpool 1
Kaiserslautern 1, Borussia
  Mönchengladbach 2
Borussia Mönchengladbach 7,
  Kaiserslautern 1
OFK Belgrade 3, Twente 2
Twente 2, OFK Belgrade 0

243

**Semi-finals**

Liverpool 1, Tottenham
   Hotspur 0

Tottenham Hotspur 2,
   Liverpool 1

Borussia Mönchengladbach 3,
   Twente 0

Twente 1, Borussia
   Mönchengladbach 2

**Final**

Liverpool, 10 May 1973

Liverpool 3, Borussia Möchengladbach 0

*Liverpool:* Clemence; Lawler, Lindsay; Smith, Lloyd, Hughes; Keegan, Cormach, Toshack, Heighway (Hall), Callaghan.

*Borussia:* Kleff; Netzer, Danner, Michallik, Vogts, Bonhof, Kulik, Jensen, Wimmer, Rupp (Simonsen), Heynckes.

*Scorers:* Keegan (2), Lloyd for Liverpool.

Mönchengladbach, 23 May 1973

Borussia Mönchengladbach 2, Liverpool 0

*Borussia:* Kleff; Vogts, Surau, Netzer, Bonhof, Danner, Wimmer, Kulik, Jensen, Rupp, Heynckes.

*Liverpool:* Clemence; Lawler, Lindsay; Smith, Lloyd, Hughes; Keegan, Cormack, Heighway (Boersma), Toshack, Callaghan.

*Scorer:* Heynckes (2) for Burussia Möchengladbach.

## UEFA CUP 1973-74

England's hold on the UEFA Cup was broken at last when Feyenoord beat Spurs in the final. The return leg, in Rotterdam, was blemished by the horrifying violence of the young Tottenham supporters, both inside and outside the stadium. Feyenoord won this match by a distance even without the suspended Van Hanegem, whose extraordinary left-footed goal from a free kick had helped them to draw at White Hart Lane.

Though having an indifferent time of it in the League, Spurs constantly found fresh inspiration, round by round, in the UEFA Cup. Grasshoppers were no problem, though Spurs' 5–1 win in Zurich absurdly flattered them, while a 4–1 win over Aberdeen at Tottenham hardly reflected the play. Ipswich Town, in the meantime, were being viciously assaulted in Rome by a Lazio team whose wild behaviour suggested the use of drugs, rather than mere revenge for the way Ipswich, with four goals by Whymark, had thrashed them in the first leg at Portman Road.

Drawing in far off Tblissi, Spurs then thrashed the Georgians 5–1 in London, exploiting their colossal superiority in the air against a team which had previously been formidable. In the same round, Leeds United virtually abdicated, putting out in Setubal a team full of reserves. Ipswich however, surpassed themselves with a double victory over the excellent young Dutch team, Twente.

The quarter-finals saw Tottenham's best performance yet, rising from the ashes of dreadful exhibitions in the League to beat Cologne in Germany. Martin Chivers at his best then brushed them aside at home. Ipswich, however, fell in Leipzig on penalties, largely because Mills, provoked into retaliation, was sent off. It fell to Spurs comfortably and forcefully to despatch Leipzig in the semi-finals. But the all round power, speed, and versatility of Feyenoord were too much for them in the final.

At Tottenham, Mike England headed their first goal, caused confusion for the second, each time at Ray Evans' free kicks. But Van Hanagem's own free kick and a late, lively one-two between De Jong and Kristensen properly brought Feyenoord the equaliser. In Rotterdam, Jennings kept them out for a time, but when his mistake allowed Rijsbergen to score, that was the end of Tottenham.

## First Round

Strömsgodset 1, Leeds United 1
Leeds United 6, Strömsgodset 1
Ipswich Town 1, Real Madrid 0
Real Madrid 0, Ipswich Town 0
Grasshoppers 1, Tottenham H. 5
Tottenham H. 4, Grasshoppers 1
Aberdeen 4, Finn Harps 1
Finn Harps 1, Aberdeen 3
Hibernian 2, Keflavik 0
Keflavik 1, Hibernian 1
Ards 3, Standard Liège 2
Standard Liège 6, Ards 1
Dundee 1, Twente Enschede 3
Twente Enschede 4, Dundee 2
Belenenses 0, Wolves 2
Wolves 2, Belenenses 1
Nice 3, Barcelona 0
Barcelona 2, Nice 0
US Luxemburg 0, Marseille 5
Marseille 5, US Luxemburg 1
Fiorentina 0, Universitatea
  Craiova 0
Universitatea 1, Fiorentina 0
Admira Wacker 1,
  Internazionale 0
Internazionale 2, Admira
  Wacker 1
Torino 1, Locomotive Leipzig 2
Locomotive Leipzig 2, Torino 1
Lazio 3, Sion 0
Sion 3, Lazio 1
Frederikstad 0, Dynamo Kiev 1
Dynamo Kiev 4, Frederikstad 0
Ruch Chorzow 4, Wuppertal 1
Wuppertal 5, Ruch Chorzow 4

BK Copenhagen 2, AIK 1
AIK 1, BK Copenhagen 1
Carl Zeiss Jena 3, Mikkelin 0
Mikkelin 0, Carl Zeiss Jena 3
Fortuna Dusseldorf 1, Naestved 0
Naestved 2, Fortuna Dusseldorf 2
Oesters 1, Feyenoord 3
Feyenoord 2, Oesters 1
Español 0, Racing White 3
Racing White 1, Español 2
Vitoria Setubal 2, Beerschot 0
Beerschot 0, Vitoria Setubal 2
Ferencvaros 0, Gwardia Warsaw 1
Gwardia 2, Ferencvaros 1
VfB Stuttgart 9, Olympiakos
  Nicosia 0
Olympiakos Nicosia 0, VfB
  Stuttgart 4
Tatran Presov 4, Velez 2
Velez 1, Tatran Presov 1
Dynamo Tblissi 4, Slavia Sofia 1
Slavia Sofia 2, Dynamo Tblissi 0
Panathinaikos 1, OFK Belgrade 2
OFK Belgrade 0, Panathinaikos 1
Fenerbahce 5, Arges Pitesti 1
Arges Pitesti 1, Fenerbahce 1
VSS Kosice 1, Honved 0
Honved 5, VSS Kosice 2
Eskisehirspor 0, Cologne 0
Cologne 2, Eskisehirspor 0
Panachaiki 2, Graz 1
Graz 0, Panachaiki 1
Sliema Wanderers 0, Locomotive
  Plovdiv 2
Locomotive 1, Sliema Wand. 0

**Second Round**

Ipswich Town 4, Lazio 0
Lazio 4, Ipswich Town 2
Leeds United 0, Hibernian 0
Hibernian 0, Leeds United 0
Aberdeen 1, Tottenham H. 1
Tottenham H. 4, Aberdeen 1
Locomotive Leipzig 3, Wolves 0
Wolves 4, Locomotive Leipzig 1
Nice 4, Fenerbahce 0
Fenerbahce 2, Nice 0
Marseille 2, Cologne 0
Cologne 6, Marseille 0
VfB Stuttgart 3, Tatran Presov 1
Tatran Presov 3, VfB Stuttgart 5
Admira Wacker 2,
   Fortuna Dusseldorf 1
Fortuna Dusseldorf 3,
   Admira Wacker 0
Vitoria Setubal 1, Racing White 0
Racing White 2, Vitoria Setubal 1
Lokomotive Plovdiv 3, Honved 4
Honved 3, Lokomotive Plovdiv 2
Feyenoord 3, Gwardia Warsaw 1
Gwardia Warsaw 1, Feyenoord 0
Dynamo Kiev 1,
   BK Copenhagen 0
BK Copenhagen 1,
   Dynamo Kiev 2
Dynamo Tblissi 3, OFK
   Belgrade 0
OFK Belgrade 1,
   Dynamo Tblissi 5
Panachaiki 1, Twente 1
Twente 7, Panachaiki 0
Standard Liège 3,
   Universitatea Craiova 0
Universitatea 1, Standard Liège 1
Ruch Chorzow 3,
   Carl Zeiss Jena 0
Carl Zeiss Jena 1,
   Ruch Chorzow 0

**Third Round**

Dynamo Tblissi 1,
   Tottenham Hotspur 1
Tottenham Hotspur 5,
   Dynamo Tblissi 1
Ipswich Town 1,
   Twente Enschede 0
Twente Enschede 1,
   Ispwich Town 2
Leeds United 1, Vitoria Setubal 0
Vitoria Setubal 3, Leeds United 1
Nice 1, Cologne 0
Cologne 4, Nice 0
Standard Liège 3, Feyenoord 1
Feyenoord 2, Standard Liège 0
Honved 2, Ruch Chorzow 0
Ruch Chorzow 5, Honved 0
Fortuna Dusseldorf 2,
   Locomotive Leipzig 1
Locomotive Leipzig 3,
   Fortuna Dusseldorf 0
Dynamo Kiev 2, VfB Stuttgart 0
VfB Stuttgart 3, Dynamo Kiev 0

**Quarter-finals**

Cologne 1, Tottenham H. 2
Tottenham H. 3, Cologne 0
Ipswich Town 1,
   Locomotive Leipzig 0
Locomotive Leipzig 1,
   Ipswich Town 0
Ruch Chorzow 1, Feyenoord 1
Feyenoord 3, Ruch Chorzow 1
VfB Stuttgart 1, Vitoria Setubal 0
Vitoria Setubal 2, VfB Stuttgart 2

**Semi-finals**

Locomotive Leipzig 1,
   Tottenham Hotspur 2
Tottenham Hotspur 2,
   Locomotive Leipzig 0
Feyenoord 2, VfB Stuttgart 1
VfB Stuttgart 2, Feyenoord 2

**Final**

Tottenham, 22 May, 1974
Tottenham Hotspur (1) 2          Feyenord (1) 2
*Spurs:* Jennings; Evans, England, Beal (Dillon), Naylor, Perryman,
Pratt, Peters, McGrath, Chivers, Coates.

*Feyenoord:* Treytel; Rijsbergen, Van Daele, Israel, Vos, Van Hanegem, De Jong, Jansen, Ressel, Schoenmaker, Kristensen.
*Scorers:* England, Israel (o.g.) for Spurs; Van Hanegem, De Jong for Feyenoord

Rotterdam, 29 May, 1974
Feyenoord (1) 2                    Tottenham Hotspur (0) 0
*Feyenoord:* Treytel; Ramljak, Israel, Van Daele, Vos, Rijsbergen, (Boscamp), De Jong, Jansen, Ressel, Schoenmaker, Kristensen.
*Spurs:* Jennings; Evans, Naylor, Pratt (Holder), England, Beal, McGrath, Perryman, Chivers, Peters, Coates.
*Scorers:* Rijsbergen, Ressel.

CHAPTER SEVENTEEN

# South American Championship and Libertadores' Cup History

## CHAMPIONSHIP

|      |              | Winners   | Runners-up |
|------|--------------|-----------|------------|
| 1917 | Montevideo   | Uruguay   | Argentina  |
| 1919 | Rio          | Brazil    | Uruguay    |
| 1920 | Valparaiso   | Uruguay   | Argentina  |
| 1921 | Buenos Aires | Argentina | Brazil     |
| 1922 | Rio          | Brazil    | Paraguay   |
| 1923 | Montevideo   | Uruguay   | Argentina  |
| 1924 | Montevideo   | Uruguay   | Argentina  |
| 1925 | Buenos Aires | Argentina | Brazil     |
| 1926 | Santiago     | Uruguay   | Argentina  |
| 1927 | Lima         | Argentina | Paraguay   |
| 1929 | Buenos Aires | Argentina | Uruguay    |
| 1937 | Buenos Aires | Argentina | Paraguay   |
| 1939 | Lima         | Peru      | Brazil     |
| 1942 | Montevideo   | Uruguay   | Argentina  |
| 1947 | Guayaquil    | Argentina | Paraguay   |
| 1949 | Rio          | Brazil    | Paraguay   |
| 1953 | Lima         | Paraguay  | Brazil     |
| 1955 | Santiago     | Argentina | Chile      |
| 1957 | Lima         | Argentina | Brazil     |
| 1959 | Buenos Aires | Argentina | Brazil     |
| 1963 | La Paz       | Bolivia   | Paraguay   |
| 1967 | Montevideo   | Uruguay   | Argentina  |

## LIBERTADORES' CUP

The South American Cup, or *Copa de Los Libertadores*, was founded in 1960 to provide a South American team to play the winners of the European Cup, for the unofficial championship of the world. It was initially confined, like the European Cup, to champions of various countries – Brazil organized a new cup tournament to find one – but when, in the later 1960s, it was enlarged to include two teams per country, Brazilian and Argentinian clubs objected and, on various occasions, withdrew. Thus, no Brazilian clubs competed in 1965, 1969 or 1970, a year in which Argentina were represented only by the South American Cup-holders and world champions, Estudiantes. The clubs now qualify in 'mini-league' groups, in two stages, for a final played at home and away, with aggregate score irrelevant.

**1960**
Penarol 1, Olimpia Paraguay 0
Olimpia Paraguay 0, Penarol 0

**1961**
Penarol 1, Palmeiras 0
(Sao Paulo)
Palmeiras 1, Penarol 1

**1962**
Santos 2, Penarol 1
Penarol 3, Santos 2
Santos 3, Penarol 0

**1963**
Santos 3, Boca Juniors 2
Boca Juniors 1, Santos 2

**1964**
Nacional 0, Independiente 0
Independiente 1, Nacional 0

1965
Independiente 1, Penarol 0
Penarol 3, Independiente 1
Independiente 4, Penarol 1

**1966**
Penarol 2, River Plate 0
River Plate 3, Penarol 2
Penarol 4, River Plate 2

**1967**
Racing Club 0, Nacional 0
Nacional 0, Racing Club 0
Racing Club 2, Nacional 1

**1968**
Estudiantes 3, Palmeiras 1
Palmeiras 3, Estudiantes 1
Estudiantes 2, Palmeiras 0

**1969**
Nacional 0, Estudiantes 1
Estudiantes 2, Nacional 0

**1970**
Estudiantes 1, Penarol 0
Penarol 0, Estudiantes 0

**1971**
Estudiantes 1, Nacional 0
Nacional 1, Estudiantes 0
Nacional 2, Estudiantes 0

**1972**
Universitario 0, Independiente 0
Independiente 2, Universitario 1

**1973**
Independiente 1, Colo Colo 1
Colo Colo 0, Indepndeiente 0
Independiente 2, Colo Colo 1

**1974**

Yet another victory for Independiente, this time at the expense of Sao Paolo, though it went to a third game, in Santiago. Sao Paolo dominated the first game but fell behind to a breakaway goal, recovering to win in the second half. Independiente then won 2–0 in Buenos Aires, necessitating a play-off in which a penalty by Pavoni, the Uruguayan defender, was decisive. Sao Paolo, too, were awarded a penalty kick, but missed it. It was a tense, mediocre game in which Independiente stayed the cooler.

13 October 1974
Sao Paolo (0) 2                          Independiente (1) 1
*Rocha, Mirandinha*                      *Saggioratto*

17 October 1974
Independiente (1) 2                      Sao Paolo (0) 0
*Bocchini, Balbuena*

Play-off, Santiago, Chile, 19 October 1974
Independiente (1) 1                      Sao Paolo (0) 0
*Pavoni (pen)*

---

## European Youth Championship 1974-75

For the fourth time in five years, the seventh in all, England's youth, team won the European title. This time the manager was Ken Burton, and the opponents in the final, beaten only after extra time, were, most unexpectedly, Finland.

To win Group B, England took full points from the two Irelands and Switzerland, the hosts, were actually thrashed 4–0, two of the goals going to the Chelsea captain, the inside-forward Ray Wilkins. Another Chelsea player, the left-back John Sparrow, scored twice with tremendous long shots against Hungary, beaten 3–1 in the semi-final.

The Finns, surprise of the tournament, had in the past won only five such matches in 28 years. But they pushed England hard in the final, and only after five minutes' extra time did Ray Wilkins take a pass from West Ham's Alan Curbishley to score. Under the new rules, that automatically brought the game to an end and gave England the Cup.

**Final**  Berne, 19 May, 1975
England (0) 1                          Finland (0) 0
*England:* Middleton; Wicks, Smith, Robson, Sparrow, Wilkins, Hoddle, Trewick (Langley), Nightingale (Curbishley), Bertschin, Barnes.
*Finland:* G. Lindholm; P. Ulmonen, Laamanen, Koskinen, Ilula, Pulliainen, Lappailanen, Houtsonen, Ismail, H. Lindholm.
*Scorer:* Wilkins.

# CHAPTER EIGHTEEN

# UEFA and the Lobo–Solti Affair, continued.

There are signs that the Solti Affair is reaching crescendo; that evidence will now uncover the alleged connection between the Hungarian 'fixer', Deszo Solti, and Juventus.

In March 1973, Solti went to Lisbon and tried to bribe the Portuguese referee, Francisco Marques Lobo, to favour Juventus in their return European Cup semi-final with Derby County. Lobo sturdily refused, reported the matter to his Federation, took a tape of a subsequent telephone conversation with Solti, and gave evidence in Zurich to UEFA, the European governing body.

UEFA's Disciplinary Committee demanded that Solti be made *persona non grata* throughout European football, but the Executive Committee did not accede. Nor did they even implement their own decision to notify all their members of Solti's behaviour. Meanwhile, UEFA had mysteriously and totally absolved Juventus, the obvious beneficiaries, of all blame.

Keith Botsford and I, hearing of this, carried out an investigation for *The Sunday Times* which is still proceeding. The first fruits were the appointment of an Ad Hoc Investigating Committee consisting of Lucien Schmidlin (Switzerland) and Jacques Georges (France) in May 1974. But their brief was absurdly limited, they came up with no new information, and when UEFA's Executive Committee met in Budapest in December 1974, all that happened was that Solti finally *was* declared *persona non grata*, and the case closed.

*The Sunday Times* returned to the attack, publishing a long analysis not only of the Solti Affair but of the chicanery of the three leading Italian clubs – Inter, Juventus, and Milan – over the previous dozen years, showing how certain referees had been used by them time and again, to their immense benefit. Once more UEFA had to move, and to re-open the case, reconstituting the ad Hoc Committee, with the promise that it would be expanded by a further member, probably an English Q.C., and that it would work in conjunction with *The Sunday Times* inquiry.

A name which perpetually cropped up in the investigation was that of Italo Allodi, General Manager of Juventus at the time of the attempt to bribe Lobo, Secretary of Internazionale when Solti was unquestionably on their pay roll, now in charge of an 'investigation' into the running of the Federal Technical Centre of the Italian FA, in Florence.

Though there seemed every prospect of some at least of the birds coming home to roost after what *The Sunady Times* called 'The Years of the Golden Fix', the abysmal refereeing of the Leeds–Bayern

European Final of 1975 suggested that perhaps UEFA should keep its own permanent investigating body, preferably one with time, teeth, and financial resources. It was also good to hear that UEFA were belatedly getting round to appointing the *best* referees for a European Final, rather than one from the country where that game was being played.

# THE SUNDAY TIMES
## SPORTS PAGES

### *Best informed.... Best written....*
### *Most outspoken*

**SOCCER**
BRIAN GLANVILLE
ROB HUGHES

**CRICKET**
ROBIN MARLAR
Former captain of Cambridge University and Sussex
JACK FINGLETON
Former Australian opening batsman

**RUGBY**
VIVIAN JENKINS
Former Welsh International and Glamorgan cricketer

**RACING**
BROUGH SCOTT
A famous amateur jockey

**GOLF**
DUDLEY DOUST
HENRY LONGHURST

**ATHLETICS**
CLIFF TEMPLE

**TENNIS**
JOHN BALLANTINE

The "Alternative Voice"
MICHAEL PARKINSON

**MOTOR RACING**
KEITH BOTSFORD
An original view

**Plus**
INSIDE TRACK
The Controversial Column

From the Sports Pages of

## THE SUNDAY TIMES

December 2, 1973

The Football Association appointed a committee with an average age of about 70 to investigate the game. BRIAN GLANVILLE responded with:

### You Are Old, Councillor William

*"You are old, Councillor William," the young man roared,*
*"And are obviously quite out of touch:*
*"And yet you incessantly travel abroad.*
*"Don't you think, at your age, it's too much?"*

*"In my youth," Councillor William replied with disdain,*
*"I spent all my time making money.*
*"But now I can go round the world without paying,*
*"I really don't see what's so funny."*

*"You are old," said the youth, "as I've mentioned before,*
*"And are greatly reluctant to think.*
*"And yet for an ancient, reactionary bore,*
*"It's amazing how much you can drink."*

*"When Sir Alf," said the Councillor, "took over the side,*
*"He robbed me of any real function.*
*"So drinking for England's my joy and my pride,*
*"Nor have I the slightest compunction."*

*"You are old," said the youth, "and you stand in the way*
*"Of anyone younger than you;*
*"And yet you're eternally having your say*
*"On what English football should do."*

*"I am old," said the sage, "you are perfectly right,*
*"But I'd rather be old than be clever.*
*"Do you think you can change the whole game overnight?*
*"Be off, or I'll stay here for ever!"*

With apologies to Lewis Carroll.

From the Sports Pages of

# THE SUNDAY TIMES

November 3–10, 1974

### HEAD DAMAGE

Overriding all shades of opinion are the facts. In records at this newspaper, 55 players have died at football since 1931. Of these, 26 had head injuries, and eight were attributed at coroners' inquests to heading the ball and nothing else . . .

It is an absurd paradox that, whereas the British play their football in the air, they concentrate their coaching and medical awareness below the belt . . . The coaches, in schools and at clubs, can improve on the alarming lack of formal education in heading. ROB HUGHES

June 1, 1975

Nausea! That, I am afraid, is my first reaction to this storm tossed match at Brisbane's Rallymore Park, where Australia beat England once again . . . From the first kick-off, the Australians made it plain that they intended to be no respecters of persons; the boots went in with a viciousness that made even the committed watcher wince. VIVIAN JENKINS

Niki Lauda got his first and second cars from his two grandmothers. He hasn't really looked back. The first he got by telling his grandmother he had wrecked a friend's car. That tells you three things: his family could afford his ambitions, that possible accident is always in a corner of his mind and Niki Lauda is determined to get what he wants. KEITH BOTSFORD

The purblind mandarins of Lords, joined at the hip by the majority of cricket commentators, will tut-tut about that bounder Boycott while ignoring the basic fundamental question he has posed. Boycott has challenged the hypocrisy of English cricket and will no doubt pay the price, but unless the lesson is learned the game will be the final loser. MICHAEL PARKINSON

### THE SOLTI AFFAIR

In March, 1973, a Hungarian called Dezso Solti, domiciled in Milan, went to Lisbon and unsuccessfully tried to bribe Francisco Marques Lobo, Portuguese referee of the Derby County–Juventus European Cup semi-final, to favour Juventus. UEFA, the

European body, heard the case but did nothing. In April, 1974, KEITH BOTSFORD and BRIAN GLANVILLE exclusively revealed the scandal, demanding action. In May, a two man Ad Hoc Investigating Committee was appointed by UEFA. In December, 1974, Solti was declared *persona non grata* by UEFA. In March, 1975, Botsford and Glanville insisted this was not enough, revealed a web of Italian corruption in European football over at least 12 years. UEFA re-appointed the sub-committee, asked Botsford and Glanville for help. It has been forthcoming . . .

### May 4, 1975

In the Madrid hotel somebody banged on the wall, but Hal Underwood, the lanky golfer from Texas, hunched over his guitar and kept on strumming and wailing away:

> *Ah went out in thirty-two, Lord,*
> *And Ah had mah baby by mah side,*
> *Then Ah put it in the bunker,*
> *And Ah left it in the bunker.*
> *And mah baby she done left mah side.*
> *Ah got those double-bogey blues . . .*

DUDLEY DOUST

The saddest and most desperate thing about the jockey-snatching, lad-bashing events last Thursday is that anyone could talk of "winning". . . . On the lads' side, the violence and abuse, which started with the breaking of horse box windows and culminated in the "duffing-up" of Willie Carson, was just the sort of behaviour their hard line "put the chukka boot in" opponents had been waiting for. But the Establishment's "over the rails and at 'em" reaction was even more frightening, irresponsible and damaging.

BROUGH SCOTT

### April 20, 1975

The fun will come from people. People who can communicate the joy of cricket. Whether it be Tony Greig, whom I see now in Melbourne, garlanded more by the bikini-clad beauties than by the carnations they were carrying; or the middle-order-batsman-cum-lay-preacher in the Haig Village Match who no sooner left the pavilion for the pulpit than he had to return whence he had come.

ROBIN MARLAR